Absorbing the Blow

Absorbing the Blow

Populist Parties and their Impact on Parties and Party Systems

Edited by Steven Wolinetz
and Andrej Zaslove

ecpr PRESS

ROWMAN &
LITTLEFIELD
INTERNATIONAL

London • New York

Published by Rowman & Littlefield International, Ltd.
6 Tinworth Street, London SE11 5AL, United Kingdom
www.rowmaninternational.com

In partnership with the European Consortium for Political Research,
Harbour House, 6-8 Hythe Quay, Colchester, CO2 8JF, United Kingdom.

Rowman & Littlefield International Ltd. is an affiliate of Rowman & Littlefield
4501 Forbes Boulevard, Suite 200, Lanham, Maryland 20706, USA
With additional offices in Boulder, New York, Toronto (Canada), and Plymouth (UK)
www.rowman.com

British Library Cataloguing in Publication Data
A catalogue record for this book is available from the British Library

ISBN: HB 978-1-78552-149-2
         PB 978-1-78661-314-1

Library of Congress Cataloging-in-Publication Data
Names: Wolinetz, Steven B., 1943– editor. | Zaslove, Andrej, 1963– editor.
Title: Absorbing the blow : populist parties and their impact on parties and
    party systems / edited by Steven Wolinetz and Andrej Zaslove.
Description: London ; New York : Rowman & Littlefield International, Ltd,
    [2018] | Includes bibliographical references and index.
Identifiers: LCCN 2017054304 (print) | LCCN 2017041441 (ebook) | ISBN
    9781785521492 (cloth) | ISBN 9781786613141 (paperback) | ISBN 9781786606396
(electronic)
Subjects: LCSH: Political parties—Europe. | Populism—Europe. | Right-wing
    extremists—Europe. | Europe—Politics and government—21st century.
Classification: LCC JN50 .A33 2018 (ebook) | LCC JN50 (print) | DDC
    324.2094—dc23
LC record available at https://lccn.loc.gov/2017054304

Contents

Part I

INTRODUCTION

Chapter 1

The Impact of Populist Parties on Party Systems

Steven Wolinetz and Andrej Zaslove

We have all seen it happen. Imagine a large family, a set of friends, a group of co-workers, a class or a team. Within this unit, there are likes and dislikes as well as conventions about what can or cannot be said and how to get along with one another. One or more newcomers might arrive and behave differently enough that they alter the group dynamic. The same can occur if one of the regular members changes his or her behaviour. The group can respond in a myriad of ways. It can close ranks and marginalise newcomers. It can divide, with some members of the group interacting more with the newcomers and less with those who were there before. To be sure, not every newcomer alters or upsets pre-existing dynamics; indeed, some are easily assimilated into pre-existing norms and behaviour. However, others are not, and their presence forms an alternate pole that changes the unit and how its members interact through force of personality or because of who these new members are or what they do.

Readers could be forgiven for asking what this narrative has to do with European political parties and party systems. The answer is a good deal. Coping with newcomers – or with parties whose style and behaviour has changed – is something with which older parties in many European countries have had to wrestle. In the first few decades following Second World War, most Western European party systems were sufficiently static that, following Lipset and Rokkan (1967), they could be characterised as frozen (Bartolini and Mair 2007; Mair 1997). Rooted in class and religious cleavages, many parties simply relied on electorates of belonging whose support they managed to cultivate and renew. Some older parties still do, but party systems are less firmly anchored than they once were. Rates of electoral volatility and the frequency of high volatility elections have increased, and many party systems are now more fragmented than they were in the 1950s and 1960s (Chiaramonte and Emanuele 2017; Mair 2008, 2013). Reflecting transitions to democracy in southern and east central Europe, the universe of party systems in liberal democracies is also larger.

Two new party families – 'Green' and left libertarian parties (henceforth, collectively referred to as 'Greens'), on one hand, and populist radical right parties, on the other – have emerged and become credible and, in some instances, formidable competitors, while Communist parties have all but disappeared or have been replaced by radical left parties (including a few that have themselves developed into populist parties). Articulating points of view different from mainstream parties, Green parties and populist parties were potential threats to the dominant position that mainstream parties previously enjoyed. Giving voice to concerns about environment, the quality of life and the quality of democracy, Green parties drew support from younger, educated voters coveted by Social Democrats. Populist parties presented a different challenge. Articulating a Manichean view that juxtaposed the demands of the people and what they truly wanted to an uncaring establishment deaf to these demands, populist parties were a potential threat not only to parties of the right but also to parties on all parts of the spectrum.

Not all the parties that forced others to sit up and take note were newcomers: in Switzerland, mainstream parties had to react to one of their own, the Swiss People's Party (SVP), that not only assumed a populist stance but also brought about a substantial shift in the party balance in so doing. Similarly, the Austrian Freedom Party (FPÖ) originated as a smaller nationalist and liberal party whose first impact on the party system was to provide the Socialists with a parliamentary majority in 1983. However, under Jörg Haider, the FPÖ redefined itself as a populist party and an outsider that was a newcomer for all intents and purposes.

In this volume, we examine the impact (if any) that populist parties have on the party systems of which they have become a part. Party systems are more than collections of parties. Instead, characterised by regular recurring interactions, they embody the fraternal relations among parties that regularly work together and the less-friendly relations among others that do not cooperate as readily or often. As we have noted, populist parties are not the only parties that have intruded on European party systems. Green parties often preceded them, appearing when older parties still retained more support from loyal voters; however, Green parties did not create the same stir and did not produce the same unsettling effect that some populist parties have in part because they grew more slowly. In contrast, as figure 1.1 demonstrates, populist parties have surged rapidly and often introduced an element of uncertainty into electoral competition that Green parties – despite the challenge to establishment practices that they initially presented – did not.

Classifying populist parties has been notoriously difficult. This has to do with several issues: First, there has been significant disagreement over how to define populism (see next). Second, we need to determine which parties fit the criteria of being a populist party. Third, we find populist parties across

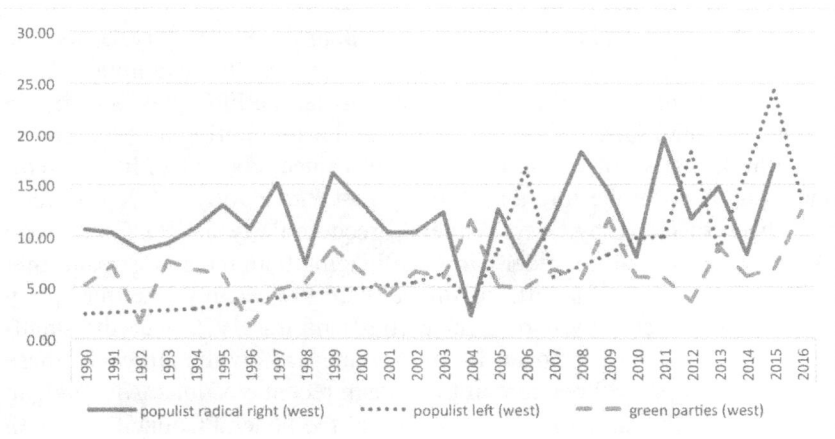

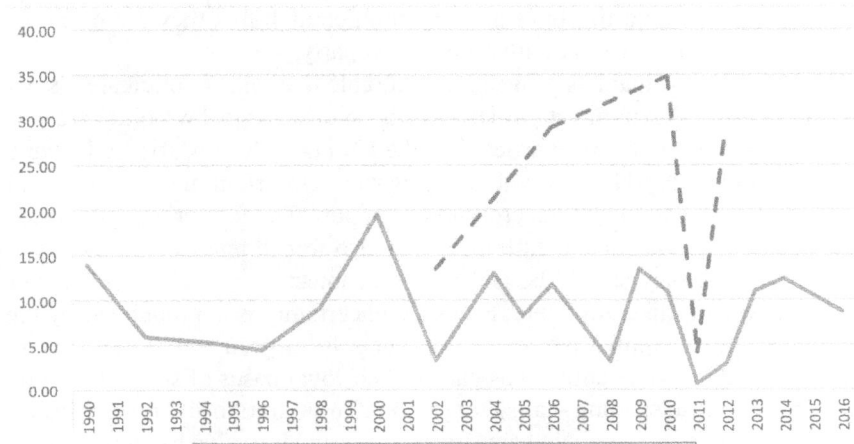

Figure 1.1

Source: Populist parties based on author's original dataset compiled using van Kessel 2015 and Döring and Manow 2017.[1]

the left/right ideological spectrum. This is confirmed in figure 1.1 where we compare the share of the vote won by populist radical right, Green parties, and the populist left in elections from 1990 to 2016. Both the populist radical right and the populist left are on a small but steady climb. In particular, we see that the populist left has done well in the last ten years. However, we have to be careful because the number of cases is small. We also see that there has been a steady increase in the populist radical right in Western Europe. In most cases, the populist radical right has fared better in Western Europe than Green parties (*see* figure 1.1).

Some of these populist parties – the Freedom parties in Austria and the Netherlands and the Front National (FN) in France, for example – have become part of the political landscape. In Austria, the FPÖ grew steadily in the 1990s and then suffered a sharp decline and a split during its stint in government in the early 2000s, but its support has since rebounded. In the Netherlands, populism broke through with the List Pim Fortuyn (LPF) in 2002 and has been sustained by Geert Wilders' Freedom Party (PVV). Established in 1972, France's FN is an older party challenging both the mainstream right and, to a lesser degree, the left. In Austria, the FPÖ began as the third party in a system dominated by two larger parties, and the SVP, once the smallest of four parties sharing power in Switzerland, is now the largest of these parties, garnering 26–29 per cent of the vote in recent elections. Although an insider – the SVP continues to share power in the Federal Council – it often assumes the position of an outsider, sponsoring referenda opposing government policy. Obviously, these parties are no longer minor players: In several countries, populist parties have grown strong enough that they are often the second or third and, occasionally, the largest party.

Surging support that has proven more durable than many anticipated is not the only reason that populist parties have been unsettling. Two other reasons are the association of some parties (e.g. the FN under Jean-Marie Le Pen and the FPÖ under Jörg Haider) with an earlier extreme right and the ability of some populist parties to attract cross-class support. The former not only raised the spectre of old fashioned extremism but also forced mainstream parties to decide whether they should be isolated and subject to a *cordon sanitaire* or treated as a party like any other. Strategic uncertainty is compounded by the ability of many populist parties to win votes from groups that mainstream parties had at one time counted as part of their loyal bases of support. Giving voice to – but also shaping – misgivings about immigration and multiculturalism and a European Union that can appear alien and intrusive has transformed some populist parties into viable competitors. Nor is this their only source of support. Several of these parties have also cast themselves as champions of welfare state entitlements that mainstream parties – struggling to stay within EU budgetary norms – have found themselves forced to trim. However, many would restrict benefits to those who 'deserve' them, that is, native-born citizens and those who have integrated as opposed to less deserving outsiders (Häusermann and Kriesi 2015). Adopting welfare chauvinist positions has enabled populist parties to win the support of those in routine occupations who in earlier decades might have supported Social Democratic or, in some instances, Christian Democratic parties. Notably, populist parties are increasingly drawing support from manual workers (Häusermann and Kriesi 2015; Oesch 2008, 2013; *see also* Jupskås, chapter 5, this volume).

Mainstream parties are not without advantages of their own, but they bear the burden of defending policies that may be unpopular and may find it difficult to deliver desired results or to translate them into support at the polls. The position they find themselves in is different from the immediate postwar decades. Then mainstream parties benefitted from sustained economic growth and full employment and could claim that they had delivered on their promises. By contrast, parties that govern today must grapple with intertwined problems – the cost of entitlements, the problems of interdependent economies and coping with immigration and diversity – that are proving to be far less tractable than they once were.

Populist parties have become prominent in party systems not only in older Western European democracies but also in younger East Central European democracies. Their party systems differ from those in older democracies in several key respects. Most are less firmly anchored in society, and parties position themselves differently on key dimensions (Rohrschneider and Whitefield 2012). Some have also proven fertile ground, if not for populist parties, then for parties employing populist appeals. In Hungary, Fidesz – initially a smaller liberal party and more recently a conservative and increasingly dominant nationalist party – leans towards populism. Along with a newer populist right party, Jobbik, Fidesz gives Hungarian politics a distinctly populist tinge. In Slovakia, the governing party in the 1990s, the People's Party – Movement for a Democratic Slovakia (HZDS), was a left populist party (Deegan-Krause and Haughton 2009). As Casal Bértoa and Guerra (chapter 9, this volume) demonstrate, populism has been a persistent element in Polish political discourse. In the early 2000s, two populist parties, the League of Polish Families (LPR) and Self Defence (SRP), gained strength until their agenda was taken over by a conservative nationalist party, Law and Justice (PiS), an older political force rooted in the Solidarity Movement.

The emergence of populist parties has triggered the growth of a literature that has attempted to define and explain the phenomenon. In the next section, we consider what populism means, how populist parties differ from other parties and the ways in which they affect both competition for votes and competition for government.

DEFINING POPULISM

Studies of populism paralleled the growing success of populist parties. Debates regarding how populism should be defined and conceptualised ensued[2]: scholars studied and debated whether populism is an ideology, a style or a strategy and whether it is left-wing or right-wing (see Canovan 1999; Jagers and Walgrave 2007; March 2007; Moffitt and Tormey 2014; Mudde 2004, 2007; Weyland 2001). Although disagreements persist (particularly between Latin American and European scholars, cf. Weyland 2001), in the European context, there has been less controversy over how to conceptualise populism than some maintain (Akkerman et al. 2014). Most scholars now accept Mudde's notion that populism is a thin-centred ideology (Mudde 2004, 2007) to which other ideologies become attached. The thin-centred ideological perspective argues that populism reflects a coherent set of ideas about the world, representation and democracy, but that this worldview is not broad enough to stand on its own and that populists thus attach this worldview to other ideologies (Mudde and Kaltwasser 2013; Stanley 2008).

The thin-centred ideological approach focuses on four core components: populism begins with the 'pure people' (Akkerman et al. 2014; Mudde 2004). Focusing on 'the pure people', however, is insufficient, and 'the pure people' are thus juxtaposed with the elites, that is, those who are thought to be corrupt (Mudde 2004). In addition, populism espouses a Manichean worldview in which the two worlds are at odds with one another. The tension between 'the pure people' and the elites is framed as a battle between good and evil (Hawkins 2009; Mudde 2004). Finally, populists contend that representation is about asserting the general will (Mudde 2004), a point that Mudde articulates succinctly. Populism is

> a thin-centred ideology that considers society to be ultimately separated into two homogenous and antagonistic groups, 'the pure people' versus the 'corrupt elite', and which argues that politics should be an expression of the *volonté générale* (general will) of the people. (Mudde 2007: 23)

Because it is a thin-centred ideology, populism must attach itself to other ideologies. In Europe, populism has attached itself to radical right, market liberal and left-wing or socialist ideologies. The most common variant is the populist radical right. The ideology of the populist radical right is defined, in addition to populism, by its nativism and authoritarianism (Mudde 2007). However, populist liberals are neither nativist nor authoritarian, and they do not focus exclusively on law and order or moral traditionalism; moreover, immigration is not as important as it is for populist radical right parties. Notably, populist liberal parties are less prevalent in Europe, although Forza

Italia (Go Italy/FI) and the List Dedecker in Belgium are clear examples of this phenomenon (Pauwels 2010; Zaslove 2008).

Populist left-wing parties fuse populism with socialist or social democratic ideologies. Left populists frequently define themselves in opposition to neo-liberalism and globalisation (March 2007). Although some left populist parties make anti-immigration claims, more often than not they support ethnic pluralism. Nevertheless, their principal focus is on economic issues such as regulation, redistribution and income equality. In addition, opposition to the EU – and to EU-mandated austerity measures in particular – is common. Left populist parties include the Dutch Socialist Party, the German Left Party, and more recently Podemos in Spain, as well as SYRIZA in Greece. The Five Star Movement (M5S) in Italy is often classified as a left populist party, but its left/right status is increasingly less clear (Hough and Kon 2009; Kioupkiolis 2016; Otjes and Louwerse 2015; Stavrakakis and Katsambekis 2014; Van Kessel 2015; Verbeek and Zaslove 2016).

POPULISM AND PARTY SYSTEMS

Populist parties have become significant players in several European party systems, sometimes winning as many votes as mainstream parties. Our premise is that such parties have become sufficiently strong and that their presence is sufficiently unsettling that they may have an impact on these party systems. Whether and to what extent they affect party systems is the subject of this book.

To date, most research on populism and party systems has focused on populist radical right parties and why they arise and from whom they derive their support. Several studies focus on the effects of the party system on the success and/or failure of populism. For example, Ignazi (2006) and Kitschelt and McGann (1995) emphasise the extent to which the divergence (or radicalisation/polarisation) or convergence of political parties towards the middle creates opportunities for the rise of populist radical right parties. Divergence (radicalisation/polarisation) primes voters (Ignazi 2006), making them open to populist perspectives. Ignazi (2006) states, 'Radicalization and polarization, together with the politicization of new, salient, and mis-conceived issues, seem to be at the heart of the dynamic that fostered the rise of extreme right parties' (p. 212). By contrast, Kitschelt and McGann (1995) argue that convergence creates room at the margins for populist parties to emerge. Meguid (2005, 2008) approaches the problem from a different perspective by focusing on how mainstream parties decide how to react to populist radical right parties once they appear. How they respond – whether and how consistently they take dismissive, accommodative or adversarial stances vis-à-vis the newcomer – influences the electoral fortunes of populist radical right parties.

Although numerous studies examine why different types of voters support populist parties, there is little research on how this support affects party systems. Most studies focus on attitudes, socio-economic characteristics and political allegiances, and these studies mainly conclude that immigration is the most important issue explaining why voters support populist radical right parties (Ivarsflaten 2008; van der Brug et al. 2013). By contrast, immigration is less salient for supporters of left-wing populists (or those with a left-wing ideology), and economic issues are more important (Akkerman and Zaslove 2014; Visser et al. 2014). Although the homogeneity of support for the populist radical right must not be overstated, younger men and (increasingly) the working class tend to support these parties (Arzheimer 2013; Mudde 2007; Van der Brug et al. 2013). Conversely, radical left parties, some of which are populist, are supported by both less-educated and better-educated voters as well as voters who identify as working class and are union members (Ramiro 2016).

These findings are important but do not tell us how voters' demands for certain types of positions translate into a supply of parties representing them. Scholars such as Kriesi et al. (2008, 2012) bridge these approaches. Treating both demand and supply, they focus on the ways in which parties respond to changing dimensions of conflict as well as the emergence of new parties. Their premise is that globalisation has opened up economic and cultural divides that separate globalisation winners and globalisation losers. These divides have transformed older class and religious cleavages and in some instances have led to the emergence of new parties. Mainstream parties must then decide whether to reposition in light of transformed cleavages and new competition. Populist parties are key players but their impact depends on the ease with which they can win seats and the extent to which older parties modify their positions (Grande 2008; Kriesi et al. 2008, 2012).

The few studies that consider the impact that populist parties have on party systems reach different conclusions. Bale (2003) argues that populist radical right parties reinforce the right in party systems. As mainstream right parties adopt themes from the populist radical right, they move their political agenda to the right, enabling these mainstream parties to invite the radical right parties into coalitions. Drawing these conclusions some fourteen years ago, Bale argued that party systems had become increasingly bipolar as a result. Focusing on the Netherlands, Pellikaan et al. (2003) take a different approach and argue that populist parties such as LPF have politicised a cultural dimension that has not been present in the Netherlands, which has ramifications for the ways in which parties compete over dimensions and issues. Much like Kriesi et al. (2008, 2012) and Bornschier (2010a, 2010b), Pellikaan et al. (2003)

tap into arguments regarding the dimensional bases of party competition and the extent to which the new cultural dimension intersects the more classical left-right divide.

Mudde takes a different position. In two related articles, Mudde (2013, 2014) argued that populist radical right parties are neither as strong as others have indicated, nor have they had much impact on party systems. Mudde (2013) argues that although populist parties are the most successful post-war political family, their average electoral strength is only moderate across Western Europe. They have not had a strong presence in government and have not influenced attitudes on issues such as immigration, which were already changing. More restrictive policies on immigration and integration reflect the changing positions of mainstream right parties, which have been responding to shifts in public opinion. Although populist radical right parties may have accelerated shifts to the right, they did not cause these shifts. However, Mudde wrote in 2013 and focuses on average strengths across Western European party systems, including several in which it has been negligible.

Mudde (2014) uses Sartori's typology to consider the extent to which populist radical right parties have caused 'alterations in the systemic interactions of the relevant parties in a country' (Mudde 2014: 218). There have been no changes from two-party to multiparty systems or vice versa, nor is there any evidence of changes from one of Sartori's (1976) types to another. Although populist parties challenge some liberal democratic values, they are not anti-system parties because they are not opposed to democracy. Moreover, they have not had blackmail or coalition potential, and they have not been relevant in the sense that Sartori indicated. Further, there is no evidence of the increased bipolarisation that Bale (2003) predicted. Some countries with strong populist radical right parties have two-bloc polarised party systems but many more do not. The same is true for countries without such parties.

Mudde's (2014) argument is consistent with the insistence of students of party systems that electoral change is not the same as party system change (Mair 1997), but it leaves key questions open about the impact that stronger populist parties have had on party competition. As we have already seen, populist parties in many party systems have become significant competitors that rival mainstream parties. If we want to know what impact they have, we need to examine what difference parties that have blackmail potential and are clearly relevant make in electoral politics and competition for government. Of crucial importance is how mainstream parties respond to competition from populist parties: Do parties change strategies, altering the ways in which they approach voters, or modify positions and the ways in which they present themselves? Competition for government is different: here we want to know whether shifts in party strength and the presence of populist parties (a) precludes parties from forming coalitions that they had previously preferred and

(b) opens opportunities for the formation of alternate coalitions that would not otherwise be possible.

In addition, Mudde's (2014) argument focuses on whether party systems have changed from one of Sartori's (1976) types to another – that is, from a two-party system to a multiparty system or vice versa, or from moderate to pluralist.[3] Sartori's typology is a masterful instrument, but it is based on party systems as they were in the 1960s and 1970s, and it no longer differentiates party systems as effectively as it once did. Over time, the category of polarised pluralism – distinguished by the presence of not only anti-system parties but also centrifugal drives and a hollowing out of the centre (Sartori 1976: 131–138) – has emptied and most cases now fit under moderate pluralism, albeit with more parties than Sartori anticipated (Mair 1997, 2006; Wolinetz 2006). This development leaves open questions about variations among systems of moderate pluralism and whether there may be changes occurring in them. Before considering changes from one type of party system to another, we must investigate whether there have been changes in the ways in which parties organise two key activities, competition for government and competition for votes. Competition for government is the facet of party competition that Mair (1997, 2006) urged students of party systems to consider as opposed to changes among types. Competition for votes takes us into the electoral arena. It includes not only how parties contest elections but also how they frame issues and define what competition is about. This is the facet of party competition that Schattschneider (1960) alluded to when he wrote about changes in the scope of conflict.

Populist radical right parties are the single most successful new post-war political family. Mobilising around thin-centred ideologies that combine a Manichean view of elites who are deaf to what the people really want with diverse points of view – opposing immigration, multiculturalism and the European Union with a social populism that defends the entitlements of native-born citizens in the case of many populist radical right parties – they have mounted a substantial challenge to mainstream parties. As a result, there have been changes in electoral alignments. Many populist parties are now as large as, if not larger than, the mainstream parties with which they compete. If we want to understand their impact on party systems, we need to examine what happens not only when populist parties appear but also what happens when they grow. Our discussion suggests two key facets: competition for votes and the ways in which parties frame what elections are about and the ways in which they organise competition for government. To be sure, party systems are not determined by a single party but are the products of the collective interaction of multiple parties. However, that does not prevent us from examining the ways in which mainstream parties react to the challenges that populist parties mount and from considering whether these reinforce or weaken changes in party competition that were already underway, or, more broadly, the impact that they have on party systems.

Framework for Analysis

Two broad categories emerge from our discussion: competition for votes and competition for government. These go to the heart of what party systems are about.

Competition for Votes

Competition for votes refers not only to election campaigns and the positions that parties take when they publish manifestos but also to how parties frame issues and define what elections are about. Parties and party systems provide voters with definitions of the choices facing them. Once election campaigns are underway, these definitions may not prevail, but they are important starting points if we want to understand what occurs in elections. They also vary over time and across party systems. It is that variation and the contribution that populist parties make to it that interests us.

One thing that populist parties are said to do is to reset agendas, forcing other parties to address issues that they might otherwise neglect. This resetting of agendas is explicit not only in arguments such as those made by Kitschelt and McGann (1995) that attribute their rise to issue space left open by mainstream parties but also in arguments that discuss the ways in which other parties respond. Thus, Meguid (2005, 2008) argues that mainstream parties respond to populist radical right parties in one of three ways – dismissing or ignoring what the populist party has to say; accommodating it, in effect taking on their demands; or opposing it directly – and that this response affects how well the challengers do. Although Meguid focuses primarily on electoral outcomes, she is also discussing ways in which agendas are set and reset. So too are others such as Mondon (2013), who argues that populist parties not only put issues such as immigration on the agenda but also encourage parties on the right to incorporate their positions. Whether and to what extent these positions are incorporated is a matter that subsequent chapters consider. In some instances, mainstream parties may have already modified their positions before populist parties appear in responding to the electorate.

Defining what party competition involves speaks not only to the ways in which issues are defined but also to the underlying dimensions along which parties compete. It was commonplace to note that although voters regularly placed not only parties but also themselves on left-right scales that most Western European party systems divided not only along social class and redistribution lines but also along lines involving religion and religiosity

(Lijphart 2012). Many scholars argue that these alignments are changing and that a new cultural divide, the integration-demarcation dimension, has either supplanted or transformed an earlier one, religion and religiosity (Bornschier 2010a; Kriesi et al. 2008, 2012). This re-alignment can occur in different ways: In some instances, the socio-cultural dimension replaces religion and religiosity as a second dimension dividing parties and voters. In others, differences between those with Green, alternative, or left-libertarian perspectives and those who begin from more traditional, authoritarian, or nationalist points of view load on the left-right dimension, so that competition takes place on a single modified dimension. The chapters that follow explore this notion by considering whether the scope of conflict from election to election is defined in the same manner and the degree to which elections themselves have become an argument about the scope and definition of what conflict should be.

Competition for Government

As with competition for votes, competition for government speaks directly to reasons why students of politics pay attention to parties and party systems. Competition for government involves the roles that parties play in narrowing the available alternatives and supporting governments. Much of the literature considers parties in parliamentary systems in which the durability of cabinets depends on the ability of parties to form governments and to provide them with sustained support. Competition for government is different in presidential and semi-presidential systems but is no less important.

Noting that Sartori's typology no longer differentiated as well as it once did, Mair (1997, 2006) proposed an alternate scheme based on competition for government. Mair proposed investigating whether patterns of coalition formation are open, with frequent recourse to novel coalitions; partially closed, with incomplete or partial alternation among combinations of parties that had occurred before; or closed, with full alternation in government. Mair also suggested a second facet, the extent to which parties resorted to previous combinations or had recourse to novel coalitions, which directed attention away from classification and towards the structure of competition.

Examining the structure of competition provides an additional way to assess the impact of populist parties. Building on Mair's analysis of the impact of Green parties, Bale (2003) argues that the presence of populist parties has led to a bipolarisation of party systems, with governments on the left alternating with a centre-right strengthened by support from the populist radical right. Denmark and Norway provide support for Bale's hypothesis, but other cases do not fit this mould. In Austria, the FPÖ and the Alliance for the Future of Austria (BZÖ) have narrowed rather than enlarged coalition opportunities, leading to the repeated formation of increasingly narrow versions of the grand coalitions that governed Austria from 1945 to 1966.

STRUCTURE OF THE BOOK

If we want to know more about the impact that populist parties have, we must look more closely at parties and party systems. The chapters that follow provide an opportunity to do so. In choosing cases, we have attempted to keep several things in mind. First, we wanted to have a regional cross section. Thus, we have chosen party systems from Scandinavia, Southern Europe, Northern Continental Europe, and Central and Eastern Europe. We have also included diverse types of party and political systems. All are multiparty systems, but some are simpler, whereas others are extended multiparty systems with more rather than fewer parties (Wolinetz 2006). The former include Austria, Norway, Sweden, Switzerland and Hungary, and the latter include Denmark, the Netherlands, Finland, France, Italy and Poland. Of these, several are bipolar: the principal competition is between completing blocs, sometimes but not always dominated by a single larger party and sometimes competing in distinct clusters, as parties do in Fifth Republic France, Second Republic Italy and Poland. We also include several countries considered to be consensual democracies (Denmark, Norway and Sweden), three sometimes considered to be or to have been consociational democracies (Austria, the Netherlands and Switzerland), two newer democracies (Hungary and Poland) and semi-presidential France. All have or have had strong populist radical right parties. However, some, such as the Netherlands, have left populist parties, and the post-1994 Italian party system includes not only a populist radical right, the Lega Nord (LN), but also the People of Freedom (PdL), which is, like its predecessor, FI, a liberal populist party, and, more recently, Beppe Grillo's M5S, a left populist party.

The chapters that follow fall into overlapping groups. We begin with Austria, Switzerland and the Netherlands and then consider the Scandinavian countries and Finland, France and Italy, and Hungary and Poland. In so doing, we begin with three countries considered not only consensual democracies but also consociational systems and then move on to Denmark, Norway, Sweden and Finland, four countries also considered consensual democracies. We then consider France and Italy, both bipolar multiparty systems in which parties often compete in blocs or clusters, and finally, two newer democracies, Hungary and Poland. Arranging chapters in the order we have chosen, we invite readers to consider a variant of a hypothesis that is common in the literature: Kitschelt (2002) argued that consensual democracies are a breeding ground for populist parties because populists react to the putatively closed and elitist decision making that frequently occurs before and after elections. As a core purpose of populism is to break consensus, then we should expect populist parties to have their greatest impact on consensual democracies' party systems. However, the chapters that follow demonstrate that there is considerable difference between the Scandinavian countries (which have had sharper patterns of government and opposition, with coalitions of the left and right alternating in power) and Austria, Switzerland and the Netherlands. Although it may be disputed whether any or all should be labelled consociational, there is no doubt that the latter three have had a wider incidence of power sharing and less complete alternation in government than Denmark, Norway and Sweden.

The first four chapters offer an opportunity to explore the differential effects that populist parties have had in several countries considered more consensual than others. In chapter 2, Franz Fallend and Reinhard Heinisch examine the impact of Jörg Haider's FPÖ on the Austrian party system. They begin with the transformation of the FPÖ into a populist party and then trace its rise in a system characterised by cartelisation, long periods of grand coalitions and neo-corporatist decision making. Initially, the steady rise of the FPÖ appeared to transform the Austrian party system. Its entrance into government in 2000 appeared to solidify an increase in the number of parties, producing the first signs of polarisation and the move to a bipolar party system. However, subsequent divisions in the FPÖ, the formation of a new party (the BZÖ), the FPÖ's reversion not only to voting seeking but also to earlier populist radical right positions and renewed coalitions between the Social Democrats and the Christian Democrats raise questions about the extent of change. Nevertheless, the FPÖ placed new issues – opposition to migration, Islam and the EU – on the agenda and injected the mass-elite dichotomy into a party system that is now more polarised. However, the Social Democrats and Christian Democrats shared power until the 2017 election and – along with unions and employers – drove public policy.

There are similarities between Austria and Switzerland. In his chapter on the SVP, Oscar Mazzoleni also traces the transformation of an established party into a populist party in the 1990s. The SVP – and the Zurich wing of the party under the leadership of Christoph Blocher in particular – reacted against the established elites and consensus decision making. Mazzoleni concludes that the party system and competition for the Swiss Federal Council have undergone significant changes, including de-institutionalising the rules that govern the decision-making process. Under pressure from the SVP and the inter-party dynamic that it triggered, cooperative rules which sustained the Swiss power-sharing model for several decades have weakened. Pursuing an 'insider-outsider' strategy, the SVP cooperates with other parties in government, but it also uses referenda to pursue its own objectives. There have been important shifts in the party balance. In addition, a more competitive pattern has gradually developed in Swiss politics, which is reflected in higher levels of volatility, electoral mobilisation in diverse settings and an increasingly adversarial logic in parliamentary arenas and referenda. Nevertheless, these changes are more limited than changes in other European countries.

Sarah de Lange's chapter on the Netherlands analyses the considerable changes that have occurred in the Dutch party system since 2002, including the transformation of a party system divided by communitarian, economic and ethical dimensions into a two-dimensional system divided by economic and cultural concerns; shifts in party positions in both dimensions; and increased fragmentation, polarisation and volatility, resulting in shorter-lived cabinets. The Dutch party system changed from moderate pluralism, albeit with a large number of parties, to a system bordering on polarised pluralism. Whether these developments can be attributed to populist parties is another matter. Although many of these developments have been exacerbated by the success of populist parties, all were evident before either the LPF or the PVV had appeared and reflect the weakened position of mainstream parties, particularly the Christian Democratic Appeal (CDA).

In chapter 5, Anders Jupskås compares the impact that first and second generations of populist parties have had on the Danish, Norwegian and Swedish party systems. Jupskås argues that the first generation mobilised anti-establishment feelings. By contrast, the second generation has challenged the dominant structural cleavage by tapping into a social cultural dimension. However, the impact of the second generation of populist parties on competition for government has been the same. The first generation of populist parties led to an eclectic range of governments, particularly in Denmark. By contrast, the second-generation Danish People's Party (DF) and, to a lesser extent, the Norwegian Progress Party (FrP) have been incorporated into bipolar patterns of competition for government, in which the former has served as a support party for governments of the right and the latter has served both as a support party and coalition partner for governments of the right. By contrast, neither the Sweden Democrats (SD) nor its predecessor, New Democracy (ND), have been deemed suitable coalition partners in Sweden. Nevertheless, Swedish parties have sustained a bipolar competition and have resorted to cross-bloc arrangements to prevent populist challengers from exercising influence.

In chapter 6, David Arter examines the impact of the Finns Party (PS) and its predecessor, the Finnish Rural Party (SMP), on the Finnish party system. Populism in Finland has been a 'family business' dominated first by Veikko Vennamo, then his son, and, more recently, a chosen heir apparent, Timo Soini. Both parties found support among displaced populations and people opposed to a foreign influence. Neither the PS nor the SMP, the oldest of the populist parties treated in this book, have had much effect on competition for government. The SMP was initially excluded from coalitions because of personal animosity between Vennamo and Finland's long-time president, Uhro Kekkonen, but was eventually included once Kekkonen had left office. Its successor, the PS, was not formally excluded but was not included in coalition formation negotiations until the 2011 and 2015 elections. However, including the SMP in 1983 and the PS in 2015 led to no change in what was already an eclectic and innovative pattern of competition for government.

In chapter 7, Gilles Ivaldi traces the development of the FN and examines the impact that it has had on the French party system. One of the oldest parties of its type, the FN is a well-organised party that has cultivated a loyal base of support. In so doing, it has entrenched itself in the French party system. Ivaldi explores the paradoxes of the populist radical right in France: Mainstream parties have attempted to maintain a *cordon sanitaire* around the FN, but this boundary has eroded over time. The majoritarian electoral systems that elect France's President and National Assembly have limited the FN's impact on competition for votes to the role of 'nuisance' (primarily for the right but for the left as well, on occasion). However this 'limitation' has not prevented the FN from influencing the policy agendas of other parties. Notably, parties of the right have adopted some of its positions on immigration and law and order. Nevertheless, through 2016, the FN had not altered the bipolar character of the French party system, which continues to be characterised by competition between blocs dominated by the Socialist Party (SP) on the left and the Union for a Popular Majority (UMP) on the right. Historically, these blocs (particularly on the right) periodically regroup and reorganise under new banners.

In chapter 8, Bertjan Verbeek, Andrej Zaslove and Matthijs Rooduijn examine the impact of populist parties on Italy's First Republic and Second Republic party systems and consider whether populism might be ushering in a further transformation. Although present at the beginning of the First Republic, populist parties did not play a major role in Italian politics until the late 1980s. Since then, their presence in a substantially reconstructed party system has increased. The LN is a populist party, but so are the PdL and the M5S. In the 2013 elections, some 50 per cent of the vote went to one of the three. These authors argue that the regionalist populism of the LN was an integral part of the fall of the post–Second World War party system, whereas the move towards a fragmented bipolar system after 1994 was facilitated by the ability of the centre-right to appeal to high levels of voter dissatisfaction with political elites and by its ability to establish an anti-left coalition. The chapter concludes with some reflections on the rise of Beppe Grillo's M5S.

Chapters 9 and 10 address the cases of Poland and Hungary, two Central European countries that have or have had electorally significant populist parties. Both are newer democracies, but the two have very different party systems. Of the two, the Hungarian party system institutionalised earlier and has fewer parties. By contrast, the Polish party system institutionalised later and has ended up with more parties and a bipolar pattern of competition that includes not only competition between blocs of parties on the left and right but also competition within the blocs. In chapter 9, Ferdinand Casal Bértoa and Simona Guerra examine the impact of populist parties in Poland. Populism has been a persistent element in Polish political discourse. However, populist parties were only represented in the Sejm from 2000 to 2007. These parties triggered a ninety-degree change in the axes of political competition, but the positions they espoused were taken over by the conservative nationalist party, PiS. The absence of any prolonged representation has meant that populist parties have had only a minimal impact on the party system, but the PiS' appropriation of populism and the positions advanced by populist parties are present in the current divisions between transition winners and losers.

In chapter 10, Zsolt Enyedi and Dániel Róna examine recent changes in the Hungarian party system. Central to their discussion is a shift to the right that has not only provided a popular majority to a conservative nationalist party (Fidesz) that is increasingly populist but also led to the rise of a populist radical right party (Jobbik) that won 17 per cent of the vote in the 2010 parliamentary elections. Enyedi and Róna focus on the interaction between Fidesz and Jobbik, examining not only the ways in which they influence one another's positions but also the ways in which Fidesz uses Jobbik to stake out positions that it sometimes later adopts. In so doing, Enyedi and Róna describe an asymmetrical pattern in which the Hungary Socialist Party (MSZP), Fidesz and Jobbik compete for votes, but only the MSZP and Fidesz compete for government.

In chapter 11, Steven Wolinetz compares the impact that populist parties have had on competition for votes and competition for government. Taken together, these cases indicate that populist parties have had a substantial impact on what party competition is about. As with Green parties, populist parties have been vehicles through which new issues and concerns have found expression in party systems or, if issues like these have already been taken up by mainstream parties, receive additional emphasis because populist parties take ownership of them. One consequence is that competition increasingly takes place on a new socio-cultural dimension, sometimes but not always orthogonal to the state-market dimension. In contrast, changes in competition for government have been more muted. Variations depend not on the type of political system or the initial structure of competition but rather the degree to which populist parties have been incorporated into older structures of competition. Although the initial response to the emergence of populist parties was typically been to quarantine them through a formal or informal *cordon sanitaire*, such arrangements often break down. In several instances, populist parties have been incorporated into the politics of coalition formation in ways that preserve key features of the system, such as bipolar competition. However, incorporating these parties has come at a price. Mainstream parties no longer command the support that they once did. In some instances, they have preserved their position only by enlisting parties on their flanks as supporting parties or coalition partners. Whether populist parties have an impact depends whether they have grown large enough to prevent mainstream parties, their support diminished, from forming coalitions they would have otherwise preferred or, alternatively, makes it possible to form coalitions that would not otherwise be possible. As such, populist parties are one of several factors contributing to changes in party systems. Wolinetz concludes by reflecting on party system change and the ways in which we study it. Although the literature emphasises the considerable continuity that Western European party systems have shown, it may be time to think more about the changes that have occurred.

NOTES

1 Some parties have been reclassified (i.e. the Dutch Socialist Party) and some added since they did not exist when Kessel compiled the list (i.e. Podemos). Ideological orientation and electoral results are based upon ParlGov. "Radical right" was preferred over "right-wing." Some ideological orientations have been recalibrated when the authors, based on the literature, disagreed with the classification (i.e. the Dutch Freedom Party was classified as Radical Right and not as conservative). For a full list of additions and changes, please contact the authors.

2 Arguments made in this section are based upon previous work. See, for example, Akkerman et al. 2014; Akkerman and Zaslove 2014.

3 Mudde also considers whether populist parties have affected vertical (pillarisation), horizontal (politics on different levels of government) or functional dimensions of competition, but he does not indicate why we should expect populist radical right parties to affect these dimensions.

BIBLIOGRAPHY

Akkerman, A., Mudde, C. and Zaslove, A. (2014) 'How populist are the people? Measuring populist attitudes in voters', *Comparative Political Studies*, 47(9): 1324–1353.

Akkerman, A. and Zaslove A. (2014) 'We the people or we the peoples? A comparison of left- and right-wing populists', ECPR General Conference, University of Glasgow, Glasgow, 3–6 September 2014.

Alapuro, R. and Allardt, E. (1985) *Small states in comparative perspective: Essays for Erik Allardt*, Norvège: Norwegian University Press.

Arzheimer, K. (2013) 'Working class parties 2.0? Competition between centre left and extreme right parties', in J. Rydgren (ed.) *Class politics and the radical right*, London: Routledge pp. 75–90.

Bale, T. (2003) 'Cinderella and her ugly sisters: The mainstream and extreme right in Europe's bipolarising party systems', *West European Politics*, 26(3): 67–90.

Bartolini, S. and Mair, P. (2007) *Identity, competition and electoral availability: The stabilisation of European electorates 1885–1985*, Colchester: ECPR Press.

Blondel, J. (1968) 'Party systems and patterns of government in Western democracies', *Canadian Journal of Political Science*, 1(2): 180–203.

Bornschier, S. (2010a) *Cleavage politics and the populist right: The new cultural conflict in Western Europe*, Philadelphia: Temple University Press.

———— (2010b) 'The new cultural divide and the two-dimensional political space in Western Europe', *West European Politics*, 33(3): 419–444.

Canovan, M. (1999) 'Trust the people! Populism and the two faces of democracy', *Political Studies*, 47(1): 2–16.

Chiaramonte, A. and Emanuele, V. (2017) 'Party system volatility, regeneration and de-institutionalization in Western Europe (1945–2015)', *Party Politics*, 23(3): 376–88.

Dahl, R. A. (1966) *Patterns of opposition: Political oppositions in Western democracies*, New Haven: Yale University Press.

Deegan-Krause, K. and Haughton, T. (2009) 'Toward a more useful conceptualization of populism: Types and degrees of populist appeals in the case of Slovakia', *Politics & Policy*, 37(4): 821–841.

Döring, H. and Manow, P. (2017) Parliaments and governments database (ParlGov): Information on parties, elections and cabinets in modern democracies. Accessed May 1, 2017.

Grande, E. (2008) 'Globalizing Western European politics: The change of cleavage structures, parties and party systems in comparative perspective', in H. Kriesi et al. (eds.) *West European politics in the age of globalization*, Cambridge, UK: Cambridge University Press pp. 320–344.

Häusermann, S. and Kriesi, H. (2015) 'What do voters want? Dimensions and configurations in individual-level preferences and party choice', in P. Beramendi, S. Hausermann, H. Kitschelt and H. Kriesi (eds.) *The politics of advanced capitalism*, New York: Cambridge University Press pp. 202–230.

Hawkins, K. A. (2009) 'Is Chavez populist? Measuring populist discourse in comparative perspective', *Comparative Political Studies*, 42(8): 1040–1067.

Hough, D. and Kon, M. (2009) 'Populism personified or reinvigorated reformers? The German Left Party in 2009 and beyond', *German Politics and Society*, 27(2): 76–91.

Ignazi, P. (2006; paperback edition first published 2003) *Extreme right parties in Europe*, Oxford: Oxford University Press.

Ivarsflaten, E. (2008) 'What unites right-wing populists in Western Europe? Re-examining grievance mobilization models in seven successful cases', *Comparative Political Studies*, 41(1): 3–23.

Jagers, J. and Walgrave, S. (2007) 'Populism as political communication style: An empirical study of political parties' discourse in Belgium', *European Journal of Political Research*, 46(3): 319–345.

Kioupkiolis, A. (2016) 'Podemos: The ambiguous promises of left-wing populism in contemporary Spain', *Journal of Political Ideologies*, 21(2): 99–120.

Kitschelt, H. (2002) 'Popular dissatisfaction with democracy: Populism and party systems', Y. Meny and Y. Surel (eds.) *Democracies and the populist challenge*, Houndmills, UK: Palgrave.

Kitschelt, H. and McGann, A. (1995) *The radical right in Western Europe: A comparative analysis*, Ann Arbor: University of Michigan Press.

Kriesi, H., Grande, E., Dolezal, M., Helbling, M., Höglinger, D., Hutter, S. and Wüest, B. (2012) *Political conflict in Western Europe*, Cambridge: Cambridge University Press.

Kriesi, H., Grande, E., Lachat, R., Dolezal, M., Bornschier, S. and Frey, T. (2008) *West European politics in the age of globalization*, Cambridge: Cambridge University Press.

Laakso, M. and Taagepera, R. (1979) ' "Effective" number of parties: A measure with application to west Europe', *Comparative Political Science*, 12(1): 3–27.

Lijphart, A. (2012) *Patterns of democracy: Government forms and performance in thirty-six countries*, second ed., New Haven: Yale University Press.

Lipset, S. M. and Rokkan, S. (1967) 'Cleavage structures, party systems, and voter alignments: An introduction', in S. Martin Lipset and S. Rokkan (eds.) *Party systems, and voter alignments: Cross-national perspectives*, New York: Free Press pp. 1–64.

Mackie, T. T. and Rose, R. (1991) *The international almanac of electoral history*, third ed., London: Macmillan.

Mair, P. (1997) *Party system change: Approaches and interpretations*, Oxford: Clarendon Press.

———— (2006) 'Party system change', in R. S. Katz and W. Crotty (eds.) *Handbook of party politics*, London: Sage Publications pp. 63–73.

———— (2008) 'Electoral volatility and the Dutch Party system: A comparative perspective', *Acta Politica*, 43(2–3): 235–253.

———— (2013) *Ruling the void: The hollowing of Western democracy*, London, England: Verso.

March, L. (2007) 'From vanguard of the proletariat to vox populi: Left-populism as a "shadow" ', *SAIS Review*, 27(1): 63–77.

Meguid, B. M. (2005) 'Competition between unequals: The role of mainstream party strategy in niche party success', *American Political Science Review*, 99(3): 347–359.

———— (2008) *Competition between unequals: Strategies and electoral fortunes in Western Europe*, Cambridge: Cambridge University Press.

Moffitt, B. and Tormey, S. (2014) 'Rethinking populism: Politics, mediatisation and political style', *Political Studies*, 62(2): 381–397.

Mondon, A. (2013) *The mainstreaming of the extreme right in France and Australia: A populist hegemony?*, Farnham, England: Ashgate.

Mudde, C. (2004) 'The populist zeitgeist', *Government and Opposition*, 39(4): 542–563.

———— (2007) *Populist radical right parties in Europe*, Cambridge: Cambridge University Press.

———— (2013) 'Three decades of populist radical right parties in Western Europe: So what?', *European Journal of Political Research*, 52(1): 1–19.

———— (2014) 'Fighting the system? Populist radical right parties and party system change', *Party Politics*, 20(2): 217–226.

Mudde, C. and Kaltwasser, C. R. (2013) 'Exclusionary vs. inclusionary populism: Comparing contemporary Europe and Latin America', *Government and Opposition*, 48(2): 147–174.

Oesch, D. (2008) 'Explaining workers' support for right-wing populist parties in Western Europe: Evidence from Austria, Belgium, France, Norway, and Switzerland', *International Political Science Review*, 29(3): 349–373.

––––––– (2013) 'The class basis of the cleavage between the new left and the radical right: An analysis for Austria, Denmark, Norway, and Switzerland', in J. Rydgren (ed.) *Class politics and the radical right*, London: Routledge pp. 31–51.

Otjes, S. and Louwerse, T. (2015) 'Populists in Parliament: Comparing left-wing and right-wing populism in the Netherlands', *Political Studies*, 63(1): 60–79.

Pauwels, T. (2010) 'Explaining the success of neo-liberal populist parties: The case of Lijst Dedecker in Belgium', *Political Studies*, 58(5): 1009–1029.

Pellikaan, H., Van der Meer, T. and De Lange, S. (2003) 'The road from a depoliticized to a centrifugal democracy', *Acta Politica*, 38(S1): 23–49.

Ramiro, L. (2016) 'Support for radical left parties in Western Europe: Social background, ideology and political orientations', *European Political Science Review*, 8(1): 1–23.

Rohrschneider, R. and Whitefield, S. (2012) *The strain of representation: How parties represent diverse voters in Western and Eastern Europe*, Oxford: Oxford University Press.

Sartori, G. (1976/2005) *Parties and party systems: A framework for analysis*, Colchester: ECPR Press.

Schattschneider, E. (1960) *The Semisovereign people: A realist's view of democracy in America*, New York: Holt, Rinehart and Winston.

Smith, G. (1989) 'A system perspective on party system change', *Journal of Theoretical Politics*, 1(3): 349–363.

Stanley, B. (2008) 'The thin ideology of populism', *Journal of Political Ideologies*, 13(1): 95–110.

Stavrakakis, Y. and Katsambekis, G. (2014) 'Left-wing populism in the European periphery: The case of SYRIZA', *Journal of Political Ideologies*, 19(2): 119–142.

Van der Brug, W., Fennema, M., De Lange, S. and Baller, I. (2013) 'Radical right parties: Their voters and their electoral competitors', in J. Rydgren (ed.) *Class politics and the radical right*, London: Routledge pp. 52–74.

Van Kessel, S. (2015) *Populist parties in Europe: Agents of discontent?*, London: Palgrave Macmillan.

Verbeek, B. and Zaslove, A. (2016) 'Italy: A case of mutating populism?', *Democratization*, 23(2): 304–323.

Visser, M., Lubbers, M., Kraaykamp, G. and Jaspers, E. (2014) 'Support for radical left ideologies in Europe', *European Journal of Political Research*, 53(3): 541–558.

Weyland, K. (2001) 'Clarifying a contested concept: Populism in the study of Latin American politics', *Comparative Politics*, 34(1): 1–22.

Wolinetz, S. B. (2006) 'Party systems and party system types', in R. S. Katz and W. Crotty (eds.) *Handbook of party politics*, London, New Delhi and Thousand Oaks: Sage Publications pp. 51–62.

Zaslove, A. (2008) 'Here to stay? Populism as a new party type', *European Review*, 16(3): 319–336.

Part II

SIMPLE AND EXTENDED
MULTIPARTY SYSTEMS

Chapter 2

The Impact of the Populist Radical Right on the Austrian Party System

Franz Fallend and Reinhard Heinisch

INTRODUCTION

This chapter examines the impact of the populist radical right on mainstream parties in Austria and on the Austrian party system as a whole. In the Austrian context, the label 'populist radical right' is most unambiguously attributable to the Freedom Party of Austria (*Freiheitliche Partei Österreichs*, FPÖ), after Jörg Haider was elected party chairman in 1986. Under his leadership, the former national-liberal party adopted a political style of fundamental opposition, directed in particular against the two mainstream parties that had dominated national politics since 1945, that is, the Christian Democratic Austrian People's Party (*Österreichische Volkspartei*, ÖVP) and the Social Democratic Party of Austria (*Sozialdemokratische Partei Österreichs*, SPÖ). Within 13 years, the FPÖ managed to achieve more than a fivefold increase in its electoral share in national parliamentary elections. With 26.9 per cent of the votes, it even temporarily displaced the ÖVP as the second strongest party in 1999. Both parties formed a coalition government, which broke down in 2002 because the FPÖ proved unable to reconcile its populist base with the necessary compromises that governing requires. Finally, in 2005, the party split and the Alliance for the Future of Austria (*Bündnis Zukunft Österreich*, BZÖ) broke away. While the ÖVP continued its coalition with the more moderate BZÖ (which, paradoxically, also included Haider until his death in 2008), the FPÖ returned to the opposition benches. After 2007 – as was the case from 1987 to 2000 – the country was again governed by an SPÖ-ÖVP 'grand coalition', which faced opposition from the FPÖ, BZÖ and the Green party. Under new leadership, the Freedom Party revived its populist strategies of the past, whereas the BZÖ followed a model closer to that of the German

Free Democrats (FDP). Although it moved in a right-wing liberal direction, Haider's new party hardly showed any populist features. However, in the general elections of 2013, the BZÖ failed to clear the necessary threshold to re-enter parliament, and it will likely fade from the political scene.

Austria is an important case for understanding the effects of the populist radical right on the party system for three principal reasons: First, the political system was so clearly defined in the post-war period by its ultra-stability and consensus orientation that Austria became a textbook example of the quint-essential neo-corporatist party state. Politics were dominated by a duopoly, that is, the ÖVP and the SPÖ, whereas third parties found themselves frozen out of the institutions of power (Luther 1999: 124–125; Müller 1994: 51–52). Thus, the FPÖ was clearly facing greater odds than comparable parties elsewhere if it was to have an impact. Second, the political system has been exposed longer than most others to the attacks of a dynamic populist radical right party, which had unprecedented success, captured enormous interna-tional attention, and became a model for others to follow. Third, given that the FPÖ has withstood crucial challenges including internal rifts, a temporary collapse in the polls, the exodus and subsequent death of its erstwhile leader, and the establishment of a close rival, it is no longer possible to refer to the success of the populist radical right as merely a 'flash in the pan' (Rose and Mackie 1988), as nothing more than a temporary counter-reaction to an entrenched *partitocrazia*. Surviving a political near-death experience, repeat-edly consolidating its position and achieving a resurgence under new leader-ship all attest to the FPÖ's political prowess, the resonance of its message, and the relative strength of its organisation.

Further in the text, we analyse in what respects the Austrian party system has changed since the emergence of the populist radical right. Starting with an analysis of the properties of the party system, we then summarise competi-tion for governing power. We then examine competition for votes, focusing on the nature and extent of the FPÖ's electoral appeal, and the ways in which the other parties, especially the mainstream SPÖ and ÖVP, have adapted their strategies to the newest challenger. Finally, we weave the different strands together and analyse the FPÖ's impact on the party system, particularly concerning changes in the number and size of the relevant parties, electoral volatility, and government formation.

PROPERTIES OF THE PARTY SYSTEM

Until the rise of the populist radical right, the fundamental characteristics of the Austrian party system had been stability, consensus, and order. Party elites wanted to avoid a return to the contentious and polarised politics of the interwar period, which had resulted in a civil war and the breakdown of democracy in 1934. As a result, post-war Austria developed into an ultra-stable consociational democracy that was based on an elaborate power-sharing arrangement, the so-called Proporz (proportionality) system. To ensure mutual control and to foster political trust, influence over the nation's most important institutions of political, economic, and civic power was proportionately allocated to the Social Democrats and Christian Democrats based on the parties' respective success at the polls (Lehmbruch 1967; Lijphart 1977). This system also allowed the two major parties to pursue clientelistic linkage strategies with voters, which, in turn, gave rise to excessive influence peddling and favouritism (Müller 2006b: 192) and accounted for the extraordinarily high levels of party membership (Mair and van Biezen 2001: 9). Moreover, the ÖVP and the SPÖ respected each other's spheres of influence, even during the periods of the one-party government of the ÖVP (1966–70) and the SPÖ (1970–83). However, this respect was not only a question of mutual tolerance but also one of practicality because both parties had links to the major labour market associations (the ÖVP to those of employers and the SPÖ to the trade unions), whose cooperation every government hoped to secure. The characteristics of the Austrian party system and the rise of the Freedom Party as a political outsider must be understood in this context. However, as the subsequent discussion makes clear, the rise of the Freedom Party was not the principal cause of the change of the party system; instead, this change resulted from societal changes that preceded the emergence of the populist radical right in Austria.

Classification of the Party System

In the comparative literature, various measures have been developed to classify party systems (Wolinetz 2006), which may help us refine the qualitative description of the Austrian party system above (*see* table 2.1). If we apply Sartori's (1976) well-known scheme, based on a party's relevance in terms of its coalition or blackmail potential and the system's ideological polarisation, Austria can be classified as a moderate pluralist system from 1945 to 1966, as a two-party system from 1966 to 1983 (when first the ÖVP and then the SPÖ had absolute majorities and formed one-party governments) and again as a moderate pluralist system from 1983 to 1986 (Müller 2006a: 295). According to Siaroff (2000: 179; 2003: 272; cf. Müller 2006a: 292), after 1949, Austria was a two-and-a-half-party system, characterised by the two strongest parties' joint share of 80–95 per cent of the parliamentary seats and the absence of a dominant party. However, with the exceptions of 1949, 1953 and 1962, the share of the two major parties (the ÖVP and the SPÖ) was very close to or even above the 95 per cent mark, that is, Siaroff's threshold for pure two-party systems. Using the continuous measure of the 'effective number of parties', as proposed by Laakso and Taagepera (1979), in the period between 1945 and 1986, the effective number of electoral parties (ENEP) was, on average, 2.43, and the effective number of parliamentary parties (ENPP) was 2.24 (*see* table 2.1). Despite such nuances, all classifications and indices highlight that, until 1986, the Austrian party system was highly concentrated. From 1959 to 1986, the legislature included only three parties: the SPÖ, the ÖVP, and the FPÖ.

Table 2.1 Parameters of the Party System

Typology	Pre-'Haider-FPÖ'	'Haider-FPÖ' and Thereafter
Mair (1996) Siaroff (2000)	Two-and-half party system (1945–1986)	Moderate multiparty system with two main parties (1986–1994) Moderate multiparty system with balance among parties (1994–2013)
Sartori (1976)	Moderate pluralism (1945–1966) Two-party system (1966–1983) Moderate pluralism (1983–1986)	Moderate pluralism (1986–2005) Polarised pluralism (since 2005)
Number of parliamentary parties	Typically 3	Typically 4–5
Effective number of electoral parties (ENEP) (Laakso and Taagepera 1979)	2.43	3.70
Effective number of parliamentary parties (ENPP) (Laakso and Taagepera 1979)	2.24	3.44
Electoral volatility (Pedersen Index)	4.19	11.52
Effective number of parties in the cabinet (NC) (Blau 2008)	1.61	2.08
Open/closed party access to government office (Mair 1996)	Closed: 8 contests Open: 4 contests (ratio = 2)	Closed: 5 contests Open: 4 contests (ratio = 1.25)
Full or partial changes of government (Mair 1996)	4/13 (ratio = 0.30)	3/9 (ratio = 0.33)
Party composition of government (Mair 1996)	Familiar pattern: 9 Innovative pattern: 4 (ratio = 2.25)	Familiar pattern: 8 Innovative pattern: 1 (ratio = 8)

The stability of the Austrian party system up until 1986 is also reflected in the Pedersen index, which captures changes in electoral volatility (Pedersen 1979). In fact, Pedersen's original article featured Austria as an extreme case that exhibited the least volatility in his sample of European party systems (cf. Pedersen 1979: 7; figure 13.1, table 13.1). He also presented a decade-by-decade comparison between 1948 and 1977, in which Austria's low volatility scores remained virtually unchanged, even declining toward the end of the period studied. For the eleven elections prior to 1986, the index amounted to a low score of 4.2 (*see* table 2.1).

Third Parties

Third parties stood completely outside this system. As such, the FPÖ – founded in 1956 and appealing to former Nazi sympathisers but also independent, libertarian, and anti-clerical middle-class voters – remained a relatively marginal party for thirty years. Hovering around the 5 per cent mark in national elections, it played a significant role only twice. Once it supported a Social Democratic minority government in 1970, and, from 1983 to 1986, it became the junior partner in a coalition government with the Social Democrats; it is only in this moment that the FPÖ – like its distant German cousin, FDP – occupied a 'hinge' position (Siaroff 2003: 276, 285–286). The liberal orientation of the party's national leadership and the government coalition's lack of success galvanised the right-wing grassroots in the provinces and allowed Jörg Haider, the most aggressive of the regional FPÖ leaders, to be installed as the new party head in 1986 (Riedlsperger 1998: 28–34; Morrow 2000: 41–48). Subsequently, he transformed the FPÖ into a substantively new party. Figure 2.1 shows the development of the electoral support of the FPÖ, together with its changing orientations.

Party De-alignment and Party System Change

Although the Freedom Party was the first Austrian party to challenge the two-party hegemony of Social Democrats and Christian Democrats, the FPÖ was not the sole source of party system change. In fact, significant societal changes that affected the party system were under way by the mid-1970s, and they are well documented in the literature (cf. Luther 1999: 130–134; Müller et al. 2004: 147–152). Austria had become a full-fledged middle-class society, triggering de-alignment processes in party electorates. By the early 1980s, demographic and socio-economic change, along with the influx of neoliberal ideas, had created fertile conditions for party/political change. According to a voter analysis, the period of the late 1960s and early 1970s is characterised by 'structural de-alignment'

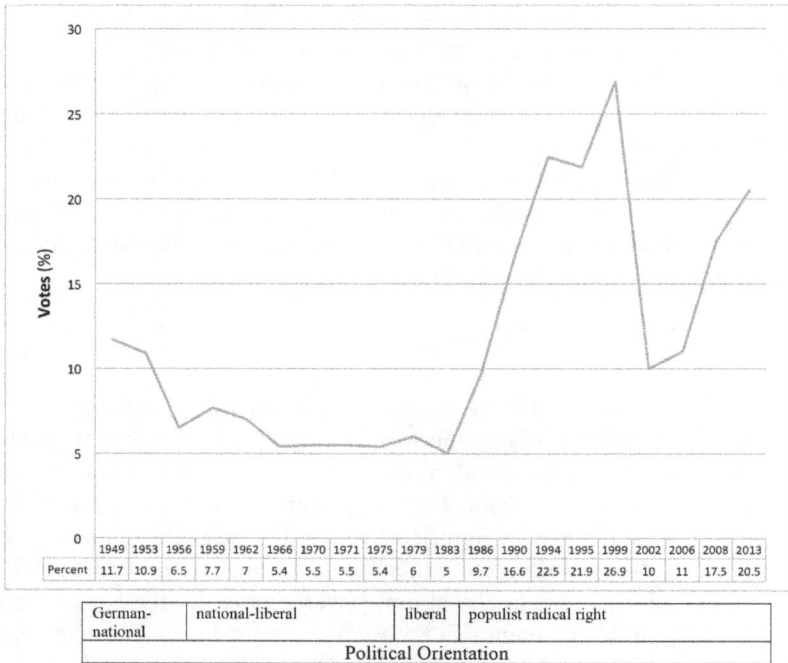

The chart shows "Votes (%)" on the y-axis ranging from 0 to 30, with the following data table:

Year	1949	1953	1956	1959	1962	1966	1970	1971	1975	1979	1983	1986	1990	1994	1995	1999	2002	2006	2008	2013
Percent	11.7	10.9	6.5	7.7	7	5.4	5.5	5.5	5.4	6	5	9.7	16.6	22.5	21.9	26.9	10	11	17.5	20.5

German-national	national-liberal	liberal	populist radical right
	Political Orientation		

Figure 2.1 The Results of General Elections and the Political Orientation of the FPÖ

[1] 1949 and 1953: League of Independents (VdU), the predecessor of the FPÖ.

Source: Federal Ministry of the Interior.

(i.e. the increase in electoral volatility and the breakdown of closed ideological camps due to the emergence of a middle-class society). A second
phase from the late 1970s to the mid-1980s can be considered a period of
'affective de-alignment' (i.e. complete alienation from traditional politics,
anti-elitist sentiments, profound distrust of politicians and preferences for
alterative and non-traditional political movements), which was followed
by a third period in the late 1980s and 1990s that was characterised by an
increasing protest orientation and growing active opposition to the political
status quo (the emergence of a culture of voter protest) (Plasser et al. 2000:
72, 74). The FPÖ was the party that stood to gain most from this development, but it was not the only one to benefit from this trend. The Greens
and, a decade later, the Liberal Forum also profited from it. However, the
FPÖ managed not only to break out of its niche position but also to grow
considerably, potentially threatening the position of the major parties at the
national and sub-national levels.

COMPETITION FOR GOVERNMENT

The FPÖ's exclusion from government until 1983 supports Mair's (2006: 64) assertion that knowledge about the number of parties in a system – in the Austrian case, the notion of a 'two-and-a-half-party system' – 'can tell us next to nothing in itself about how the party system works'. Instead, the structure of competition for executive control, which to Mair is the core of any party system, has to be considered. He defines this structure using three components: (1) the pattern of alternation in government (continuance, wholesale or partial change of the governing parties), (2) the extent of new, innovative government formulae and (3) the open versus limited access of parties to the government (Mair 2002; 2006: 65–66).

If we apply this scheme to the Austrian case, we see that the pattern of government formation was rather stable until 1986. Of the thirteen governments formed in this period, nine followed an established pattern. The party composition of the government changed four times, at one time fully (1970) and three times partially (1947, 1966 and 1983). In the same four cases, the party composition of government was also innovative: these changes occurred when the Communists left the government (1947); when Austria changed from grand coalitions to successive single-party rule, first under the ÖVP (1966) and then under the SPÖ (1970); and when the Social Democrats, after losing their absolute majority and needing a coalition partner, found one in the Freedom Party (1983) (cf. Müller 2006a: 298; figure 2.1).

Thus, the party system was highly cartelised (or closed) from 1949 to 1966 (Katz and Mair 1995), when grand coalitions between the ÖVP and the SPÖ were the norm. It became more competitive (or open) from 1966 to 1986, when both parties struggled for absolute majorities to form one-party governments (Müller 2006a: 300–301). The FPÖ's coalition with the SPÖ in 1983 was intended to complete the evolution of the FPÖ into a 'normal' party with coalition potential. However, Haider's unexpected ascendency to the leadership initiated a process that radically transformed the party, rendering it politically ineligible as a coalition partner for the centrist mainstream parties.

Cordon Sanitaire: Government Formation in the Face of the Rise of the Populist Radical Right

In the early 1980s, after more than a decade out of power, the ÖVP was gaining momentum and appeared on the verge of overtaking the Social Democrats. In 1983, the ÖVP had already come within 4.3 per cent of defeating the SPÖ (*see* table 2.2). In 1986, new party leadership and a neoconservative international trend seemed likely to carry the Christian Democrats to victory.

However, the ÖVP fell short by a mere 1.8 per cent, which it would have needed to close the gap with the SPÖ. The political momentum had shifted to the new FPÖ leader, Jörg Haider. He quickly repositioned the party as a right-of-centre, anti-government protest party, thereby appealing especially to conservative and middle-class voters. By not having a stake in the neo-corporatist system, the Freedom Party could far more credibly make the case for economic liberalisation than the ÖVP. Thus, in 1986, the Christian Demo-crats missed a historic opportunity to claim the chancellorship, such that their only option to return to government lay in the SPÖ's offer to make the ÖVP the junior partner in a grand coalition. The new pattern aimed to exclude the FPÖ from public office, which was to become the standard pattern through 1999 and 2006 onwards.

From 1986 to 1999, the FPÖ increased its electoral share from 5 to 26.9 per cent of the vote (*see* table 2.2) and the party's share of parliamentary seats grew from five to fifty-two seats. The rise of the Haider-FPÖ primar-ily changed the competition between the main parties by precluding any alternative coalition. Neither of the major parties could pursue a policy of winning majorities, and they relied instead on the (shrinking) margin of oversized majorities. Forming a grand coalition forced both parties to

Table 2.2   Elections to the National Parliament (Lower House, *Nationalrat*)

Year of election[2]	Greens	Social Democrats (SPÖ)	People's Party (ÖVP)	Freedom Party (FPÖ)	Alliance (BZÖ)	Team Stronach	Liberals
1983		47.7	43.2	5.0			
1986	4.8	43.1	41.3	9.7			
1990	4.8	42.8	32.1	16.1			
1994	7.3	34.9	27.7	22.5			6.0
1995	4.8	38.1	28.3	21.9			5.5
1999	7.4	33.2	26.9	26.9			
2002	9.5	36.5	42.3	10.0[3]			
2006	11.1	35.3	34.3	11.0	4.1		
2008	10.4	29.3	26.0	17.5	10.7		
2013	12.4	26.8	24.0	20.5	–	5.7	5.0

Political Parties[1] (percentage of vote share)

[1] The parties are ordered along the left-right dimension. Grey cells indicate the parties that form the govern-ment after the respective elections.
[2] Legislative and government periods do not always correspond exactly. General elections often take place at the end of the calendar year, which is why most new governments only take office at the beginning of the following year (e.g. this was the case in 1987, 1996, 2000, 2003 and 2007).
[3] The second ÖVP-FPÖ cabinet lasted only until April 2005, when the BZÖ formally replaced the FPÖ as the ÖVP's coalition partner, without new elections being called.

Source: Federal Ministry of the Interior.

explain and defend the government's record, thereby reducing areas of competition for the sake of maintaining coalition stability. The smaller these majorities became, the less each major party would have an incentive to jeopardise the continuation of the grand coalition, as an incalculable loss of political power and influence would have occurred without it. Thus, whereas the People's Party commanded 44.2 per cent of the seats in the legislature in 1983, its margin shrank to 28.4 per cent eleven years later (*see* table 2.2). During the same period, the SPÖ plunged from 49.1 to 38.7 per cent of the seats. Unsurprisingly, given its more precarious position, the ÖVP would defect from its coalition with the SPÖ and instead form a government with the FPÖ.

In 1994, when the grand coalition eventually dropped for the first time below the important two-thirds majority with which Austrian governments could pass bills as 'constitutional laws' and thus protect themselves from judicial interference, legislation became more susceptible to challenges. As the FPÖ's membership in parliament rose, it became better positioned to take advantage of certain legislative procedures – especially the so-called right of 'requests' (*Anfragen*) and 'urgent requests' (*dringliche Anfragen*) – to 'harass' the government, and the major parties responded by being even less transparent in their political manoeuvring. Although the absolute number of government-initiated bills passed increased in the 1990s, fewer of them actually underwent a modification in the legislature. Fearing that opposition challenges to controversial legislation might affect caucus discipline or antagonise their bases of support, the major parties resorted to policymaking through negotiated pacts, often presenting legislation as *fait accompli* when they introduced the bill. To reduce the impact of other parties or outside actors, such as the neo-corporatist social partnership, a growing number of bills were introduced as private member bills (*Initiativanträge*), not government bills. Thereby, the governing parties could eschew the right of interest groups to comment on government bills and accelerate the legislative process (Fischer 1997: 104–107).

By the end of the 1990s, the Freedom Party had also greatly expanded its power at the regional and local levels, emerging as the second-largest party in five of Austria's nine provinces (including the capital of Vienna) and the dominant party in Carinthia (cf. Dachs 2008: 97–99). While the *cordon sanitaire* vis-à-vis the Haider-FPÖ was maintained at the national level until 2000, this policy was somewhat disrupted by regional developments. In seven of the nine provinces, so-called Proporz governments granted all major parties a constitutional right to take part in government according to their share of parliamentary seats. As a result, by the end of the 1990s, the FPÖ was represented in all of them, contributing to a gradual erosion of the general principle of exclusion (Fallend 2010: 181–182).

Bound Together: The Limitations and Political Costs of the 'Grand Coalition'

Since the FPÖ's transformation into a party of the populist radical right, the interactions between government parties and the Freedom Party were shaped by a set of general political factors. First, the FPÖ's success at the polls meant that absolute majorities ceased being realistic goals for the major parties. Instead of an all-out competition for vote maximisation, they pursued a strategy of winning enough votes to ensure the continuation of their partnership. In fact, a study by Schedler (1995) and new data by Heinisch (2011) suggest that once the Freedom Party had emerged as a successful vote-seeking opposition force, competition between the SPÖ and the ÖVP declined, even though the issue-related divergence between the two mainstream parties actually increased over time. Second, the FPÖ's radical positions, especially regarding European integration, generally precluded coalitions with Haider (and Heinz-Christian Strache, the FPÖ's new chairman since 2005) because of the political costs involved and the overriding importance of EU membership. Third, the nature of grand coalition politics, especially when major policy reforms were costly for the core voting groups of either major party, required policymaking through finely calibrated package deals, opaque compromises and closed-door negotiations, which, in turn, reduced competition. Fourth, although the Freedom Party asymmetrically weakened the Social Democrats and the Christian Democrats, the former weakened less than the latter, meaning that competition for the number two spot in Austrian politics intensified, whereas an otherwise weak SPÖ was locked in place as the dominant political force, at least until the 1999 elections. However, as the ÖVP shrank to middle-party status, its de facto central role as an indispensable coalition partner for the Socialists increased because, without the Christian Democrats, the SPÖ could not form a government. This interdependent relationship naturally led to great resentment between the two, as the Christian Democrats felt that they were paying a high price and the Social Democrats were upset that they had to cater by equal measure to the interests of a substantially smaller coalition partner.

Breaking the *Cordon Sanitaire*: The ÖVP-FPÖ Coalition

In 2000, the political constellation fundamentally changed. In the 1999 general elections, the ÖVP had fallen to an all-time low in terms of its share of the vote and crossed the finish line as third strongest party (415 votes behind the FPÖ). Nevertheless, party chairman Wolfgang Schüssel seized the opportunity to escape the unloved 'grand coalition' with the SPÖ and formed the first ÖVP-FPÖ coalition in Austria. In hindsight, the grand coalition's inability to sustain its dominance after a thirteen-year run should come as no surprise. The general political constraints ensured a continued political haemorrhaging that the smaller of the two mainstream parties, the ÖVP, was less well equipped to survive. The ÖVP was no longer in a position to bargain for favourable terms for a grand coalition. For the Christian Democrats the best chance to extricate themselves from this untenable situation was to form an alliance with the Freedom Party; the latter still required a coalition partner with government experience and was not yet strong enough to dictate terms. The main question was whether the Freedom Party would moderate its position on key questions, particularly on the EU, which, in the end, Haider signalled he was willing to do. He, too, had to be concerned that, after not moving any closer to elected office in nearly fifteen years, his vote-seeking strategy could not be continued with impunity – he was not getting any younger. To avoid endangering the formation of the ÖVP-FPÖ coalition, Haider eventually resigned, allowing his confidante Susanne Riess-Passer to be elected party leader and to thus become vice-chancellor.

The new government changed the patterns of party competition in Austria. The ÖVP and the FPÖ followed a 'majoritarian' strategy, meaning that they attempted to maximise the influence of the government and parliament. Above all, this strategy was directed against the 'unofficial' arena of social partnership, which was considered a gateway for SPÖ influence and an obstacle to reform. In contrast to the style of muddling through terms, which had prevailed for past grand coalitions, the new government aimed to realise substantial reforms in a speedy manner. In addition, both parties appointed loyalists to key positions in the public sector to replace the officials who were faithful to the SPÖ (Müller and Fallend 2004: 809–817). In the electoral and parliamentary arenas, polarisation between the government (the ÖVP and the FPÖ) and the opposition (the SPÖ and the Greens) was growing (Müller and Fallend 2004: 817–818, 823–224). On the other hand, government policies from 2000 to 2002 'generally [did] not bear the mark of right-wing extremism or excessive populism' (Heinisch 2003: 106; see also Luther 2003: 138). However, in the end, government participation could not completely 'tame' the FPÖ, which became evident when the party's populist-oriented rank and file, dissatisfied with the government's neoliberal reforms, toppled its own party leadership and the government in 2002 (Luther 2003: 139–141).

Nonetheless, the ÖVP continued its coalition with the FPÖ after the 2002 general elections. The Christian Democrats had achieved an impressive victory (42.3 per cent of the vote, 15.4 per cent more than in the last elections), while the Freedom Party had experienced its Waterloo, falling from 26.9 to 10 per cent. Continuing the governing partnership offered the ÖVP greater spoils in office than would have been possible with a much stronger coalition partner, such as the SPÖ. Moreover, coalescing with the smaller Freedom

Party, which had struggled to develop effective legislative proposals even at the height of its power, ensured the Christian Democrats' clear domination in the policymaking arena. This outcome also prevented the FPÖ from regrouping and reasserting itself as an opposition party (Luther 2003: 148–149). However, the Schüssel II cabinet (2003–2007) was far less politically successful than its predecessor. The Social Democrats, recognising that their best chance lay in trying to reactivate their core voters (rather than converting new voters), took advantage of the unpopularity of the government's social policy reforms, especially the changes in the pension system, health care policy and home nursing care, and mounted a successful campaign in the 2006 elections, culminating in the surprising defeat of the Christian Democrats, who lost 8 per cent of their voters from 2002.

Restoring the *Cordon Sanitaire*: The Revival of the 'Grand Coalition'

In early 2007, the grand coalition, now led by Chancellor Alfred Gusenbauer (SPÖ), was restored. The FPÖ; its breakaway group, the BZÖ; and the Greens served as the parliamentary opposition. The BZÖ and the Greens could have served as potential coalition partners of both the SPÖ and the ÖVP, but both were too small to achieve a winning governing majority with either of the two mainstream parties (especially because the Greens had decreased in size). The resulting role of the FPÖ remains unclear. In the late 1990s, the SPÖ and the Greens continued to categorically rule out any coalition with the FPÖ (now under Heinz-Christian Strache). The FPÖ was not invited to any serious coalition negotiations after the 2006 elections or the 2008 elections. During the 2006 election campaign, even ÖVP representatives denounced the FPÖ as a 'band of hooligans' (*Der Standard*, 14 September 2006). In 2008, FPÖ party chairman Strache excluded himself from forming a coalition by demanding excessive conditions (e.g. an immediate national referendum on the EU's Lisbon treaty). In addition, the global financial crisis pressured the SPÖ and the ÖVP to once again take over the responsibility of governing to avoid passing the reins to a seemingly irresponsible and unpredictable Freedom Party. Its stance on Europe, which is substantially more anti-European than those of the major parties, seems to make the entry of the ÖVP or the SPÖ into an official coalition with the party very difficult.

Given that the number of relevant parties in Austria is limited, the few options for forming coalitions have, under these circumstances, resulted in successive grand coalitions, which will likely remain in power until the SPÖ and the ÖVP can no longer muster the requisite majority (cf. table 2.2). At the same time, the other parties – the Greens, the new liberal party NEOS, and the new anti-system, protest-oriented 'Team Stronach' (founded and financed by the wealthy Austro-Canadian industrialist Frank Stronach and consisting primarily of former BZÖ members) – are too small for the creation of a two-party coalition. A three-party coalition would be a new government formula for Austria (if we disregard the ÖVP-SPÖ-Communist government of the two immediate post-war years). When this chapter was written (January 2016), it seemed rather unclear if the grand coalition would last through the full legislative term until 2018. Because of the rather harsh political climate surrounding the two coalition partners, the government record is generally regarded as meagre, and the FPÖ, profiting from the continuing financial crisis in the EU and the increasing salience of the immigration issue, leads in the polls.

COMPETITION FOR VOTES

Until the 1980s, the two mainstream parties felt relatively safe in their 'cartel' position and, for a long time, did not realise that fundamental de-alignment processes were underway in the electorate (Müller et al. 2004: 152–153). The decline in class voting and party identification in an increasingly educated and prosperous electorate allowed bourgeois parties to more directly challenge the strongly redistributive and interventionist policies that the Social Democrats had enacted under Chancellor Bruno Kreisky in the 1970s. This strategy was first taken up by the ÖVP, which became more neoconservative on cultural issues and more neoliberal on socio-economic issues. When the Christian Democrats failed in their objective in the watershed 1986 election, the Freedom Party took the opportunity to present themselves as the champions of liberal economic reform, at least until the early 1990s. Over the course of the campaign, Haider shifted his party's approach from an office-seeking strategy to a vote-seeking strategy, and he took complete control of its political messaging (cf. Heinisch 2002: 94–95; Luther 2006: 368–371). At the time, the FPÖ's constituency consisted of approximately 10 per cent more former ÖVP voters (32 per cent) than former Social Democratic voters (22 per cent) (Plasser and Ulram 2000: 228–231). In fact, 7 per cent of former ÖVP voters switched to the Freedom Party, and 2 per cent switched to the Greens (Hofinger et al. 2000: 131). Moreover, the ÖVP was losing middle-class support to the newly formed Greens, who had adopted a rather bourgeois posture in Austria.

The shift towards the FPÖ among middle-class voters continued in the 1990 election. However, this changed when Haider began targeting the Social Democratic bastions in the larger cities and industrial regions. By embracing social populism, thus appealing to the SPÖ's traditional supporters in the lower-middle and working classes, the Freedom Party began chipping away at the support for both major parties.

The Battle over Issues and Framing: The Impact
of the FPÖ's Political Agenda

In the first years of Haider's leadership, the FPÖ recast itself as an 'anti-statist populist party'. Public debate focused on an overbearing corporatist state, *partitocrazia* and clientelism and favoured a more grassroots democracy and green politics (Kitschelt and McGann 2005: 151; cf. Heinisch 2008: 78, 80; Müller 2002: 157–158). Nonetheless, Haider's vote-seeking strategy also implied that the party had committed itself to ideological flexibility and political opportunism, adopting popular positions that conflicted not only with those of the government but also with positions that were previously held by the FPÖ. The best-known examples are the party's reversal of its position on EU accession and its shifts from pan-Germanic to Austro-patriotic, from anti-clerical to traditionalist Catholic, and from liberal to protectionist positions. As a parallel strategy, Haider developed an image-making campaign by presenting himself as the 'champion of ordinary Austrians', who had run afoul of powerful elites who were intent on destroying him (cf. Ottomeyer 2000).

Another set of issues that improved the Freedom Party's opportunity structure involved questions of identity and national culture in the wake of European integration, globalisation and the collapse of communism to Austria's south and east. A key event in this regard was the so-called Waldheim Affair in 1986, which could be dubbed the 'Austrian culture war'. When former UN Secretary-General and later Austrian President Kurt Waldheim was internationally accused of having been implicated in Nazi war crimes, Austrians rallied around the embattled Christian Democratic politician. This episode provided Haider with an opportunity to appeal to bourgeois and conservative voters by becoming a defender of Austria's national honour (Gehler 1996). The FPÖ eventually came to dominate the extreme conservative end of the socio-cultural issue spectrum, campaigning on their objections to the influx of foreigners and European integration.

By the early 1990s, the process of European integration and the collapse of communism on its doorstep had imposed a new agenda on Austria. Preparing Austria for EU accession required painful economic adjustment processes. Coupled with the fallout from the instability in Eastern Europe and the Balkans in the form of large influxes of migrant workers and refugees, this presented Social Democrats and Christian Democrats with a series of unpopular political choices. The Freedom Party cast itself as the only credible alternative for those who were concerned about issues such as the increasing wealth gap, austerity measures designed to allow Austria to meet the EU Maastricht convergence criteria, the impact of globalisation, mass immigration, and rising crime rates. Thus, Haider moved the Freedom Party towards a sharply anti-European stance and began emphasising a social populist agenda, targeting Social Democratic voters in regions of the country that had previously been beyond the FPÖ's reach (Müller 2002: 162–170). In the fall of 1992, the Freedom Party launched its 'Austria First' initiative, through which it proposed a constitutional amendment declaring that Austria was not a country of immigration. The initiative advocated a catalogue of measures against foreigners, covering everything from education, health, public welfare, housing and crime (Riedlsperger 1998: 36). At the heart of the FPÖ's racist and xenophobic mobilisation efforts were persistent charges linking foreigners with crime.

Following a worse-than-expected showing in the 1995 national elections – the FPÖ lost 0.6 per cent of the vote from the previous elections – Haider shifted from social populism to an even more xenophobic and anti-European rhetoric. In 1996, in European elections and local elections in the capital of Vienna, Nazi-style terminology (such as *Überfremdung*, referring to the 'over-foreignisation' of the Austrian people) became a public controversy (Plasser and Ulram 2000: 227). The Freedom Party eventually made such strong inroads in the blue-collar urban electorate that it edged out the Social Democrats as the largest blue-collar party in the 1999 elections (Luther 2008: 113).

From Dismissive to Accommodative Strategies

Social Democrats and Christian Democrats initially sought to politically isolate the Freedom Party in response to its surge after 1986, applying what Meguid (2008) called a 'dismissive strategy'. In particular, the Social Democratic party leader, Chancellor Franz Vranitzky, publicly committed himself to a *cordon sanitaire* with respect to Haider and his party. Using the concept of the 'constitutional arch', both parties declared that the FPÖ was not fit to govern ('*regierungsfähig*') as long as its leadership continued its 'cultural revolution', opposed Austria's consensus democracy and social partnership, rejected European integration and only half-heartedly distanced itself from Nazism (Fallend 2012: 120; Luther 2010: 81–82). The governing parties sought to marginalise the FPÖ by representing themselves as engaged in a challenging but momentous reform agenda and by portraying Haider as a politically irresponsible firebrand and opportunist who was exploiting difficult circumstances for personal power. The strategy of excluding the FPÖ from political dialogue was intended as a signal to the electorate that votes for the Freedom Party were essentially wasted. This strategy was more difficult for the ÖVP because many in its Christian Democratic rural base believed that Haider was championing not only positions that appealed to them but also ones that their party had seemingly neglected. In practice, the disqualification of the FPÖ as coalition partner was clearly and repeatedly emphasised by leading representatives of the SPÖ, the Greens and the Liberals, though less clearly by representatives of the ÖVP (Art 2007: 342–343; Müller 2000: 94–95).

In the second half of the 1990s, the dismissive strategy adopted by the major parties towards the FPÖ was tacitly but increasingly abandoned. The shift to an accommodative strategy was most pronounced in the areas of immigration and, to a lesser extent, law and order. During the 1990s, Austrian immigration and asylum policy became continually more restrictive as SPÖ-ÖVP governments tightened immigration rules and restricted asylum policies (Bauböck and Perchinig 2006: 732–735). The appointment of hardliners to head the Ministry of the Interior, first by the SPÖ until 2000 and then by the ÖVP after 2000, was seen as indicative of how much the FPÖ had changed the public debate about immigration and crime. For example, in 1997, in a show of symbolic politics, the Social Democrats replaced their well-known liberal Minister of the Interior with a hardliner, who, unlike any other Social Democrat to hold the position, cultivated a reputation of being a law-and-order man and openly maintained political contacts with the FPÖ. Thus, even during its opposition years, the Freedom Party managed to exercise considerable influence on other parties' behaviours and legislative outcomes by framing the issues of immigration and European integration, including the very controversial issue of EU enlargement.

The ascendency of culturally conservative but economically neoliberal groups within the Christian Democrats implied a political convergence between the ÖVP and at least some quarters of the FPÖ. This convergence was recognised by Haider, who was also increasingly afraid that, despite winning elections, his party was not getting any closer to entering the national government, and was thus in danger of overplaying its hand. Moreover, Haider's image as a youthful and iconoclastic political rebel could not be maintained indefinitely. In the latter part of the 1990s, Haider began developing a more policy-oriented focus (Luther 2010: 81–82), proposing, among other things, a flat tax that was tailored to appeal to the business faction within the ÖVP. The Freedom Party simultaneously began defending Catholic traditionalism, presented a family-oriented social policy agenda that clearly corresponded with ideas that were popular with the conservatives in the ÖVP, and unveiled a new party program in 1997 that was rather measured in tone. In doing so, the FPÖ laid the ideological and political groundwork for an alliance with the Christian Democrats and the emergence of a two-bloc party system consisting of competing ÖVP-FPÖ and SPÖ-Green alliances (cf. Müller and Fallend 2004).

The Social Democratic Response

In the general elections in 1995, the SPÖ, the stronger mainstream party at the time, reverted briefly to a social protectionist posture to shore up its blue-collar base. Soon afterwards, it returned to a middle-of-the-road course that sought to protect the interests of its traditional base while appealing to middle-class voters. The SPÖ did so by pursuing a cautious modernisation and reform agenda. However, this agenda made the Social Democrats vulnerable to losses from both blue-collar and middle-class supporters. On the one hand, blue-collar workers felt abandoned by their party. In 1994, 24 per cent of the FPÖ voters had switched over from the SPÖ, while only 12 per cent had transferred from the Christian Democrats (Hofinger et al. 2000: 130). Subsequent analyses suggested that, after 1994, blue-collar workers were about twice as likely to opt for the FPÖ as they were in 1986. The trend was especially pronounced among younger labourers and among males (male workers: 38 per cent; female workers: 21 per cent; Plasser et al. 2000: 83). On the other hand, many middle-class voters, especially those employed in the private sector, were not convinced by the SPÖ's reform agenda, and they switched from the SPÖ to the FPÖ (Plasser et al. 2000: 87–89).

Following a disastrous showing in the 1996 elections to the European Parliament, in which the FPÖ did particularly well, the Social Democrats also replaced their party leader. Recruiting Viktor Klima, a telegenic former manager from the oil industry and later the Minister of Finance, for the chancellorship, the governing SPÖ clearly hoped to challenge Haider more directly. No stranger to populist rhetoric, Klima opened his personal life more widely to tabloid media scrutiny than previous party leaders had and came to be associated with U.S. style political marketing and campaigning at the expense of the party's traditional ideology.

The Christian Democratic Response

The ÖVP, the weaker of the two mainstream parties in the 1980s and 1990s, found its ability to pursue its reform agenda constrained when it joined the Social Democrats as the junior partner in a new grand coalition. On issues such as European integration, economic modernisation, welfare state reform, and budgetary retrenchment, the SPÖ moved closer to the ÖVP's positions (Müller et al. 2004: 163–164), making it more difficult for the latter to stake out a distinct profile. In some areas, such as administrative reform, economic governance, and European economic integration, the Christian Democrats had their own clientele groups to protect and could not adopt as radical a reform posture as that of the Freedom Party. In addition, the Christian Democrats had to contend not only with the greatest vote share loss of any party

(1983–1995: 14.9 per cent) but also with frequent changes in leadership. In the years since Haider began courting Christian Democratic voters – less than a decade – the People's Party had four different party leaders.

In 1995, the Christian Democrats selected a new leader, Wolfgang Schüssel. He had been a leading functionary in the business wing of the party. Fed up with the ÖVP's position as the junior partner in the grand coalition, he wanted to give the party a clearer profile and immediately took steps to move the party ideologically to the right, arguing that the SPÖ was unprepared to back necessary policy reforms in the fields of budget consolidation, public transportation and pension policy (Luther 2003: 136–138). Schüssel was also a far better political tactician than the ÖVP party leaders before or after him. This tactical advantage enabled him to remain at the helm of his party for eleven years and, for the most part, to succeed in managing complicated coalition governments, first with the FPÖ (2000–2003, 2003–2005) and then with the BZÖ (2005–2007). Both these parties encountered internal difficulties when they entered government. Traditionally focused on protest politics and previously campaigning on popular but often incongruous or unachievable goals (i.e. by making both neoliberal and protectionist demands), the Freedom Party was suddenly faced with the constraints of public office and the demands of a coalition partner that was significantly more experienced in government (Heinisch 2010). In the run-up to the coalition with the Freedom Party, the ÖVP increasingly converged with the FPÖ in areas such as family policy, national administrative and deregulatory reform, expanded privatisation, national security (i.e. NATO membership), crime fighting and immigration and asylum policy. A survey of the national MPs conducted in 1997–1998 revealed that, on socio-economic and socio-cultural matters, ÖVP members of parliament were closer to FPÖ MPs than to SPÖ MPs (Müller and Jenny 2000: 143–151). Particularly, at the provincial and local levels, demands increasingly called for the ÖVP to abandon its coalition with the SPÖ in favour of an alliance with the FPÖ.

Managing the Issue of European Integration

During the years of the SPÖ-ÖVP coalition, the goal of EU membership and the broader agenda of European integration had been the glue that held the grand coalition together. It was also a popular political objective in Austria. However, in the latter part of the 1990s, the issue suddenly became a political boomerang for the major parties (cf. Falkner 2006). This sentiment not only reflected the austerity programmes that Austrians had to endure as the price of integration but also stemmed from grievances over unresolved differences with the EU on several policy issues (e.g. truck traffic through the Alpine valleys and anonymous bank accounts) and from growing concern about the negative effects of the EU's easterly expansion on Austria's crime rate and labour market. Therefore, the government found marketing policy successes, such as Austria's first EU presidency in 1998, difficult. In response, both the SPÖ and the ÖVP shifted towards the Eurosceptical positions of the Freedom Party. For example, they attempted to make labour market access to Eastern European labourers as restrictive as possible under EU law. After 2000, the ÖVP-led Austrian government also raised the issue of 'absorption capacity' – the EU's capacity to absorb additional members – in the European Council. Under Schüssel's chancellorship, the Christian Democrats also vehemently opposed Turkish accession to the EU, and, in 2008, the Social Democratic leaders publically committed themselves to submitting future EU treaty changes to a referendum.

In 2000, the EU 'issue' took on an especially sensitive quality for all Austrian political actors, as fourteen EU member states imposed so-called sanctions on the Austrian government. The action aimed to undermine the FPÖ's government participation, but it was directed against Schüssel for abandoning the *cordon sanitaire* against the FPÖ. The measures taken by Austria's EU partners caused many Austrians, even those critical of the ÖVP-FPÖ coalition, to rally behind the government (for a detailed overview, see Heinisch 2002: 242–259).

Even after the sanctions and the end of the Schüssel government, Austrian Euroscepticism remained higher than it did in most older member states. Nonetheless, after 2008, the economic recession and financial crisis absorbed most of the political attention and left less room for party political manoeuvring. The FPÖ has continued to be Austria's hard Eurosceptical party; however, it did not advocate leaving or breaking up the EU and instead preferred to renationalise many EU competencies.

Meanwhile, both the SPÖ and the ÖVP have struggled to maintain their pro-European positions despite a relatively Eurosceptical public. Particularly, at the local and regional levels, where Brussels appears distant but nonetheless intrusive, Christian Democratic officials have found explaining the party's position difficult in the face of relentless FPÖ criticism.

'Old' Issues and New Political Actors

When the FPÖ returned to its role as a populist radical right party in 2005, it needed to rebuild its base. Thus, it revived the issues that had provided the Freedom Party with the most political traction: foreign immigrants, crime, Islam, public corruption, and European integration. To some extent, these issue domains were also contested by Haider's BZÖ, which was positioned as a more moderate and office-seeking alternative to the FPÖ. By 2008, the Freedom Party and the BZÖ together achieved roughly the same vote share as the FPÖ, under Haider, had obtained about a decade earlier. Changing party leaders seemed to have little effect on the political fortunes of the SPÖ and the ÖVP: their election results in both 2008 and 2013 were dismal. In 2013, the FPÖ's vote share grew by 3 per cent to 20.5 per cent, whereas the main parties had their worst showing to date (*see* table 2.2). The pattern of an increasingly diminished and unpopular centrist SPÖ-ÖVP coalition, confronted with an aggressive and populist Freedom Party challenger led by a youthful and rhetorically gifted leader, appeared to be a replay of the politics of the 1990s. The position of the FPÖ became even more favourable after the demise of the BZÖ, following Haider's sudden death in 2008. After 2013, the third grand coalition in succession was formed, but it got off to a rocky start by nearly collapsing over disagreements about how to lower income taxes while simultaneously reducing the budget deficit. Following a cabinet reshuffle in 2014 and the selection of yet another ÖVP leader – Reinhold Mitterlehner is the fourth party chairman since Schüssel's resignation in 2007 – widespread agreement held that this moment represented the 'last chance' for the grand coalition to improve its standing with the public.

THE OVERALL EFFECT OF THE POPULIST RADICAL RIGHT ON THE PARTY SYSTEM

Since 1986, the rise of the FPÖ has changed the Austrian party system, including the structure of competition for executive control. Since the mid-1980s, either four or five parties have crossed the threshold into parliamentary representation (*see* table 2.2). Although the emergence of the Greens, who entered parliament in 1986, and the FPÖ's growing strength had already begun eroding the dominance of the major parties, a clear systemic shift did not occur until the 1994 national elections, when the Freedom Party came within 5 per cent of the People's Party. The party system has been characterised by a moderate multiparty structure, with initially (1986–1994) two main parties and subsequently (1994–2013, with the exceptions of the elections in 2002 and 2006) three bigger parties (the SPÖ, the ÖVP, and the FPÖ) and one or more significantly smaller parties. In 1994, 2008, and 2013, the Social Democrats and Christian Democrats lost votes to the Freedom Party to such an extent that even grand coalitions no longer garnered the important two-thirds majority in parliament, which governments use to enact bills as constitutional laws to protect them from judicial challenges by the Constitutional Court.

In electoral politics, the rise of the Freedom Party went hand in hand with a significant electoral realignment (for a detailed analysis, see Plasser et al. 2000). For one, an important gender and generational realignment among younger voters had taken place; in particular, men under thirty years of age tended to gravitate towards the Freedom Party. Second, an unprecedented realignment of the blue-collar working class was occurring as an increasing number of former SPÖ voters were shifting their support to the FPÖ. Third, the emergence of a new political cleavage in society pitted the post-materialist and libertarian values represented by the Greens against the traditionalist and authoritarian orientations advocated by the Freedom Party.

In addition, other indices indicate that substantial changes have occurred in the Austrian party system since the mid-1980s (*see* table 2.1). The average effective number of electoral parties (ENEP) increased from 2.63 to 3.7. When we consider only the period after the momentous 1994 elections, the results become even more pronounced. The highest ENEP value (5.15) appeared in 2013. With respect to the ENPP, we obtain an average of 2.24 prior to 1986 and of 3.44 thereafter, with the highest coefficient (4.59) appearing again in 2013. The Pedersen index shows a similar development. With the ascendency of the Haider-led Freedom Party after 1986, we find substantial increases in electoral volatility. By comparing the average volatility for the eleven elections prior to 1986 with the corresponding coefficient for the eight elections thereafter, we notice an increase from 4.19 to 11.52. As figure 2.1 clearly indicates, volatility substantially increased after the critical 1994 elections, peaking at nearly 21 per cent in 2002.

Despite the FPÖ's substantial effect on the party system, its overall influence on governing has been less pronounced (*see* table 2.1). The index suggested by Blau (2008: 173–174) to capture the effective number of parties in terms of their influence in the cabinet (NC) shows an overall NC value of 1.61 for the twelve governments before 1986, compared with an average NC of 2.08 for the nine governments thereafter. If we do not count the BZÖ's substitution for the FPÖ as the ÖVP's coalition partner in 2005 as a change of government, the party composition changed three times (1986, 2000 and 2006) in the eight government formations from 1986 to 2008. If we consider the ratios of 4 of 13 and 3 of 9, respectively, we see few differences in terms of full and partial changes in government before and after 1986 (*see* table 2.3).

In fact, since 1986, only one government formation (in 2000) can be considered 'innovative' because it broke with a previously established pattern. The ÖVP-FPÖ coalition established in 2000 was also surprising – to use Siaroff's (2003: 276) terms – insofar as the FPÖ under Jörg Haider had gradually left its 'hinge' position (between the two major parties) and moved to a 'wing' position on the far right. However, this position change makes sense if we consider the general political constraints of the grand coalitions and the strategic considerations of the ÖVP party leadership described earlier in the text.

Table 2.3   Full and Partial Changes of Government in Austria (according to Mair 2002, 2006)

	No Change	Partial Alternation	Full Alternation
Pre-1986	1949	1947	1970
	1953	1966	
	1956	1983	
	1959		
	1962–1963		
	1971		
	1975		
	1979		
Post-1986		1986–1987	
	1990	1999–2000	
	1994	2006–2007	
	1995–1996		
	2002–2003		
	2008		
	2013		

Applying Mair (2002) to this analysis, we conclude that the party system, which was cartelised in the 1986–99 period, became highly competitive in the 1999–2002 period (see Müller 2006a: 301). The inclusion of the FPÖ in the government in 2000, ending one of the most durable party constellations since 1945 and introducing a new formula (the ÖVP-FPÖ coalition), led Müller and Fallend (2004: 804) to conclude that the post-2000 party system was more open than the pre-2000 system. However, according to the authors (Müller and Fallend 2004: 832), this change led only to a 'weak version of a two-bloc system' because the relationships between the parties in each bloc remained strained and fluid. When the FPÖ, under its new party leader Strache, returned to a polarising style of opposition, the bloc character of the party system declined even further.

When we compare the Austrian party system in terms of its key characteristics, two contradictory developments emerge. In terms of volatility, effective parties and relevant players (an increased ratio of open contests for government), the system has clearly changed by becoming more volatile, more open and more polarised. As such, the tone of the political discourse is now harsher. On the other hand, the polarising style of the FPÖ under Strache again called into question its 'governing fitness' (a term used in the public debate of the late 1990s). Paradoxically, the radical nature of the FPÖ made it an undesirable political partner and reduced the available coalition options, increasing the cartelisation of the party system.

In fact, the smaller the share of the electorate that the major parties manage to obtain, the more the SPÖ and the ÖVP cater to their most loyal constituent groups, making the coalition parties appear closed to the interests of large voter segments and depressed voter turnout. Whereas electoral participation had been above 90 per cent in Austria until the 1980s, turnout declined from 90.5 per cent in 1986 to 80.4 per cent by 1999 and 74.9 per cent by 2013.

While the Austrian party system has clearly moved beyond its two-and-a-half configuration, the system's current configuration remains unclear. If we follow Sartori's (1976) classification, Austria evolved into a moderate pluralist system in 1983. Müller (2006a: 295) argued that, in 2006, before the future development of the FPÖ and the BZÖ was clear, the party system had not yet crossed the border into polarised pluralism. However, several aspects have changed since then. Above all, the major parties, the SPÖ and the ÖVP – the political centre, so to speak – have been severely weakened by the 2006, 2008 and 2013 elections, while the reconstituted FPÖ, under its new chairman Strache, has grown stronger by following an increasingly polarising course. In addition, the BZÖ and Team Stronach represent two new parties that occupy relatively extreme positions and espouse similarly extreme rhetoric. If we accept Mair's (2006: 65) observation that, in many classifications of party systems, including Sartori's, the multiparty or moderate pluralist category is 'overcrowded and undifferentiated' and thus increasingly less appropriate for capturing distinctions in the real world, we may conclude that the Austrian party system is moving in the direction of a polarised pluralist model due to the FPÖ's strongly polarising course after 2005.

CONCLUSION

Summarising the programmatic and strategic behaviour of the Austrian parties from the time of the FPÖ's transformation into a populist radical right party, we see that, in the late 1970s, the classic left-right political dimension was augmented by a new issue cleavage that centred on Green-alternative and libertarian ideas ('GAL' – cf. Hooghe et al. 2002). Although the Freedom Party (before Haider) had emphasised liberal ideals, its transformation resulted in the FPÖ's occupation of the diametrically opposed part of this new post-materialist spectrum, which researchers have described as marking traditionalism/authoritarianism/nationalism ('TAN' – cf. Hooghe et al. 2002). The Freedom Party has remained the only Austrian party that can credibly claim ownership of this issue dimension. By contrast, the BZÖ appeared to be more firmly committed to typical neoliberal ideas.

The discourse changed as well. The Freedom Party introduced a type of populist rhetoric that was largely absent in national-level Austrian politics; it did so by explicitly emphasising the mass-elite cleavages, by making regular appeals to a conception of the 'people' without divisions of interest or class, and by explaining political outcomes in terms of conspiracies or threats posed by sinister out-groups. Nonetheless, this rhetoric did not rub off on Austria's mainstream parties and remained relegated to the FPÖ and individual members of the BZÖ. More than any other party, the FPÖ embraced identity politics, making Islam and the threats posed by European integration the central concerns in political campaigns. Thus, national identity was no longer understood in terms of Austria's relationship with Germany; instead, it was understood as Austria's relationship with Europe and the wider world (Heinisch 2008: 78–81).

Despite the decline in the electoral fortunes of the major parties in favour of new political actors, access to the levers of political power in terms of government participation and legislative influence has not been as pronounced. In other words, public policy is still driven nearly exclusively by Social Democrats and Christian Democrats and by internal factions within them.

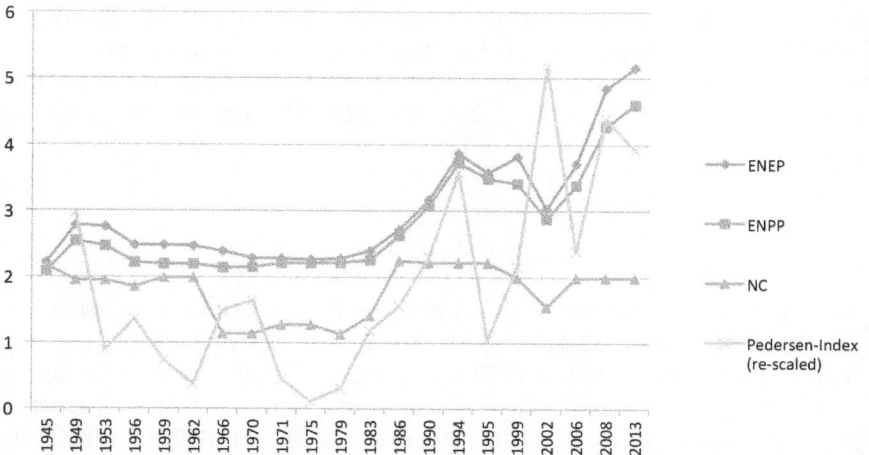

Figure 2.2 Effective Number of Party-Indices[1] and Electoral Volatility[2] – Austrian Party System, 1945–2013[3]

[1] ENEP = effective number of electoral parties; ENPP = effective number of parliamentary parties; NC = effective number of parties in the cabinet.
[2] The Pedersen-Index (0–100) is created by totalling the net changes for each party, which are then divided by 2. For purposes of a better fit with the chart above, the coefficients were rescaled by dividing them by 4.
[3] The calculations were made based on all the parties that received at least 1 per cent of the vote. Changes in the number of parliamentary seats or government positions that occurred during a legislative period were not considered.

Therefore, legislative outcomes depend less on strategic competition with and input by the opposition and primarily on areas of consensus between the government parties. In addition, appealing to important internal factions and key constituent groups, such as public sector workers, business and farming interests and pensioner advocacy groups, have thus far been effective means of securing albeit diminishing majorities for Social Democrats and Christian Democrats.

BIBLIOGRAPHY

Art, D. (2007) 'Reacting to the radical right: Lessons from Germany and Austria', *Party Politics*, 13(3): 331–349.

Bauböck, R. and Perchinig, B. (2006) 'Migrations- und Integrationspolitik', in H. Dachs (ed.) *Politik in Österreich: Das Handbuch*, Vienna: Manz pp. 726–742.

Blau, A. (2008) 'The effective number of parties at four scales: Votes, seats, legislative power and cabinet power', *Party Politics*, 14(2): 167–187.

Dachs, H. (2008) 'Regional elections in Austria from 1986 to 2006', in G. Bischof and F. Plasser (eds.) *The changing Austrian voter* (*Contemporary Austrian Studies*, vol. 16), New Brunswick, NJ: Transaction Publications pp. 91–103.

Falkner, G. (2006) 'Österreich als EU-Mitglied: Kontroversen auf internationaler und nationaler Ebene', in E. Tálos (ed.) *Schwarz-Blau: Eine Bilanz des 'Neu-Regierens'*, Vienna-Münster: LIT-Verlag pp. 86–101.

Fallend, F. (2010) 'Austria: From consensus to competition and participation?', in J. Loughlin, F. Hendriks and A. Lidström (eds.) *The Oxford handbook of local and regional democracy in Europe*, Oxford: Oxford University Press pp. 173–195.

———— (2012) 'Populism in government: The case of Austria (2000–2007)', in C. Mudde and C. Rovira Kaltwasser (eds.) *Populism in Europe and the Americas: Threat or corrective for democracy?*, Cambridge: Cambridge University Press pp. 113–135.

Fischer, H. (1997) 'Das Parlament', in H. Dachs (eds.) *Handbuch des politischen Systems Österreichs*, Vienna: Manz Verlag pp. 96–117.

Gehler M. (1996) '. . . eine grotesk überzogene Dämonisierung eines Mannes . . .? Die Waldheim-Affäre (1986–1992)', in Gehler, M. and Sickinger, H. (eds) *Politische Affären und Skandale in Österreich: Von Mayerling bis Waldheim*, Thaur/Vienna/Munich: Kulturverlag pp. 614–666.

Heinisch, R. (2002) *Populism, proporz and pariah – Austria turns right: Austrian political change, its causes and repercussions*, Huntington and New York: Nova Science Publishing.

———— (2003) 'Success in opposition – failure in government: Explaining the performance of right-wing Populist Parties in Public Office', *West European Politics*, 26(3): 91–130.

———— (2008) 'Austria: The structure and agency of Austrian Populism', in D. Albertazzi and D. McDonnell (eds.) *Twenty-first century populism: The spectre of Western European democracy*, Houndmills, Basingstoke/New York: Palgrave Macmillan pp. 67–83.

——— (2010) 'Unremarkably remarkable, remarkably unremarkable: Schüssel as Austria's foreign policymaker in a time of transition', in F. Plasser and G. Bischof (eds.) *The Schüssel years in Austria* (*Contemporary Austrian Studies,* vol. 18), New Orleans: University of New Orleans Press pp. 119–158.

——— (2011) 'Returning to gridlock – as populism grows, mainstream party competition declines' paper presented at the Eighteenth Conference of the Council for European Studies, Barcelona, June 2011.

Hofinger, Ch., Jenny, M. and Ogris, G. (2000) 'Steter Tropfen höhlt den Stein. Wählerströme und Wählerwanderungen 1999 im Kontext der 80er und 90er Jahre', in F. Plasser, P. A. Ulram and F. Sommer (eds.) *Das Österreichische Wahlverhalten,* Vienna: Signum Verlag pp. 117–140.

Hooghe, L., Marks, G. and Wilson, C. J. (2002) 'Does left/right structure party positions on European integration?', *Comparative Political Studies,* 35(8): 965–989.

Katz, R. S. and Mair, P. (1995) 'Changing models of party organization and party democracy: The emergence of the Cartel Party', *Party Politics,* 1(1): 5–28.

Kitschelt, H. and McGann, A. J. (2005) 'The radical right in the Alps: Evolution of support for the Swiss SVP and Austrian FPÖ', *Party Politics,* 11(2): 147–171.

Laakso, M. and Taagepera, R. (1979) 'Effective number of parties: A measure with application to West Europe', *Comparative Political Studies,* 12(1): 3–27.

Lehmbruch, G. (1967) *Proporzdemokratie: Politisches System und Politische Kultur in der Schweiz und in Österreich,* Tübingen: Mohr.

Lijphart, A. (1977) *Democracy in plural societies: A comparative exploration,* New Haven: Yale University Press.

Luther, K. R. (1999) 'Austria: From moderate to polarized pluralism?', in D. Broughton and M. Donovan (eds.) *Changing party systems in Western Europe,* London/ New York: Pinter Publishing House pp. 118–142.

——— (2003) 'The self-destruction of a right-wing populist party? The Austrian parliamentary election of 2002', *West European Politics,* 26(2): 136–152.

——— (2006) 'Die Freiheitliche Partei Österreichs (FPÖ) und das Bündnis Zukunft Österreich (BZÖ)', in H. Dachs (eds.) *Politik in Österreich: das Handbuch,* Vienna: Manz Verlag pp. 364–388.

——— (2008) 'Electoral strategies and performance of Austrian right-wing populism, 1986–2006', in G. Bischof and F. Plasser (eds.) *The changing Austrian voter,* New Brunswick, NJ: Transaction Publications pp. 104–122.

——— (2010) 'Governing with right-wing populists and managing the consequences: Schüssel and the FPÖ', in G. Bischof and F. Plasser (eds.) *The Schüssel era in Austria,* New Orleans: Uno Press/Innsbruck University Press pp. 79–103.

Mair, P. (1996) *Party system change,* Oxford: Oxford University Press.

——— (2002) 'Comparing party systems', in L. LeDuc, R. G. Niemi and P. Norris (eds.) *Comparing democracies 2: New challenges in the study of elections and voting,* London: Sage Publications pp. 88–107.

——— (2006) 'Party system change', in R. S. Katz and W. Crotty (eds.) *Handbook of party politics,* London/Thousand Oaks/New Delhi: Sage Publications pp. 63–73.

Mair, P. and van Biezen, I. (2001) 'Party membership in twenty European democracies, 1980–2000', *Party Politics,* 7(1): 5–21.

The Impact of the Populist Radical Right on the Austrian Party System   53

Meguid, B. (2008) *Competition between unequals: Strategies and electoral fortunes in Western Europe*, Cambridge: Cambridge University Press.

Morrow, D. (2000) 'Jörg Haider and the New FPÖ: Beyond the democratic pale?', in P. Hainsworth (ed.) *The politics of the extreme right: From the margins to the mainstream*, London/New York: Pinter Publishing House pp. 33–63.

Müller, W. C. (1994) 'The development of Austrian party organizations in the post-war period', in R. S. Katz and P. Mair (eds.) *How parties organize: Change and adaptation in party organizations in Western democracies*, London/Thousand Oaks: Sage Publications pp. 51–79.

────── (2000) 'Austria: Tight coalitions and stable government', in W. C. Müller and K. Strøm (eds.) *Coalition governments in Western Europe*, Oxford: Oxford University Press pp. 86–125.

────── (2002) 'Evil or the "engine of democracy"? Populism and party competition in Austria', in Y. Mény and Y. Surel (eds.) *Democracies and the populist change*, Palgrave Macmillan pp. 155–175.

────── (2006a) 'Parteiensystem: Rahmenbedingungen, format und Mechanik des Parteienwettbewerbs', in H. Dachs (eds.) *Politik in Österreich: Das Handbuch*, Vienna: Manz Verlag pp. 279–304.

────── (2006b) 'Party patronage and party colonization of the state', in R. S. Katz and W. Crotty (eds.) *Handbook of party politics*, London/Thousand Oaks/New Delhi: Sage Publications pp. 189–195.

Müller, W. and Fallend, F. (2004) 'Changing patterns of party competition in Austria: From multipolar to bipolar system', *West European Politics*, 27(5): 801–835.

Müller, W. C. and Jenny, M. (2000) 'Abgeordnete, Parteien und Koalitionspolitik: Individuelle Präferenzen und politisches Handeln im Nationalrat', *Österreichische Zeitschrift für Politikwissenschaft*, 29(2): 137–156.

Müller, W. C., Plasser, F. and Ulram, P. A. (2004) 'Party responses to the erosion of voter loyalties in Austria: Weakness as an advantage and strength as a handicap', in P. Mair, W. C. Müller and F. Plasser (eds.) *Political parties and electoral change: Party responses to electoral markets*, London: Sage Publications pp. 145–178.

Ottomeyer, K. (2000) *Die Haider show*, Klagenfurt, Austria: Drava-Verlag.

Pedersen, M. N. (1979) 'The dynamics of European party systems: Changing patterns of electoral volatility', *European Journal of Political Research*, 7(1): 1–26.

Plasser, F., Seeber, G. and Ulram, P. A. (2000) 'Breaking the mold: Politische Wettbewerbsräume und Wahlverhalten Ende der neunziger Jahre', in F. Plasser, P. A. Ulram and F. Sommer (eds.) *Das Österreichische Wahlverhalten*, Vienna: Signum Verlag pp. 55–115.

Plasser, F. and Ulram, P. A. (2000) 'Rechtspopulistische Resonanzen: Die Wählerschaft der FPÖ', in F. Plasser, P. A. Ulram and F. Sommer (eds.) *Das Österreichische Wahlverhalten*, Vienna: Signum Verlag pp. 225–241.

Riedlsperger, M. (1998) 'The Freedom Party of Austria: From protest to radical right populism', in H.-G. Betz and S. Immerfall (eds.) *The new politics of the right: Neo-populist parties and movements in established democracies*, New York: St. Martin's Press pp. 27–43.

Rose, R. and Mackie, T. T. (1988) 'Do parties persist or fail? The big trade-off facing organizations', in K. Lawson and P. Merkl (eds.) *When parties fail: Emerging alternative organizations*, Princeton: Princeton University Press pp. 533–558.

Sartori, G. (1976) *Parties and party systems: A framework for analysis*, Cambridge/ New York: Cambridge University Press.

Schedler, A. (1995) 'Zur (nichtlinearen) Entwicklung des Parteienwettbewerbes (1945 bis 1994)', *Österreichische Zeitschrift für Politikwissenschaft*, 24(1): 17–34.

Siaroff, A (2000) *Comparative European party systems: An analysis of parliamentary elections since 1945*, New York: Garland Publishing.

Siaroff, A. (2003) 'Two-and-a-half-party systems and the comparative role of the "half"', *Party Politics*, 9(3): 267–290.

Wolinetz, S. (2006) 'Party systems and party system types', in R. S. Katz and W. Crotty (eds.) *Handbook of party politics*, London/Thousand Oaks/New Delhi: Sage Publications pp. 51–62.

Chapter 3

From Limited Multipartism to Extended Multipartism?

The Impact of the Lijst Pim Fortuyn, the Partij voor de Vrijheid and the Socialistische Partij on the Dutch Party System

Sarah L. de Lange

INTRODUCTION

In the Netherlands, a country with an opportunity structure favourable to the breakthrough of new parties, populist parties were largely absent until the dramatic elections of 2002. In that year, the Lijst Pim Fortuyn (LPF) came second in the national elections and assumed government responsibility. Although the LPF disintegrated only a few years after its breakthrough, other populist parties became important players in national politics in subsequent years. The Partij voor de Vrijheid (PVV) and the Socialistische Partij (SP) have been significant forces in Dutch politics. Taken together, populist parties in the Netherlands have consistently secured more than 10 per cent of the vote since the dramatic elections of 2002 (*see* figure 3.1), a figure comparable with that in other consociational democracies (Hakhverdian and Koop 2007).

Despite these parties' electoral success, few studies have systematically investigated their impact on the Dutch party system. Some commentators have suggested that the impact of Fortuyn and Wilders has been largely identical to that of Jean-Marie Le Pen or Jörg Haider. Concluding that 'Fortuyn has accelerated the development towards a political landscape in which left-right relations no longer explain everything', Kanne (2011: 61) describes Fortuyn as the great catalyst or accelerator. However, no one has established whether this change has also affected the basic characteristics of the party system, such as the degree of fragmentation and polarisation, the level of volatility, and the competition for office and votes that underpins the system.

For many years, the Dutch party system was known for its continuity and stability. Described as a classic example of a frozen party system, it was profoundly shaped by consociationalism and pillarisation (Lipset and Rokkan 1967). Coalition governance and elite cooperation, on the one hand, and fragmentation and ideological struggle, on the other, have characterised this system (Lijphart 1968). Because of these features, as well as the absence of anti-system parties, the Dutch party system has also been characterised by limited multipartism (Wolinetz 2006).[1] If the electoral success of populist parties has indeed affected the Dutch party system, the system may have moved from limited to extended multipartism.

This chapter examines the impact of populist parties on the Dutch party system. First, it sketches the history of populism in the Netherlands, focusing on the LPF, the PVV and the SP. Because these parties have different ideological origins, their impact on the party system also differs. Second, this chapter discusses the changes in the Dutch party system that have taken place in recent years, including increasing volatility, polarisation and fragmentation, and relates these changes to the success of the SP, the PVV and the LPF. Third, it investigates the impact of these parties on competition for votes, arguing that discursive or programmatic responses to the growth of the LPF and the PVV have reshaped the Dutch political space and competition for political office. Finally, this chapter assesses whether the Dutch party system has indeed moved from limited to extended multipartism as a result of the pressures exerted by the LPF, the PVV, and, to a lesser extent, the SP. It concludes that Dutch populist parties have indeed been catalysts for party system change. However, this catalytic role does not stem from these parties' populism. Instead, their core ideologies shape their impact on the party system.

POPULIST PARTIES IN THE NETHERLANDS

For many years, Dutch commentators and political scientists believed that the Dutch electorate was immune to populist temptations (e.g. Mudde and Van Holsteyn 2000; Rydgren and Van Holsteyn 2005). Although the agrarian populist Boerenpartij (BP) and radical right-wing populist Centrum Democraten (CD) and Centrum Partij (CP) contested elections in the 1970s and 1980s and 1990s, respectively, these parties had never been particularly successful (Lucardie and Voerman 2012). Additionally, when the social populist SP gained representation in 1994 after participating unsuccessfully in national-level elections since 1977, the party's breakthrough was not interpreted as a populist surge, even though it was one of the first social populist parties to be elected to a Western European parliament.

In 2002, the Dutch situation changed significantly. In February, Pim Fortuyn announced that he would participate in the May 2002 elections. His vehicle was a new party – the Lijst Pim Fortuyn (LPF). Fortuyn's party quickly soared in the polls, increasing from 3 per cent in mid-February to 15 per cent in late March. However, on 6 May 2002, Fortuyn was assassinated by an environmental activist. When elections were held nine days later, many voters still expressed their support for the slain leader. The LPF gained 17.0 per cent of the vote and 26 seats, making it the second-largest party in the Lower House. The Christen-Democratisch Appel (CDA) and the Volkspartij voor de Vrijheid en Democratie (VVD) invited the LPF to participate in the first Balkenende cabinet. The cabinet included four LPF ministers and five LPF junior ministers. However, this cabinet proved short-lived, and early elections were called. The LPF was decimated in the 2003 elections and disappeared from parliament in 2006. In the same year, the Freedom Party (PVV), founded by Geert Wilders in 2005, gained the support of 5.9 per cent of voters and, along with the SP, which continued to grow slowly but steadily, became a force in the Lower House (Van Holsteyn 2007). In 2010, the PVV made significant inroads into the electorates of mainstream parties, gaining the support of 15.5 per cent of voters, and became a key player in coalition negotiations. Although the CDA and the VVD refused to give the PVV cabinet portfolios, they invited the PVV to act as a supporting party in their minority government. The coalition fared relatively well until 2012. The economic and financial crisis forced the participating parties to renegotiate their coalition agreement. During these negotiations, the PVV refused to support extensive cuts, and, as a result, early elections were called. In the 12 September 2012 election, the PVV lost some of its support but retained 10.1 per cent of the vote and 15 seats in parliament.

The LPF, the PVV and the SP share a populist view regarding the functioning of Dutch democracy (e.g. De Lange and Rooduijn 2011; Lucardie 2010). Their opposition to the 'establishment', which they claim is out of touch with reality, unites them. They argue that politicians from the established parties – not only the CDA, the Partij van de Arbeid (PvdA), and the VVD but also Democraten 66 (D66) and GroenLinks – act contrary to the interests of the average man in the street. To correct this, ordinary citizens should have more to say in politics – for example, through referenda. However, populism is not the core ideology of the LPF, the PVV or the SP; it is instead a thin ideology attached to their core ideologies (Mudde 2004). The parties differ fundamentally in their ideological outlooks and are located on opposite sides of the political spectrum, with the SP on the left wing and the LPF and PVV on the right wing.

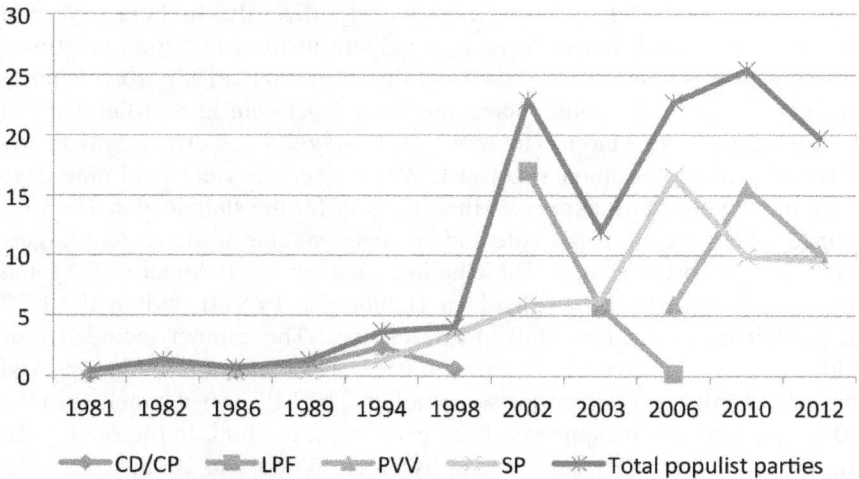

Figure 3.1 Percentage of the Vote Won by Populist Parties 1981–2012

Although the LPF and the PVV are often included in the family of radical right-wing populist parties (e.g. De Lange and Rooduijn 2015), they have different ideological profiles (e.g. Mudde 2007). Because its emphasis on socio-economic neoliberalism and its critique of Dutch immigration policy and multiculturalism are liberal in character (Akkerman 2005; Mudde 2007), the LPF best qualifies as a neoliberal populist party. The LPF's nationalism is relatively moderate and, contrary to the CD, the Flemish Vlaams Belang (VB) and the French Front National (FN), the party has never campaigned in favour of national preference or remigration policies (e.g. Lucardie and Voerman 2002). By contrast, because of nativism's centrality to the party's ideology, which manifests itself in its anti-Islam campaigns, the PVV is best described as a national-populist party (e.g. Lucardie 2007; Mudde 2011; Vossen 2010, 2011). As a consequence, the LPF has been sceptical about immigration, while the PVV is opposed to immigration (cf. Decker 2004). Nevertheless, the two parties have been functional equivalents. They have attracted similar voters and fulfilled similar roles in the Dutch parliament and party system.

While the PVV and the LPF belong to the family of radical right-wing populist parties, the SP belongs to the group of social populist parties (March and Mudde 2005). The party campaigns against the consensus politics of 'The Hague', which the SP argues is founded on neoliberal principles. It defends the interests of working-class citizens against a conglomerate composed of banks, employer organisations, lobbyists and multinational corporations. To enhance its position or to reach ordinary citizens, the SP supports a wide range of direct democratic measures, which it considers complementary to intermediate political structures (Lucardie 2010; Voerman 2009). It combines these populist stances with classic left-wing, socialist positions, for example, with regard to pensions and welfare state benefits.

Reflecting differences in their core ideologies, the roles that these parties play vary considerably. The LPF and the PVV are 'prophets', while the SP is a 'purifier'. Prophets promote a new ideology, whereas purifiers promote an ideology that 'has been betrayed or diluted by established parties' (Lucardie 2000: 175). The radical right-wing populism to which the PVV and the LPF adhere can be considered an ideology that was previously not represented successfully in the Netherlands, hence explaining their classification as prophets. In many respects, the SP is a populist and more radical version of the PvdA, campaigning on the same socio-economic issues as this social-democratic party.[2] It is best labelled a purifier. Thus, the three populist parties take different positions on socio-economic questions, immigration and integration and most other issues. They are only united in their opposition to the EU (Otjes and Louwerse 2015).

As demonstrated further, the impact that the LPF and the PVV have had on the Dutch party system has been more pervasive than that of the SP. Campaigning on immigration and integration issues, radical right-wing populist parties have influenced the dimensionality of the Dutch political space and thereby the party system. Because the issues that the SP promotes are less distinct from the ones on which mainstream parties campaign, it has played a smaller role. Therefore, the chapter concentrates primarily (but not exclusively) on the LPF and the PVV.

THE PARAMETERS OF THE PARTY SYSTEM: THE DUTCH PARTY SYSTEM IN A STATE OF FLUX

For many years, scholars believed that the Dutch party system was frozen (Lipset and Rokkan 1967). Reflecting pillarisation and the absence of anti-system parties, volatility, polarisation and governmental alternation were extremely low, and the Dutch party system was usually considered to reflect limited multipartism (Wolinetz 2006). However, this system has been in flux since the 1994 elections (for detailed election results, *see* table 3.1A). De-pillarisation, a consequence of secularisation and the rise of the middle class, has led to electoral emancipation and a sharp rise in electoral volatility. The emergence of new parties, some of which have been populist, has affected fragmentation and polarisation levels. Together, these factors have influenced patterns of government formation and alternation.

In the post-war era, Dutch voters rarely changed party preferences. Prior to 1994, less than 15 per cent of voters changed allegiances between elections (see table 3.1). From 1946 to 1963 and from 1977 to 1989, volatility was below 10 per cent. However, since 1994, volatility has risen significantly. The 2002 elections (30.7 per cent) and 2012 elections (30.6 per cent) were the most volatile elections in Western Europe since Second World War. With volatility percentages above 20 per cent, the elections in 1994, 2006 and 2010 also showed comparatively high volatility (Mair 2008). High volatility levels might leave readers with the impression that Dutch voters are adrift. However, they mask relatively stable attitudinal and electoral preferences (Aarts and Thomassen 2008). Because voters have coherent sets of choices, typically consisting of two to three parties (see the section on the competition for votes), changes in party preferences from one election to the next occur largely within ideological blocs. Although intra-bloc volatility is high, inter-bloc volatility is relatively low (Van der Brug et al. 2013; Van der Meer, Lubbe et al. 2012).

Volatility is partly due to the emergence of new parties, some of which are populist. For example, in 2002, the emergence of the LPF encouraged citizens to leave the mainstream parties – the CDA, the PvdA and the VVD – and support the new radical right-wing populist party. In 2003, many LPF voters returned to mainstream parties, contributing again to a high level of volatility. Similarly, the emergence of the PVV in 2006 encouraged voters to shift away from the CDA and the VVD. The SP's gradual growth between 1994 and 2006 also contributed to the increased volatility; voters increasingly abandoned mainstream parties, especially the PvdA, for the SP. However, part of the volatility results from voters switching between mainstream parties, as occurred in the 1994 and 2012 elections, or to non-populist newcomers, such as the elderly party over fifty and the animal rights party *Partij voor de Dieren* (PvdD). Therefore, increased volatility thus both causes and results from the emergence of new non-populist and populist parties (cf. Bartolini and Mair 1990).

As a result of the volatility in the 1990s and 2000s, the fragmentation of the Dutch parliament has fluctuated in recent decades (see table 3.1). Because few new parties have been able to maintain their parliamentary representation (Krouwel and Lucardie 2008), the absolute number of parties in the Lower House has changed little since 1994. However, the effective number of parliamentary parties has been relatively high (7.0 in 2010 and 6.0 in 2002) and low (5.0 in 2003 and 5.1 in 1998) in recent years. Unsurprisingly, the fragmentation has been particularly high in years in which relative newcomers, including social populist and radical right-wing populist parties, have succeeded at the expense of mainstream parties. In recent years, the Dutch parliament has been populated by many medium-sized parties with vote shares no larger than 20 to 25 per cent. For example, in 2010, the largest party, the VVD, obtained only 20.7 per cent of the seats, while another four parties obtained from 9.9 and 19.6 per cent of the seats. These support percentages are much lower than those in the second half of the twentieth century, when the Dutch party system was characterised by a few larger and many smaller parties. For example, the CDA, the largest party until 1994, was still supported by 35 per cent of voters in the late 1980s. As demonstrated next, the presence of many mid-sized parties has important implications for government formation.

Although the Dutch party system has not consistently become more fragmented, it has become more polarised. Polarisation scores have increased considerably between the early 1980s and the most recent elections (*see* table 3.1). The sharp rise in polarisation stems from the breakthrough of new parties. Because of the emergence of fringe parties on both the left (GroenLinks and the SP) and the right (the LPF and the PVV), the political spectrum has been expanded. The subsequent growth of these parties – at

Table 3.1 Electoral Dimension of Party System Change in the Netherlands

Year	Electoral Volatility	# Parties	ENEP	ENPP	New Parties	Polarisation
1946		7	4.7	4.5		0.38
1948	5.6	8	5.0	4.7	KPN	0.36
1952	5.6	8	5.0	4.7		0.34
1956	4.1	7	4.3	4.1		0.33
1959	5.7	8	4.5	4.1	PSP	0.30
1963	5.0	10	4.8	4.5	BP, GPV	0.31
1967	10.8	11	6.2	5.7	D66	0.31
1971	12.0	14	7.1	6.4	DS70, NMP, PPR	0.33
1972	12.2	14	6.9	6.4	RKPN	0.37
1977	12.8	11	4.0	3.7	*CDA*	0.33
1981	8.8	10	4.6	4.3	RPF	0.34
1982	9.4	12	4.2	4.0	CP, EVP	0.35
1986	10.2	9	3.8	3.5		0.34
1989	4.7	9	3.9	3.8	CD, *GL*	0.40
1994	21.5	12	5.7	5.4	AOV, SP, Unie55+	0.36
1998	16.6	9	5.1	4.8		0.40
2002	30.7	10	6.0	5.8	*CU*, LN, LPF	0.44
2003	16.0	9	5.0	4.7		0.40
2006	20.3	10	5.8	5.5	PvdD, PVV	0.49
2010	22.4	10	7.0	6.7		0.49
2012	30.6	11	5.9	5.7	50+	0.46

Note: Based on indicators identified by Mair 1997; italics: merger of existing parties.

Source: Döring and Manow (2012); Krouwel and Lucardie (2008); Mair (2008: 250).

the expense of centrist mainstream parties – has created bipolar tendencies. Mainstream parties have also moved away from the centre, contributing to a further increase in the level of polarisation (Pellikaan et al. in press, Pennings and Keman 2008).

Fragmentation, polarisation and volatility have had important implications for the composition of governments. Until the late 1980s, Dutch governments were composed of the CDA and either the PvdA or the VVD. Partial alternation between centre-left and centre-right governments was the norm (*see* table 3.2). Only in the early 1970s, when polarisation was particularly high, were new parties, such as D66, DS70 and the PPR, included in coalition governments. Because they lacked majorities in parliament, two-party coalitions have not been feasible since the early 1990s.[3] Instead, coalition formulae

Table 3.2   Governmental Dimension of Party System Change in the Netherlands

Year	Coalition Composition	Coalition Identity	Alternation	Innovation	Newly Governing Party
1946	KVP-PvdA-PvdV	Centre-left-right			
1948	KVP-PvdA-CHU-VVD	Centre-left-right	Partial	Yes	CHU
1952	PvdA-KVP-ARP-CHU	Centre-left	Partial	Yes	ARP
1956	PvdA-KVP-ARP-CHU	Centre-left	No	No	
1959	KVP-VVD-ARP-CHU	Centre-right	Partial	No	
1963	KVP-VVD-ARP-CHU	Centre-right	No	No	
1967	KVP-VVD-ARP-CHU	Centre-right	No	No	
1971	KVP-VVD-ARP-CHU-DS70	Centre-right	Partial	Yes	DS70
1972	PvdA-KVP-ARP-PPR-D66	Centre-left	Partial	Yes	D66, PPR
1977	CDA-VVD	Centre-right	Partial	No	
1981	CDA-PvdA-D66	Centre-left	Partial	Yes	
1982	CDA-VVD	Centre-right	Partial	No	
1986	CDA-VVD	Centre-right	No	No	
1989	CDA-PvdA	Centre-left	Partial	No	
1994	PvdA-VVD-D66	Left-right	Partial	Yes	
1998	PvdA-VVD-D66	Left-right	No	No	
2002	CDA-LPF-VVD	Centre-right	Partial	Yes	LPF
2003	CDA-VVD-D66	Centre-right	Partial	Yes	
2006	CDA-PvdA-CU	Centre-left	Partial	Yes	CU
2010	CDA-VVD-(PVV)	Centre-right	Partial	Yes	PVV
2012	VVD-PvdA	Left-right	Partial	Yes	

Note: Based on indicators identified by Mair 1997.

Source: Döring and Manow (2012).

have become highly innovative. Many coalition governments formed in the 2000s have incorporated parties without previous executive experience, including the LPF in 2002, the CU in 2006 and the PVV in 2010. In recent years, parties have also opted for minority government coalitions, surviving with the help of opposition parties that support the government (e.g. the PVV in 2010). This development is an important deviation from the practice of (oversized) majority coalitions that prevailed in the Netherlands until 2002. Thus, the diversity of coalitions has been greater in the twenty-first century than in the second half of the twentieth century. Nevertheless, alternation in the Netherlands remains partial, with all coalition governments including two of the three mainstream parties (e.g. the CDA and the PvdA in 2006, the CDA and the VVD in 2002, 2003 and 2010 and the PvdA and the VVD in 1994, 1998 and 2012).

The Dutch party system remains in a state of flux. The effective number of parties continues to fluctuate from one election to the next, suggesting that neither the number of parties represented in the Lower House nor the balance of power among them has been determined. As a consequence, no clear and decisive new pattern of government formation and, in turn, alternation has emerged. The Dutch party system has also become more polarised and volatile. However, these trends started with the collapse of the CDA in the mid-1990s and pre-date the rise of the populist newcomers: the LPF, the PVV and the SP.

Second, some of the changes that have taken place are not novel. If the indicators for 1994–2012 are compared with those for the late 1960s and early 1970s, these periods demonstrate similar levels of fragmentation, polarisation and government alternation. In the literature on the Netherlands, this period is known for its 'politics of the extremes'. During this period, left-wing parties used a strategy of politicisation and polarisation to force full governmental alternation (Daalder 1986). Interestingly, the current developments in the Dutch party system look relatively similar. However, one difference is that the right, rather than the left, is now pursuing a strategy of polarisation. More-over, despite the emergence of new parties in the late 1960s (e.g. D66, DS70 and the PPR), the levels of volatility were relatively low, and mainstream parties remained rather large. In that respect, the current changes have the potential to affect the competition for office more fundamentally, thereby transforming the direction of competition from centripetal to centrifugal. Of course, the kind of parties that emerged in the late 1960s not only were funda-mentally different ideologically from those that have emerged in recent years but also appealed to different segments of the population. Nevertheless, they performed similar functions, opening up the party system to new dynamics of competition, for example, by changing coalition practices and redefining the relationship between parties.

The observations mentioned earlier in the text suggest that changes in the Dutch party system may be cyclical in nature, with periods of depolarisation followed by periods of polarisation. In table 3.2, the four phases in Dutch party politics can clearly be distinguished based on their characteristics: depolarisation in the 1950s, polarisation in the 1960s and 1970s, depolarisation in the 1980s and 1990s and polarisation in the twenty-first century. The cyclical dynamics in the Dutch party system might stem from the lack of contestation and conflict in calmer periods. In those periods, mainstream parties tend to collide, which hampers representation. When representation is not optimal, citizens may respond to prolonged periods of depolarisation by supporting challengers that seek to redefine or extend conflict.

COMPETITION FOR VOTES

In the past, the Dutch electorate displayed relatively stable patterns of party switching. The rise of the SP, the PVV and the LPF has significantly influenced patterns of competition in the Netherlands. Because existing parties have lost supporters to populist challengers, they have adjusted their electoral strategies. However, the effect has not been uniform because populist parties compete with different established parties for votes. The electorate of the PVV overlaps primarily with that of other right-wing parties. Of the VVD voters in the 2010 elections, 42.1 per cent considered supporting the PVV in subsequent elections, as did 17.4 per cent of SGP voters and 11.9 per cent of CDA voters. The SP has the greatest overlap with left-wing parties, particularly the PvdA (31.5 per cent considered supporting the SP) and GroenLinks (27.5 per cent). However, the SP also shares voters with the PvdD (13.5 per cent) and D66 (12.6 per cent). In addition, considerable overlap exists between the SP and the PVV: 18.1 per cent of SP voters consider voting for the PVV, and 13.4 per cent of PVV voters feel an affinity with the SP (Van der Meer, Van Elsas et al. 2012: 32–34; see also Van der Brug et al. 2013).

First and foremost, the ideological similarities among parties can explain the overlap in electoral constituencies. For example, the electorates of the CDA, the PVV, the SGP and the VVD share programmatic orientations, including their traditional stances on right-wing issues such as law and order and nationalism (Van Kersbergen and Krouwel 2008). The SP, the PvdA, and GroenLinks think alike on socio-economic issues, arguing in favour of more state intervention in the economy to address inequality and to protect the vulnerable. The SP and the PVV differ in many ways, but they attract voters with similar socio-economic and demographic characteristics. Their typically less-educated voters are Eurosceptic and cynical about politics – stances that the two populist parties also embrace (Schumacher and Rooduijn 2013).

As a result of electoral competition between the mainstream and populist parties, the former have reacted quite strongly to the success of the latter, most notably by changing their discourse and programmes (Bale 2008; Bale et al. 2010; Meguid 2005). Because the PVV and the LPF have gained support by campaigning on immigration and integration issues, mainstream parties have primarily responded by altering their stances on these issues. However, they have also changed positions on the EU and law and order.[4] By contrast, the SP campaigns primarily on socio-economic issues. Because these issues concern the traditional left-right dimension, the SP's impact on the party system has been less substantial than those of the PVV and the LPF.

Some mainstream parties have reacted by devoting more attention to immigration and integration issues. However, these issues were gaining salience prior to the rise of radical right-wing populist parties (*see* table 3.3). Remarkably, several parties devoted less attention to immigration and integration questions in their manifestos in 2002, the year in which the LPF emerged, than in 1998. The notable exception is the VVD, which responded to the LPF's success in the polls with an overhaul of the immigration and integration paragraphs of its programme. At its April 2002 party congress, the VVD rewrote its programme, further emphasising the integration of immigrants into Dutch society (Van Kersbergen and Krouwel 2008). In 2006, the first year in which Geert Wilders' PVV participated in the elections for the Lower House, the attention devoted to immigration and integration issues in the manifestos of the CU, GroenLinks, the PvdA, and the SGP increased, but other parties paid less attention to these issues. In addition, in 2010, immigration and integration problems became less salient in all parties except the VVD. The lack of attention given to these issues probably stemmed from the 2008 financial crisis (Van Heerden et al. 2014).

The fluctuations in the importance of immigration and integration issues are only partly related to the electoral success of radical right-wing populist parties. Although a few parties have responded directly to the electoral threat posed by these parties (most notably the VVD), other parties, such as the CDA and the PvdA, seemingly react more indirectly. The latter group have seemingly reacted to the rising salience of immigration and integration issues among citizens (*see* table 3.3). Until the late 1980s, voters who were asked to name the most important problem facing the country rarely mentioned immigration. Instead, they considered employment to be the most important problem. However, in 1994, immigration and integration issues suddenly became one of the most often cited problems facing the country. Although the percentage of voters who mentioned immigration and integration issues gradually declined – from 26 per cent in 1994 to 11 per cent in 2006 (Aarts and Thomassen 2008) – it has likely increased again in recent years.

Mainstream parties have also reacted by adopting different frames and emphasising different facets when they discuss immigration and integration (*see* table 3.4). In recent years, the cultural integration of immigrants, as opposed to their socio-economic integration, has been emphasised (Van Heerden et al. 2014). However, these changes commenced in 1998 and thus pre-date the emergence of the LPF and the PVV.

In addition, mainstream parties have reacted by adopting more restrictive stances on immigration and integration (e.g. Davis 2012; Van Heerden et al. 2014). A shift from more multicultural to more monocultural positions can be observed in the manifestos of the larger mainstream parties (the CDA, the PvdA and the VVD), albeit for different reasons. However, mainstream parties have not changed their programmes to the same extent. Certain parties (e.g. the CDA and the VVD) have moved to the 'right' more rapidly than others (e.g. D66, GroenLinks, PvdA, and SP). Such positional shifts depend both on the extent to which immigration and integration issues cause intraparty tensions and on the composition of parties' electorates (Davis 2012; Van Heerden et al. 2014). Because the CDA and the VVD have greatest overlap

Table 3.3 Salience of Immigration and Integration Issues in Dutch Manifestos

	1994 (%)	1998 (%)	2002 (%)	2006 (%)	2010 (%)
CDA	1.35	3.13	2.52	2.04	1.48
CU	1.24*	1.63*	0.59	2.67	2.07
D66	1.38	1.80	1.70	0.65	0.52
GL	2.11	2.48	2.11	4.69	2.75
PvdA	0.93	1.75	0.84	2.35	1.04
SGP	1.50	1.30	1.77	2.64	1.28
SP	2.26	2.51	2.61	1.89	1.85
VVD	1.47	1.56	3.29	1.36	3.30
Radical right	6.02	5.23	5.00	14.94	7.09
Voters	26	19	16	11	22

* Average of the GPV and RPF

Source: Aarts and Thomassen (2008); Van Heerden et al. (2014).

Table 3.4 Salience of Different Immigration and Integration Frames in Dutch Manifestos

	1994 (%)	1998 (%)	2002 (%)	2006 (%)	2010 (%)
Immigration	41.5	40.7	46.7	45.6	45.8
Integration – cultural	17.2	25.1	20.1	28.7	31.5
Integration – legal	0.0	0.9	2.9	3.8	3.5
Integration – socio-economic	41.0	33.3	30.3	21.8	19.2

Source: Van Heerden et al. (2014).

in voter preferences with the PVV and the LPF, they have the strongest incentives to co-opt their positions (cf. Van Spanje 2010). Consequently, a growing level of polarisation characterises the Dutch debate about immigration and integration issues (Oosterwaal and Torenvlied 2010). A clear distinction exists between parties with monocultural orientations, on the one hand, and parties with multicultural orientation, on the other. Because of the emergence of radical right-wing populist parties, the politics of immigration and integration is more divided than ever before.

More importantly, the immigration and integration debate does not pit left-wing parties against right-wing parties. Although traditional left-right positions and parties' positions on immigration and integration correspond considerably (Davis 2012; Van Heerden et al. 2014), notable exceptions to this rule prevent immigration and integration issues from being subsumed in the left-right dimension. Two examples are telling: D66 combines a right-wing position on socio-economic issues with multiculturalism, making placing the party on a general left-right spectrum difficult. The PVV programme combines monoculturalism and welfare chauvinism; thus, interpreting its programme in general left-right terms is not easy.

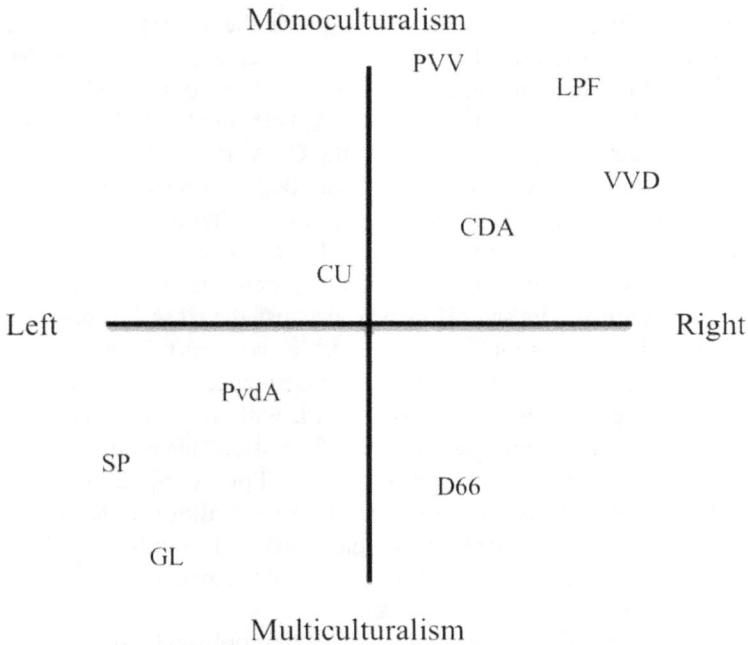

Figure 3.2 Dutch Political Space after 2002

Source: Based on Pellikaan et al. (2003, 2007).

Immigration and integration issues can be considered an independent new dimension that structures the Dutch political space (e.g. Otjes 2011; Pellikaan, et al. 2003, 2007), which is orthogonally related to the socio-economic dimension.[5] Consequently, Dutch parties can take a left-wing monocultural (the ChristenUnie, CU), a left-wing multicultural position (GroenLinks, the PvdA and the SP), a right-wing monocultural position (the CDA, the LPF, the PVV, the SGP and the VVD) or a right-wing multicultural position (D66) in this political space (*see* figure 3.2). Thus, since the emergence of the LPF, the Dutch political space has differed considerably from that of previous decades, when communitarian issues, ethical issues and socio-economic issues structured competition and cooperation among the parties (Pellikaan et al. 2003).

COMPETITION FOR GOVERNMENT

Changes in the dimensionality of the political space have made coalition formation in the Netherlands more complex and protracted. Until the early 1990s, Dutch parties aimed to form coalition governments that were connected along the left-right dimension because doing so would ensure coherent policy production (De Vries 1999). With the emergence of the new two-dimensional structure of the political space, the possibilities to form coherent coalitions have increased considerably. Coalitions can be connected along the left-right dimension (e.g. the CDA, D66 and the VVD in 2003), the libertarian-authoritarian dimension (e.g. the CDA, the PVV and the VVD in 2010), or both (e.g. CDA, LPF and VVD in 2002). Moreover, the fragmentation and polarisation that have occurred in the Netherlands have created an 'empty heart' in the Dutch political space. In post-war politics, the CDA was at the centre of the political space, dominating coalition bargaining because of its central position and its size. However, because the CDA has become more right-wing and has lost much of its support, a 'core party' can no longer be identified (Pellikaan et al. in press). As a consequence, competition for office and votes has become more centrifugal and, without a core party that can dominate the formation process, coalition formations have become difficult, and governments are now inherently instable. For example, between 2002 and 2015, the Netherlands was governed by five coalitions, and the country held an equally high number of general elections. This number stands in stark contrast to the figures from the 1980s and 1990s, when most government coalitions endured a full four-year term.

The changes in the dimensionality of the political space have also affected the ways in which coalition agreements are reached. Coalitions are increasingly formed based on logrolling (the quid pro quo principle), rather than on classic compromises (the meet-in-the-middle principle). Radical right-wing populist parties have been important for this development. Because these parties campaign on different issues than mainstream parties, trade-offs are possible. In 2010 and, to a lesser extent, in 2002, the CDA and the VVD decided to give their radical right-wing coalition partners free rein in the domain of immigration and integration policy in exchange for the latter's support in economic, financial and social reforms (De Lange 2012b).

The changes in coalition practices can be illustrated by examining the government formation in 2002, when the LPF assumed office, and in 2010, when the PVV became a supporting party for a Rutte I minority cabinet. When Fortuyn first emerged on the scene in 2002, the approach of the media and politicians was quite similar to that used with respect to its predecessor, Janmaat's CD. Initially, mainstream parties and politicians, with the exception of the CDA, were quite hostile towards the LPF. This hostility reflected a deeply shared sense of unease about Fortuyn's immigration policies and electoral considerations (Van Heerden 2014). As opponents frequently attacked Fortuyn, his supporters began claiming that he was being demonised. Although such demonisation certainly occurred initially, attitudinal and behavioural changes arose at the local level in late March 2002, most notably in Rotterdam. After Fortuyn's local party *Leefbaar Rotterdam* (LR) became the largest party in the city's municipal council, Fortuyn invited all parties for exploratory talks and ultimately formed a coalition with the CDA and the VVD.[6] After the assassination of Fortuyn and the electoral victory of the LPF, national politicians' attitudes towards the party also changed dramatically. After the 2002 elections for the Lower House, a broad consensus emerged that the LPF should be invited to discuss coalition alternatives with the other winners – the CDA and the VVD. This new consensus deviated from the informal norm that had previously prevailed. Before 2002, parties were typically included in coalition governments because of their relative size and their ideological proximity.

At the start of the coalition formation process, most leading politicians interpreted the election results as a clear demand for political change.[7] Minutes from parliamentary debates during the 2002 coalition negotiations reveal that most mainstream parties believed that the election results reflected a clear preference on the part of the electorate for a government coalition of the CDA, the LPF and the VVD.[8] Thus, the landslide victory of the newly founded LPF made a centre-right government of the CDA, the LPF and the VVD the 'only realistic option' (Lucardie 2003: 1034). According to Lucardie and Voerman, several new coalitions could have been formed, but only one was considered viable based on the clear message that voters had sent by supporting the LPF:

> Even the dramatic 2002 election results allowed several options: a 'Scandina-vian option' of a minority government led by the largest party – the CDA – and supported by the VVD, the LPF and/or the small Protestant parties; a centre-left coalition of the CDA, the PvdA and GroenLinks; or a 'Flemish option' of a grand coalition of the CDA, the PvdA, and the VVD imposing a cordon sanitaire on the LPF. However, these options were incompatible with the consociational political culture of the Netherlands. Consociationalism required a reconciliation of the emerging conflict between the populist opposition and the elitist govern-ment, in other words, involving the LPF in a coalition to pacify the unrest and discontent mobilized by Fortuyn and exacerbated by his violent death. (Lucardie and Voerman 2007: 252–253)

The coalition negotiations between the CDA, the LPF and the VVD were smooth and quick, with the parties easily reaching a coalition agreement.[9] The negotiations were concluded after sixty-seven days of bargaining – a relatively short period by Dutch standards.[10] On immigration and integration, as well as on other issues prominent in the campaign for the 2002 elections (e.g. education, healthcare and security), the parties promoted stances that were largely similar (De Lange 2012a, 2012b). At the outset of the coalition negotiations, the LPF underlined the policy rationale for a centre-right cabi-net when it declared the following:

> Especially the CDA and the VVD have priorities similar to ours. According to us, the differences can also be overcome in the domain of migration policy. Even though our party declares without hesitation that the Netherlands is not an immigration country, our stance is not fundamentally different from that of the CDA or the VVD.[11]

However, despite these shared policy orientations, the coalition collapsed after only three months in office. Continuous fights between LPF ministers and between different groups within the LPF encouraged the CDA and VVD to 'pull the plug'.[12] These fights were a direct consequence of Fortuyn's assassination; the LPF failed to find a legitimate leader to succeed him (Art 2011, De Lange and Art 2011).

The failure of the coalition between the CDA, the VVD and the radical right-wing populists (the LPF) did not signal a return to exclusionary mecha-nisms. Instead, the approach by both the media and parties towards Geert Wilders and his PVV has been cooperative from the start. Wilders had been a representative of the mainstream VVD before he founded his own party and was thus on friendly terms with the vast majority of members of parliament, which partly explains this cooperative approach. In addition, the way of thinking about the efficacy of exclusionary mechanisms and the attitudes of citizens, journalists and politicians changed. Exclusionary mechanisms were increasingly perceived as counterproductive and anti-democratic. Bans on discrimination and hate speech increased the salience of questions regarding these groups' freedom of speech. In addition, the assassinations of Fortuyn and van Gogh, as well as 11 September 2001, affected attitudes towards Islam and multiculturalism, increasing the acceptability of radical right-wing populist parties. Although a *cordon sanitaire* was briefly discussed in media outlets in the summer of 2009 and again in September 2013 and March 2014 – when Wilders made some of his most radical statements – mainstream parties have never thought seriously about systematically ostracising the party. Instead, prior to the 2010 elections, most parties decided to cooperate with the PVV. Although left-wing parties (the CU, D66, GroenLinks, the PvdA and the SP) declared that they did not see any grounds for cooperation because of ideological differences, the CDA and the VVD stated they were unwilling to rule out any coalition a priori. Although these stances were partly informed by ideological considerations (i.e. the policy distance between parties), strategic motivations also came into play. Because the CDA and the VVD risked losing votes to the PVV, they were careful to not offend potential PVV supporters (Akkerman 2016).

Because the 2010 elections did not produce a clear majority for previously formed coalitions, complex negotiations followed. When exploratory talks among the CDA, the PVV and the VVD, similar to those conducted in Austria in 2000, failed in June 2010, other alternatives were discussed. These included a 'purple-plus' coalition of D66, GroenLinks, the PvdA and the VVD. Because the foundation for these coalitions proved inadequate, formal negotiations between the CDA, the PVV and the VVD commenced more than two months after the elections.[13] Although negotiations were abandoned briefly in early September 2010, a minority government of the VVD and the CDA, supported by the PVV, assumed office in October 2010.[14] The decision to exclude the PVV from the cabinet and to sign a separate support agreement with the party was partially motivated by ideological differences, most notably with regard to the position of Islam. The support agreement indicated that the parties fundamentally disagreed about 'the characterization of Islam as either a religion or a (political) ideology', but they nevertheless saw enough common ground to cooperate on issues such as the budget, crime, eldercare and immigration and integration. However, this separate agreement also reflected opposition to the PVV within the CDA – the CDA believed that the alliance went against the core principles of the party – and the PVV's reluctance to take responsibility for all government policies (Akkerman 2016). Thus, although the inclusion of the LPF and the PVV has been the dominant approach, radical right-wing populist parties have never been considered mainstream or 'normal' parties (Akkerman et al. 2016).[15]

FROM LIMITED MULTIPARTISM TO EXTENDED MULTIPARTISM?

Although party competition in the 1980s and 1990s was essentially depolarised and centripetal, it has become increasingly polarised and centrifugal since 1994 (Pellikaan et al. in press). The competition for office and votes is oriented more towards the extremes of the political space than it has been in previous decades. However, party competition is not fully bipolar. Because the CDA, despite losing the dominant position it once enjoyed, continues to periodically play a significant role, the Dutch party system is not (yet) identical to the bipolar systems that can be found in Denmark, Norway and Sweden. For example, between 2002 and 2010, the CDA was the largest party and thus led the government coalitions that assumed office. As a result, bipolar drive was relatively contained in this period. However, the CDA's role is clearly changing because it has moved in a more right-wing and authoritarian direction in recent years. As a consequence, bipolar tendencies have become stronger, and the resemblance between the Dutch party system and the Scandinavian systems may become more pronounced. Moreover, both in practical and structural terms, the dynamics of competition increasingly resemble those of the Danish party system. The minority government that ruled in the Netherlands in 2010 highlights that resemblance, as it concerns a coalition formula that is identical in composition and type (liberals and conservatives or Christian-democrats supported by radical right-wing populists) to the one that governed in Denmark from 2001 to 2011. However, because complete alternation has never occurred, the resemblance is not perfect.

At the same time, because of the complex dimensionality of the political space in the Netherlands, the pattern of competition could also increasingly be considered multipolar rather than bipolar. If this trend continues, the Netherlands might develop in a direction in which minority governments play a role, though in a different way than in the Scandinavian countries. In that case, alternation will remain partial, with continuously changing alliances and highly innovative government compositions. Notably, fluctuations, instability and volatility characterise the current dynamics of the Dutch party system. Because of the two-dimensionality of the political space and the frequent shifts in voter support, the patterns of conflict and cooperation have continuously shifted in recent elections. These shifts will likely continue to be an essential part of party politics in the Netherlands. In other words, the Dutch party system is seemingly increasingly characterised by de-institutionalisation, a trend that has also been observed in other Western European countries (Chiaramonte and Emanuele 2017). As a result, the Dutch party system does not fall neatly into any of the standard categories that we have used to classify party systems, especially when a medium- to long-term perspective is taken.

This point can be illustrated by attempting to classify the Dutch party system. Most developments in the party system – the emergence of relatively successful populist parties on the fringes of the political space, increased polarisation and the reversal of previous centripetal tendencies – point to extended multipartism with greater polarisation (Wolinetz 2006). However, the Netherlands does not fit Sartori's (1976) model of polarised multipartism. Dutch populist parties cannot be characterised as anti-system parties in the relational sense that Sartori indicated (see Capoccia 2002) because they are clearly *Koalitionsfahig*. Radical right-wing populist parties have assumed office or supported governments, and the SP is a potential partner for the PvdA and GroenLinks, making coalition formation fundamentally different from Sartori's classic cases of polarised pluralism in France during the Fourth Republic, in Italy during the First Republic, or in Weimar Germany.

As a result of the described changes, existing party system typologies no longer fruitfully distinguish among Western European party systems. One shortcoming of these typologies is that they assume that party systems are relatively stable over time and that countries fall in a clear category election after election (see also Wolinetz 2006). The Dutch party system demonstrates that this assumption does not necessarily reflect reality. Another shortcoming of these typologies is that they implicitly or explicitly assume that competition between parties is structured by the left-right dimension (e.g. Blondel 1968; Sartori 1976; Siaroff 2000; Wolinetz 2006). However, the preceding analysis demonstrates that competition is no longer structured in this way. Instead, the two-dimensional nature of the political space in Western Europe has an impact on the competition for office and votes. Analytical tools that consider this two-dimensionality are needed if we are to classify party systems more effectively (see also Pellikaan et al. in press).

CONCLUSION

Once known for its stability because of pillarisation, the Dutch party system has been in a state of flux since the early 1990s. The emergence of populist parties in 1994 (the SP), 2002 (the LPF) and 2006 (the PVV) has coincided with changes in the Dutch party system. The most notable party system changes include (a) increasing fragmentation, (b) increasing polarisation, (c) increasing volatility and (d) increasing alternation in government. These changes reflect changes in the competition for office and votes, including (a) changes in the number of the dimensions that make up the Dutch political space, (b) changes in the content of these dimensions and (c) changes in parties' positions on these dimensions. Although not features of classic party system typologies, these changes in party positions have also resulted in new modes of government formation and coalition maintenance (e.g. shorter negotiations and agreements based on logrolling), shorter life spans for government coalitions and more frequent elections.

The developments that we have described are interconnected. Changes in the party system reflect changes in the competition for office and votes because the changing electoral playing field has affected the discursive, programmatic and strategic behaviour of the mainstream parties. These behavioural changes have, in turn, shaped patterns of coalition formation and thus affect a fundamental feature of the party system, namely, the direction of competition. These changes have partly resulted from the electoral pressures exerted by the LPF, the PVV and, to a lesser degree, the SP; these parties siphoned votes away from mainstream parties, setting in motion the process described in the chapter. Of these three parties, the LPF and the PVV have had the greatest impact because these prophetic parties have put new issues on the agenda and thereby contributed to the emergence of new lines of conflict. The SP's effect on growth has been smaller because, as a purifier party, it reinforces existing lines of conflict. However, the parties' populism does not affect the mainstream parties and thereby set change in motion; instead, these parties' core ideologies (e.g. nativism in the case of radical right-wing populist parties) and the ways in which these appeal to (certain groups of) voters trigger such change.

However, many of these developments were set in motion by Dutch mainstream parties at a time when no successful populist parties were represented in the Dutch parliament. Therefore, we cannot conclude that the electoral success of the LPF, the PVV and the SP sparked these developments and thus reshaped the Dutch party system (see also Mudde 2014). Instead, the success of these populist parties is both a cause *and* an effect of party system change. Developments in the Dutch party system also relate to exogenous factors, such as societal change and the emergence of new parties that do not belong to any of the populist party families. Thus, the Dutch party system as a whole seemingly responds first and foremost to the electorate, that is, changes in voter preferences and attitudes. Importantly, parties do not seem to respond to the average voter rather than to their electoral constituencies. In other words, they operate as genuine catch-all parties (Kirchheimer 1966), albeit not always successful ones. Thus, Dutch party politics and the Dutch party system function as an electoral market in which supply and demand interact. This strategic interaction between parties and voters eventually leads to party system change.

Nevertheless, the parties' direct and indirect influences should not be underestimated. At the very least, populist parties' electoral successes have accelerated and promoted changes that were already taking place. The LPF, the PVV and, to a lesser extent, the SP have certainly contributed to party system change in the Netherlands. The observation that populist parties are the great catalysts or accelerators of Western European party system change is thus correct. Based on these developments, the Dutch party system can no longer be classified as a limited or moderate multiparty system; it is better characterised as an extended multiparty system. However, the exact contours of the party system remain vague, with some indications that it is becoming increasingly polarised but also more multipolar. Regardless, few hints reveal that the party system is completely disintegrating or turning into a polarised multiparty system similar to those that Sartori (1976) described.

Table 3.1A Results Dutch Elections 1994–2012

	1994 (%)	1998 (%)	2002 (%)	2003 (%)	2006 (%)	2010 (%)	2012 (%)
AOV	3.6						
CD	2.5						
CDA	22.2	18.4	**27.9**	**28.6**	**26.5**	**13.7**	8.5
CU			2.5	2.1	**4.0**	3.3	3.1
D66	**15.5**	**9.0**	5.1	**4.1**	2.0	6.9	8.0
GL	3.5	7.3	7.0	5.1	4.6	6.6	2.3
GPV	1.3	1.2					
LN			1.6	0.4			
LPF			**17.0**	5.7	0.2		
PvdA	**24.0**	**29.0**	15.1	27.3	**21.2**	19.6	**24.7**
PvD				0.5	1.8	1.3	1.9
PVV					5.9	**15.5**	10.1
RPF	1.8	2.0					
SGP	1.7	1.8	1.7	1.6	1.6	1.7	2.1
SP	1.3	3.8	5.9	6.3	16.6	9.9	9.6
Unie 55+	0.9						
VVD	**20.0**	**24.7**	**15.4**	**17.9**	14.6	**20.4**	**26.5**
50+							1.9

Note: Bold: governing party.

Source: Döring and Manow (2012).

Table 3.2A Elections Results 2017

	Seat Share (%)
CDA	12.7
CU	3.3
D66	12.7
DENK	2.0
FvD	1.3
GL	9.3
PvdD	3.3
PvdA	6.0
PVV	13.3
SGP	2.0
SP	9.3
VVD	22.0
50+	2.7

POSTSCRIPT

After 2012, the populist surge in the Netherlands continued. On 15 March 2017, parliamentary elections were held in the Netherlands in which at least five populist parties competed: the early-mentioned PVV and SP, as well as the new radical right-wing populist parties Forum voor Democratie (FvD), Geen Peil (GP) and Voor Nederland (VNL). Of the new populist parties, only the FvD gained parliamentary representation; it currently has two seats in the Tweede Kamer.

The outcome of the 2017 elections confirms the trends observed in this chapter about the Dutch party system. The seat shares of the three traditional parties have diminished even further, while the seat shares of newer challenger parties, including the populist ones, have increased sharply. The largest party in the system, the conservative liberal VVD, has merely 22 per cent of the seats in parliament (see table 3.2A).

As a consequence, the effective number of parties has risen significantly, from 5.7 in 2012 to 8.1 in 2017. The fragmentation of the party system has made the coalition formation process extremely complicated. At least four parties were needed to form a majority government coalition, and multiple bargaining attempts failed before such a majority could be found. The negotiations were the longest in Dutch history, with the VVD, D66, CU, and CDA taking 225 days to finalize their coalition agreement.

NOTES

1 Others have classified the Dutch party system as moderate multipartism (Sartori 1976), a multiparty system without a dominant party (Blondel 1968) or a multiparty system with balance among the parties (Siaroff 2000).

2   At the same time, the LPF's anti-establishment attitudes and behaviours and its Euroscepticism set it apart from the PvdA.

3   The PvdA and the VVD only had a parliamentary majority in 1998 and 2012. However, in 1998, the parties decided to continue with the 'purple' government that they had formed in 1994 with D66.

4   The LPF, the PVV and the SP have together politicised the issue of European integration, for example, by campaigning for a 'no' vote in the 2005 referendum. In the process of politicisation, Dutch mainstream parties have become increasingly Eurosceptic (e.g. Harmsen 2004). However, systematic research on the contagion effect of Eurosceptic parties in the Netherlands and elsewhere is still lacking. Moreover, as with the politicisation of immigration and integration issues, changes in citizens' attitudes notably accompanied or preceded the growth of Euroscepticism among political parties (Lubbers and Jaspers 2011).

5   In the comparative literature, this dimension is commonly referred to as the cultural, GAL-TAN, libertarian-authoritarian, or socio-cultural dimension and also comprises issues such as democratic participation, ethical questions, individual life-styles and safety and security (e.g. Hooghe et al. 2002; Kitschelt 1995; Kriesi et al. 2008). However, in the Netherlands, issues related to democracy and participation have not been shown to be part of this dimension (De Lange 2007).

6   Contrary to Dutch tradition, the coalition negotiations were public.

7   CDA leader Jan Peter Balkenende stated that 'the results of the elections held on Wednesday 15 May 2002 show that the Dutch population has a clear desire for change', while his GroenLinks colleague Paul Rosenmöller concluded that 'the large gains of the CDA and LPF, and the fact that these parties together with the VVD have become the three largest parties of the country, point in one direction. The voter wants the pendulum to swing to the right' (Kamerstukken 61855).

8   Handelingen 7434A02; Kamerstukken 61855.

9   They managed to conclude a strategic agreement after a mere sixty-eight days at the negotiating table, which is relatively quick according to Dutch standards.

10   The Netherlands has the long-lasting coalition bargaining, with an average of 70.6 negotiation days and two inconclusive negotiation rounds before reaching a coalition agreement (De Winter and Dumont 2008: 130).

11   *Handelingen* 7434A02.

12   The main conflicts were between the Minister of Economic Affairs Herman Heinsbroek and the Minister of Health, Sport and Welfare Eduard Bomhoff and between the chairman of the party, the members of parliament and the regional representatives.

13   The informateurs Opstelten and Rosenthal both assessed the likelihood of the formation of a CDA-PVV-VVD coalition, but they concluded that it was unrealistic. After other possibilities proved unfeasible as well, informateur Tjeenk Willink recommended that the option be explored again.

14   The situation in the Netherlands resembles that in Denmark between 2001 and 2011, although the minority government construction is largely unprecedented in Dutch politics.

15   The same goes to for the social populist SP, which has never been actively excluded from political decision making because of a *cordon sanitaire*. Initially, most parties did not consider the party Koalitionsfähig because it rejected NATO membership and the Dutch monarchy and was unwilling to compromise on key stances, such as the

retirement age, market liberalisation and dismissal legislation (Keith 2010). However, since 2006, these stances have been relaxed little by little, and the party's populism has diminished (De Lange and Rooduijn 2011). Moreover, in the run-up to the 2012 elections, the SP organised a special party congress in which it indicated that it was willing to take up government responsibility and compromise. As a consequence, the SP has especially become an acceptable coalition partner to the social democratic PvdA and the green GroenLinks. In recent years, closer cooperation on these three left-wing parties has been discussed extensively, but, because of the structural lack of a left-wing majority in the Netherlands, the SP has not yet governed at the national level.

BIBLIOGRAPHY

Aarts, K. and Thomassen, J. (2008) 'Dutch voters and the changing party space 1989–2006', *Acta Politica*, 43(2–3): 203–234.

Akkerman, T. (2005) 'Anti-immigration parties and the defence of liberal values: The exceptional case of the list Pim Fortuyn', *Journal of Political Ideologies*, 10(3): 337–354.

——— (2016) 'The Party for Freedom: Balancing between mission, votes and office', in T. Akkerman, S. L. De Lange and M. Rooduijn (eds.) *Radical right-wing populist parties in Western Europe: Into the mainstream?*, London: Routledge pp. 144–168.

Akkerman, T., De Lange, S. L. and Rooduijn, M. (2016) 'Into the mainstream? A comparative analysis of the programmatic profiles of radical right-wing populist parties in Western Europe over time', in T. Akkerman, S. L. De Lange and M. Rooduijn (eds.) *Radical right-wing populist parties in Western Europe: Into the mainstream?*, London: Routledge pp. 31–52.

Art, D. (2011) *Inside the radical right: The development of anti-immigrant parties in Western Europe*, New York, NY: Cambridge University Press.

Bale, T. (2008) 'Turning round the telescope: Centre-right parties and immigration and integration policy in Europe', *Journal of European Public Policy*, 15(3): 315–330.

Bale, T., Green-Pedersen, C., Krouwel, A., Luther, K. R. and Sitter, N. (2010) 'If you can't beat them, join them? Explaining Social Democratic responses to the challenge from the populist radical right in Western Europe', *Political Studies*, 58(3): 410–426.

Bartolini, S. and Mair, P. (1990) *Identity, competition, and electoral availability: The stabilisation of European electorates 1885–1985*, Cambridge: Cambridge University Press.

Blondel, J. (1968) 'Party systems and patterns of government in Western Democracies', *Canadian Journal of Political Science*, 1(2): 180–203.

Capoccia, G. (2002) 'Anti-system parties: A conceptual reassessment', *Journal of Theoretical Politics*, 14(1): 9–35.

Chiaramonte, A. and Emanuele, V. (2017) 'Party system volatility, regeneration and de-institutionalization in Western Europe (1945–2015)', *Party Politics*, 23(3): 376–388.

Daalder, H. (1986) 'Changing procedures and changing strategies in Dutch coalition building', *Legislative Studies Quarterly*, 11(4): 507–532.

Davis, A. (2012) *The impact of anti-immigration parties on mainstream parties: Immigration positions in the Netherlands, Flanders and the UK*, Florence: European University Institute pp. 1987–2010.

De Lange, S. L. (2007) 'A new winning formula? The programmatic appeal of the radical right', *Party Politics*, 13(4): 411–435.

――――― (2012a) 'New alliances: Why mainstream parties govern with radical right-wing populist parties', *Political Studies*, 60(4): 899–918.

――――― (2012b) 'Radical right-wing populist parties in office: A cross-national comparison', in U. Backes and P. Moreau (eds.) *Extreme right in Europe: Current trends and perspectives*, Göttingen: Vandenhoeck and Ruprecht pp. 171–194.

De Lange, S. L. and Art, D. (2011) 'Fortuyn versus Wilders: An agency-based approach to radical right party building', *West European Politics*, 34(6): 1229–1249.

De Lange, S. L. and Rooduijn, M. (2011) 'Een populistische tijdgeest in Nederland? Een inhoudsanalyse van de verkiezingsprogramma's van politieke partijen', in R. Andeweg and J. Thomassen (eds.) *Democratie doorgelicht: Het functioneren van de Nederlandse democratie*, Leiden: Leiden University Press pp. 319–334.

――――― (2015) 'Contemporary populism, the agrarian and the rural in central Eastern and Western Europe', in D. Strijker, I. Terluin and G. Voerman (eds.) *Rural protest groups and populist political parties*, Wageningen: Wageningen Academic Publishers pp. 163–190.

De Vries, M. W. M. (1999) *Governing with your closest neighbour: An assessment of spatial coalition formation theories*, Nijmegen: Radboud University Nijmegen.

De Winter, L. and Dumont, P. (2008) 'Uncertainty and complexity in cabinet formation', in K. Strom, W. C. Muller and T. Bergman (eds.) *Cabinets and coalition bargaining: The democratic life cycle in Western Europe*, Oxford: Oxford University Press pp. 123–157.

Decker, F. (2004) *Der neue Rechtspopulismus*, Opladen: Leske+Budrich.

Döring, H. and Manow, P. (2012) 'Parliament and government composition database (ParlGov): An infrastructure for empirical information on parties, elections and governments in modern democracies', *Version*, 10(11): 6.

Downs, W. M. (2012) *Political extremism in democracies: Combating intolerance*, Basingstoke: Palgrave MacMillan.

Hakhverdian, A. and Koop, C. (2007) 'Consensus democracy and support for populist parties in Western Europe', *Acta Politica*, 42(4): 401–420.

Harmsen, R. (2004) 'Euroscepticism in the Netherlands: Stirrings of dissent', *European Studies: A Journal of European Culture, History and Politics*, 20: 99–126.

Hooghe, L., Marks, G. and Wilson, C. J. (2002) 'Does left/right structure party positions on European integration?', *Comparative Political Studies*, 35(8): 965–989.

Kanne, P. (2011) *Gedoogdemocratie: Heeft stemmen eigenlijk wel zin?*, Amsterdam: Meulenhoff.

Keith, D. (2010) 'Ready to get their hands dirty: The Socialist Party and GroenLinks in the Netherlands', in D. Hough, J. Olsen and M. Koß (eds.) *Left parties in national government*, Basingstoke: Palgrave MacMillan pp. 155–172.

Kirchheimer, O. (1996) 'The transformation of the Western European party systems', in J. LaPalombara and M. Weiner (eds.) *Political parties and political development*, Princeton, NJ: Princeton University Press, pp. 177–200.

Kitschelt, H. (1995) *The radical right in Western Europe: A comparative analysis*, Ann Arbor, MI: University of Michigan Press.

Kriesi, H., Grande, E., Lachat, R., Dolezal, M., Bornschier, S. and Frey, T. (2008) *West European politics in the age of globalization*, Cambridge: Cambridge University Press.

Krouwel, A. and Lucardie, P. (2008) 'Waiting in the wings: New parties in the Netherlands', *Acta Politica*, 43(2–3): 278–307.

Lijphart, A. (1968) *The politics of accommodation: Pluralism and democracy in the Netherlands*, Berkeley, CA: University of California Press.

Lipset, S. M. and Rokkan, S. (1967) *Party systems and voter alignments: Cross-national perspectives*, Toronto: Free Press.

Lubbers, M. and Jaspers, E. (2011) 'A longitudinal study of Euroscepticism in the Netherlands: 2008 versus 1990', *European Union Politics*, 12(1): 21–40.

Lucardie, P. (2000) 'Prophets, purifiers and prolocutors: Towards a theory on the emergence of new parties', *Party Politics*, 6(2): 175–186.

——— (2003) 'The Netherlands', *European Journal of Political Research*, 42(7–8): 1029–1036.

——— (2007) 'Rechts-extremisme, populisme of democratisch patriotisme? Opmerkingen over de politieke plaatsbepaling van de Partij voor de Vrijheid en trots op Nederland', in *Jaarboek DNPP 2007*, Groningen: R.U.G. pp. 176–190.

——— (2010) 'Tussen establishment en extremisme: Populistische partijen in Nederland en Vlaanderen', *Res Publica*, 52(2): 149–172.

Lucardie, P. and Voerman, G. (2002) 'Het gedachtegoed van Fortuyn: Liberaal patriot of nationaal populist?', *Socialisme en Democratie*, 59(4): 31–42.

——— (2012) *Populisten in de polder*, Amsterdam: Uitgeverij Boom.

Mair, P. (1997) *Party system change: Approaches and interpretations*, Cambridge: Cambridge University Press.

——— (2008) 'Electoral volatility and the Dutch party system: A comparative perspective', *Acta Politica*, 43(2–3): 235–253.

March, L. and Mudde, C. (2005) 'What's left of the radical left? The European radical left after 1989: Decline and mutation', *Comparative European Politics*, 3(1): 23–49.

Meguid, B. M. (2005) 'Competition between unequals: The role of mainstream party strategy in niche party success', *American Political Science Review*, 99(3): 435–452.

Mudde, C. (2004) 'The populist zeitgeist', *Government and Opposition*, 39(4): 542–563.

——— (2007) *Populist radical right parties in Europe*, Cambridge: Cambridge University Press.

——— (2011) 'Radical right parties in Europe: What, who, why?', *Participation* 35(1): 12–15.

——— (2014) 'Fighting the system? Populist radical right parties and party system change', *Party Politics*, 20(2): 217–226.

Mudde, C. and Van Holsteyn, J. (2000) 'The Netherlands: Explaining the limited success of the extreme right', in P. Hainsworth (ed.) *The politics of the extreme right: From the margins to the mainstream*, London and New York: Pinter Publishing House pp. 144–171.

Oosterwaal, A. and Torenvlied, R. (2010) 'Politics divided from society? Three explanations for trends in societal and political polarisation in the Netherlands', *West European Politics*, 33(2): 258–279.

Otjes, S. and Louwerse, T. (2015) 'Populists in parliament: Comparing left-wing and right-wing populism in the Netherlands', *Political Studies*, 63(1): 60–79.

Pellikaan, H., De Lange, S. L. and Van der Meer, T. (2007) 'Fortuyn's legacy: Party system change in the Netherlands', *Comparative European Politics*, 5(3): 282–302.

Pellikaan, H., Van der Meer, T. and De Lange, S. L. (2003) 'The road from a depoliticized to a centrifugal democracy', *Acta Politica*, 38(1): 23–49.

Pellikaan, P., De Lange, S. L., Van der Meer, T. (in press) 'The centre does not hold: Coalition politics and party system change in the Netherlands 2002–2012', *Government and Opposition*.

Pennings, P. and Keman, H. (2008) 'The changing landscape of Dutch politics since the 1970s: A comparative exploration', *Acta Politica*, 43(2–3): 154–179.

Rydgren, J. and Van Holsteyn, J. (2005) 'Holland and Pim Fortuyn: A deviant case or the beginning of something new?', in J. Rydgren (ed.) *Movements of exclusion: Radical right-wing populism*, Hauppage, NY: Nova Science Publishers pp. 41–63.

Sartori, G. (1976) *Parties and party systems: A framework for analysis*, Cambridge: Cambridge University Press.

Schumacher, G. and Rooduijn, M. (2013) 'Sympathy for the "devil"? Voting for populists in the 2006 and the 2010 Dutch general elections', *Electoral Studies*, 32(1): 124–133.

Siaroff, A. (2000) *Comparative European party systems: An analysis of parliamentary elections since 1945*, New York: Garland Publishing.

Otjes, S. (2011) 'The Fortuyn effect revisited: How did the LPF affect the Dutch parliamentary party system?', *Acta Politica*, 46(4): 400–424.

Van der Brug, W., Fennema, M., De Lange, S. L. and Baller, I. (2013) 'Radical right parties: Their voters and their electoral competitors', in J. Rydgren (ed.) *Class politics and the radical right*, London: Routledge pp. 52–74.

Van der Meer, T., Lubbe, R., Van Elsas, E., Elff, M. and Van der Brug, W. (2012) 'Bounded volatility in the Dutch electoral battlefield: A panel study on the structure of changing vote intentions in the Netherlands during 2006–2010', *Acta Politica*, 47(4): 333–355.

Van der Meer, T., Van Elsas, E., Lubbe, R. and Van der Brug, W. (2012) *Kieskeurige kiezers: Een onderzoek naar de veranderlijkheid van Nederlandse Kiezers*, Amsterdam: University of Amsterdam pp. 2006–2010.

Van Heerden, S. (2014) *What did you just call me? A study on the demonization of political parties in the Netherlands between 1995 and 2011*, Amsterdam: University of Amsterdam.

Van Heerden, S., De Lange, S. L., Van der Brug, W. and Fennema, M. (2014) 'The immigration and integration debate in the Netherlands: Discursive and programmatic reactions to the rise of anti-immigration parties', *Journal of Ethnic and Migration Studies*, 40(1): 119–136.

Van Holsteyn, J. (2007) 'The Dutch parliamentary elections of 2006', *West European Politics*, 30(5): 1139–1147.

Van Kersbergen, K. and Krouwel, A. (2008) 'A double-edged sword! The Dutch centre-right and the "foreigners issue"', *Journal of European Public Policy*, 15(3): 398–414.

Van Spanje, J. (2010) 'Contagious parties: Anti-immigration parties and their impact on other parties' immigration stances in contemporary Western Europe', *Party Politics*, 16(5): 563–586.

Voerman, G. (2009) 'Van Mao tot marketing: Over het populisme van de SP', *Socialisme & Democratie*, 66(9): 26–32.

Vossen, K. (2010) 'Populism in the Netherlands after Fortuyn: Rita Verdonk and Geert Wilders compared', *Perspectives on European Politics and Society*, 11(1): 22–38.

——— (2011) 'Classifying Wilders: The ideological development of Geert Wilders and his Party for Freedom', *Politics*, 31(3): 179–189.

Wolinetz, S. B. (2006) 'Party systems and party system types', in R. S. Katz and W. Crotty (eds.) *Handbook of party politics*, London: Sage Publications pp. 51–73.

Chapter 4

Political Achievements, Party System Changes and Government Participation: The Case of the 'New' Swiss People's Party

Oscar Mazzoleni

INTRODUCTION

This chapter examines the impact that a party of the so-called populist right, the Swiss People's Party (SVP), has had on other Swiss parties and the Swiss party system. Once the smallest of the four parties that share government power in Switzerland, with 29.4 per cent of the vote in the October 2015 elections of the federal parliament, the SVP is now the largest. Initially a centre-right party with agrarian roots, the SVP is currently not only the leading Swiss party with right-wing, nationalist and populist tendencies (Albertazzi and McDonnell 2015; Betz 1994, 2009; Mazzoleni 2008; Skenderovic 2009a) but also the largest and electorally most successful radical right-wing party in Western Europe.[1] Although the 'new' SVP is not the only party with a recognised populist style and rhetoric that has shared power, it is the only one that has been continuously present in coalition governments both before and since its radicalisation (e.g. Mazzoleni 2016; Mazzoleni and Skenderovic 2007).

The radicalisation of the SVP, its electoral advance and its competition for government seats in the 1990s and the 2000s represent a real challenge for the Swiss party system. Studies of Swiss politics frequently focus on the ways in which Swiss institutions and politics differ from those of the countries surrounding it. Scholars such as Lehmbruch (1967) and Lijphart (1999) have characterised Switzerland as a *Proporzdemokratie* or a 'consensual' democracy that has used cooperative decision-making to respond to socio-cultural and institutional segmentation. Multiple facets – including cantonal autonomy and its continued recourse to power sharing in federal politics, the uses that are made of referenda and popular initiatives and its steadfast neutrality and reluctance to join the EU – make Switzerland different from the smaller European democracies with which it is frequently compared. However, in the last decades, these facets also include the SVP's strength, its position as an established party rather than a new one and the way that it has managed to be both an insider, sharing power in national governments and an outsider, opposing policies that the cabinets in which it has served have put forward.

In the sections that follow, we examine the impact that the SVP's transformation from a smaller agrarian party to a much stronger party with distinct populist tendencies has had both on the mainstream parties with which it competes and shares power and on the party system as a whole. As in other chapters in this volume, we consider not only how other parties position themselves but also how they influence the shape of the party system and competition for government (Mair 1997). In doing so, we consider so-called Swiss exceptionalism. In a country in which sharing power has been the norm, the different forms that change takes compared with those in other countries should come as no surprise. Switzerland once had one of the most stable party systems in Europe. We examine the extent to which it has changed and the degree to which these changes resulted directly or indirectly from the rise and consolidation of the 'new' SVP. Although the literature has explored these questions to some degree (Bochsler, Hänggli and Häusermann 2015; Ladner 2007; Sager and Zolliger 2011; Vatter 2008), the role played by the SVP on the party system has not been fully addressed, particularly once this system is seen as a by-product of real interactions among parties. In the current Swiss party system, mainstream parties continue to share power, but the ways in which they do so are different not only from those of other countries but also from previous decades.

We begin by examining the ways in which the cooperative rules that shaped the 'golden' era of Swiss politics have been challenged by the SVP and the issues that these challenges have catalysed. We then consider how other Swiss parties have reacted to the SVP's transformation and electoral success. Finally, we investigate how these changes have influenced the party system and competition for representation in its collegial executive, the Federal Council. In doing so, we consider not only competition for votes, competition for government seats and the parameters of the party system but also the extent to which the norms and practices that frame these items have changed.

THE STABILITY OF THE PARTY SYSTEM WITHIN COOPERATIVE RULES

Since the 1940s, especially from 1959 to 2003, the partisan composition of the Federal Council remained constant. The four largest parties won a substantial portion of the popular vote and seats in parliament. Until the 1990s, the rates of electoral volatility were low, and, at best, minimal changes occurred in the parties' shares of the vote and seats in parliament. Once elected, the lower and upper chambers of the federal parliament were responsible for selecting the Federal Council. The Council's seven seats were distributed according to a 'magic formula', which allocated two seats to the three larger parties, the Socialist Party (SP), the Christian Democrats (CVP) and the Liberals (FDP), and one to the smaller SVP. This formula produced grand coalitions whose position was reinforced by the distribution of the popular vote and seats in parliament (Burgos et al. 2011; Deschouwer 2001; Kerr 1987) and by a party system that, despite the number of smaller parties contesting elections, could be described as 'moderate pluralism' (Sartori 1976; Wolinetz 2006).

Otto Kirchheimer (1966) characterised the crystallisation of power relations in party organisations and party systems, as in the Swiss system, as a manifestation of established rules of cooperation and negotiations among the main parties that limited electoral competition (see also Mair 1997: 162–165). The convergent use of rules offered parties few incentives to switch to 'catch-all' strategies, delaying the development of more professional capital-intensive campaigning. Swiss parties oscillated between policy seeking and office seeking, with vote seeking coming in second, if not third, place. This development was self-perpetuating: The stability of the party system was matched by accommodative strategies that governed interactions among parties in their competition for votes and seats in parliament. The constraints of the electoral market and the opportunity structure faced by the parties represented in government encouraged others to employ similar strategies. Their withdrawal not only discouraged vote seeking but also consolidated the party system. These practices – continually reproducing and applying the 'magic formula' and allocating the same number of cabinet seats to the same four parties in successive elections between the 1960s and the 1990s – discouraged vote seeking. The parties typically limited their actions in the electoral arena to defending and maintaining the system. This strategy not only guaranteed stable power relations in parliament but also allowed parties that invested minimal money and personnel to win seats in the Federal Council. This pattern was not simply a product of Swiss political culture. Instead, continued cooperation in the party system and the Swiss model of government reflected the convergent interests and strategies of the mainstream parties (Mazzoleni and Rayner 2009). This cooperation was reinforced by a 'language of politics' (Mair 1997) that valued power sharing and problem-solving practices, which, in turn, were framed by a widespread national discourse that emphasised Swiss exceptionality as a model of consensual and peaceful democracy (Burgos et al. 2011).

At the same time, this non-alteration of power was the product of institutional, social and economic conditions that contributed to enduring parliamentary stability and reinforced cooperative rules. Thus, power sharing emanated not only from the common values and strategies of political leaders (Pappalardo 1981) but also from the opportunity structures that these actors faced. Therefore, we must consider not only Switzerland's crosscutting institutional, linguistic and cultural cleavages but also the factors that favoured the fragmentation of cleavages and provided weak national parties with their raison d'etre (e.g. Kerr 1987). In addition, other elements reinforced the compact and crystallised nature of Switzerland's 'consensual' democracy. Although these approaches are typically viewed as alternatives in the literature, one of the conditions for Swiss political power sharing has been the consolidation of a 'liberal-corporatist' model that, for several decades in the twentieth century, characterised Switzerland as a small, economically open country in the heart of Western Europe (Katzenstein 1984).

This model is characterised by the institutionalisation of bargaining agreements between business associations and trade unions and collusive practices among Swiss economic elites. Beginning in 1937, the former neutralised conflicts in the labour market. Borne out by the high number of cartels that dominated significant portions of the economy during the twentieth century, the latter were strongly embedded in the Swiss political system (Mach 2006). Other factors include the development of the welfare state and the unprecedented economic growth that Switzerland experienced in the post-war decades. Switzerland was not the only country to enjoy the 'Trente glorieuses', but it had the added advantage of incurring no costs for post-war reconstruction, which helped limit socio-economic conflicts and promoted convergence among the main parties. Power sharing was also fostered by foreign policy that was based on neutrality and the policy of 'good offices' between the East and the West, which was endorsed by all the mainstream parties during the Cold War. Thus, in the 1960s and 1970s, Switzerland was widely acclaimed as a model of political integration (e.g. Deutsch 1976).

This model was based on the strong stability of the party system. According to a comparative analysis on electoral volatility between 1948 and 1977, the Swiss parliamentary elections showed the lowest rate of volatility (along with Austria) among thirteen Western democracies (Pedersen 1979). Some changes occurred in the 1970s, when small right-wing and left-wing parties emerged, challenging the government parties in the streets, in the federal parliament, and especially in referenda. This period witnessed not only the emergence of green political movements but also challengers who opposed immigration and demanded the defence of national integrity (Altermatt and Kriesi 1995; Gentile 1996). However, until the 1990s, smaller parties and movements had, at best, a marginal impact on the party system. The new left, the Greens, and the nationalist parties were unable to undermine the 'magic formula' and the system of power sharing that it guaranteed. The two largest parties in government, the FDP and the CVP, had begun to decline electorally in the 1970s; ongoing secularisation was underway; and post-materialism was emerging, weakening traditional cleavages. However, through the 1980s, the Swiss party and government systems appeared to be strongly entrenched. Consequently, the government system maintained the same composition, avoiding any significant challenge until the 1990s.

CHALLENGING THE COOPERATIVE PATTERN

The late 1980s and early 1990s constituted a turning point in Swiss politics. The fall of the Berlin Wall was one of several factors signalling change. At home, Switzerland experienced deep-seated socio-economic and geopolitical shifts. Increasing unemployment and job insecurity stood in sharp contrast to the prosperity that Swiss citizens enjoyed during the *Trente glorieuses*. Expressing new expectations, business elites – for the most part, less nationally embedded than in previous decades – prioritised competitiveness in international markets. Increased social conflict not only damaged the corporatist model but also made national borders less important (Trampusch and Mach 2011). In addition, the changing international climate (Church 2006) made neutrality more difficult to maintain. Reflecting this shift, Switzerland's foreign policy and its emphasis on neutrality and national independence became crucial issues, as did Switzerland's relationship with the rest of Europe.

The accelerating pace of European integration and economic globalisation ushered in a period of uncertainty that an increasingly radicalised SVP turned to its advantage. This international focus was reflected in referenda: Swiss citizens were asked to vote frequently, not only on domestic but also on European issues. The 1992 referendum on the European Economic Area provided a crucial opportunity for a new generation of radicalised politicians led by billionaire Christoph Blocher, the chair of the SVP's Zurich branch, to challenge the political establishment. Based in Zurich, the SVP's radical faction not only marginalised the previously dominant moderate wing of the national SVP but also helped Blocher become the party leader. Important changes in the SVP's strategy and position followed. Muting its accommodative posture and replacing it with a more assertive style, the SVP sought support from new segments of the electorate. As was the case for other mainstream parties, the SVP had been an office- and policy-seeking party. Under Blocher, it moved into new policy areas and became not only a vote-seeking party but also one with a pronounced right-wing nationalist and populist stance (Mazzoleni 2016).

This new stance contrasted sharply with the moderate conservatism that characterised the SVP when it was primarily an agrarian party. The SVP's more assertive strategy gave form to a new political cleavage dividing advocates of national independence and those who were more disposed to open borders and transnationalism. The SVP largely monopolised the defence of national integrity as opposed to other parties in government that, to varying degrees, embraced openness with Europe, integration and membership in supranational organisations (e.g. the UN). In addition, the SVP emphasised typically right-wing themes, including law and order and economic liberalism. Presenting itself as the defender of the 'exceptional' wealth of the post-war period and the advantages of a liberal economy, the SVP stood against the excessive costs of the welfare state (Mazzoleni and Skenderovic 2007). Accusing the federal government of siding with European and left-wing interests, the party adopted an anti-establishment style. It blamed various ills on the 'fatal' effects of collaboration among parties, which were accused of defending their interests instead of those of the Swiss people. Increasing their use of referenda to counter government decisions or to introduce their issues through popular initiatives, the SVP's leadership were able to shape the national agenda and mobilise followers.

Along with the systematic use of referenda, the SVP strengthened its electoral support. In lower chamber elections, which take place under proportional representation, the SVP advanced from 15 per cent of the vote in 1995 to 29.4 per cent in 2015 – the most rapid and durable electoral growth of any Swiss party in the last century. Instead of organising in barely half of the Swiss cantons, in the 1990s, the party set up cantonal branches and hundreds of new local party organisations throughout the country. It could thus present candidates and gather electoral support in all cantons (Mazzoleni 2012). At the same time, the SVP attempted to undermine the established composition and practices of 'all-party' government. Since 1999, the party has tried to challenge not only the government's composition – securing a second seat – but also the competition rules, including a popular initiative demanding the direct election of the national executive. Although this initiative was rejected by most Swiss voters in June 2013, it helped reinforce the party's anti-establishment posture. The party's strategy and its electoral advance are directly linked to its changing organisational features (Skenderovic 2009b). In contrast to the amateur organisational model that had hitherto characterised Swiss parties, the SVP moved towards more centralised organisational forms and shifted towards more professional, capital-intensive campaigns (Mazzoleni and Rossini 2016; Skenderovic 2009b; Weinmann 2009). These organisational changes gave the party greater strategic and ideological autonomy from the surrounding parties, strengthening its capacity to mobilise support.

POPULISM, PRAGMATISM AND COMPETITION FOR GOVERNMENT SEATS IN THE 1990S AND BEYOND

Despite its radicalisation, the SVP continued to be part of the federal government, taking part in governments without alternation or significant compositional changes in the 1990s or the 2000s. In this sense, although the SVP attempted to challenge the dominant pattern, no relevant change occurred. Several factors explain this stability. Despite its electoral and parliamentary strength, the SVP was not able to build or assemble the support that it would need to shift Switzerland towards a majoritarian system of government. Nor did its changed posture alter its relationship with other mainstream parties, which continued to recognise the 'new' SVP as a rightful member of the government. Although this recognition was not uncritical, especially for the left, it came from all the mainstream parties, no matter where they were located on the political spectrum. The SVP's reputation was one reason that it received such recognition; it could still be regarded as an older 'government' party with longstanding relationships with other government parties. Moreover, despite its radicalisation and challenges to other parties and pre-existing norms and practices, the SVP retained a pragmatic wing and could show a pragmatic face. This ambivalence, along with its history as a 'government' party, was an essential factor in the SVP's acceptance as a government partner. Although the Blocher SVP was a reformed and radicalised version of the old farmers' party, it retained the name associated with its continuing role in government. Moreover, through 2003, the SVP's representative in the Federal Council was invariably someone from its moderate wing. In addition, the SVP did not engage in obstructionism on issues such as membership in international economic organisations (e.g. the IMF). The SVP also pragmatically accepted the initial adoption of bilateral agreements with the EU and the incorporation of European law into the Swiss legal system. This pragmatism was reinforced to some degree by the role that the SVP played in parliamentary coalitions on a wide range of issues. Because Swiss parliamentarians cannot propose non-confidence motions, members of parliament from governing parties are free to form coalitions on individual issues. This freedom has allowed other mainstream parties to converge with the SVP on some issues even though they vote against them on others (Mazzoleni 2016).

Other factors may explain the continued inclusion of the 'new' SVP in the governing coalition. Despite its transformation, the 'new' SVP's rapid growth helped it gain legitimacy. Mainstream parties believed that the 'strongest' party could not be excluded from the federal government. In other words, their generally permissive or, in Meguid's (2008) terms, accommodative response reflects the SVP's ability to mobilise in different arenas. However, other factors contributed to this response. In Switzerland, any law passed by parliament can be put to a referendum. Other parties also knew that the SVP or the factions within it could initiate more referenda that might reject their legislation. Excluding a stronger party, such as the SVP, might have put the entire policymaking process at risk because referenda are usually tools for oppositional parties and movements.

Thus, direct democracy is a crucial consideration. The SVP's participation in government presumes the persistence of power sharing and widespread inter-partisan agreement among parties. The principle that governing coalitions should be large coalitions became the crystallised norm or general rule for governing during the twentieth century. This principal acknowledged that parties' representatives in the Federal Council, their representatives in parliament, and their organisations outside parliament are mutually autonomous and that each one can operate independently from any other. Therefore, although the norms of collegiality require that members of the government support the government's majority positions, party organisations remain free to organise referenda on individual laws proposed by the government.

Moreover, the mainstream parties do not perceive the use of referenda as a systemic threat. Until the 1990s, primarily the socialists – who were often in the minority in both the government and parliamentary coalitions – but also other parties used referenda in this way. This legacy helped legitimise the ambivalent posture of the 'new' SVP, which simultaneously sits in government, opposes its actions and regularly launches challenges against it. However, tolerance for the use of direct democracy by Swiss mainstream parties relates to its perceived threat to the work of the government. This tolerance decreases if opposition becomes systematic and the party behind the referenda or popular initiatives rejects compromise on certain matters that are at the top of the government's agenda, such as European issues in the 2000s. Nevertheless, the main parties acknowledge that recourse to direct democracy does not challenge the government's legitimacy (Church 2006; Kobach 1993). The lack of a shared government platform and the absence of a vote of confidence reinforce the idea that direct democracy is not a threat.

The SVP's major party status also explains its treatment in the media. Ambivalence towards the party, despite its strong Eurosceptic strategy and criticism of other mainstream parties, is reflected in journalists' discourse. In the last decade, the Swiss media have alternated between two positions. On the one hand, the SVP is described as a 'populist', 'nationalist' and 'far-right' party; on the other, more traditional terms, such as 'conservative', are used. As a result, the SVP is frequently regarded as a governing party that belongs to the *bürgerliche Parteien* (i.e. bourgeois parties) (Mazzoleni 2007). This ambivalence has taken different forms, including the ways that its leader has been framed in the media. For instance, through 1999, columnists from the main Swiss papers considered SVP leader Christoph Blocher unsuitable for entry into government based on collegial rules. However, when Blocher claimed a second seat in government in 2003, the leading Swiss dailies lent legitimacy to his candidacy. Above all, since 2007, the mainstream newspapers have often provided a more explicit criticism against the 'enfant terrible' Blocher, although widely recognising him as a clever 'political animal'.

PARTY RESPONSES: OTHER MAINSTREAM PARTIES VERSUS THE SVP?

The parties' recognition of the 'new' SVP is also linked to the interests, positions and ambivalence of the centre-right government parties. The rise of the SVP has electorally damaged Switzerland's two main centre-right parties, the FDP and the CVP, the most. Both have been continuously represented in the federal executive since the nineteenth century (Burgos et al. 2011; Gruner 1977). Until the end of the 1990s, their main positions reflected their strong attachment to Switzerland's government pattern; they minimised their electoral decline by insisting that their pivotal role in government (Mair, Müller and Plassner 2004) had not been challenged by increasing electoral volatility and the rise of populism. This perspective slowed attempts to professionalise the parties or to make their election campaigns more capital-intensive. They rejected changes in funding for parties and election campaigning (Mazzoleni 2009). Indeed, policy-seeking strategies remain dominant in Swiss mainstream parties. All maintain a problem-solving attitude and remain open to alliances with the SVP on many issues.

All centre-right parties continue to rely on SVP votes to set agendas and make policy. From this perspective, the SVP's continued presence in the Federal Council does not differ greatly from the entry of other European populist parties into coalition governments (Bale 2003; De Lange 2007). In the 2000s, the centre-right was amenable to the arguments that the SVP presented about the welfare state and/or immigration and asylum. Thus, the SVP triggered a shift to the right on these issues (Mazzoleni 2016). The response of the only party on the left in the Swiss government, the SP, took place in two stages. Through 2008, the period in which SVP support was increasing steadily, the SP emphasised its opposition to the SVP on right-wing issues (e.g. immigration and the free market), but it did not deny the right of the SVP's moderate representatives to participate in the government. Since 2008, the SP has become even more pragmatic. On the one hand, it continues to oppose the SVP on many issues, believing that the SVP enjoys an unjustified competitive advantage. For this reason, the SP demanded, along with the Greens, federal regulation of election and referendum campaign expenses and public funding for parties; on the other, the SP has recognised several issues (e.g. security and foreign criminals) that it had not previously acknowledged. The SP has also not been above supporting the SVP in parliament on issues such as public pensions. This support has served an additional purpose – minimising the dominant weight of centre-right parties in policymaking. The FDP, albeit with some ambivalence, more frequently allied itself with the SVP in legislative coalitions and in government elections. In addition, the CVP, which sought alternate coalitions opposing the government on policymaking, continues to converge with the SVP on some issues.

In competition for positions in the federal cabinet, the mainstream parties' responses have varied over time. For instance, in 2003, the SVP challenged the 'magic formula', not only by seeking a second seat but also by designating Christoph Blocher as the candidate for this seat. Blocher won the seat, reducing the CVP's representation from two seats to one. The parties' recognition of the SVP's institutional legacy partially explained their support of Blocher's government candidacy in 2003. Some mainstream parties, especially the FDP, also thought that Blocher's inclusion in the federal executive would encourage the SVP to be more cooperative and would temper his anti-establishment stance. However, once he was part of the federal executive, Blocher did little to realise their hopes. As a member of the government, he was repeatedly accused of violating the rules of collegiality. In 2007, other parties reacted by forming an inter-party coalition of Socialists, Greens, Christian Democrats and a handful of Liberal Party MPs and voting to replace Blocher with a less radical SVP candidate for government, Eveline Widmer-Schlumpf.

The December 2007 election had major consequences not only for the SVP but also for the strategies adopted by the other main parties, competition for government seats and the party system itself. Blocher's expulsion and replacement caused a crisis within the SVP. Until then, the radical and moderate wings of the SVP managed to coexist. However, in early 2008, the national party, with the support of the majority of the parliamentary group, decided to expel the newly elected SVP member of the federal government, and the Graubünden branch that had backed her. Shortly thereafter, parts of the SVP in Berne and other moderate branches, including Graubünden, left to form a new party, the Conservative Democratic Party of Switzerland (CDPS). Because the CDPS was more moderate than the SVP and more amenable to European integration, it was able to corral those leaving or expelled from the SVP. A few months later, parliament once again elected an SVP candidate, Ueli Maurer, to the federal executive. A former president of the SVP, Maurer belonged to the Blocher wing of the party. However, unlike Blocher, Maurer showed greater acceptance of the government's collegial style. In a similar vein, in 2015, the mainstream parties, from the centre-right and the socialists, elected a second member of the SVP, the French-speaking Guy Parmelin, who is not considered a strict follower of Blocher, to the government.

In sum, the increasing ambition of the SVP challenges the traditional rules of the competition for government seats, which implies change but also maintains inter-partisan relations. What stands out is the considerable continuity with which parties relate to and work with one another. Of course, shifts in the party balance, which have worked to the advantage of the SVP and to the detriment of centre-right parties, have occurred. Overall, at most, subtle changes have occurred in terms of how parties compete – or, in this case, fail to compete – for seats in the federal executive. Nevertheless, electoral, strategic and ideological changes and changes in the rules that govern inter-party relations have occurred. Longstanding rules have been called into question, and, in some instances, new practices and trends have emerged.

COMPETITION FOR VOTES, POLARISATION AND FRAGMENTATION

Of course, distinguishing between the impact of general geopolitical and socio-economic changes on a small country, such as Switzerland, and the specific impact of the SVP on inter-partisan dynamics is difficult. However, the SVP likely played a crucial role. The party took advantage of opportunities that emerged from institutional settings, developing socio-economic and cultural crises, and inter-party relationships. As a result, the rise and consolidation of the 'new' SVP has resulted in a more open form of competition in referenda and in parliamentary and government elections.

Let us look at some of these changes in greater detail. First, a higher degree of volatility exists in the party system. As table 4.1 shows, during the 1970s and 1980s, levels of volatility remained relatively constant, which was different from those of other 'consensual' democracies, such as the Netherlands and Belgium. By the 1980s and 1990s, both were experiencing higher levels of volatility and more pronounced change in the party balance and in competition for government (Deschouwer 2001: 219–222). Although the transformation of the Swiss party system has been slower and more gradual, in 1995 and especially in 1999, overall electoral volatility in lower chamber elections increased. Although it dipped in 2007, volatility remained high in 2011, when new centre-right wing parties arose. By contrast, in 2015, the volatility weakened, despite the success of the SVP.

As noted, the institutionalisation of the 'magic formula' was based on segmentation and high levels of electoral and parliamentary stability. In elections from 1971 to 1991, SVP support ranged from a low of 9.9 per cent in 1975 to a high of 11.9 per cent in 1991. It then won 14.9 per cent in 1995, 22.5 per cent

Table 4.1 The Strength of the Mainstream Parties and General Electoral Volatility (Lower Chamber Elections, 1971–2015)

Year	Liberal Party	Christian Democratic Party	Socialist Party	Swiss People's Party	Volatility (Pedersen index) of all parties
1971	21.8	20.3	22.9	11.1	7.4
1975	22.2	21.1	24.9	9.9	5.2
1979	24.0	21.3	24.4	11.6	6.2
1983	23.3	20.2	22.8	11.1	5.1
1987	22.9	19.6	18.4	11.0	6.4
1991	21.0	18.0	18.5	11.9	6.6
1995	20.2	16.8	21.8	14.9	7.0
1999	19.9	15.9	22.5	22.5	8.7
2003	17.3	14.4	23.3	26.7	7.8
2007	15.8	14.5	19.5	28.9	6.6
2011	15.1	12.3	18.7	26.6	10.3
2015	16.4	11.6	18.8	29.4	4.7

Source: Federal statistical office, Berne.

in 1999, and 26.7 per cent in 2003; increased to 28.9 per cent in 2007; declined somewhat to 26.6 per cent in 2011; and peaked at 29.4 per cent in 2015. The number of parties also evolved (*see* table 4.2), partly reflecting the disappearance of populist parties such as the Swiss Democrats and the Freedom Party in the 1980s and early 1990s. More recently, an increase in the effective number of electoral and parliamentary parties (*see* 2011 in table 4.2) reflected the rise of a second and more moderate Green party, the Liberal Green Party and the Conservative Democratic Party, which both declined in the last election. Thus, to some extent, in contrast with the 1970s and the 1980s, because of the increasing support for the SVP and the strength of the SP and the Greens, more polarisation occurred in the 2000s and 2010s, undermining the legacy of 'moderate pluralism' in Switzerland. This change reflects the SVP's increasing electoral strength, which introduces new issues in the electoral arena and helps shape a new cleavage between national independence and supranational integration (Bornschier 2015; Kriesi 2012; Lachat 2008).

Second, increased party competition reflects shifting patterns in electoral mobilisation. This shift combined with an equivalent transformation in the media and changes in election campaigning. Engaging in more capital-intensive campaigns, parties modernised the ways in which they mobilised support (Ladner 2005; Marcinkowski 2007; Skenderovic 2009b). A partial re-politicisation of citizens also occurred. During the era of the 'magic formula', the logic of inter-party cooperation went hand in hand with relatively depoliticised elections

Table 4.2 Effective Number of Parties in the Swiss Lower Chamber and Its Government (1971–2015)

Year	Effective Number of Parties (electoral), ENEP	Effective Number of Parties in Parliament, ENPP	% of Parties in Government	Number of Parties in Government
1971	6.08	5.52	76.1	4
1975	5.8	5.01	78.1	4
1979	5.51	5.14	81.3	4
1983	6.04	5.31	77.5	4
1987	6.82	5.74	72.0	4
1991	7.38	6.7	69.4	4
1995	6.79	5.6	73.7	4
1999	5.87	5.16	80.8	4
2003	5.44	5.01	81.7	4
2007	5.61	4.97	78.7	4
2011	6.35	5.57	78.1	5
2015	5.95	5.12	80.3	5

for the federal parliament. As noted earlier, parties engaged primarily in office and policy seeking. In the 1960s and 1970s, Switzerland had lower rates of participation in national elections than other European democracies. By contrast, the rise of the SVP corresponded with an increased turnout in federal elections (Giugni and Sciarini 2008; Kriesi 2005; Lutz 2012).

Third, division among government parties in parliamentary decision making and referenda has increased (Bühlmann et al. 2012: 198ss; Schwarz 2009). In parliament, the frequency of legislative coalitions that included all government parties sharply declined between the mid-1990s and 2013, partly because the SVP increasingly adapted its own positions on controversial issues, particularly those related to immigration and welfare policies (Afonso and Papadopoulos 2015; Traber 2015). While the distance between the SVP and the SP generally increased, at times they converged, placing the centre-right mainstream parties in the minority. These trends also altered the relations between the upper and lower chambers. Because the upper chamber is dominated by traditional centre-right parties, a new – and, for the Swiss system, novel – imbalance between the two chambers occurred, resulting in an unprecedented rise in the incidence of laws that either required conciliation measures or were blocked because the two chambers could not agree (Mazzoleni 2013).

Fourth, the SVP's increased strength in parliament and the competitive posture that it adopted challenged several of the informal rules that regulated federal government elections. Blocher's election in 2003 challenged unwritten rules that had been in place for several decades. For instance, an outgoing government candidate once had the right to stand for the Federal Council, and if he or she did so, he or she would be re-elected. Another unwritten rule ensured that the distribution of seats in the Federal Council remained the same. Although these 'rules' had been unchallenged for almost forty years, after 2003, they could no longer be taken for granted. When the SVP won a seat that was usually held by the CVP, a government or party could no longer be 'guaranteed' its seat(s) in the Federal Council. In both 2003 and 2007, government elections excluded a member who stood for re-election, changing the rules governing competition for the government. As a result, other parties modified their strategies and tactics (Burgos et al. 2011).

Putting these changes into context is important. All are modest when compared to changes in other countries; all took place gradually; and, in many crucial respects, they are true to Swiss traditions that are characterised by institutional segmentation. Although the SVP moved towards 'nationalisation', establishing branches in all cantons and gaining a more homogeneous distribution of votes throughout the country, the party largely remains stronger in the German-speaking part than in the French-speaking part of Switzerland. This divide also reflects the difficulties that Blocher's party encountered in attempting to simultaneously manage a centralised party and acknowledge the autonomy of cantonal organisations. In addition, few organisational changes occurred in other mainstream parties, which instead for the most part maintained policy- and office-seeking strategies (Mazzoleni 2016). Moreover, institutional constraints stemming from cantonal segmentation limited both the advance of the SVP and the broader processes of party and party system change. The upper chamber elections, which take place under majoritarian electoral systems, were limited in this way. To win seats, competitors must manage large electoral coalitions in each constituency or canton. Moreover, although the 'new' SVP's ideological autonomy gave it a competitive advantage in elections for the lower chamber and in sub-national legislative elections, both of which are held under proportional representation, this advantage did not carry over into upper chamber elections. The same autonomy that shaped activists and party elites also made it more difficult for the SVP to find candidates who could reach beyond their core support.

CONCLUSION

Since the 1990s, the ways in which the Swiss political system operates have changed. The rules that governed Switzerland in the first decades after the Second World War are less firmly entrenched and institutionalised than they once were. Without a doubt, the main party that has contributed most to these changes is the 'new' SVP led by Christoph Blocher. The SVP's consolidation as Switzerland's largest national party and its adversarial strategy are at stake. The SVP, the old agrarian party that radicalised in the 1990s and 2000s, had an impact on the party system via competition for votes and competition for government seats. Moreover, by adopting a vote-seeking strategy and attempting to maximise votes, the SVP helped undermine the unwritten rules that limited competition for decades.

The electoral advance of the 'new' SVP contributed to the strongest party system change in decades. In contrast with the 1950s and the 1960s, since the 1990s, the Swiss party system has been experiencing higher volatility and fragmentation, moving beyond the crystallisation underlined by Kirchheimer (1966). Overall, in the 2000s and 2010s, the number of parties declined, moving towards an increasingly polarised party system. As higher levels of volatility, shifting electoral mobilisation settings and an increasingly adversarial logic in parliamentary and referendum arenas indicate, a more competitive pattern has gradually taken hold in Swiss politics. The governing pattern based on the formation of large coalitions without any alternation remains unchanged, but the fight for government seats has certainly become more competitive. After more than forty years in which seats in the Federal Council were distributed in the same proportions among the same four parties, including the 'old' SVP, government elections have become much less predictable. These changes provide an undermining trend against the Swiss model of 'consensus' democracy, which has been consolidated since the 1950s and 1960s.

However, current changes in the Swiss political system do not necessarily foreshadow sudden or drastic changes in competition for votes in the party system or in competition for government. Despite its radicalisation and its anti-establishment and populist claims, the SVP has remained in some respects a pragmatic government party, which benefits from the mainstream parties' persistent, though ambivalent, recognition as a 'government party'. This recognition helps explain why the overall process of adaptation has been gradual and why Switzerland retains an aura of exceptionality that makes the SVP's continued presence in government unique. Based on non-alternating coalitions, the Swiss government differs from 'consensus' government elsewhere in Europe. This will likely continue. As a result, compared with those of other countries, changes in the party system and in competition for votes and the national government remain rather limited in Switzerland.

NOTE

1   With Betz (2009: 99), we argue that 'the SVP quickly adopted the core elements and rhetoric of right-wing populist ethno-nationalism and made them central to its mobilization campaigns' around the mid-1990s. Other 'populist' parties in Switzerland currently include the *Lega dei Ticinesi* and the *Mouvement des Citoyens Genevois*. Both are regional parties, active in Canton Ticino and Canton Geneva, respectively.

BIBLIOGRAPHY

Afonso, A. and Papadopoulos, Y. (2015) 'How the populist radical right transformed Swiss welfare politics: From compromise to polarization', *Swiss Political Science Review*, 21(4): 617–635.

Albertazzi, D. and McDonnell, D. (2015) *Populists in power*, London: Routledge.

Altermatt, U. and Kriesi, H. (Hg.) (1995) *Rechtsextremismus in der Schweiz. Organisationen und Radikalisierung in den 1980er und 1990er Jahren*, Zurich: Neue Zürcher Zeitung Verlag.

Bale, T. (2003) 'Cinderella and her ugly sisters: The mainstream and extreme right in Europe's bipolarising party systems', *West European Politics*, 26(3): 67–90.

Betz, H.-G. (2004) *Radical right-wing populism in Western Europe*, New York: St. Martin's Press.

——— (2009) 'The Swiss populist right in the West European context', in M. A. Neggli (ed.) *Right-wing extremism in Switzerland: National and international perspectives*, Baden-Baden: Nomos pp. 92–101.

Bochsler, D., Hänggli, R. and Häusermann, S. (2015) 'Introduction: Consensus lost? Disenchanted democracy in Switzerland', *Swiss Political Science Review*, 21(4): 475–490.

Bornschier, S. (2015) 'The new cultural conflict, polarization, and representation in the Swiss party system, 1975–2011', *Swiss Political Science Review*, 21(4): 680–701.

Bühlmann, F., Botkin, C. S. and Farago, P. (eds.) (2012) *Rapport social 2012: Générations en jeu*, Zurich: Seismo.

Burgos, E., Mazzoleni, O. and Rayner, H. (2011) *La formule magique: Conflit et consensus dans l'élection du Conseil Fédéral*, Lausanne: Presses Polytechniques et universitaires romandes.

Church, C. H. (ed.) (2006) *Switzerland and the European Union: A close contradictory and misunderstood relationship*, London: Routledge.

De Lange, S. (2007) 'From pariah to power broker: The radical right-wing and government in Western Europe', in P. Delwit and P. Poirier (eds.) *The new right-wing parties and power in Europe*, Bruxelles: Editions de l'Université de Bruxelles pp. 21–40.

Deschouwer, K. (2001) 'Freezing pillars and frozen cleavages: Party systems and voter alignments in the consociational democracies', in Karvonen, L. and Kuhnle, S. (eds.) *Party systems and voter alignments revisited*, London: Routledge, 205–221.

Deutsch, K. W. (1976) *Die Schweiz als ein Paradigmatischer Fall politischer Integration*, Bern: Haupt.

Gentile, P. (1996) *Les trajectoires de la droite radicale 1984–1993*, Genève: Université de Genève.

Giugni, M. and Sciarini, P. (2008) 'Polarisation et politisation en Suisse', in C. Suter, S. Perrenoud, R. Levy, U. Kuhn, D. Joye and P. Gazareth (eds.) *Rapport social 2008*, Zurich: Seismo.

Gruner, E. (1977) *Die Parteien der Schweiz*, Bern: Francke.

Katzenstein, P. J. (1984) *Corporatism and change: Austria, Switzerland, and the politics of industry*, Ithaca and London: Cornell University Press.

Kerr, H. H. (1987) 'The Swiss party system: Steadfast and changing', in H. Daalder (ed.) *Party systems in Denmark, Austria, Switzerland, the Netherlands, and Belgium*, London: Pinter pp. 107–192.

Kirchheimer, O. (1966) 'The transformation of the Western European party system', in J. LaPalombara and M. Weiner (eds.) *Political parties and political development*, Princeton: Princeton University Press pp. 177–200.

Kobach, K. W. (1993) *The referendum: Direct democracy in Switzerland*, Dartmouth: Aldershot.

Kriesi, H. (2005) *Der Aufstieg der SVP: Acht Kantone im Vergleich*, Zürich: NZZ Verlag.

———— (2012) 'Restructuring the national political space: The supply side of national electoral politics', in H. Kriesi, E. Grande, M. Dolezal, M. Helbling, D. Hoglinger, S. Hutter and B. Wuest (eds.) *Political conflict in Western Europe*, Cambridge: Cambridge University Press pp. 96–126.

Lachat, R. (2008) 'Switzerland: Another case of transformation driven by an established party', in H. Kriesi, E. Grande, R. Lachat, M. Dolezal, S. Bornschier and T. Frey (eds.) *West European politics in the age of globalization*, Cambridge: Cambridge University Press pp. 131–153.

Ladner, A. (2005) 'Die Parteien in der politischen Kommunikation. Mediendemokratie: Herausforderungen und Chancen für politische Parteien', in P. Donges (ed.) *Politische Kommunikation in der Schweiz*, Bern: Haupt pp. 57–74.

———— (2007) 'Political parties', in U. Klöti et al. (eds.) *Handbook of Swiss politics*, Zurich: NZZ Verlag pp. 309–334.

Lehmbruch, G. (1967) *Proporzdemokratie: Politisches system und politische kultur in der Schweiz und in Österreich*, Tübingen: Mohr.

Lijphart, A. (1999) *Patterns of democracy: Government forms and performance in thirty-six countries*, New Haven and London: Yale University Press.

Lutz, G. (2012) *Eidgenössische Wahlen 2011: Wahlteilnahme und Wahlentscheid*, Lausanne: Selects-FORS.

Mach, A. (2006) *La Suisse entre internationalisation et changements politiques internes: La législation sur les cartels et les relations industrielles dans les années 1990*, Genève-Zürich: Seismo.

Mair, P. (1997) *Party system change: Approaches and interpretations*, Oxford: Clarendon Press.

Mair, P., Müller, W. G. and Plassner, F. (eds.) (2004) *Political parties and electoral change: Party responses to electoral markets*, London: Sage Publishing House.

Marcinkowski, F. (2007) 'Media system and political communication', in U. Klöti (ed.) *Handbook of Swiss politics*, Zurich: NZZ Verlag pp. 381–402.

Mazzoleni, O. (2007) 'Définir le parti: Un enjeu scientifique et politique', in O. Mazzoleni, P. Gottraux and C. Péchu (eds.) *L'Union Démocratique de Centre. Un Parti, son action et ses soutiens*, Lausanne: Editions Antipodes pp. 17–47.

———— (2008) *Nationalisme et Populisme en Suisse: La Radicalisation de la 'Nouvelle' UDC*, Lausanne: Presses Polytechniques et universitaires romandes.

———— (2009) 'Des partis gouvernentaux face à la 'crise': Les cas du Parti libéral-radical et du Parti démocrate-chrétien', in O. Mazzoleni and H. Rayner (eds.) *Les partis politiques en Suisse: Traditions et renouvellements*, Paris: Houdiard Editeur pp. 410–442.

———— (2012) 'Between centralisation and nationalisation: The case of the Swiss People's party', in G. Pallaver and C. Wagemann (eds.) *Challenges for Alpine parties: Strategies of political parties for identity and territory in the Alpine regions*, Studienverlag: Innsbruck pp. 17–34.

———— (2013) 'Ungewöhnliche Konvergenzen. Die Schweizerische Volkspartei un die Sozialdemokratische Partei in der parlamentarischen Arena der Eidgenossenschaft', in O. Mazzoleni and O. Meuwly (eds.) *Die Parteien in Bewegung: Nachbarschaft und Konflikte,* Zurich: Neue Zürcher Zeitung Verlag pp. 99–121.

———— (2016) 'Staying away from the mainstream: The case of the Swiss People's party', in T. Akkerman, L. S. de Lange and M. Rooduijn (eds.) *Radical right-wing populist parties in Western Europe: Into the mainstream?*, New York: Routledge pp. 252–275.

Mazzoleni, O. and Rayner, H. (2009) *Les partis politiques en Suisse: Traditions et renouvellements,* Paris: Houdiard Editeur.

Mazzoleni, O. and Rossini, C. (2016) 'The Swiss People's party', in R. Heinisch and O. Mazzoleni (eds.) *Understanding populist party organisation: The radical right in Western Europe*, Basingstoke: Palgrave Macmillan.

Mazzoleni, O. and Skenderovic, D. (2007) 'The rise and impact of the Swiss People's party: Challenging the rules of governance in Switzerland', in P. Delwit and P. Poirier (eds.) *The new right-wing parties and power in Europe*, Bruxelles: Editions de l'Université de Bruxelles pp. 85–116.

Meguid, B. M. (2008) *Party competition between unequals: Strategies and electoral fortunes in Western Europe*, Cambridge: Cambridge University Press.

Pappalardo, A. (1981) 'The conditions for consociational democracy: A logical and empirical critique', *European Journal of Political Research*, 9(4): 365–390.

Pedersen, M. N. (1979) 'The dynamics of European party systems: Changing patterns of electoral volatility', *European Journal of Political Research*, 7(1): 1–26.

Sager, F. and Zolliger, C. (2011) 'The Swiss political system in comparative perspective', in C. Trampusch and A. Mach (eds.) *Switzerland in Europe: Continuity and change in the Swiss political economy*, London and New York: Routledge pp. 27–42.

Sartori, G. (1976*) Parties and party systems: A framework for analysis*, Cambridge: Cambridge University Press.

Schwarz, D. (2009) *Zwischen Fraktionszwang und freiem Mandat. Eine Untersuchung des fraktionsabweichenden Stimmverhaltens im Schweizerischen Nationalrat zwischen 1996 und 2005,* Norderstedt: Books on Demand.

Skenderovic, D. (2009a) *The radical right in Switzerland: Continuity and change, 1945–2000*, New York: Berghahn.

———— (2009b) 'Campagnes et agenda politiques. La transformation de l'Union démocratique du centre', in O. Mazzoleni and H. Rayner (eds.), *Les partis politiques en Suisse: Traditions et renouvellements*, Paris: Michel Houdiard pp. 378–409.

Traber, D. (2015) 'Disenchanted Swiss Parliament? Electoral strategies and coalition formation', *Swiss Political Science Review*, 21(4): 702–723.

Vatter, A. (2008) 'Swiss consensus democracy in transition: A re-analysis of Lijphart's concept of democracy for Switzerland from 1997 to 2007', *World Political Science*, 4(2): 1–38.

Weinmann, B. (2009) *Die Amerikanisierung der Politischen Kommunikation in der Schweiz. Bestandsaufnahme und Experteninterviews vor dem Hintergrund der Eidgenössischen Parlamentswahlen 2007*, Zürich: Rüegger.

Wolinetz, S. B. (2006) 'Party systems and party system types', in R. Katz and W. Crotty (eds.) *Handbook of party politics*, London: Sage pp. 51–62.

Chapter 5

Shaken, but Not Stirred: How Right-wing Populist Parties Have Influenced Parties and Party Systems in Scandinavia

Anders Ravik Jupskås

INTRODUCTION

Despite frequent portrayals as a consensual, egalitarian and progressive region of Europe, Scandinavia seems to be a fertile garden for right-wing populist parties. In fact, the rise and, in some cases, subsequent persistence of this new party family is perhaps one of the most significant post-war political developments in this region (Jungar and Jupskås 2014; Widfeldt 2015a). Contemporary parties such as the Danish People's Party (*Dansk Folkeparti*, DF), the Progress Party (*Fremskrittspartiet*, FrP) in Norway and the Sweden Democrats (*Sverigedemokraterna*, SD) are either the second-largest (DF) or third largest (FrP and SD) in their respective party systems in terms of electoral support and parliamentary representation. Moreover, some of the parties have even been in government (FrP) or have acted as stable support parties for governing coalitions (DF). While only the FrP has existed for many decades, both the DF and the SD have had notable right-wing populist predecessors, including the Progress Party (*Fremskridtspartiet*, FrPd) in Denmark and New Democracy (*Ny Demokrati*, ND) in Sweden. Against the backdrop of the successful breakthrough and persistence of right-wing populist parties in Scandinavia, this chapter asks the following question: To what extent have these parties impacted on mainstream parties, as well as on the party system as a whole?

The chapter proceeds as follows. First, it provides a short overview of the rise of Scandinavian right-wing populism, distinguishing between a first and second generation of populist parties based on core ideology, degree of institutionalisation, and position in the party lifespan.[1] The second part will first assess whether these populist parties have affected three core aspects of the party system: (1) key parameters such as fragmentation, polarisation and volatility; (2) competition for votes; and (3) competition for government. Then the chapter will deal with the extent to which the rise of populist parties has changed (4) the strategies and policy positions of mainstream parties. The data come from the Comparative Manifesto Project, which in the Danish case has been heavily criticised (Hansen 2008), national election surveys, and the existing literature on government formation and party strategies in the Scandinavian countries. Towards the end, the chapter summarises the main findings and briefly discusses some of the most important implications.

TWO GENERATIONS OF RIGHT-WING POPULIST PARTIES IN SCANDINAVIA

If populism is conceptualised as a thin ideology that pits the ordinary and virtuous people against the corrupt and ignorant elite (Mudde 2004; Canovan 2002), the first generation of right-wing populist parties emerged in the so-called electoral earthquakes of 1973 in Denmark and Norway (e.g. Goul Andersen and Bjørklund 1990).[2] While the FrPd astonishingly gained 15.9 per cent of the vote in Denmark, a similar party that was initially called Anders Lange's Party for a Strong Reduction in Taxes, Duties and Public Intervention (*Anders Langes parti til sterk nedsettelse av skatter, avgifter og offentlige inngrep*, ALP), but later renamed FrP, gained 5 per cent of the vote in Norway (*see* figure 5.1). As part of what von Beyme (1988) called the 'second wave' of far-right mobilisation in post-war Europe, these parties were primarily anti-tax movements rather than nationalist parties. Programmatically, they opposed increased taxes, the growing bureaucracy, the expansion of the (Scandinavian) welfare state and foreign aid (Goul Andersen and Bjørklund 2000). The two leaders – Lange in Norway and Glistrup in Denmark – were particularly hostile towards the established parties, although they also attacked bureaucrats and intellectuals (Bjørklund 1981: 4).

The FrPd and the FrP seemed unable to institutionalise. Both parties suffered from unstable electoral support (*see* figure 5.1), organisational problems and profound factionalism (Jupskås 2016a; Ringsmose 2003). With the exception of a short-lived recovery in the late 1980s, the FrPd gradually lost support until another more successful right-wing populist party, the DF, replaced it in the mid-1990s. The Norwegian FrP also experienced instability in the electoral arena and ideological conflicts in its first two decades of existence. Although it gained some electoral support after playing the 'immigration card' for the first time in 1987, a growing ideological division between the nationalist, Christian-conservative and libertarian wing resulted in diminished electoral support in the early 1990s. After an agonising party convention in 1994 where the invaluable party leader since 1978, Carl I.

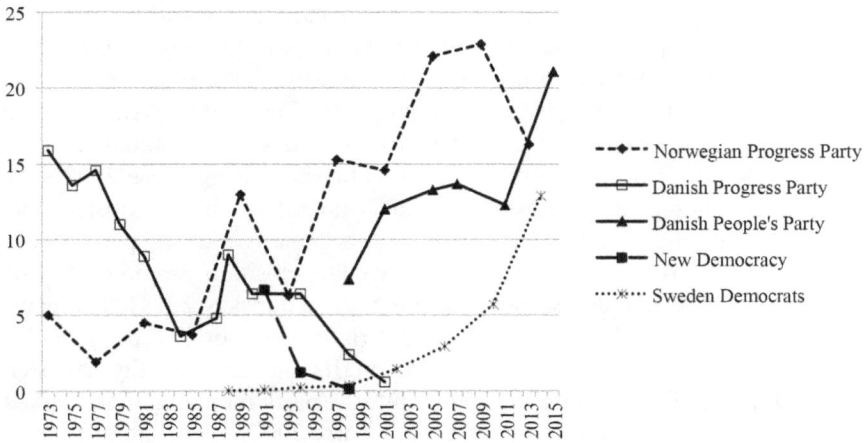

Figure 5.1 Electoral Support for Scandinavian Right-Wing Populist Parties in General Elections, 1973–2015 (in per cent)

Note: The Norwegian Progress Party was initially called Anders Lange's Party for Strong Reduction in Taxes, Duties and Public Intervention.

Source: Official electoral statistics from three Scandinavian countries.

Hagen, eventually sided with the two other factions against the libertarians, most of the libertarians left the party. Neither the FrPd nor the FrP were considered as a possible coalition partner by other established right-wing parties; instead, they were viewed as unreliable and politically extreme (Bille 1989: 46; Heidar 1989: 147).

In Sweden, the first generation of right-wing populism did not emerge until the early 1990s, although similar parties had been active at the sub-national level in the southern part of Sweden in the 1980s (e.g. Peterson et al. 1988).[3] The ND appeared more or less out of nowhere and entered the parliament with 6.7 per cent of the vote in 1991. The party primarily criticised the elitism of the established parties and the level of taxation, although welfare chauvinism and ethno-pluralism also constituted parts of the party's programmatic appeal (Rydgren 2006: 46ff). Despite its initial electoral success, support eroded rapidly, largely due to organisational weaknesses and internal factionalism. In the next parliamentary election in 1994, the ND received a mere 1.2 per cent of the vote, and six years later, in 2000, the party was declared bankrupt. Like the first generation of right-wing populist parties in Norway and Denmark, the ND was not invited to take part in any governing coalition. However, the established right-wing parties were less confrontational in Sweden than in the other Scandinavian countries, even though the ND was also perceived as an unreliable party (Widfeldt 2004: 159).

The second generation of right-wing populist parties emerged in the 1990s. Again, the development first occurred in Denmark and Norway. In Denmark, several prominent MPs who had defected from the FrPd, most notably the former party leader, Pia Kjærsgaard, founded the DF in 1995. Although the reasons behind the party split were primarily related to organisational matters (Ringsmose and Pedersen 2005) and personal rivalry (Ringsmose 2003: 88), the DF also adopted a more explicit national-populist position. Most importantly, anti-immigration and Euroscepticism became two of the party's core issues (Meret 2010: 102ff), and the anti-welfare position promoted by the FrPd was slowly abandoned (see also Jungar and Jupskås 2014). The party quickly replaced the FrPd as the dominant right-wing populist party, and it embarked on a process of institutionalisation. Its electoral stability has been remarkable (*see* figure 5.1). Moreover, while the party for a long time seemed dependent upon its founder (Andersen and Borre 2007), its electoral support actually increased further after the leadership succession from Kjærsgaard to Kristian Thulesen Dahl. Becoming an institutionalised party is perhaps even more impressive knowing that the DF simultaneously acted as a stable support party for Denmark's right-wing minority government between 2001 and 2011. Although the party did not hold any government portfolios, it was consistently part of the parliamentary majority needed to pass legislation and the annual state budget (Christiansen 2012). In the most recent election, the DF emerged as the largest right-wing party, gaining more than one-fifth of the popular vote. However, the party decided to stay out of office and remain an influential support party of the right-wing government.

In Norway, the FrP emerged as a more clear-cut national-populist party after the split in 1994 when most of the libertarian wing left the party (Jupskås 2016b; Goul Andersen and Bjørklund 2000: 206). While the party retained some of its right-wing issues, it also adopted a new programmatic appeal that mostly emphasised anti-immigration and welfare chauvinism. This appeal proved electorally beneficial, and the party gained more than one-fifth of the vote in several elections.[4] However, despite being the largest right-wing party in several elections, mainstream parties continued to view the party as un-coalitionable for more than a decade. This stance changed in 2013 when the party entered office as a junior partner in a right-wing minority coalition government with the Conservatives. Simultaneously, the party has become less anti-establishment, although it retained its radical profile on niche issues such as immigration and law and order (Jupskås 2016b).

Characterised by the absence rather than the presence of a national-populist party (or even a functional equivalent), Sweden for a long time was considered an 'exceptional case' (Rydgren 2008). The ND certainly mobilised on anti-immigration sentiments, yet the party was primarily concerned with economic issues and ended up as a flash party (see earlier in the chapter). However, in the 2010 national elections, the state of exceptionalism ended.

With 5.7 per cent of the vote, the SD entered the parliament for the first time. Though this party had been founded in the late 1980s, its extreme-right origins and history turned out to be 'an obstacle on the attempted route to a national breakthrough' (Widfeldt 2008: 275). By the time the SD gained parliamentary representation, its ideology had been somewhat moderated and was more in line with that of other national-populist parties (Widfeldt 2015a: 193–202). Since the parliamentary breakthrough, its electoral support has further increased. In 2014, the SD became the third largest party, gaining 12.9 per cent of the popular vote. By and large, however, the party remains politically isolated due to a *cordon sanitaire* erected by all other parties, though the Conservative Party no longer rules out collaboration on specific issues.

To sum up: the first generation of populist parties in Scandinavia (FrPd, ND and FrP before the party split) was electorally unstable, ideologically neoliberal and unwanted as coalition partners. The second generation (DF, SD and FrP after the party split), on the other hand, has (thus far) proved to be more institutionalised, more oriented towards nationalism, and is – with the notable exception of the SD – accepted as possible governing parties. The next section considers the extent to which the two generations of populist parties have influenced certain key aspects of the Scandinavian party systems.

SHIFTING PARAMETERS OF SCANDINAVIAN PARTY SYSTEMS

For a long time, the Scandinavian countries had some of the most stable party systems in Europe – they were 'frozen' (Lipset and Rokkan 1967: 51). The conceptualisation of Scandinavia's party system was largely based upon the Swedish experience, which has been described as a 'five-party model' because it consisted of a far-left party (either a communist or a socialist party), a social democratic party, an agrarian party, a liberal party and a conservative party (Berglund and Lindström 1978). In Norway, however, there was also a smaller non-socialist Christian party, whereas the Danish parliament had a small centrist party inspired by Georgism, *Retsforbundet*, until the late 1970s. The social democrats were much larger than the other parties in terms of electoral and parliamentary size, although the Danish Social Democrats were always less dominant than their Scandinavian counterparts. According to Sartorian counting rules,[5] all these parties – five in Sweden and six in Denmark and Norway – were relevant parties. They were either governing parties or held blackmailing power (i.e. the communists or left-wing socialists vis-à-vis the social democrats) (Bille 1989: 43). Following the typology introduced by Blondel (1968), Denmark, Sweden and Norway had limited multiparty systems with a predominant party.

Furthermore, the effective number of parties *in the legislative arena* was extremely stable in all the Scandinavian countries. In the first decades of the post-war period, there were approximately three in Sweden and Norway and approximately four in Denmark (*see* figure 5.2). The effective number of parties *in the electoral arena* was somewhat higher in all the countries, particularly in Norway, but was equally stable (figure not shown here). The party systems were consensus oriented with relatively low levels of ideological polarisation, although anti-system parties (i.e. the communists) were present in the parliaments. In Sartorian terminology, the Scandinavian party systems are characterised by moderate rather than polarised pluralism. Finally, all countries have low levels of volatility – both at the aggregate and, to the extent that surveys exist, the individual level (Aardal and Bergh 2015: 20; Oscarsson and Holmberg 2013: 164; Stubager et al. 2013: 30; *see also* figure 5.3).

The first generation of populist parties contributed significantly to increased fragmentation, polarisation and volatility in the Scandinavian party systems (see also Arter 1999b; Demker and Svåsand 2005). As some of the few new parties in post-war Scandinavia, the FrPd, the FrP and the ND were definitely relevant parties in their party systems. While none of them were perceived as potential coalition partners, they surely had blackmail potential, as was the case from the very beginning in Denmark and Sweden, where the FrPd and the ND's parliamentary seats were needed to secure any centre-right coalition. Especially in Denmark, government formation and the strategies of the established parties were affected by the rise of the FrPd (Bille 1989). In Norway, by contrast, the FrP's seats were not needed by any centre-right coalition until 1985, more than a decade after the party had been founded (Heidar 1989: 147). Since then, the FrP's parliamentary strength has been crucial for the survival of any non-socialist government.

With the breakthrough of populist parties, the number of effective parties in parliament increased significantly in all the countries: from 3.9 in 1971 to an astonishing 6.9 in 1973 in Denmark, from 3.2 in 1969 to 4.1 in 1973 in Norway and from 3.7 in 1988 to 4.2 to 1991 in Sweden (*see* figure 5.2). However, fragmentation decreased again as these populist parties gradually lost their initial electoral support: back to just above 3 in the early 1980s in Norway, approximately 5 in the late 1980s in Denmark and 3.5 in 1994 in Sweden. Nevertheless, Wörlund's (1992: 142) observation from Sweden in the early 1990s holds for all the Scandinavian countries: 'the durable . . . five-party system is now definitely dead and gone'. Of course, populist parties were not the only new parties to emerge in Scandinavia after 1970, but their electoral strength surpassed that of most other newcomers. Consequently, these populist parties were the main drivers of a rapid shift from limited to extreme pluralism, even though the rise of Christian, green, new left parties and, in the Danish case (see Bille 1989: 47), new centrist parties also impacted on the fragmentation of the party system.[6]

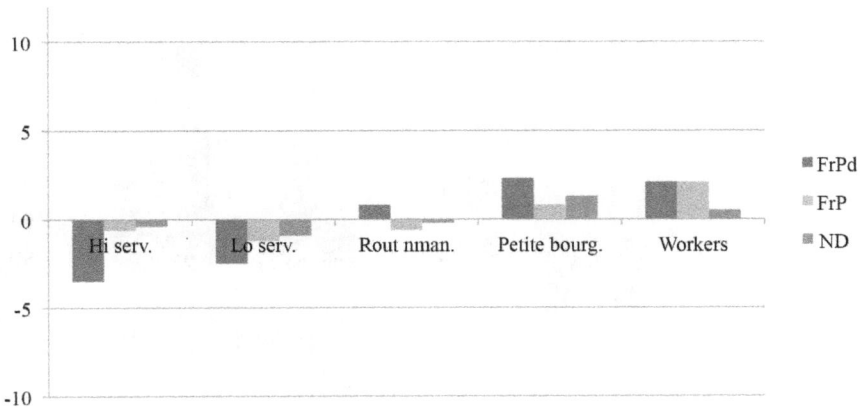

Figure 5.2 Number of Effective Parties in Scandinavian Parliaments, 1945–2015

Note: The effective number of parties is an index introduced by Laakso and Taagepera in which the parties' relative strength is taken into consideration when counting the number of parties in a country's party system.

Polarisation increased too, primarily along the dominant socio-economic left-right cleavage. Arguably, these populist parties and the rise of new left parties (especially in Denmark and Norway) should be interpreted as *new* expressions of *old* class politics, that is, the conflict between employees and employers (Valen 1981: 67). In Norway, a party to the right challenged the Conservatives for the first time in the post-war period. The FrP's first manifesto exclusively focused on typical right-wing policies such as the anti-tax issue and the alleged paternalistic policies of the social democratic state (Bjørklund 1981: 9). Data from the Comparative Manifesto Project also put the FrP far to the right on the socio-economic dimension between 1973 and 1985 but not particularly far to the right on socio-cultural issues (*see* figure 5.4; Bilstad 1994). In Denmark, the FrPd was usually the most right-wing party on economic issues, although it faced strong competition from both the Liberal and the Conservative parties (*see* figure 5.5). Its position on socio-cultural issues, however, was more moderate, at least until the late 1990s. In Sweden, the ND contributed to increased polarisation along the traditional socio-economic cleavage. Rydgren (2006: 51) refers to the ND as the 'product of a process of "outbidding"'. While the Moderate Party – the conservative party in Sweden – continued to promote right-wing policies during this period, the ND always suggested even more radical policies, especially with regard to tax policies. Manifesto data also show that in comparison

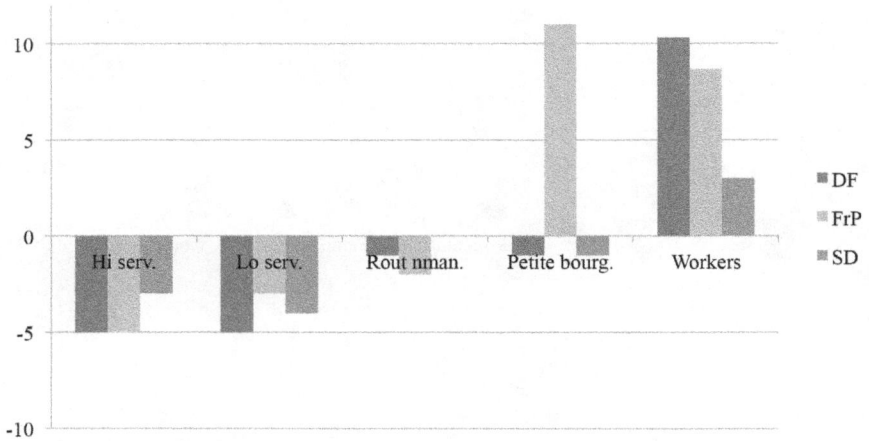

Figure 5.3 Levels of Electoral Volatility at the Individual Level in Scandinavia, 1960–2014

Note: In contrast to the aggregate electoral volatility measured by Pedersen's index, this figure shows volatility at the individual level on the basis of national electoral surveys. Only those voting in both elections are included.

Source: Aardal and Bergh (2015: 20); Oscarsson and Holmberg (2015: 5); Stubager et al. (2013: 28).

with the Moderate Party, the ND's economic position was slightly to the right on the socio-economic dimension but equally authoritarian on the socio-cultural dimension (*see* figure 5.6).

However, the (socio-economic) polarisation of the party system in the wake of the populist upsurge was not only a matter of degree, as one might interpret from the discussion presented earlier in the chapter – it also represented something qualitatively new in the Scandinavian context. Although these parties do not quite fit the notion of anti-systemic, they were anti-establishment and profoundly sceptical of the Scandinavian welfare system and consensus politics (Arter 1999a: 150–151). In this sense, the party systems, at least in some periods, drifted towards polarised pluralism. Wolinetz (2006: 60) has suggested that *extended* rather than *extreme* multipartism is more useful when characterising multiparty systems that include parties that do not challenge the democratic system, yet push 'the boundaries of political correctness and force the other parties to take up some of their claims'.

Finally, the first generation of populist parties contributed to rising levels of volatility – on the one hand, by being able to mobilise disgruntled

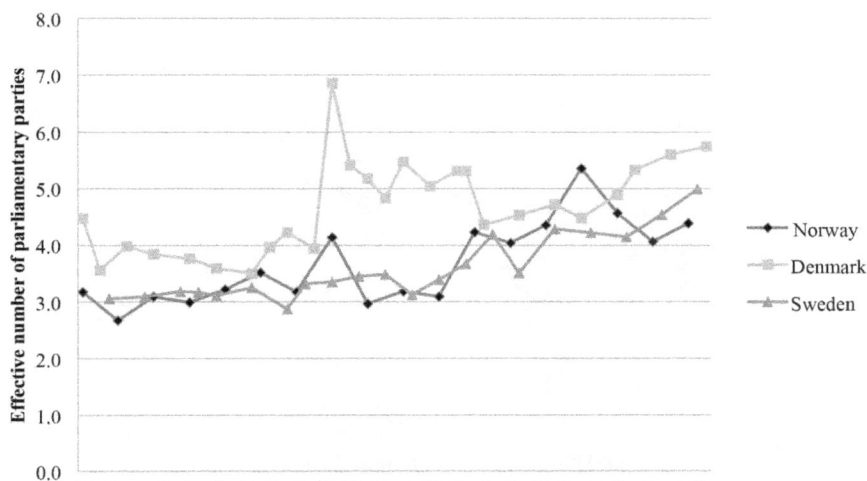

Figure 5.4 Socio-Economic Polarisation in Norway, 1945–2009

Note: The socio-economic index has been created by including only those items in the Comparative Manifesto Project that directly relate to economic policies. It is calculated by subtracting the share of statements in the manifestos characterised as economically left wing from the share of statements characterised as economically right wing. The economic right is defined as 303 (decentralisation positive), 401 (free enterprise positive), 402 (incentives positive), 407 (protectionism negative), 414 (economic orthodoxy positive), 505 (welfare state limitation positive), 702 (labour groups negative) and 704 (middle class and professional groups positive). The economic left is defined as 404 (economic planning positive), 406 (protectionism positive), 409 (Keynesian demand management), 412 (controlled economy), 413 (nationalisation positive), 415 (Marxist analysis positive), 503 (social justice positive), 504 (welfare state expansion positive) and 701 (labour groups positive). Abbreviations: SV = Socialist Left Party, Ap = Labour Party, H = The Conservative Party and FrP = The Progress Party.

Source: The Comparative Manifesto Project (Volkens et al. 2013).

voters from the established parties and, on the other hand, by being unable to turn those protest voters into loyal partisans (*see* figure 5.3). In Denmark, volatility increased from 17 per cent in 1971 to 44 per cent in 1973. It remained at a high level in two subsequent elections but decreased somewhat during the 1980s. The FrPd gained most of their voters from the Social Democrats, the Conservatives, the Agrarian Liberals and the Social Liberals (Borre 1974: 202). In Norway, volatility increased much less than in Denmark; yet it went from 24 per cent in 1969 to 32 per cent in 1973. Similar to its Danish peer, most of the FrP voters had previously voted for the Conservatives or the Labour Party (Bjørklund 1981: 42). Moreover, the FrP attracted voters who had previously abstained from voting or were first-time voters. While the level of volatility decreased when the FrP lost support in the late 1970s and early 1980s, it reached

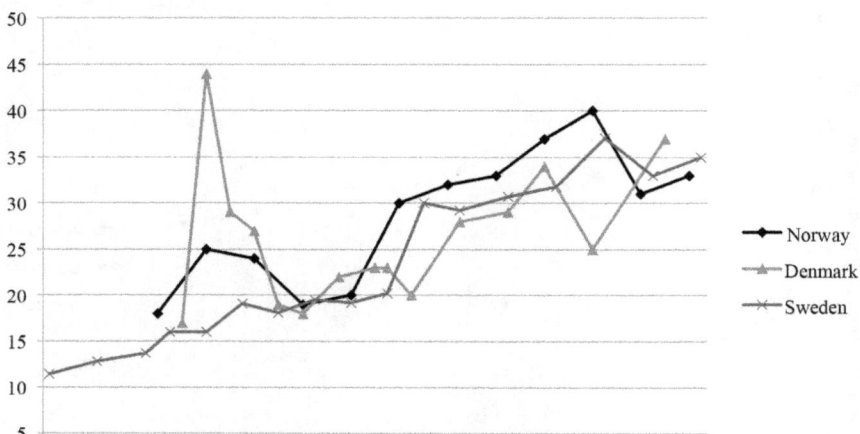

Figure 5.5 Socio-Economic Polarisation in Denmark, 1945–2011

Note: See previous figure. Abbreviations: SF = Socialist People's Party, S = Social Democrats, V = The Liberal Party, KF = The Conservative People's Party, DF = Danish People's Party and FrP = Progress Party.

Source: The Comparative Manifesto Project (Volkens et al. 2013).

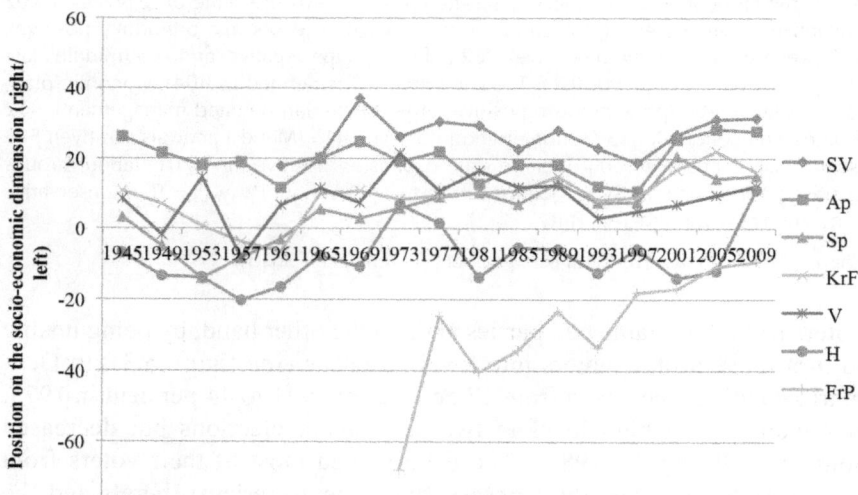

Figure 5.6 Socio-Economic Polarisation in Sweden, 1944–2010

Note: See figure 5.5. Abbreviations: V = Left Party, S = Social Democrats, M = Conservative Party, SD = Sweden Democrats and ND = New Democracy.

Source: The Comparative Manifesto Project (Volkens et al. 2013).

new heights in the late 1980s after the party politicised immigration for the first time. Again, most of the voters came from either the Conservatives or the Labour Party (Valen et al. 1990: 30). In Sweden, volatility increased from 20 per cent in 1988 to 30 per cent in 1991. The ND voters had previously voted for the Social Democrats (24 per cent), the Moderates (20 per cent), had abstained from voting (18 per cent), or they were voting for the first time (11 per cent) (Gilljam and Holmberg 1993: 73). In addition to these observations, it is worth noting that these parties' capacity to attract both the working class (which previously voted for the social democratic parties) and the petty bourgeoisie (which previously voted for non-socialist parties) contributed strongly to a new phenomenon in Scandinavia, namely electoral volatility across the dominant blocs (e.g. Oscarsson 2016: 17).

However, because they were protest-oriented, entrepreneurial-issue parties without any consolidated organisation (Harmel and Svåsand 1993; Goul Andersen and Bjørklund 1990), the first generation of populist parties struggled to turn disgruntled voters into a loyal electorate. In all elections prior to the party split, less than half of the FrP voters in one election also voted for the party in the subsequent election (Aardal and Valen 1995: 29; Valen et al. 1990: 23; Aardal and Valen 1989: 159; Valen and Aardal 1983: 50). With the exception of some elections in the 1980s (Tonsgaard 1989: 149), the pattern was similar in Denmark: only 23 and 11 per cent of FrPd voters were loyal to the party in 1998 and 2001, respectively (Nielsen 1999a: 53; Nielsen and Thomsen 2003: 65). The ND lost almost all of their voters in the first election after a breakthrough; most of its voters defected back to where they came from (Gilljam and Holmberg 1995: 33). Not surprisingly, surveys suggest very low levels of party identification among ND voters: only 28 per cent and 14 per cent in 1991 and 1994, respectively (Oscarsson and Holmberg 2011: 33).

The rise of a second generation of populist parties had a different impact on Scandinavian party systems than the first generation. To some extent, the party systems became even more fragmented, as the DF and the FrP (after the party split in 1994) have proven more electorally successful and have been increasingly accepted as support parties (DF in 2001) or governing parties (FrP in 2013). Having seen these parties move into the mainstream, the party systems in Denmark and Norway are definitely no longer characterised by extreme multipartism. In fact, even labelling them as extended multipartism (see earlier in the chapter) might be an example of conceptual stretching. In Sweden, however, the SD continues to be a pariah party, although it could be considered a relevant party due to its electoral strength and its ability to affect the strategies of the other parties (e.g. Aylott and Bolin 2015). Although not reaching the exceptional level of fragmentation after the 'earthquake election' in Denmark, the electoral success and institutionalisation of the second generation of populist parties have contributed to a further increase in the number of effective parties in the legislative arena. The number of effective parties increased from 4.2 in 2006 to 5 in 2014 in Sweden, from approximately 4.5 in the 1990s to 5.7 in 2015 in Denmark and from 3.1 in 1985 to 4.4 in 2013 in Norway (*see* figure 5.2). Similar developments can be observed in the electoral arena (figure not shown here). As previously noted, these figures also reflect the rise of other new party families (i.e. the greens and the Christians), but populist parties are by far the largest, attracting, for example, almost twice as many voters as the greens. Moreover, and quite interestingly, some of the other new parties have been founded as a direct consequence of the rise of the populist right. In Denmark, *Ny Alliance* (New Alliance, NA) was founded in 2007 with the explicit motive of diminishing the influence of the DF in Danish politics. Similarly, in Sweden, *Feministisk initiativ* (Feminist initiative, FI) was established prior to the SD's parliamentary breakthrough, but it has recently positioned itself as the main opponent of the SD (Aylott and Bolin 2015: 733).

In terms of polarisation, the second generation of populist parties has had less impact on the socio-economic dimension than on the socio-cultural dimension. In Norway, the FrP remains the most right-wing party in economic policies, yet it has drifted significantly towards a more centrist position (figure 5.4). However, with regard to socio-cultural issues, the party has moved away from the other parties and currently occupies the most authoritarian position in the party system (*see* figure 5.7). In Denmark, too, the DF gradually became economically centrist while consistently holding the most authoritarian position. In contrast to the Norwegian party system, however, several parties in Denmark have contributed to polarisation along the socio-cultural dimension (*see* figure 5.8; see also Rydgren 2010). The DF faces competition from other right-wing parties, and there are several parties with an increasingly pronounced libertarian agenda. Nevertheless, the impact of the second generation of populist parties is perhaps even more telling in Sweden. In the Swedish party system, the SD holds a quite centrist position on the socio-economic dimension but a profoundly radical position on the socio-cultural dimension (*see* figure 5.9). With the exception of the Christian party, which has occasionally mobilised on traditional values, there was virtually no polarisation along socio-cultural issues in Sweden prior to the entrance of the SD.

Levels of volatility have remained high (*see* figure 5.3), but populist parties are no longer the main drivers of electoral instability. In fact, the SD had the most loyal voters of all parliamentary parties between 2010 and 2014. While most parties struggled with disloyal voters (with the exception of the Social Democrats, less than two-thirds were loyal), as many as 87 per cent of the

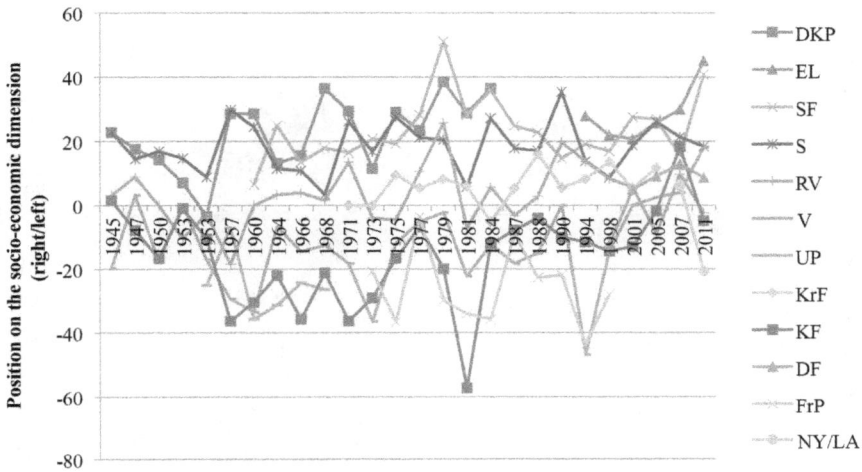

Figure 5.7 Socio-Cultural Polarisation in Norway, 1945–2009

Note: The socio-cultural index has been created by including only those items in the Comparative Manifesto Project that directly relate to non-economic policies such as the military, national way of life, law and order, moral issues and multiculturalism. It is calculated by subtracting the share of statements in the manifestos characterised as libertarian from the share of statements characterised as authoritarian. Libertarian is defined as 105 (military negative), 602 (national way of life negative), 604 (traditional morality negative), 607 (multiculturalism positive) and 705 (underprivileged minority groups positive). Authoritarian is defined as 104 (military positive), 601 (national way of life positive), 603 (traditional morality positive), 605 (law-and-order positive) and 608 (multiculturalism negative). Abbreviations: SV = Socialist Left Party, Ap = Labour Party, H = The Conservative Party and FrP = The Progress Party.

Source: The Comparative Manifesto Project (Volkens et al. 2013).

SD's voters in 2010 voted for the party again in 2014 (Oscarsson and Holmberg 2016: 154). Similarly, in Denmark, the DF has been able to cultivate a loyal electorate. After its second parliamentary election in 2001, the party had the second most loyal electorate, partly because the other parties suffered from truly disloyal voters (Nielsen and Thomsen 2003: 65). In 2011 and 2015, its loyalty increased further to 74 per cent and 90 per cent, respectively (Møller Hansen and Stubager 2017: 36; Stubager et al. 2013: 29). In Norway, the FrP's electorate seemed to be somewhat more loyal after the party split: it increased from 31 per cent in 1993 to 65 per cent in 1997 (Aardal 1999: 36). However, in recent years, it has decreased again – from 58 per cent in 2009 to 46 per cent in 2013 (Aardal 2007: 26; 2011b: 24; Aardal and Bergh 2015: 21). This means that the party has among the most disloyal voters of all parties in parliament.

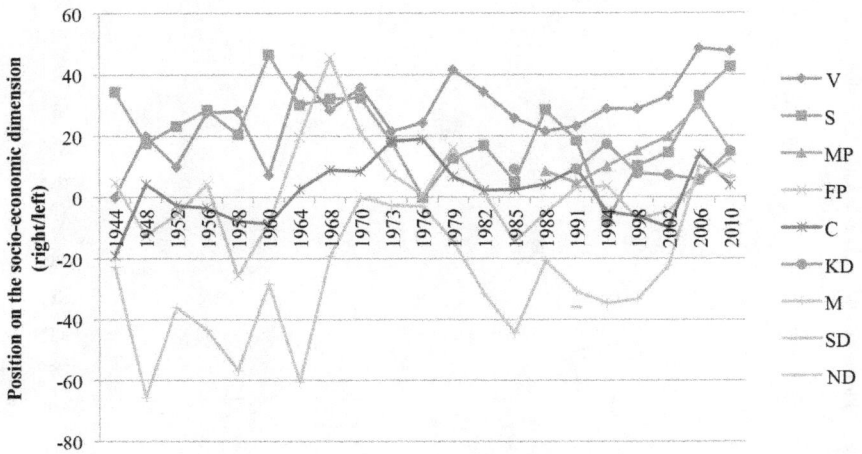

Figure 5.8 Socio-Cultural Polarisation in Denmark, 1945–2011

Note: See previous figure. Abbreviations: SF = Socialist People's Party, S = Social Demo-crats, V = The Liberal Party, KF = The Conservative People's Party, DF = Danish People's Party and FrP = The Progress Party.

Source: The Comparative Manifesto Project (Volkens et al. 2013).

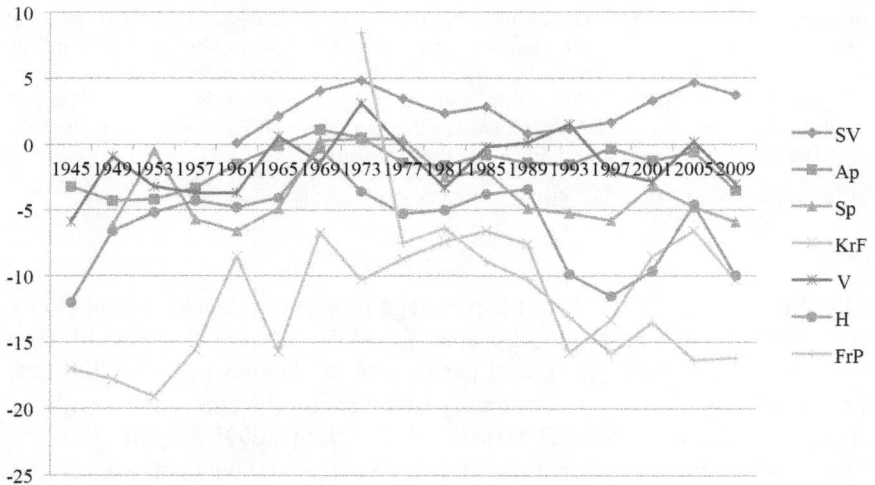

Figure 5.9 Socio-Cultural Polarisation in Sweden, 1944–2010

Note: See previous figure. Abbreviations: V = Left Party, S = Social Democrats, M = The Conservative Party, SD = The Sweden Democrats and ND = New Democracy.

Source: The Comparative Manifesto Project (Volkens et al. 2013).

COMPETITION FOR VOTES

Prior to the rise of the right-wing populist parties, the Scandinavian party system was dominated by a class cleavage, although religious-secular and centre-periphery cleavages were present as well, especially in Norway.[7] In fact, in the 1950s and 1960s, the Scandinavian countries experienced the strongest class voting in Western Europe (Knutsen 2006). The strong relationship between occupational status and party choice meant that most voters voted according to their class position: workers voted for left-wing parties, employers for Conservatives, and farmers for agrarian parties. In addition, part of the urban middle class voted for liberal parties, and Christian voters voted for small Christian parties. Moreover, both voters and parties could be placed on a left-right continuum (Bengtsson et al. 2013: 161). The communists were furthest to the left, followed by the Social Democrats, the three centrist parties (the Liberals, the Christians and the Agrarians), and the Conservatives were furthest to the right. The party system was characterised by strong alignment, including quite high levels of party membership and party identification (e.g. Aylott 2011: 305–309).

The first generation of populist parties did not fundamentally alter the existing cleavages. Instead, these parties politicised anti-establishment attitudes. As argued by Borre (1974: 203), the 1973 election in Denmark 'introduced a protest or distrust dimension . . . rather than following the conventional ideological dimension'. Beyond any doubt, 'Mr. Glistrup was the first to seize this dimension and the most successful in channelling the feelings of dissatisfaction into mass voting behavior' (Borre 1974: 203). Surveys suggested that voting for or sympathising with the FrPd correlated more strongly with indicators of political distrust than with indicators of conservative ideology. In fact, even though the FrPd was located socio-economically on the right, its voters were neither particularly right-wing nor members of a particular social class: what united them was their mistrust of the political system and their anti-establishment attitudes (Nielsen 1979: 168).

Similarly, the ALP's (as the FrP was initially called) voters were also characterised by political distrust. While the voters of another fairly new party, the SV, were somewhat more dissatisfied with the responsiveness of the political system as a whole, the ALP's voters were more critical of established politicians (Bjørklund 1981: 13–14). Moreover, as in the Danish case, neither the voters nor the members were particularly right-wing on economic issues. In fact, on most issues, they were to the left of the Conservatives (Bjørklund 1981; Saglie 1994), which suggests that the party was not (exclusively) the product of the centrist turn of the Conservative Party (in the late 1960s and early 1970s) and the social democratic policies of the non-socialist government (between 1965 and 1971).

Similar to the two progress parties in the 1970s, the ND seems to owe a great deal of its electoral success to protest voting (Wörlund 1992). Not only did the party emerge after a period of rising political discontent in the electorate, a majority of the voters also justified their voting behaviour by referring to different protest motives (Rydgren 2006: 40). Moreover, approximately four out of five voters expressed very or fairly little confidence in Swedish politicians, which was far more than in the electorate as a whole (Gilljam and Holmberg 1993: 173). Rydgren (2006: 49) further demonstrates how 'voters having low trust in politicians and voters strongly believing that political parties are uninterested in the opinion of the voters . . . were more than three times as likely to vote for the [ND]'. Although some specific socio-economic (i.e. less state involvement) and socio-cultural issues (i.e. law and order and opposition to foreign aid) were associated with voting for the ND, most issues related to authoritarianism, xenophobia and distributive politics were not (Rydgren 2006: 47–48). Additionally, while the party was located to the right of the Conservatives, when comparing the two manifestos, the ND's voters viewed themselves as being more centrist (Gilljam and Holmberg 1993: 139).

Given their protest elements, it may not come as a surprise that the first generation of populist parties had no distinct class basis. The lack of a clear-cut class profile is a typical feature of a protest-oriented party. Crudely distinguishing between five different classes, surveys from the early 1990s suggest that these parties were only marginally overrepresented among the working class and the petty bourgeoisie and were marginally underrepresented among the higher and lower service class (*see* figure 5.10). In most cases, the difference was no more than 1–2 percentage points from the average support across all classes.

In contrast to the first generation of populist parties, the second generation has had a more profound impact on competition for votes in the Scandinavian party systems. As argued by Bengtsson et al. (2013: 184), 'there is no doubt that the [current] populist parties [in particular] have challenged the traditional cleavage structure' in Scandinavia. Protest and political distrust are certainly still important features of the voters of these parties (Listhaug and Aardal 2011: 299; Meret 2003: 385; Oscarsson and Holmberg 2016: 257; Sannerstedt 2014: 454), but these attitudes seem to be more related to emerging new cleavages rather than diffuse opposition to the established parties as a whole. More specifically, the rise of these parties has resulted in a more complex cleavage structure in which the traditional socio-economic-based class cleavage has been partly replaced by a new socio-cultural dimension, sometimes referred to as a libertarian-authoritarian divide (e.g. Kitschelt and McGann 1995).[8] Although different scholars conceptualise this dimension somewhat

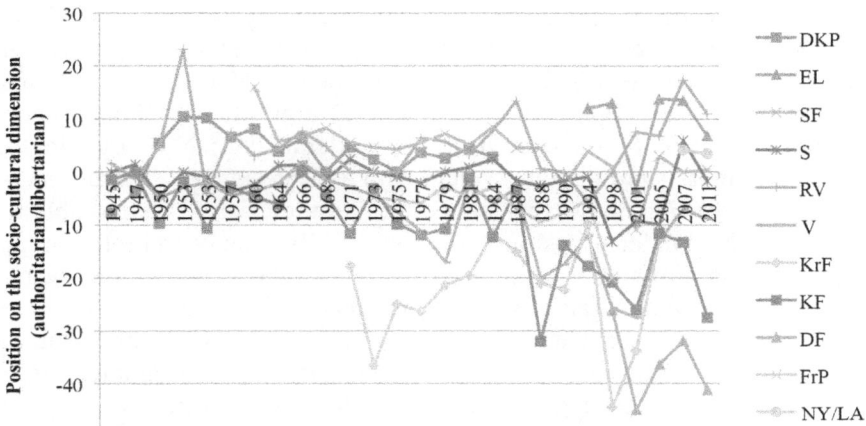

Figure 5.10 Class Profile of First Generation of Populist Parties

Abbreviations: Hi serv. = Higher service class, Lo serv. = Lower service class, Rout nman. = Routine non-manual employees, Petite bourg. = Petite bourgeoisie and Workers = Skilled and unskilled manual workers.

Source: Knutsen (2004).

differently, it usually includes issues related to immigration, multiculturalism, feminism, the environment, security, law and order and European integration. For the second generation of right-wing populist parties in Scandinavia, opposition to immigration has been by far the most important issue.

In Denmark, the socio-cultural dimension certainly became increasingly important and the socio-economic dimension decreasingly important in terms of explaining voting behaviour already by the late 1980s and early 1990s (e.g. Borre 1995). However, the rise of the DF reinforced the stability and saliency of this new cleavage (Goul Andersen 2003: 188; Rydgren 2010: 63). The share of voters stating that immigration was among the most important political issues in Denmark increased from 16 per cent in 1994 to 43 per cent in 1998, the first election in which the DF participated (Nielsen 1999b: 23). Three years later, immigration completely dominated the agenda, and the socio-cultural dimension surpassed the socio-economic dimension for the first time in terms of explaining voting behaviour in general (Møller Hansen and Goul Andersen 2013: 207). While the financial crisis, which emerged in 2008, brought economic issues back on the political agenda, the socio-cultural division between libertarians and authoritarians regained its prominence in Danish politics in 2015 (Møller Hansen and Stubager 2017: 403). Notably, this cleavage is important not only for the DF but pre-eminently also for mainstream parties like the Social Liberals (which mobilise on libertarian positions) and the Liberals (which mobilises on authoritarian positions).

As in Denmark, a libertarian-authoritarian cleavage (based upon views related to gender equality, integration, foreign aid and abuse of social security) emerged as a quite important cleavage in Norway in the 1980s (Aardal and Valen 1989: 65). Furthermore, opposition to immigration gained some salience in the late 1980s (Bjørklund 1988). Not surprisingly, the FrP's voters were the only voters with a clear authoritarian and anti-immigrant position. However, this new cultural cleavage was not able to challenge the dominant position of old politics (economy and religion) as quickly or as profoundly as in Denmark. While the socio-cultural cleavage was equally important as traditional class politics for the first time in 1997 in terms of explaining voting behaviour, this was rather due to decreasing importance of the socio-economics than increasing importance of socio-cultural cleavage (Aardal 2015: 94). Moreover, less than 10 per cent mentioned immigration as one of two important issues between 1989 and 2005 (Karlsen and Aardal 2011: 135). More recently, the socio-economic cleavage has clearly regained its prominence, even if more voters mention immigration as an important issue – 16 per cent and 12 per cent in 2009 and 2013, respectively. In terms of explaining support for individual parties, the immigration issue is the most important only for the FrP. To be sure, the Socialist Left also mobilises on this issue (but with a pro-immigrant posture), but distributive politics and environmental issues matter more (Aardal 2015: 96).

The traditional left-right division dominated Swedish politics longer than in Denmark and Norway, although it was partly challenged by the emergence of the Green Party in the 1980s. Furthermore, with the rise of the ND in 1991 and the short-lived mobilisation on anti-immigration sentiments by the Liberal Party in 2002, 'the contours of an alternative cleavage dimension began to surface' (Rydgren 2006: 40). However, since the entrance of the SD in 2010, the socio-economic dimension has 'been complemented by [a new cleavage] on which issues of immigration and national identity are debated, and on which the Sweden Democrats stand opposed to all the other parties' (Aylott and Bolin 2015: 783). Immigration was mentioned by as many as two-thirds of the SD's voters as the reason for voting for the party, which was far more than any other party (Oscarsson and Holmberg 2013: 186). During its first period in parliament, the SD seems to have had a significant impact on the political agenda. Since the mid-1980s, 10 per cent or fewer of the voters mentioned immigration in an open-ended question about which issue was important for their party choice (Oscarsson and Holmberg 2016: 177). In 2014, this figure had increased to 23 per cent, making immigration the fourth most important issue in Swedish politics behind welfare, education and employment.

Comparative analyses of the electorate in the Scandinavian countries further demonstrate that the voters for the DF, the FrP and the SD hold 'extreme anti-immigration positions compared to most other parties' (Bengtsson et al. 2013: 39). These analyses also show how strongly these attitudes correlate with party choice, especially in Denmark. The position of the electorate along other dimensions provides additional support for the argument that these parties primarily mobilise on new political issues, although these results are not consistent across all countries. The DF and FrP's voters represent the most or the second most grey position on environmental issues, respectively. The SD's voters have no clear position. The voters for the SD and the DF, together with those who vote for the far left, are clearly eurosceptical, whereas the FrP's voters are more divided. The voters for all three are consistently morally conservative, but not as much as those voting for the Christian parties. Finally, the voters for the FrP and, to a lesser extent, the DF hold right-wing views on economic issues but less so than voters for the established right-wing parties. In Sweden, the SD's voters are actually located between the left-wing and right-wing blocs, though they are slightly more to the left.

While the first generation of populist parties had a diffuse class profile, it is quite different with the second generation. The differences between different classes regarding their support for populist parties have increased significantly. Today, they are all 'working-class' parties (*see* figure 5.11). Certainly, the DF has traditionally had less support among the working class than the Social Democrats and the Liberals (Andersen and Goul Andersen 2003: 210; Stubager and Møller Hansen 2013), but in the 2015 election, the DF attracted as many workers as the Social Democrats and far more than the Liberals (Goul Andersen 2017: 56). In Norway, the FrP became the most popular party among the working class in 2009 after having strengthened its position since the mid-1990s (Bjørklund 2009; Berglund et al. 2011: 28). However, while the party remained popular among the working class, Labour and the Conservatives were actually more popular in the 2013 election (Kleven et al 2015: 20). Finally, in Sweden, there is 'room for realignment' of the working class (Oskarson and Demker 2015), although approximately half of the workers still vote for the Social Democrats. From 2010 to 2014, the SD increased its share of working-class votes from 9 to 15 per cent, whereas the share decreased from 51 to 47 per cent for the Social Democrats and from 21 per cent to 16 per cent for the Conservatives (Oscarsson 2016: 42). The support among the petty bourgeoisie has changed over time and is much stronger in Norway than in Denmark and Sweden. While the second generation of right-wing populist parties in Denmark and Sweden (i.e. the DF and the SD) are more

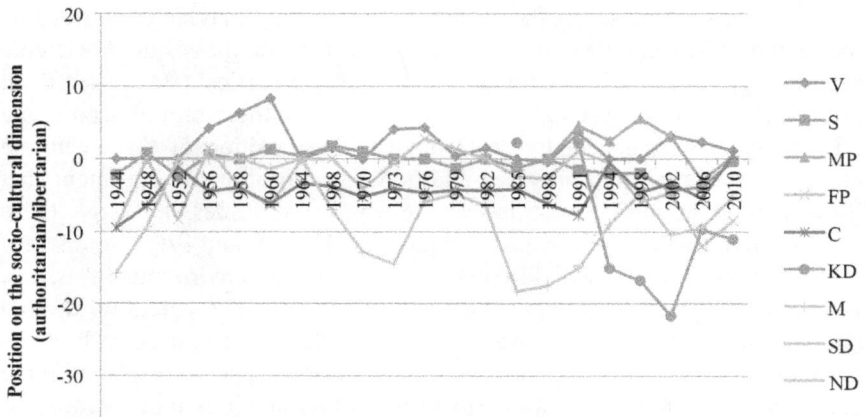

Figure 5.11 The Class Profile of the Second Generation of Populist Parties

Note: See previous figure. The data are derived from either the European Value Study in 2008 (Norway and Denmark) or the 2013 survey of the SOM Institute (Sweden). There are no data on routine non-manual employees for Sweden. Abbreviations: Hi serv. = Higher service class, Lo serv. = Lower service class, Rout nman. = Routine non-manual employees, Petite bourg. = Petite bourgeoisie and Workers = Skilled and unskilled manual workers.

Source: Langsæther (2014).

economically centrist compared to the first generation and therefore do not have much support among employers, the FrP has retained much of its neoliberal appeal (anti-tax, privatisation and de-regulation) and actually strengthened its position among employers.

COMPETITION FOR GOVERNMENT

Initially, government formation in post-war Scandinavia could be characterised by a 'predominant party' period that gradually changed into a 'balanced two-bloc system' (e.g. Heidar 2005). Moreover, following Mair's (2006) distinction between *open* and *closed* competition for office, all three countries were quite closed. There was not much alternation of parties in office, the governing constellations were familiar, and the ruling parties were old and well established (i.e. all but one was founded before 1920). The famous Norwegian political scientist Stein Rokkan (1968) therefore argued that the pattern of government and opposition in Scandinavian systems was characterised by a logic of '1 versus 3–4' (i.e. either the Social Democrats alone or a coalition of non-socialist parties).

In Sweden, the Social Democrats governed until 1976, usually in single-party cabinet but also together with the agrarian Center Party. The hegemony of the Social Democrats was challenged in the mid-1970s as different centre-right alternatives, usually a coalition of the three non-socialist parties (the Liberals, the Conservatives and the agrarian Center Party), seized office between 1976 and 1982. Similarly, in Norway, between 1945 and 1961, the Labour Party's predominant position produced single-party majority cabinets. After Labour lost its parliamentary majority in 1961, however, a new phase emerged in which voters were basically faced with two realistic governing alternatives: a Labour government with parliamentary support from the Socialist Left or a centre-right coalition, usually consisting of all four non-socialist parties (the Conservatives, the agrarian Center Party, the Liberals and the Christian People's Party). In Denmark, government formation was never as closed and unipolar as in Norway and Sweden. While the Social Democrats were also influential in Denmark, right-wing parties (the Liberals and the Conservatives) held office in the late 1940s and early 1950s. Moreover, in contrast to Norway and Sweden, several of the cabinets led by the Social Democrats included other centrist parties (the Social Liberals and the Justice Party). In addition, the Social Liberals were part of both centre-left and centre-right coalitions.

Although one cannot speak of any type of systemic revolution, the first generation of populist parties had significant impacts on government formation. In Denmark, the pattern of open competition for government was immediately reinforced by the meteoric rise of the FrPd. In the words of Bille (1989: 50), 'the shock was great, the confusion was great and the process of government formation became much more complex'. First, the Liberals tried to govern through a single-party minority cabinet based on only 22 out of 179 seats. The result was rather unsuccessful, as the opposition attacked the government from both the left and the right, and the government passed legislation only after 'long, exhausting, dramatic and complicated negotiations' (Bille 1989: 50). The Liberals called for new general elections, which despite providing the centre-right with a clear legislative majority, resulted in a social democratic government. The reason was, in short, the inability of the established centre-right parties to form an agreement with the FrPd. Although the social democratic government was more stable than the Liberal one, the polarising situation eventually resulted in the short-lived formation of a *Große Koalition* with the two main adversaries in Danish politics, the Social Democrats and the Liberals. Government formation temporarily returned to a more bipolar system in the early 1980s, with centrist parties aligning with the right-wing parties to create legislative majorities. However, the electoral success of the FrPd (and the far left) in the late 1980s once again resulted in complicated negotiations and novel government coalitions. First, the Social Liberals joined a right-wing government before the centrist parties, including the Social Liberals, switched sides and entered office with the Social Democrats.

In Norway, patterns of government formation remained stable even after the FrP entered parliament. The neoliberal wave across many post-industrial societies, including Norway, in the late 1970s and early 1980s produced a centre-right legislative majority without the seats of the FrP. Consequently, the FrP's breakthrough initially had no impact on government formation, which continued to be fairly closed and predictable. However, this situation changed in the 1985 election, when the FrP's two seats were needed for the centre-right government to remain in office. This period marked the beginning of a more 'diffuse phase' in which competition for government gradually became less bipolar, more open and more unpredictable (see Heidar 2005: 823–828). In 1986, the FrP decided not to support the budget proposed by the centre-right government (more specifically, the party opposed increasing the tax on gasoline), and the government resigned. A new attempt was made to re-establish a centre-right government approximately one year later, but the FrP once again opposed key policy proposals (this time on farming subsidies). As a result, the Labour Party held office between 1986 and 1989 despite the existence of a non-socialist majority in parliament. The Conservative elites and the centrist parties viewed the FrP as unreliable and politically extreme, and the FrP remained committed to its libertarian economic policies and vote-seeking strategy (see, e.g., Strøm 1994). The FrP's anti-immigration rhetoric and electoral growth in the late 1980s only made possible collaboration with non-socialist parties more unlikely.

In Sweden, where the first generation of populist parties turned out to be short-lived, their impact should not be overestimated. Although a new coalition (four non-socialist parties) and a new party entered office (the Christian Democrats) after the election in which the ND entered the parliament, the government was basically a continuation of previous non-socialist coalitions. Moreover, although the 1991 protest election resulted in a change in office, it probably would have also happened without the rise of the ND. The centre-right coalition was only five seats short of holding a majority of the seats in the parliament. Although the ND did 'steal' a significant number of voters from the centre-left bloc (31 per cent), slightly more voters came from the centre-right bloc (36 per cent) (Gilljam and Holmberg 1993: 73). However, the rise of the ND was not completely inconsequential for government formation. Its populist nature implied that its relationship with the centre-right government was anything but smooth, effectively reducing the bipolarity of the system. In fact, it was so precarious that the government instead opted for cross-bloc collaboration when the country was hit hard by an economic crisis in the early 1990s (Aylott 2011: 311). The subsequent election campaign in 1994 even 'raised the possibility of Sweden's first "cross-bloc" coalition government since 1957' (Aylott 1995: 421).

The second generation of populist parties has partly reversed the trend initiated by the first generation towards multipolarity and open competition for government. At least competition for government has become increasingly bipolar, but it remains rather open. This development is most clear in Denmark. While the FrPd was not considered a reliable support party for the established right-wing parties, the DF was offered substantive concessions on its key issue (immigration policy) and was unexpectedly invited to become a support party of the liberal-conservative government after the 2001 election. As noted by Pedersen (2005: 1102), the inclusion of the DF was unique in at least three ways. First, for the first time since 1929, the government would rely upon support from a party to the right of the Conservatives. Second, for the first time in the post-war period, the centrist parties did not determine government formation. Third, for the first time ever, a right-wing populist party was included in a governing coalition even though it did not receive any portfolios. At the time, the latter had so far only occurred in Austria, where the conservative Austrian People's Party (ÖVP) agreed to form a coalition government with the populist radical right Austrian Freedom Party (FPÖ) in early 2000.

While the inclusion of the DF represented a continuation of the Danish tradition of open competition for government (i.e. changes in office, new constellations and new parties included in the governing coalitions), it resulted in bipolar government formation. The nativist politics of the government alienated the Social Liberals, which instead aligned with the centre-left. Since 2001, two alternatives have been competing for office: a 'blue bloc' (the Liberals, the Conservatives, the DF, the Christian Democrats and more recently the Liberal Alliance) and a 'red bloc' (the Social Democrats, the Social Liberals, the Socialist Left Party, the Unity List and more recently a green party called the Alternative). The former bloc quickly turned out to be a solid and electorally successful formation, not least due to the DF's ability to attract working-class voters who previously voted for the Social Democrats. The liberal-conservative government was thus re-elected twice and remained in office until 2011. The 'red bloc' regained office in 2011, but it again lost to the 'blue bloc' in the most recent election in 2015. Somewhat surprisingly, however, the Liberals first formed a single-party cabinet, as neither the Conservatives nor the DF wanted to enter office.

The new political situation in Denmark seems like a small step towards less bipolarity. Although it seemed as if bloc politics re-emerged when the Conservatives and the neoliberal party Liberal Alliance joined the Liberal government in 2016, voting patterns from the parliament show that Social Democrats actually support the right-wing government more often than other

left-wing parties (*Information* 2017). Moreover, and perhaps more importantly, the DF seems 'more ready to exploit its position as a large party more
centrally placed on the redistributive left-right scale, from where it shares
interests with the [red bloc]' rather than the 'blue bloc' (especially the Liberal Alliance) (Kosiara-Pedersen 2015: 876). In 2017, the party leaders of the
DF and the Social Democrats even suggested that they might collaborate in
government in the future (*Politiken* 2017).

In Norway, the FrP initially contributed to the emerging patterns of more
open competition for government and decreasing bipolarity. In 1997, the FrP
replaced the Conservatives as the largest right-wing party, and a new non-
socialist coalition without the Conservatives – the centrist alternative – gained
office for the first time. However, after the turn of the millennium, government formation again became increasingly bipolar, although it remained
open. To some extent, Norwegian politics, as in Denmark, has been divided
into two 'blocs' since 2001: a centre-right bloc (the Conservatives, the Liberals, the Christians and the FrP) and a red-green alternative (the Labour party,
the Socialist Left and the agrarian Centre Party). A centre-right government
supported by the FrP was in office between 2001 and 2005, whereas the Liberals and the Christians support the Conservative/FrP government, which has
been in office since 2013. The novel red-green alternative formed a majority
cabinet between 2005 and 2013.[9]

In contrast to Denmark, however, the relationship among the parties within
the centre-right bloc has been quite complicated. The other non-socialist parties have frequently labelled FrP's immigration policies and rhetoric 'inde-
cent' (Hagelund 2003), and there was substantial ideological distance with
regard to socio-economic policies. The FrP was not accepted as a coalition
partner to the same extent as the DF. Although the centre-right government
made several policy concessions to the FrP between 2001 and 2005 (Narud
and Strøm 2011: 74), the FrP announced during the 2005 election campaign
that the party would no longer support a government in which it was not
included. Despite this ultimatum, however, the party was not accepted as
a coalition partner. In fact, the party was not accepted until after the red-
green alternative had been re-elected in 2009, the non-socialist parties had
appointed new party leaders and the grassroots seemed less hostile towards
the FrP (Jupskås 2013).[10] In 2013, the red-green alternative was defeated,
and the FrP entered government for the first time as part of a novel constellation – a 'blue-blue' coalition with the Conservative party. The centrist parties
decided for ideological reasons to stay out of office and act as parliamentary
support parties. For the time being, voters are faced with two alternatives, but
'the commitment of the Liberals and the Christian People's Party to provide
external, long-term support for the new coalition appears somewhat limited'
(Allern and Karlsen 2014: 660). In fact, the two centrist parties have recently

suggested that they in different ways will try to bring down the current government. Especially the Christian People's Party will no longer warrant that the party will support a right-wing government if it includes the FrP (*Aftenposten* 2016).

The Swedish situation has been different from the Danish and Norwegian experience. Rather than making competition for government increasingly bipolar, the rise of the SD had the opposite effect, at least initially. Moreover, the combination of the *cordon sanitaire* against the party and the SD's blackmail potential (since 2014) has resulted in both weak(er) governments and novel parliamentary arrangements. Prior to the rise of the SD, Swedish politics had become increasingly bipolarised, with two alternatives competing for a parliamentary majority: the red-green bloc (the Social Democrats, the Greens and the Left Party) and the centre-right 'Alliance' (the Moderates, the Christians, the Liberals and the Center Party) (Aylott and Bolin 2007). In 2010, voters were faced with these two governing alternatives, but none of them gained a majority of seats due to the SD's parliamentary breakthrough. As the largest bloc, the centre-right coalition remained in office, but the cabinet was significantly weakened. In order to ostracise the SD, the 'Alliance' government reached deals with the Greens on immigration and with the Greens and the Social Democrats on military presence in foreign conflict zones. Without a majority in parliament, however, little significant legislation was possible, and the red-green bloc and SD occasionally inflicted symbolic as well as policy defeats on the government throughout the period.

After the 2014 election, an even weaker centre-left government replaced this centre-right government. Realising that the SD would probably gain blackmail potential after the election, the centre-right coalition stated in the campaign that it would not oppose the formation of a centre-left government if it constituted the largest bloc after the election. A red-green coalition of the Social Democrats and the Greens entered office, while the Left party was kept out of the government in order to facilitate cross-bloc collaboration. The weakness of this government was revealed in the first budget vote, as the SD decided to break the (non-formalised) parliamentary code of conduct by supporting the budget proposed by the centre-right coalition rather than its own budget. Demonstrating its newly acquired blackmailing potential, the SD argued that it would vote against any government that did not significantly limit the number of immigrants. The result was a crisis of government, and for the first time since the 1950s, the prime minister announced that early elections would be held. However, as none of the parties (for different reasons) were particularly interested in yet another election campaign, the government reached an agreement with the centre-right 'Alliance', and the early election was called off. In order to maintain the *cordon sanitaire* against the SD, this agreement implied, simply put, that the largest bloc from now on would be allowed to pass its budget through the parliament even without a legislative majority in favour of it, and there would be cross-bloc collaboration on issues such as defence, pensions and energy (*Dagens Nyheter* December 2014). Because it effectively depoliticised major issues in Swedish politics and was portrayed as fundamentally undemocratic, the agreement became increasingly unpopular within some of the right-wing parties. In late 2015, it was abandoned after having been – somewhat surprisingly – voted down at the party convention of the Christian Democrats.

Currently, there seem to be three different ways forward (see Bergman et al. 2015). First, 'bloc politics' could continue, and there will be more weak governments and possible crises of government. Second, the *cordon sanitaire* against the SD could end, and the party will be included as part of the centre-right bloc (as in Norway and Denmark). Recent surveys suggest that support for the isolation strategy is fading among voters and politicians at the local level (*SVT* December 2014; *Dagens Nyheter* May 2015). In any case, this scenario implies the breakup of the 'Alliance', given that the Center Party and the Liberals have ruled out any collaboration with the SD. Third, existing 'bloc politics' could become less solid. While ideological disagreement *between* the 'blocs' is far from insurmountable, there is significant disagreement *within* the blocs. Moreover, the parties within the 'Alliance' coalition have recently announced that they will make budget proposals individually. The Liberals have also drifted towards a more centrist position in economic policies, which would make cross-bloc collaboration easier (*Dagens Nyheter* December 2015).

IMPACT ON MAINSTREAM PARTIES

Before right-wing populist parties emerged in Denmark and Norway, none of the mainstream parties used a populist discourse or campaigned on neoliberal (as the first generation of right-wing populist did) or nativist policies (as the second generation of right-wing populist does) (e.g. Demker and Svåsand 2005). Also in Sweden, the established parties were neither nativist nor particularly populist, but the established party of the right, the Moderates, had already adopted a neoliberal policy agenda (Rydgren 2006: 33). With the rise of right-wing populist parties, mainstream parties had to choose between dismissive, accommodative and adversarial tactics (Meguid 2005; see also Downs 2001). The latter two can both be seen as effects of right-wing populist mobilisation, but this section will put more emphasis on the cases in which mainstream parties have moved towards (i.e. accommodative tactics) rather than away from (i.e. adversarial tactics) the policy agenda of right-wing populist parties.

As expected, given its ideological focus, the first generation of right-wing populist parties was primarily able to affect the socio-economic platform of other parties, especially if not exclusively that of its main competitor, the Conservatives (see also Bjørklund and Goul Andersen 2002: 128). In Norway, the Conservative Party rapidly moved into the ideological territory of the populist contender on issues such as income taxes, total taxes, scope of government and, to a lesser extent, individual freedom (Harmel and Svåsand 1997: 324). Also in Denmark, the Conservatives moved to the right socio-economically when challenged by a neoliberal populist party. However, the Danish Conservatives only adopted more right-wing policies on issues such as the scope of government and, to a lesser extent, the total levels of taxation (Harmel and Svåsand 1997: 342). Competition from parties on their flanks seems to explain the unexpected outcome that the impact was strongest where the electoral support of a neoliberal populist party was weakest (Harmel and Svåsand 1997). While the mainstream right in Denmark had to fight a two front battle with FrPd on one side and new successful centrist parties on the other side, the centrist parties were no threat to the mainstream right in Norway. Consequently, whereas embracing (too much of) the right-wing populist agenda would be very risky for the Danish Conservatives, the Conservatives in Norway could afford to adopt an accommodative prevention strategy in order to eliminate a possible future threat.

In terms of anti-immigration policies, both the Progress parties were initially – at least until the 1990s – less successful in influencing the position of other parties, which largely responded with dismissive tactics. When the FrP first politicised the topic in late 1980s, 'all other parties shunned the issue, and spoke about it as an issue with no place in an election campaign' (Hagelund 2003: 50). Similarly, the FrPd had very little impact on the immigration policies of other parties (Green-Pedersen and Krogstrup 2008: 622–623), although 'critical voices from the right-wing parties had become stronger' throughout the 1980s (Green-Pedersen and Odmalm 2008: 371) and the mainstream right seemed to move in the direction of the FrPd in the early 1990s (Bjørklund and Goul Andersen 2002: 128). In both cases, the lack of impact was due to the logic of government formation: cutting across existing cleavages, the immigration issue would most likely split already fragile centre-right coalitions.

In Sweden, the ND had very limited influence on other parties' policy positions. Emerging much later than its Scandinavian 'sister parties', both mainstream parties – particularly the Moderates – in Sweden had shifted towards a more right-wing socio-economic platform (Wörlund 1992: 139; for voter perceptions, see Rydgren 2006: 43) and the Social Democrats had adopted more restrictive immigration policies before ND experienced an electoral breakthrough (Hinnfors et al. 2012). Although the ND was unsuccessful in pushing other parties to adopt more restrictive immigration policies (Dahl-ström and Esaiasson 2011: 354; Rydgren 2002: 39), it should be noted that this issue became somewhat more salient among voters and that the Conservative Party did propose policies similar to that of the ND a few years later (Green-Pedersen and Odmalm 2008: 372). However, mainstream parties largely continued to ignore the issue, and the only party engaging with the issue, the Liberals, actually adopted a more clear-cut liberal position (Widfeldt 2015b: 402).

Not surprisingly, the second generation of right-wing populists has been more successful when it comes to influencing the socio-cultural platform of mainstream parties, though there is significant cross-country variation. Beyond doubt, DF has had a stronger impact than FrP and SD. In Denmark, both the two established parties of the right (the Conservatives and not least the Liberals) and the Social Democrats gradually adopted significant parts of DF's nativist agenda (Bale et al. 2010: 414–415) and welfare chauvinism (Schumacher and Kersbergen 2016: 306). The only parties moving in the opposite direction were the Social Liberals and the far left party, the Unity List. To be sure, the mainstream right drifted further to the right and tried to politicise the immigration issue some years before the DF was founded in the mid-1990s, but DF's quick electoral growth and agenda-setting power certainly accelerated the process of policy co-optation (see also Green-Pedersen and Krogstrup 2008). As noted by Bjørklund and Goul Andersen (2002: 129), the Liberals 'went unusually far for an established party' and ended up resembling the Norwegian FrP. The mainstream left – the Social Democrats – was more reluctantly moving to the right. Although the Social Democratic MPs preferred a quite liberal approach for ideological as well as strategic reasons (i.e. the Social Democrats had to governed with the Social Liberals), the politicisation of the issue by right-wing parties in general and the DF in particular made it very difficult to maintain its liberal position (Green-Pedersen and Krogstrup 2008: 623). Moreover, in addition to external constraints, the party elite was under pressure from several Social Democratic mayors in immigration-dense areas who wanted a more restrictive national policy (Green-Pedersen and Krogstrup 2008: 623). Consequently, during the years of the liberal-conservative government in Denmark (2001–2011), the right-wing parties and the Social Democrats were largely accommodative, whereas other parties – particularly the Social Liberals – have been adversarial. Notwithstanding a short intermezzo in which the financial crisis made economic issues more salient than the immigration issue in Danish politics (Møller Hansen and Stubager 2017: 24), recent developments have largely reinforced existing patterns of mainstream parties' strategies. In 2015, the Liberals once again successfully politicised the immigration issue during the election campaign. The political agenda shifted immediately, the support for the right-wing bloc increased and the right-wing bloc gained office (Møller Hansen and Stubager 2017: 28). In the course of the refugee crisis some months after the election, the right-wing government pushed for even stricter policies. After a highly polarised and emotional debate in parliament, the right-wing government, DF and the Social Democrats voted in favour of quite radical measurements (e.g. allowing the police to seize refugees' assets) (*Politiken* January 2016).

In Norway, mainstream parties have been much less eager to embrace the nativist policies of the FrP – especially its anti-refugee policies (see also Gudbrandsen 2010: 256). For a long time, mainstream parties on both the left and the right pursued dismissive strategies (Bale et al. 2010: 417–418). While the policies towards immigration did become more restrictive since the mid-1970s, this reflected broader societal and political changes rather than pressure from the FrP. In fact, the policy change largely preceded the rise of the FrP. However, since 2005, the Conservatives and, to a lesser extent, Labour Party have gradually co-opted parts of FrP's anti-immigration policies (Simonnes 2013). These two parties have become stricter on asylum policies, cultural integration and, in the case of the Conservatives, family reunification. Despite drifting towards a more restrictive position on certain key issues, however, they have neither politicised the immigration issue during election campaigns nor mimicked FrP's nativist discourse. As in Denmark, parties seemed less concerned with immigration issues in the wake of the financial crisis. Moreover, a major attack on the Labour youth wing in 2011, in which the terrorist held xenophobic views, made it almost impossible to 'play the immigration card'. To be sure, mainstream parties of left and right have continuously adopted stricter policies, but they did so through broad cross-partisan agreements rather than confrontational politics. This was also the preferred strategy during the refugee crisis. Although parties with a more liberal position have occasionally opposed the introduction of more restrictive measurements, they have not made a more liberal immigration policy a key theme of their electoral campaigns. In other words, mainstream response in Norway is one of dismissal through 'pre-emptive consensus' (Bale et al. 2010) and half-hearted criticism (by immigration-friendly parties). The strategy has been rather successful, as the immigration issue has been much less salient than in Denmark, even if FrP constantly tries to put it back on the political agenda.

Swedish mainstream parties pursued dismissive strategies throughout the decade before the SD became a parliamentary party. The only exception to this pattern is the 2002 election in which 'the Liberals changed to an accommodative strategy and the Left and the Green parties responded in an adversarial way' (Dahlström and Esaiasson 2011: 360). However, this move was unrelated to pressure from a right-wing populist party – the SD was a small and insignificant party at the time. The established parties maintained dismissive strategies after SD entered the parliament. However, the media forced them to address the issue of immigration. In a televised debate with all party leaders in 2012, the moderators opened by asking, 'How much immigration can Sweden take?' (*Dagens Nyheter* October 2012). Although this certainly increased the saliency of the issue, mainstream parties refrained from accommodative tactics. In fact, on the contrary, instead of moving closer to the policies of the SD, mainstream parties eventually adopted an even more liberal discourse. During the 2014 election campaign, prime minister from the Conservatives, Fredrik Reinfeldt, asked the voters to 'open their hearts for those vulnerable people who we see around the world' (Aylott and Bolin 2015: 733). Although Reinfeldt stepped down after losing the elections, his successor initially maintained a liberal position.

In contrast to Denmark and Norway, where it simply reinforced pre-existing mainstream party strategies on immigration, the refugee crisis was a true game changer in Sweden. A relatively high number of asylum seekers – Sweden was the third-ranked country in the number of asylum applications received in 2015 – made the immigration issue more salient than ever before. In fact, although the immigration issue had emerged as the fourth most important issue already in the 2014 election (Oscarsson and Holmberg 2016: 177), in early 2016 it was by far the most important issue for Swedish voters (*Dagens Nyheter* January 2016). Not surprisingly, the support for SD increased even further, and surveys confirmed previous findings (Oscarsson and Holmberg 2016: 233): voters switching from the Moderates to the SD were above all concerned with immigration (*Dagens Nyheter* July 2016). Due to the combination of internal pressure from below and vote-seeking strategies from above, the party elite quickly adopted a more restrictive position (*Dagens Nyheter* July 2016). However, while the Conservatives have been clearest in their shift towards an accommodation strategy, the Christian Democrats and the Social Democrats have also drifted towards a more restrictive position more recently (*Dagens Nyheter* December 2015). Since the Greens are in government and therefore have reluctantly defended official policies, the Left and the Centre Party have been the most vocal defenders of (returning to) a more liberal policy (*Dagens Nyheter* January 2016).

As before, the structure of party competition seems particularly helpful in explaining cross-country variation (see also Bale et al. 2010; Green-Pedersen and Krogstrup 2008). In all countries, the mainstream right initially tried to defuse the issue knowing that it would make centre-right coalitions with (social) liberal parties much harder, if not completely impossible. However, after losing governmental power and realising that re-entering office would be very difficult without the active or passive support of the national populists, the Conservative parties gradually adopted more restrictive positions; this happened in Denmark in the 1990s, in Norway in the mid-2000s, and in Sweden in the mid-2010s. The Social Democrats were initially also keen on keeping the issue off the agenda – both because they were collaborating with liberal, green or new left parties and because of divisions in the electoral and/or internal arena (see also Odmalm 2011). However, after the mainstream right decided to politicise the key issue of the national-populist parties, defusing it was no longer a viable option. Although the social democratic parties have responded differently, they have gradually replaced dismissive with somewhat more accommodative tactics. Arguably, this development has been more pronounced in Denmark and less pronounced in Sweden.

One question that has not been addressed is whether populism spread to other parties. Such effects are largely non-existent. Judged on the basis of recent party manifestos, mainstream parties in the Scandinavian region have remained non-populist (Jupskås 2012). There is very little people-centrism and they hardly refer to key populist concepts such as common people or ordinary people. The only exception is the Centre Party in Norway, which has long been associated with so-called periphery populism (pitting people in the rural districts against the urban elites). It might be that the campaign discourse of certain parties suggest stronger contagion effects, but beyond a few anecdotal observations – for example, the (re-)introduction of the concept 'the real people' by the Christian Democrats in Sweden right before the breakthrough of the SD (Hellström 2013) – there is no systematic research on this topic.

CONCLUSION

Arditi (2007: 60) has argued that populism may challenge the existing regime in three different ways: as a new mode of representation, as politics on the more turbulent edges of democracy and as a threatening underside. In contrast to some other countries in Europe (e.g. Hungary) where populist parties seem to undermine basic aspects of liberal democracy (e.g. Pappas 2014), neither the first nor the second generation of populist parties in Scandinavia has challenged the institutional arrangements of contemporary Scandinavian democracy. However, they have had a significant impact on mainstream parties as well as the party system dynamics – not only in terms of key parameters such as fragmentation, polarisation and volatility but also with regard to the cleavages structuring voting behaviour and the logic of government formation.

In short, the analysis suggests that the first generation of populist parties (FrPd, ND and FrP in its first years) made the party systems more fragmented, socio-economically polarised and electorally volatile, politicised anti-establishment attitudes and contributed to more open competition for government. Government formation became less bipolar but more unpredictable. Uncertainty and instability seem to be two keywords characterising Scandinavian politics after the breakthrough of the populist parties. Because they were unable to institutionalise, however, these parties eventually disappeared (ND and FrPd) or experienced a transformative party split (FrP). With the emergence of a second generation of populist parties (DF, SD and FrP after the split), the party systems have remained fragmented, polarised and volatile, but polarisation now takes place along the socio-cultural dimension, and populist parties are no longer the primary producers of electoral volatility. Moreover, an ideologically embedded opposition to immigration has replaced a diffuse anti-establishment cleavage. In terms of the impact on individual parties, right-wing populist parties have mainly affected the mainstream right and, to a lesser extent, mainstream left. Although there are notable differences between the three countries, the general pattern seems to be as follows. First, the neoliberal populist parties pushed mainstream right further to the right on socio-economic issues, most notably in Norway and least notably in Sweden. Second, the national-populist parties made mainstream right *and* mainstream left more inclined to adopt restrictive immigration policies. This is most striking in the Danish case. Across cases and across the two generations of right-wing populist parties, the structure of party competition – and the office-seeking strategies that stem from this – seems crucial in order to explain when and why certain parties shift from dismissive to accommodative tactics.

Arguably, no other new party family in Scandinavia has been able to change the cleavage structure to the same extent as the second generation of populist parties. However, rather than cutting across the existing cleavage(s), the emerging socio-cultural cleavage between libertarians and authoritarians largely coincide with the socio-economic cleavage. Consequently, party competition is no longer (primarily) between the traditional left and right, but between left-wing libertarians and right-wing authoritarians. This is particularly the situation in Denmark (Altinget 2016), though Norway (Aardal 2015: 88) and Sweden (Oscarsson and Holmberg 2016: 225) have been catching up more recently. Moreover, by mobilising working-class voters who are sceptical of immigration, these parties have also reinforced the (already ongoing) decline of traditional class voting (i.e. workers voting for the left and not for the right). In other words, whereas the first generation of populist parties contributed to a process of *de-alignment* by weakening the ties between voters and the established parties, the second generation of populist parties has contributed to a process of *re-alignment* by becoming working-class parties with firm foundations in the authoritarian pole of the emerging socio-cultural cleavage.

Not surprisingly, this development has also produced rather predictable patterns of government formation. By aligning with established right-wing parties, the second generation of populist parties has made Scandinavian politics (once again) more bipolar and consequently weakened the position of the Social Democrats in the electoral, legislative and governing arenas. Because of the rise of right-wing populist parties, the Scandinavian party systems no longer have predominant parties, even if the Social Democrats remain the largest party on the left. This development has been more pronounced in Denmark and Norway than in Sweden, where the second generation of populist parties emerged more recently. In fact, in Sweden, where government formation had become quite bipolar prior to the rise of the SD, this party has actually had the opposite effect. However, there are several indications that some of the right-wing parties might break with the existing *cordon sanitaire* against the SD, although the party has a long way to go before being accepted as a coalition partner.

There are at least three lessons learned from this analysis. First, new parties can have an impact on the party system even in well-established democracies with strong parties, as in the Scandinavian region. As argued by Pedersen (1982), 'minor, especially new minor, parties [might] play an important role in the transformation of party systems' – in this case by contributing to processes of de-alignment and re-alignment and by affecting the degree of bipolarity. Moreover, new minor parties may very well have an impact on policies and strategies of mainstream parties, which will, in turn, affect the dynamics of the party system as a whole. Second, it seems as if – borrowing a distinction from Lucardie (2000) – 'prophets' who articulate a new ideology (as the second generation of populist parties have) are more likely to have an impact on the party system than 'purifiers' (as the first generation of populist parties), who only present an undiluted version of an ideology that is already promoted by other parties. Although purifiers may affect the policies of individual parties, as the two progress parties did (Harmel and Svåsand 1997), they seem less likely to alter the existing cleavage structure or patterns of government formation. Third, as opposed to the Dutch experience with Lijst Pim Fortuyn in 2002 (Pellikaan et al. 2007), this transformation has been *gradual* rather than *abrupt*. As demonstrated in this chapter, even though the first generation of populist parties played the immigration card, it was not until the second generation that this issue re-structured competition for votes and eventually affected competition for government.

NOTES

1 Admittedly, the differences between a first and a second generation of populist parties are not as distinct in practice. This is especially the case in Norway where right-wing populism is characterised by organisational continuity. In Denmark, where there are two different parties, the two generations of right-wing populist parties share several ideological features.

2 One may argue that the Independence Party (*Partiet de uafhængige*) in Denmark in the 1950s was the first populist party in post-war Scandinavia, as it combined anti-establishment orientation, anti-statism and economic liberalism (see Eriksen 1978: 71ff). However, this party will not be included in this analysis.

3 Scholars have also argued that the Center Party in Sweden channelled much of the existing populist discontent in the electorate (Fryklund and Peterson 1981).

4 The FrP's seemingly paradoxical position of being in favour of more welfare and drastic tax cuts at the same time was mainly resolved by suggesting that Norway should spend more of its income from the oil industry.

5 Sartorian counting rules rest on the assumption that parties count only to the extent that they are capable of affecting the mechanics of the party system as a whole.

6 While the party system had 'around five' relevant parties before the 'earthquake election' in 1973, there were approximately eight to nine relevant parties thereafter. The number depends on whether all parties to the left of the social democratic party are counted as relevant parties (see Bille 1989: 47).

7 In Sweden, there was also a centre-periphery cleavage before the 1970s (Bergström 1991 in Rydgren 2006: 37).

8 Danish researchers refer to the socio-cultural dimension as either 'new politics' (e.g. Borre 1995) or 'value politics' (e.g. Møller Hansen and Goul Andersen 2013). Conversely, the socio-economic dimension is referred to as either 'old politics' or 'distribution politics'. In Norway, the socio-cultural dimension is usually split into three or four specific dimensions: 'immigration/solidarity', 'green/growth', 'religious/secular' and sometimes 'global/national' (e.g. Aardal 2011a).

9 This government was a completely new experience for all of the parties in the coalition. The Labour Party governed together with other parties for the first time; the Socialist Left was in office for the first time; and the agrarian Center governed with the left-wing parties for the first time.

10 The Conservatives certainly accepted the FrP as a governing party in 2009, but they ended up campaigning for a centre-right alternative without the FrP.

BIBLIOGRAPHY

Aardal, B. (1999) 'Et utrolig velgerfolk', in B. Aardal, H. Valen, H. M. Narud and F. Berglund (eds.) *Velgere i 90-Årene*, Oslo: NKS-forlaget pp. 32–49.
——— (2007) 'Velgere på evig vandring? Hva skjedde ved stortingsvalget i 2005?', in B. Aardal (ed.) *Norske Velgere: En studie av stortingsvalget 2005*, Oslo: N. W. Damm & Søn AS pp. 13–40.

———— (2011a) 'Folkeopinionen – demokratiets grunnvoll', in B. Aardal (ed.) *Det Politiske Landskapet: En Studie av stortingsvalget 2009*, Oslo: Cappelen Damm Akademisk pp. 65–96.

———— (2011b) 'Mange blir valgt, men få blir gjenvalgt', in B. Aardal (ed.) *Det Politiske Landskapet: En Studie av stortingsvalget 2009*, Oslo: Cappelen Damm Akademisk pp. 13–39.

———— (2015) 'Politiske verdier og stemmegivning', in B. Aardal and J. Bergh (eds.) *Valg Og Velgere: En Studie av stortingsvalget 2013*, Oslo: Cappelen Damm Akademisk pp. 76–102.

Aardal, B. and Bergh, J. (2015) 'Systemskifte – fra rødgrønt til blåblått', in B. Aardal and J. Bergh (eds.) *Valg Og Velgere: En Studie av stortingsvalget 2013*, Oslo: Cappelen Damm Akademisk pp. 11–33.

Aardal, B. and Valen, H. (1989) *Velgere, Partier og Politisk Avstand*, Oslo: Statistisk sentralbyrå.

———— (1995) *Konflikt og opinion*, Oslo: NKS-forlag.

Aftenposten. (2016) 'Hareide ber statsministeren velge mellom KrF – eller FrP', 5 November 2016. URL: https://www.aftenposten.no/norge/politikk/Hareide-ber-statsministeren-velge-mellom-KrF-eller-Frp-608376b.html.

Allern, E. H. and Karlsen, R. (2014). 'A turn to the right: The Norwegian parliamentary election of 2013', *West European Politics*, 37(3): 653–663.

Altinget.dk (2016) 'Her er det nye politiske kompas', September 26, 2016. URL: http://www.altinget.dk/artikel/det-nye-politiske-kompas.

Andersen, J. and Borre, O. (2007) 'Partiledere gør en forskel', in J. G. Andersen, J. Andersen, O. Borre, K. M. Hansen and H. J. Nielsen (eds.) *Det Nye Politiske Landskab: Folketingsvalget 2005 i Perspektiv*, Århus: Academica pp. 289–306.

Andersen, J. and Goul Andersen, J. (2003) 'Klassernes forsvinden', in J. G. Andersen and O. Borre (eds.) *Politisk Forandring: Værdipolitik Og Nye Skillelinjer Ved folketingsvalget 2001*, Århus: Systime Academic pp. 207–221.

Arditi, B. (2007) *Politics on the edges of liberalism: Difference, populism, revolution, agitation*, Edinburgh: Edinburgh University Press.

Arter, D. (1999a) 'Party system change in Scandinavia since 1970: "Restricted change" or "general change"?', *West European Politics*, 22(3): 139–158.

———— (1999b) *Scandinavian politics today*, Manchester: Manchester University Press.

Aylott, N. (1995) 'Back to the future: The 1994 Swedish election', *Party Politics*, 1(3): 419–429.

———— (2011) 'Parties and party systems in the north', in T. Bergman and K. Strøm (eds.) *The Madisonian turn*, Ann Arbor: University of Michigan Press pp. 297–328.

Aylott, N. and Bolin, N. (2007) 'Towards a two-party system? The Swedish parliamentary election of September 2006', *West European Politics*, 30(3): 621–633.

———— (2015) 'Polarising pluralism: The Swedish parliamentary election of September 2014', *West European Politics*, 38(3): 730–740.

Bale, T., Green-Pedersen, C., Krouwel A., Luther, K. R., Sitter, N. (2010) 'If you can't beat them, join them? Explaining Social Democratic responses to the challenge from the populist radical right in Western Europe', _Political Studies_, 58: 410–426.

Bengtsson, Å., Hansen, K., Harðarson, Ó. Þ., Narud, H. M. and Oscarsson, H. (2013) _The Nordic voter: Myths of exceptionalism_, Colchester: ECPR Press.

Berglund, F., Reymert, I. S. and Aardal, B. (2011) _Valgundersøkelse 2009: Dokumentasjonsrapport_, Oslo/Kongsvinger: Statistisk sentralbyrå.

Berglund, S. and Lindström, U. (1978) _The Scandinavian party system (s): A comparative study_, Lund: Studentlitteratur.

Bergman, T., Bolin, N. and C. Sandström (2015) 'Det finns möligheter till blocköverskridande samarbeten'. Blog entry at Om makt och politik. https://maktochpolitik.wordpress.com/2015/04/17/det-finns-mojligheter-till-blockoverskridande-samarbeten/ (last accessed 20 May 2016).

Bille, L. (1989) 'Denmark: The oscillating party system', _West European Politics_, 12(4): 42–58.

Bilstad, K. A. (1994) 'Konfliktstruktur og partiavstand', in K. Heidar and L. Svåsand (eds.) _Partiene i Brytningstid_, Bergen: Alma Mater pp. 13–45.

Bjørklund, T. (1981) _Anders Lange og Fremskrittspartiet: Norges svar på Glistrupianismen_, Oslo: Institutt for samfunnsforskning.

––––––– (1988) 'The 1987 Norwegian local elections: A protest election with a swing to the right', _Scandinavian Political Studies_, 11(3): 211–234.

––––––– (2009) 'To mål på arbeiderklasse: Yrke og klassetilhørighet – Norske velgere og partier fra 1965 til 2005', _Norsk Statsvitenskapelig Tidsskrift_, 24(1): 5–27.

Bjørklund, T. and Goul Andersen, J. (2002) 'Anti-immigration parties in Denmark and Norway: the progress parties and the Danish People's Party', in M. Schain, A. Zolberg and P. Hossay (eds.) _Shadows over Europe: The development and impact of the extreme right in Western Europe_, New York: Palgrave Macmillan pp. 107–136.

Blondel, J. (1968) 'Party systems and patterns of government in Western democracies', _Canadian Journal of Political Science_, 1(2): 180–203.

Borre, O. (1974) 'Denmark's protest election of December 1973', _Scandinavian Political Studies_, 9(74): 193–204.

––––––– (1995) 'Old and new politics in Denmark', _Scandinavian Political Studies_, 18(3): 187–205.

Canovan, M. (2002) 'Taking politics to the people: Populism as the ideology of democracy', in Y. Meny and Y. Surel (eds.) _Democracies and the populist challenge_, Basingstoke: Palgrave MacMillan pp. 25–44.

Christiansen, F. J. (2012) 'Raising the stakes: Passing state budgets in Scandinavia', _World Political Science Review_, 8(1): 184–200.

Dahlström, C. and Esaiasson P. (2012) 'The immigration issue and anti-immigrant party success in Sweden 1970–2006: A deviant case analysis', _Party Politics_, 19(2): 343–364.

Dagens Nyheter (2012) 'Ännu splittrad opposition', 8 October 2012. URL: http://www.dn.se/ledare/huvudledare/annu-splittrad-opposition/.

––––––– (2014) 'Så fungerar decemberöverenskommelsen', 27 December 2014. URL: http://www.dn.se/nyheter/politik/sa-fungerar-decemberoverenskommelsen/.

———— (2015) 'Väljarstödet för att isolera SD luckras upp', 5 May 2015. URL: http://www.dn.se/nyheter/politik/valjarstodet-for-att-isolera-sd-luckras-upp/.

———— (2015) 'Den nya politiska kartan – så har partierna rört sig', 2 December 2015. URL: http://www.dn.se/nyheter/den-nya-politiska-kartan-sa-har-partierna-rort-sig/.

———— (2016) 'Instabila läget bäddar för mer samarbete', 14 January 2016. URL: http://www.dn.se/nyheter/sverige/ewa-stenberg-instabila-laget-baddar-for-mer-samarbete/.

———— (2016) 'Ewa Stenberg: Instabila läget bäddar för mer samarbete', 14 January 2016. URL: http://www.dn.se/nyheter/sverige/ewa-stenberg-instabila-laget-baddar-for-mer-samarbete/.

———— (2016) 'De nya hårda moderaterna', 9 July 2016. URL: http://www.dn.se/nyheter/politik/de-nya-harda-moderaterna/.

———— (2017) 'Invandring den viktigsta frågan för väljarna', 13 January 2016. URL: http://www.dn.se/nyheter/politik/invandring-den-viktigaste-fragan-for-valjarna/.

Demker, M. and Svåsand, L. (2005) *Partiernas Århundrade: Fempartimodellens Uppgång Och Fall i Norge och Sverige*, Stockholm: Santérus.

Downs, William M. (2001) 'Pariahs in their midst: Belgian and Norwegian parties react to extremist threats', *West European Politics*, 24(3): 23–42.

Eriksen, H. (1978) *Partiet De Uafhængige 1953–1960*, Odense: Odense universitetsforlag.

Fryklund, B. and Peterson, T. (1981) *Populism och Missnöjespartier i Norden: Studier i Småborgerlig Klassaktivitet*, Lund: Arkiv Förlag.

Gilljam, M. and Holmberg, S. (1993) *Väljarna Inför 90-Talet*, Stockholm: Norstedts.

———— (1995) *Väljarnas Val*, Stockholm: Fritzes Förlag.

Goul Andersen, J. G. (2003) 'The general election in Denmark, November 2001', *Electoral Studies*, 22(1): 186–194.

———— (2017) 'Portræt af vælgernes socio-demografi', in K. Møller Hansen and R. Stubager (eds.) *Oprør fra udkanten*, København: Jurist- og Økonomforbundets Forlag pp. 41–68.

Goul Andersen, J. G. and Bjorklund, T. (1990) 'Structural changes and new cleavages: The progress parties in Denmark and Norway', *Acta Sociologica*, 33(3): 195–217.

———— (2000) 'Radical right-wing populism in Scandinavia: From tax revolt to neo-liberalism and xenophobia', in P. Hainsworth (ed.) *The politics of the extreme right: From the margins to the mainstream*, London: Pinter Publishing House pp. 193–223.

Green-Pedersen, C. and Krogstrup, J. (2008) 'Immigration as a political issue in Denmark and Sweden', *European Journal of Political Research*, 47: 610–643.

Green-Pedersen, C. and Odmalm, P. (2008) 'Going different ways? Right-wing parties and the immigrant issue in Denmark and Sweden', *Journal of European Public Policy*, 15(3): 367–381.

Gudbrandsen, F. (2010) 'Partisan influence on immigration: The case of Norway', *Scandinavian Political Studies*, 33(3): 248–270.

Hagelund, A. (2003) 'A matter of decency? The Progress Party in Norwegian immigration politics', *Journal of Ethnic and Migration Studies*, 29(1): 47–65.

Hansen, M. E. (2008) 'Back to the archives? A critique of the Danish part of the manifesto dataset', *Scandinavian Political Studies*, 31(2): 201–216.

Harmel, R. and Svåsand, L. (1993) 'Party leadership and party institutionalisation: Three phases of development', *West European Politics*, 16(2): 67–88.

——— (1997) 'The influence of new parties on old parties' platforms', *Party Politics*, 3(3): 315–340.

Heidar, K. (1989) 'Norway: Levels of party competition and system change', *West European Politics*, 12(4): 143–156.

——— (2005) 'Norwegian parties and the party system: Steadfast and changing', *West European Politics*, 28(4): 807–833.

Hellström, A. (2013) 'Help! The populists are coming, appeals to the people in contemporary Swedish politics', MIM working paper series 13:4, Malmö: Institute for Studies of Migration, Diversity and Welfare (MIM), Malmö University.

Hinnfors, J., Spehar, A. and Bucken-Knapp, G. (2012) 'The missing factor: Why democracy can lead to restrictive immigration policy', *Journal of European Public Policy*, 19(4): 585–603.

Information (2017) 'Socialdemokratiet stemmer oftere med de borgerlige end med oppositionen', 6 February 2017. URL: https://www.information.dk/indland/2017/02/socialdemokratiet-stemmer-oftere-borgerlige-oppositionen.

Jungar, A. C. and Jupskås, A. R. (2014) 'Populist radical right parties in the Nordic region: A new and distinct party family?', *Scandinavian Political Studies*, 37(3): 215–238.

Jupskås, A. (2012) 'In the name of the people! Contemporary populism(s) in Scandinavia', in S. Ghergina, S. Miscoiu and S. Soare (eds.) *Contemporary populism: A controversial concept and its diverse forms*, Newcastle: Cambridge Scholars pp. 258–293.

——— (2013) 'Mangfoldig mobilisering og velsmurt valgkampmaskineri: Fremskrittspartiet runder 40 år', *Nytt Norsk Tidsskrift*, 1(30): 5–17.

——— (2016a) 'Between a business firm and a Mass Party: The organization of the Norwegian Progress Party', in R. Heinisch and O. Mazzoleni (eds.) *Understanding populist party organization: A comparative analysis*, Houndmills: Palgrave Macmillan.

——— (2016b) 'The taming of the shrew: How the progress party (almost) became part of the mainstream', in T. Akkerman, S. L. d. Lange and M. Rooduijn (eds.) *Radical right-wing populist parties in Western Europe: Into the mainstream?*, Oxon: Routledge.

Karlsen, R. and Aardal, B. (2011) 'Kamp om dagsorden og sakseierskap', in B. Aardal (ed.) *Det Politiske Landskapet: En Studie av stortingsvalget 2009*, Oslo: Cappelen Damm Akademisk pp. 131–162.

Kitschelt, H. and McGann, A. J. (1995) *The radical right in Western Europe: A comparative analysis*, Ann Arbor: University of Michigan Press.

Kleven, Ø., Aardal, B., Bergh, J., Hesstvedt, S. and Hindenes, Å. (2015) *Valgundersøkelsen 2013: Dokumentasjons- og tabellrapport*, Oslo: Statistisk Sentralbyrå.

Knutsen, O. (2004) 'Voters and social cleavages', in K. Heidar (ed.) *Nordic politics: Comparative perspectives*, Oslo: Universitetsforlaget pp. 60–80.

——— (2006) *Class voting in Western Europe: A comparative longitudinal study*, Lanham, MD: Lexington.

Kosiara-Pedersen, K. (2015) 'Tremors, no earthquake: The 2015 Danish parliamentary election', *West European Politics*, 39: 870–878.

Langsæther, P. E. (2014) Class voting and value orientations: The fourth generation, Master thesis, Department of Political Science, University of Oslo, Oslo.

Lipset, S. M. and Rokkan, S. (1967) 'Cleavage structures, party systems, and voter alignments: An introduction', in S. M. Lipset and S. Rokkan (eds.) *Party systems and voter alignments*, New York: Free Press pp. 1–46.

Listhaug, O. and Aardal, B. (2011) 'Politisk tillit: Et mål på demokratiets helsetilstand', in B. Aardal (ed.) *Det Politiske Landskap: En Studie av stortingsvalget 2009*, Oslo: Cappelen Damm Akademisk pp. 291–304.

Lucardie, P. (2000) 'Prophets, purifiers and prolocutors', *Party Politics*, 6(2): 175–185.

Mair, P. (2006) 'Party system change', in R. S. Katz and W. Crotty (eds.) *Handbook of party politics*, London: Sage Publications pp. 63–74.

Meguid, B. M. (2005) 'Competition between unequals: The role of mainstream party strategy in niche party success', *American Political Science Review*, 99(3): 347–359.

Meret, S. (2003) 'Højrepopulisme', in J. G. Andersen and O. Borre (eds.) *Politisk Forandring: Værdipolitik Og Nye Skillelinjer Ved folketingsvalget 2001*, Århus: Systime Academic pp. 375–390.

——— (2010) The Danish people's party, the Italian northern league and the Austrian freedom party in a comparative perspective: Party ideology and electoral support, PhD, Institute of History and International Social Studies AMID, Academy for Migration Studies in Denmark, Aalborg Universitet, Aalborg.

Møller Hansen, K. and Goul Andersen, J. (2013) 'En samlet model for partivalg', in R. Stubager, K. M. Hansen and J. G. Andersen (eds.) *Krisevalg: Økonomien Og Folketingsvalget 2011*, København: Jurist- og Økonomforbundets Forlag pp. 189–212.

Møller Hansen K. and Stubager, R. (2017) 'Folketingsvalget 2015 – oprør fra udkanten', in K. Møller Hansen and R. Stubaget (eds.) *Oprør fra udkanten*. København: Juris- og Økonomiforbundets Forlag pp. 21–40.

——— (2017) 'Konklusion – en samlet vælgeradfærdsmodel', in K. Møller Hansen and R. Stubaget (eds.) *Oprør fra udkanten*. København: Juris- og Økonomiforbundets Forlag pp. 385–414.

Mudde, C. (2004) 'The populist zeitgeist', *Government and Opposition*, 39(4): 542–563.

Narud, H. M. and Strøm, K. (2011) 'Coalition bargaining in an unforgiven environment: The case of Bondervik II in Norway', in R. B. Andeweg, L. D. Winter and P. Dumont (eds.) *Puzzles of government formation: Coalition theory and deviant cases*, Oxon: Routledge/ECPR Studies in European Political Science pp. 65–87.

Nielsen, H. J. (1979). *Politiske holdninger og fremskridtsstemme*, København: Forlaget politiske studier.

——— (1999a) 'De individuelle forskydninger 1994–98', in J. Andersen, O. Borre, J. G. Andersen and H. J. Nielsen (eds.) *Vælgere Med Omtanke*, Århus: Systime pp. 49–60.

——— (1999b) 'Op til valget', in J. Andersen, O. Borre, J. G. Andersen and H. J. Nielsen (eds.) *Vælgere Med Omtanke*, Århus: Systime pp. 17–28.

Nielsen, H. J. and Thomsen, S. R. (2003). 'Vælgervandringer', in J. G. Andersen (ed.) *Politisk forandring: Værdipolitik og nye skillelinjer ved folketingsvalget 2001*, Århus: Systime pp. 61–74.

Odmalm, P. (2011) 'Political parties and "the immigration issue": Issue ownership in Swedish parliamentary elections 1991–2010', *West European Politics*, 34(5): 1070–1091.

Oscarsson, H. (2016) *Flytande Väljare, vol. 21*, Stockholm: Statistiska centralbyrån.

Oscarsson, H. and Holmberg, S. (2011) *Åttapartivalet 2010. Redogörelse för 2010 års Valundersökning i Samarbete Mellan Statistiska Centralbyrån och Statsvetenskapliga Institutionen vid Göteborgs Universitet*, Stockholm: Statistiska centralbyrån.

——— (2013) *Nya Svenska Väljare*, Stockholm: Norstedts Juridik.

——— (2015) *Swedish voting behavior*, Swedish National Election Studies Program, Department of Political Science, University of Gothenburg.

Oskarson, M. and Demker, M. (2015) 'Room for realignment: The working-class sympathy for Sweden democrats', *Government and Opposition*, 50(4): 629–651.

Pappas, T. S. (2014) 'Populist democracies: Post-authoritarian Greece and post-communist Hungary', *Government and Opposition*, 49(1): 1–23.

Pedersen, Karina (2005) 'The 2005 Danish general election: A phase of consolidation', *West European Politics*, 28(5): 1101–1108.

Pedersen, M. N. (1982) 'Towards a new typology of party lifespans and minor parties', *Scandinavian Political Studies*, 5(1): 1–16.

Pellikaan, H., de Lange, S. L. d and van der Meer, T. (2007) 'Fortuyn's legacy: Party system change in the Netherlands', *Comparative European Politics*, 5(3): 282–302.

Peterson, T., Stigendal, M. and Fryklund, B. (1988) *Skånepartiet: Om Folkeligt Missnöje i Malmö*, Lund: Arkiv Förlag.

Politiken (2016) 'Det sagde de: Debatten buldrede, da L87 blev til virkelighed', 26 January 2016. URL: http://politiken.dk/indland/politik/art5608230/ Det-sagde-de-Debatten-buldrede-da-L87-blev-til-virkelighed.

Ringsmose, J. (2003) *Kedeligt Har Det i Hvert Fald Ikke Været . . . : Fremskridtspartiet 1989–1995*, Odense: Syddansk universitetsforlag.

Ringsmose, J. and Pedersen, K. (2005) 'Fra protest til indflydelse: Organisatoriske forskelle mellem fremskridtspartiet og dansk folkeparti', *Politik*, 8(3): 68–78.

Rokkan, S. (1968) 'The structuring of mass politics in the smaller European democracies: A developmental typology', *Comparative Studies in Society and History*, 10(2): 173–210.

Rydgren, J. (2006) *From tax populism to ethnic nationalism: Radical right-wing populism in Sweden*, New York: Berghahn Books.

——— (2008) 'Sweden: The Scandinavian exception', in D. Albertazzi and D. McDonnell (eds.) *Twenty-first century populism: The spectre of Western European democracy*, New York: Palgrave MacMillan pp. 135–151.

——— (2010) 'Radical right-wing populism in Denmark and Sweden: Explaining party system change and stability', *SAIS Review*, 30(1): 57–71.

Saglie, J. (1994) 'Partimedlemmer og politisk avstand', in K. Heidar and L. Svåsand (eds.) *Partiene i Brytningstid*, Bergen: Alma Mater pp. 46–79.

Sannerstedt, A. (2014) 'Sverigedemokraternas sympatisörer', in A. Bergström and H. Oscarsson (eds.) *Mittfåra och Marginal: SOM-undersökningen 2013*, Göteborg: Göteborgs universitet: SOM-institutet pp. 445–458.

Schumacher, G. and van Kersbergen, K. (2016) 'Do mainstream parties adapt to the welfare chauvinism of populist parties?', *Party Politics*, 22(3): 300–312.

Simonnes, K. (2013) 'I stjålne klær? En analyse av endringer i Høyres, Arbeiderpartiets og Fremskrittspartiets innvandrings- og integreringspolitikk', *Norsk statsvitenskapelig tidsskrift*, 29(2): 144–158.

Strøm, K. (1994) 'The Presthus debacle: Intraparty politics and bargaining failure in Norway', *American Political Science Review*, 88(1): 112–127.

Stubager, R. and Hansen, K. M. (2013) 'It's the economy, stupid!', in R. Stubager, K. M. Hansen and J. G. Andersen (eds.) *Krisevalg: Økonomien og Folketingsvalget 2011*, København: Jurist- og Økonomforbundets Forlag pp. 17–44.

Stubager, R. and Møller Hansen, K. (2013) 'Social baggrund og partivalg', in R. Stubager, K. M. Hansen and J. G. Andersen (eds.) *Krisevalg: Økonomien Og Folketingsvalget 2011*, København: Jurist- og Økonomforbundets Forlag pp. 61–88.

SVT. (2014) 'Enkät: Var tredje M-kommunpolitiker säger ja till SD-samarbete'. 11 December 2014. URL: http://www.svt.se/nyheter/inrikes/var-tredje-m-kommunpolitiker-sager-ja-till-sd-samarbete (accessed 12 May 2016).

Tonsgaard, O. (1989) 'Vælgervandringer og vælgerusikkerhed', in J. Elklit and O. Tonsgaard (eds.) *To Folketingsvalg*, Århus: Forlaget Politica pp. 135–156.

Valen, H. (1981) *Valg og Politikk: Et Samfunn i Endring*, Oslo: Forbruker-og administrasjonsdepartementet.

Valen, H. and Aardal, B. (1983) *Et Valg i Perspektiv: En Studie av Stortingsvalget 1981*, Oslo: Statistisk sentralbyrå.

Valen, H., Aardal, B. and Vogt, G. (1990) *Endring og Kontinuitet: Stortingsvalget 1989*, Oslo: Statistisk sentralbyrå.

Volkens, A., Lehmann, P., Merz, N., Regel, S., Werner, A., Lacewell, O. and Promise Schultze, H. (2013) *The Manifesto Data Collection*, Manifesto Project (MRG/CMP/MARPOR), Berlin: Wissenschaftszentrum Berlin für Sozialforschung (WZB).

von Beyme, K. (1988) 'Right-wing extremism in post-war Europe', *West European Politics*, 11(2): 1–18.

Widfeldt, A. (2004) 'The diversified approach: Swedish responses to the extreme right', in R. Eatwell and C. Mudde (eds.) *Western democracies and the new extreme right challenge*, London: Routledge pp. 150–171.

——— (2008) 'Party change as a necessity: The case of the Sweden democrats', *Representation*, 44(3): 265–276.

——— (2015a) *Extreme Right Parties in Scandinavia*, Oxon: Routledge.

——— (2015b) 'Tensions beneath the surface: The Swedish mainstream parties and the immigration issue', *Acta Politica*, 50(4): 399–416.

Wolinetz, S. (2006) 'Party systems and party system types', in R. S. Katz and W. Crotty (eds.) *Handbook of party politics*, London: Sage Publications pp. 51–62.

Wörlund, I. (1992) 'The Swedish parliamentary election of September 1991', *Scandinavian Political Studies*, 15(2): 135–143.

Chapter 6

Finnish Populism: Keeping It in the Family?

David Arter

While the name of the populist True Finns Party is known abroad and foreign correspondents may well recall the word *jytky* – the term its leader used to describe the scale of the party's sensational breakthrough at the 2011 general election – Finnish populism long antedates these dramatic events. Finnish populism has run 'in the family' and, in the shape of the Finnish Rural Party (*Suomen maaseudun* puolue, SMP) between 1966 and 1995 and the True Finns (*Perussuomalainen puolue*, PS) since 1995, it has been continuously represented in the 200-seat unicameral *Eduskunta* for over half a century. Under Veikko Vennamo, the founder of the 'business', the SMP became the first Nordic populist party to break the established party system mould, registering 10.5 per cent in 1970 at the first of the Scandinavian 'earthquake elections'. Under Veikko's son, Pekka Vennamo, the SMP polled 9.7 per cent at the 1983 general election and that year became the first Nordic populist party to enter government, where it remained until 1990. Under Veikko Vennamo's 'adopted son', Timo Soini, the SMP's successor party, the PS, advanced by an unprecedented 15 percentage points at the 2011 general election and when four years later Soini led the PS into government with the Centre and Conservative parties, the PS became the first Nordic populist party to participate in a majority coalition government. In short, there appears a strong prima facie case for the claim that an institutionalised populist party lineage has had a significant impact on the Finnish party system.

This chapter inquires whether this has indeed been the case. It approaches a response to this wide-ranging question incrementally, viewing the party system as a multidimensional phenomenon and posing two questions which structure the empirical body of the piece. The first, which focuses of the *competition for votes*, asks: Has the (at times significant) support for the two populist parties contributed to a realignment of the electoral party system? The second, which concentrates on the *competition for power* (office), poses a parallel question: What has been the impact of the populist SMP and PS on the legislative party system – and the logic of coalition formation in particular? Has it contributed to a realignment of the legislative party system?

The emphasis in response to both questions is on the True Finns – technically 'The Finns' party in English. The basic argument illustrates the value of distinguishing between the legislative and electoral party system. Over the last two general elections (2011 and 2015), the PS has averaged 18.4 per cent of the vote, is currently the second-largest parliamentary party and is a member of the governing coalition, but, curiously perhaps, it has not contributed to a significant realignment of the legislative party system. Indeed, the PS' impact has arguably been greater in the electoral party arena where, despite the evident volatility in the Finnish populist vote, it has contributed to re-politicising a traditional structure-based (class) cleavage and mobilising a potentially new value-based cleavage grounded in ethnocentrism.

The structure of the paper is as follows. In order to contextualise the analysis, the introduction sets out the parameters (indeed peculiarities) of the Finnish party system. This is followed by a section analysing the variable trajectory of the SMP, which progressed from the status of 'pariah party' in the 1970s to power in a governing coalition in the 1980s only to implode in the 1990s, internecine feuding leading to a loss of votes, bankruptcy and party termination in 1995. The focus then switches to the successor PS, its rise as an 'entrepreneurial issue party' and the hard choices it had to make following the 2011 *jytky*. With the PS having entered government following the 2015 general election, the analysis then considers whether history could repeat itself. Can the demands of *external coalition* (the need for compromise politics in cabinet) be reconciled with a disparate *internal coalition* in such a way as to avoid party fragmentation? The question has assumed heightened salience in light of Soini's decision to stand down as party chair at the June 2017 party conference. The conclusion revisits the generic question of the impact of half a century of populism on the Finnish party system. The sources used include transcripts of all nine extended interviews with veteran SMP parliamentarians available in the Eduskunta library, one of which is with the SMP chair Pekka Vennamo; six extended interviews with the PS leader Timo Soini conducted by the author between 2003 and 2014; a range of documentary evidence, *inter alia* two books by the SMP's founder-entrepreneur Veikko Vennamo and two by Soini, the PS' founder-entrepreneur; biographical and autobiographical material and newspaper sources. This novel, longitudinal approach places the paper in the 'border country' between political science and political history in the hope of benefiting from both perspectives.

THE PARAMETERS OF THE FINNISH PARTY SYSTEM

Electoral party system competition – that is, competition for votes – is governed primarily by the body of rules making up the electoral system. Over the half century of populist party representation in parliament, the institutional framework governing general elections has changed relatively little. Uniquely in the Nordic region, Finland employs an open-list PR voting system with no formal qualifying threshold. Citizens are obliged to opt for a single candidate on one of the party lists and electoral competition is thus both inter-party and, importantly too, intraparty in character. In 1969, the franchise age was lowered from 21 to 18 years and the provision for multiple candidacy abolished (the SMP leader Veikko Vennamo stood in all sixteen mainland constituencies in 1962!). The number of electoral districts (constituencies) has been reduced since the 1960s and the district magnitude (seat allocation per constituency) adjusted to reflect demographic change. This has mainly involved an exodus of people from the outlying north and east and a concentration of the population in the 'deep south' – the triangle formed by the cities of Tampere, Turku and the capital Helsinki. In 2012, the amalgamation of small-magnitude districts reduced the number of constituencies from fourteen to twelve (the legal minimum), while for the 2015 general election, district magnitude ranged from seven in Lapland to thirty-five in the Uusimaa constituency in the hinterland of Helsinki. Despite the merger of two districts in the south-east and two in the north-east, the variation in district magnitude has created hidden electoral thresholds – highest in the small-m districts – and in an attempt to achieve these (particularly small) parties may forge tactical electoral alliances. Both the SMP and PS have done so at critical junctures, and to good effect, on occasions saving themselves from falling below the threshold of representation.

Within the framework of rules governing the competition for votes, populist party surges have coincided with – and almost certainly contributed to – increased voter volatility. Thus, in the nineteen Finnish general elections between 1948 and 2015, the mean Pedersen net volatility index – calculated on the basis of the sum of the gains of winning parties – was 8.1 per cent (Borg 2015a: 24). However, at the SMP's breakthrough election in 1970, it stood at 14.4 per cent; at the SMP's 'second coming' in 1983, the figure was 11.1 per cent; and at the PS' 'big bang' (*jytky*) election in 2011, it was no less than 15.9 per cent.

In the legislative arena, the populist surge of the PS has contributed to a marginal increase in the fragmentation of the parliamentary party system. On the basis of the Laakso-Taagepera index, the effective number of legislative parties increased from 5.14 in 1999 (the PS' first general election) to

Table 6.1 The Representation of the Parties in the Finnish Eduskunta, 1999–2015 (%)

	LA	SDP	Greens	PS	Centre	CD	Cons	SPP
1999	10.9	22.9	7.3	1.0	22.4	4.2	21.0	5.1
2003	9.9	24.5	8.0	1.6	24.7	5.3	18.6	4.6
2007	8.8	21.4	8.5	4.1	23.1	4.9	22.3	4.6
2011	8.1	19.1	7.3	19.1	15.8	4.0	20.4	4.3
2015	7.1	16.5	8.5	17.7	21.1	3.5	18.2	4.9

LA: Left Alliance; SDP: Social Democrats; PS: True Finns; CD: Christian Democrats; Cons: Conservatives; SPP: Swedish People's Party

5.83 in 2015. An index of fragmentation, however, indicates little, if anything, about the interaction of the parliamentary parties and should not be confused with party system polarisation. The PS has not contributed to polarised politics in the parliamentary arena. Rather, since the 1999 general election, the same eight parties (table 6.1) have been consistently represented in the Eduskunta, all eight have been office-seeking parties and (demonstrating their coalition potential) all eight have participated in government at least once since the turn of the new millennium. This stands in contrast to periods in the Cold War era when not only the SMP but also the Conservatives and Finnish Christian League were 'offside' (denied governing potential) for so-called general reasons (*yleiset syyt*), a code for being unacceptable 'in high places'.

Since Pekka Vennamo's SMP entered government in 1983 all Finnish cabinets have run their full four-year course, several have been surplus majority cabinets (despite the abolition in 1992 of a nexus of qualified majority rules), there has been the wholesale absence of bipolar dynamics and 'bloc politics', and in the legislative party arena, the logic of coalition formation has not followed conventional left-right lines. In fact, a reasonable case could be made for viewing the legislative party system in Finland as *sui generis*, or at least one that has proved problematic for the comparativist.

Writing in the mid-1960s, Sartori (1966) viewed Finland as a possible case of *extreme multipartism*, and yet the party system did not exhibit the characteristics of polarised pluralism – for example, irresponsible opposition and outbidding. Rather, the sizeable 'anti-system' (Communist-dominated) Finnish People's Democratic League (SKDL) formed an integral part of the so-called Popular Front governments of the period. With too many 'relevant parties', moreover, and lacking bipolar dynamics, Finland could not be considered a case of moderate multipartism à la Sartori either. The logic of coalition-building (or lack of it) has also confounded political scientists. Thus, the party system has spawned a high percentage of *innovative governments* in Mair's (2008) sense of governments that have not previously held office in that form. Over the fourteen general elections since the SMP entered parliament in 1966, 92.9 per cent resulted in innovative governments involving combinations of parties that had not previously governed together. Since 1987, moreover, exactly half have included the main parties of left and right, the Social Democrats and Conservatives. The 2011–2014 coalition comprised Conservatives (the prime minister's party), the Social Democrats (post-communist), Left Alliance, Greens, Swedish People's Party and Christian Democrats. Not surprisingly, I have referred in the Finnish context to 'anything goes' governments.

A final point on the parameters of the party system is in order. Whereas in Denmark, Norway and Sweden, the left-right and GAL-TAN dimensions correlate and are overlapping, this is much less the case in Finland. On the basis of the Chapel Hill survey (remember it was conducted before the 2011 'big bang'), the PS was positioned slightly to the left of centre on an economic left-right scale, well to the right on the GAL-TAN scale (only the renamed Christian Democrats were further to the right) and closest of all the parties to the centre on a general left-right continuum (figure 6.1). On this basis, at least the PS in 2010 was a case of centrist populism.

Before moving on to the SMP/PS impact on the competition for votes and office, a note on constitutional change is necessary as a backdrop to understanding some of the changing inter-party dynamics in the legislative arena. The 1919 constitution, enacted two years after Finnish independence, prescribed a semi-presidential form of government (Arter 1999). While the government was responsible to parliament, the president was vested with

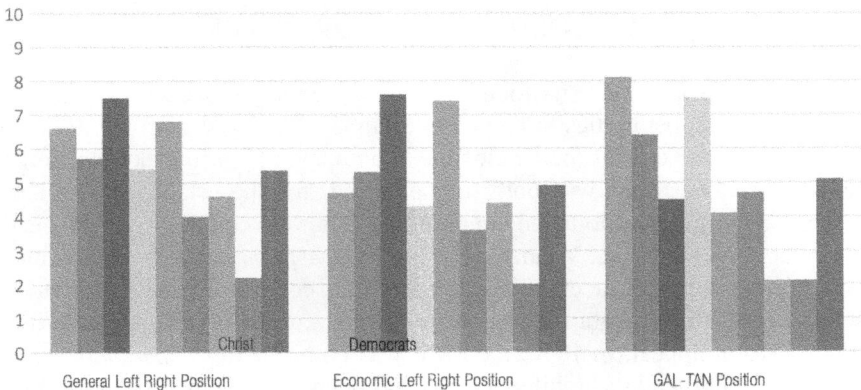

Figure 6.1 The Chapel Hill Mean Positions for the Finnish Political Parties (2010)

legislative (law-making), executive (government-nominating) and federative (foreign relations–directing) powers, while, following the Second World War, the paramount need to build and maintain amicable relations with the Soviet Union elevated the importance of the federative function. The long-serving former Agrarian prime minister, president Urho Kekkonen (1956–1981), exercised the powers of his office proactively, and particularly salient for our purposes was the way he built a Gaullist-style presidential *majorité* which made him the dominant political actor of his day and, putting it baldly, not somebody to get on the wrong side of. The relationship between Veikko Vennamo and Urho Kekkonen broke down shortly after Kekkonen became head of state in 1956 (Vennamo had supported Kekkonen's campaign) and the enmity between the two grew ever deeper as the years rolled on (Vennamo 1987).

Kekkonen's resignation on health grounds in 1981, coupled with the subsequent collapse of the Soviet Union and Finland's membership of the European Union in 1995, formed the backdrop to a period of constitutional change and a progressive reduction in the powers of the head of state. There was the introduction of presidential term limits (two consecutive six-year terms) in 1988; the shift from an American-style electoral college system to the direct, French-style, two-round popular election of the head of state in 1994; and the enactment of a new constitution substantially reducing the powers of the president, which came into force in 2000. The president no longer plays an active role in government formation and the direction of foreign relations (article 94) is shared with the government. It would be stretching the point to describe Finland in 2017 as a semi-presidential system.

THE COMPETITION FOR VOTES

In 1970, the SMP, under its founder Veikko Vennamo, became the first of the Nordic populist parties to break the established party system mould, registering 10.5 per cent at the first of the Scandinavian 'earthquake elections' (table 6.2). The result was both dramatic and, for the established parties, traumatic. It also dumbfounded the psephologists, who could not comprehend an advance on that scale. Vennamo's populism (*vennamolaisuus* – Vennamo-ism), propounded by a charismatic politician, combined a leftist-inclined social populism and right-leaning socio-cultural conservatism and had a diffuse electoral appeal. In 1970, the SMP was unmistakably a *personal party* (Lucardie 2000) and its architect, Veikko Vennamo, the archetypal APE, that is anti-political-establishment crusader.

Table 6.2 The Performance of the SMP at General Elections, 1966–1995

Year	% vote	Eduskunta Seats
1966	1.0	1
1970	10.5	18
1972	9.2	18
1975	3.6	2
1979	4.6	7
1983	9.7	17
1987	6.3	9
1991	4.9	7
1995	1.3	1

Vennamo was a member of a generation that had experienced the so-called danger years in the late 1940s (when rumours of an impending Communist coup were rife) and he feared Finland would succumb to socialism and join the Eastern bloc. Consequently, he sought to create a party that would appeal to leftist-thinking voters and protest voters but one that would lock them into the non-socialist camp.[1] Vennamo-ism was strongly anti-communist. Yet, significantly, the four years before the 1970 general election had seen the Communist-driven SKDL participate in a broad Popular Front government backed by a leftist-controlled legislature. Moreover, against the backdrop of the secularisation and libertarianism of the Popular Front years, Vennamo-ism espoused the traditionalist values of 'home, religion and fatherland'. There was no GAL-TAN scale then but the SMP would have been well to the right on the TAN dimension and it could perfectly well be depicted – the populist 'sloganising' aside – as a Christian social party.

Vennamo's social populism appealed to what Ford and Goodwin (2014) refer to as the 'left behind' in society. Vennamo's highly original, innovative and colourful populist rhetoric,[2] grounded in a visceral anti-elitism (*her-raviha*), juxtaposed the 'forgotten nation' and the corrupt, sybaritic state. The SMP's election slogan 'In Defence of the Forgotten People and Against the Abuses of Power' (*Unohdetun kansan puolesta vallan väärinkäyttöä vastaan*)[3] targeted those living in extreme hardship and in need of welfare. It mobilised those marginal and alienated groups that felt abandoned by society. These included war veterans, war widows, pensioners, invalids and those families (parents) in high-unemployment areas hit by the exodus of young people to the towns and cities of southern Finland and factories in Sweden. In short, Vennamo's populist rhetoric resonated in the economic and geographic peripheries.

For some SMP adherents, however, Vennamo was a lone anti-political-establishment 'ranger', confronting what he dismissively characterised as Kekkonen's 'civilian junta', namely, the president and his minions, who had no qualms about playing the 'Moscow card' (the threat of Soviet sanctions) in order to pull the domestic political strings. In this scenario, Vennamo was viewed as a *bravura* figure, ready boldly to challenge the obsequious *Ostpolitik* of Kekkonen and 'his gang'. Symptomatically, J. Juhani Kortesalmi, one of the 1970 tranche of SMP legislators, noted that Vennamo was the only Finnish politician clearly to condemn the Soviet/Warsaw Pact invasion of Czechoslovakia in August 1968. This expressly political (federative) dimension in Veikko Vennamo's populism has been curiously neglected (wittingly or otherwise) in earlier studies of the SMP's 1970 breakthrough election (Sänkiaho 1971).

Whether the PS, founded in autumn 1995, only months after the demise of the SMP, should be considered a new party must be open to serious question. The PS was nominally and legally a new party. However, its solitary parliamentarian between 1995 and 2003, Raimo Vistbacka, argued at the time that changing the SMP's name and collecting the 5,000 signatures *formally to found a new party* could well be the clearest route out of the party's bankruptcy dilemma. He continued that a change of name was in any event overdue as the 'Finnish Rural Party' had a dated ring.[4] Certainly at the grassroots, the PS was seen in some active quarters as no more than a change of name. Toivo Mäkelä (an SMP member since 1972, for nearly four decades a member of the local council in Kaustinen, and for over twenty years the chair of the SMP-PS Keski-Pohjanmaa district) has related how, living in a small community where everybody knows everybody else, the SMP's *change of name* affected the party's support very little.[5] He added that the PS defends the 'small person's interests' just as the SMP had done earlier.[6] Significantly, there were continuities at the elite level: 39 per cent of the very small number of PS candidates at its first general election in 1999 ($n = 54$) had stood for the SMP *at some point* in its existence between 1966 and 1995. Crucially, the party passed back into 'family hands' when Timo Soini assumed the PS party leadership in 1997 since Soini modelled his entire political persona on that of his mentor Veikko Vennamo.

At its first general election in 1999, the PS described itself as a 'right-wing party of the poor' (*köyhien oikeistopuolue*)[7] – in other words, it espoused the SMP's mix of social populism and socio-cultural conservatism. However, the PS added an element of ethno-nationalism to its appeal and, in this connection, Soini announced the following year 2000 that if in five years' time, there was not in Finland the same type of right-wing [anti-immigrant] populist party as in Norway and Austria, he would have failed (author's parentheses).[8] In fact, in the early 1990s, an electorally declining and divided SMP had sought survival by playing the anti-immigrant card and, during the 1991 general election campaign, Soini (then deputy-chair) felt compelled to write a measured letter to the national daily *Helsingin Sanomat* defending the SMP against charges of being a 'racist populist party'.[9]

PS party (re-)building was a gradual process and for fifteen years (1995–2010), its electoral impact was very limited (figure 6.2). Slow, incremental progress was made by (i) building up a field organisation, (ii) forging advantageous electoral alliances, (iii) seeking to exploit the open-list electoral system by attracting – where possible – 'celebrity candidates' with high name-recognition, (iv) using local government elections as a candidate recruitment base, (v) contesting presidential elections and (vi) pursuing an open-door management style, which attracted hard-line anti-immigrant elements to the party. In sum, as the PS grew and its potential influence likewise, so too did the heterogeneity of its activist base, which contained members of the 'old SMP guard', persons previously active in other parties, those new and inexperienced in politics and racist elements operating through their own website *Hommaforum*. As Soini was later to comment: 'Sometimes the sheer diversity of the party wears me out. It's like a bazaar – we've got a bit of everything and it's open day and night' (Soini 2014: 170).

The upturn in the PS' fortunes in the opinion polls began in summer 2010, but nobody forecast the extent of the party's success nine months later. Indeed, the *scale* and *exclusivity* of the PS' general election victory in 2011 were unprecedented. The PS advanced by 15 percentage points on the general election four years earlier, claiming 19.1 per cent of the active electorate and tying with the Social Democrats as the second-largest party on the basis of the popular vote (table 6.3). No 'winning party' in Finnish history had gained on that scale and the gains, moreover, were exclusive – the PS was the *only* winning party. Of those who voted for the PS in 2011, 9 per cent had voted

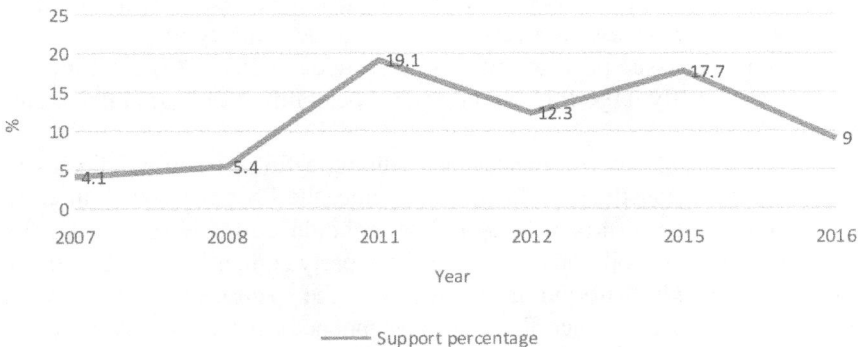

Figure 6.2 The PS Support Rates, 2007–2016

Chapter 6

Table 6.3 The Performance of the PS at Finnish General Elections, 1999–2015

Year	% vote	Eduskunta Seats
1999	1.0	1
2003	1.6	3
2007	4.1	5
2011	19.1	39
2015	17.7	38

Conservative four years earlier, 23 per cent had backed the Social Democrats and 10 per cent the Centre Party, and18 per cent had abstained or were not entitled to vote in 2007 (Borg 2012: 198). Geographically, the PS did well in strong Centre Party support areas (rural municipalities), drew support from the Conservatives and Social Democrats in urban areas (Westinen 2014) and did particularly well in its 1983 strongholds. However, it gained ground in all fourteen mainland constituencies. On a self-assessment basis relating to occupational class, 60 per cent of PS voters in 2011 identified themselves as either working class (31 per cent) or pensioners (29 per cent), a proportion exceeded only by the Social Democrats (70 per cent) (Borg 2012: 195). The PS in 2011 mobilised a type of working-class conservatism previously absent from Finnish electoral politics.

In April 2011, the PS could perhaps best be described as an *entrepreneurial-issue party* (Harmel and Svåsand 1993). Timo Soini, the entrepreneur, led the party into the election and was its dominant actor and it was 'his' issue – a strongly Eurosceptic line – which largely defined the PS' campaign. The PS had other election themes in 2011 and the party's acerbic critique of assistance to ailing Eurozone economies was not the crucial determinant for all its supporters by any means. However, the high issue saliency of a Eurosceptic stance and clear issue position ownership (Mudde 2010: 1180) combined to create a potentially large PS vote and Soini personified that potential (Arter 2016: 20).

In eschewing electoral alliances and running a full slate of candidates in every mainland constituency for the first time, the PS gave voters an extra option (the presence of a local candidate emboldened many to vote for the PS) and intensified both inter-party and intra-party competition (Arter 2013). The PS' advance bit hard into the Centre vote (the Centre recorded its lowest poll – 15.9 per cent – since Finnish independence), not least because there were elements in that party that had opposed EU membership at the 1994 referendum and continued to be strongly Eurosceptic. However, the PS not only re-politicised an existing class-based cleavage – concern about the loss of traditional industrial jobs in the new global market-place – but also mobilised a new value-based cleavage steeped in ethno-centric concern about the erosion of Finnish-ness (*suomalaisuus*) at the hands of multi-cultural orthodoxies.

COMPETITION FOR OFFICE

Following its legislative breakthrough in 1970, the SMP and its 18-strong PPG occupied 'on paper' a pivotal position in the government-formation process. Alignment with the two leftist parties would have yielded a parliamentary majority and so, too, an association with the non-socialist parties (Vennamo 1989: 150, 214). That, however, presumed a 'free-market polity', and the reality was very different. Under Veikko Vennamo, the SMP's 'coalition potential' (Sartori 1976) and access to office were constrained by the need for (i) presidential approval, (ii) Soviet acquiescence and (iii) the Finnish Communists' willingness to co-operate. The SMP fell short on all three counts. First, the personal animosity between Kekkonen and Vennamo ran deep. The president mistrusted and disliked Vennamo. The latter presented himself as the victim of a sham democracy run by a Stalin-style dictator who both threatened him and set out to destroy the SMP (Vennamo 1989: 154, 221). Second, the SMP was regarded in Moscow as a fascist party and, reduced to two MPs following the 1975 general election, it was relocated to the right of the Conservatives in the Eduskunta. For the Soviets, the SMP was an 'extreme nationalist, anti-Soviet party that practised deception politics' (Isohookana-Asunmaa 2006: 264). Finally, the Finnish Communists were unequivocal in their refusal to entertain the idea of co-operation with the SMP. The latter was formally involved in government talks following the 1970 general election but was ultimately excluded from office. The SMP became a pariah party.

Under Veikko's son Pekka Vennamo, the SMP polled 9.7 per cent at the party's 'second coming' in the 1983 general election and became the first Nordic populist party to enter government where it remained until 1990. The scale of its advance – +5.1 percentage points – was only about half that in 1970 but the following three contextual factors facilitated the SMP's pathway to power: (i) Kekkonen had resigned on health grounds and the SMP had gained the approval of the new president Mauno Koivisto by supporting him at the electoral college round of voting the previous year, (ii) Pekka Vennamo was less distrusted in Moscow than his father and the president was able to act as collateral, vouching for the SMP's 'good behaviour' in government, and (iii) the Finnish Communists were also badly divided and suffered their worst election result since SKDL's formation in 1944. Koivisto denied that he had anything to do with the SMP's inclusion in government (Suomi 2005: 305), though clearly he could, if necessary, have prevented it. Rather, the SMP's incorporation into the governing coalition in 1983 was at the initiative of the Social Democrat chair, Kalevi Sorsa.

The PS' road to government was long and hard. However, there was no suggestion of a *cordon sanitaire* mentality among the 'old' parties when, at the 2011 general election, the PS made the greatest gains of any party in the post–Second World War period, advancing by 15 percentage points compared with four years earlier (*see* table 6.3). Rather, the leaders of both the Conservatives, which emerged as the largest party for the first time in Finnish history, and the Social Democrats, which in contrast recorded their worst-ever result, publicly expressed the expectation that, in line with the democratic will of the people, the PS would join the new government. Soini also indicated, albeit in coded rhetoric, that he hoped PS involvement in government might be possible.[10] The door to office appeared open – or at least ajar – and the anticipation was that a three-party Conservative-Social Democrat-PS coalition would ultimately emerge despite their 'chalk-and-cheese' differences on 'Europe'. It would not be easy going: Katainen, the Conservatives' chair and minister of finance in the outgoing Centre-led coalition, had defended the Greek bail-outs, and now he had the task of leading negotiations on a new government with a mildly (or at least tactically) Euro-sceptic party (Social Democrats) and an unequivocally anti-EU party (PS).

Katainen, however, was nothing if not resourceful. Under pressure from Soini, he offered to exclude a Portuguese bail-out and both the temporary and permanent EU crisis-funding mechanisms from the negotiations on a new government programme. Katainen wanted the PS in the cabinet; the Conservatives were the largest party, and a three-party Conservative-Social Democrat-PS coalition would have a comfortable parliamentary majority and facilitate a Conservative prime ministership for the first time in twenty years. Katainen also doubtlessly calculated that it would be easier to govern with the PS than an eclectic mix that might well include the post-communist Left Alliance. The personal chemistry between Katainen and Soini was good; they had known each other for over ten years and both had contested the Kuopio constituency in 1999 – Katainen successfully. Soini even gave Katainen six hours' notice of the PS leader's highly EU-critical article opposing bailouts, which appeared in the *Wall Street Journal* on 9 May 2011 (during Katainen's soundings on a new government).[11] Katainen, of course, had tactical motives for seeking to include the PS. The PS' involvement in government would probably have neutered some of the party's support (cf. De Lange 2012: 914) as it had the SMP by 1987. Failing the PS' participation, Katainen also wanted to ensure that, by offering to keep the bailouts separate, Soini could not assume martyr status by inferring that the PS was summarily excluded from the government-formation process. Insofar as Soini pulled the PS out of the government talks, this could be interpreted as a tactical victory for Katainen although his first preference was for a Conservative-Social Democrat-PS coalition.

While parties have numerous goals, they also have a *primary goal* (Harmel and Janda 1994), and for Soini and the PS following the 2011 *jytky* the primary goal was office – participation in government – as a means of influencing the very issue (EU policy) which had largely identified the PS during the election campaign. Office seeking as a primary goal was a high-risk strategy that, as Soini well knew, would involve 'hard choices' (Strøm and Müller 1999) and at very least a degree of credible compromise. Soini had drafted a ministerial list and had been offered six cabinet portfolios. He would have accepted bail-outs for Ireland, Greece and Portugal but would then, as minister of finance, have pursued a hawkish, British-style 'strictly in Finland's interests' policy (Interview with Soini 23 November 2012). This was not acceptable to Katainen, who gained a compromise agreement on the euro-crisis funding machinery with the Social Democrats the day before Soini pulled out. Before that, Soini had tried to deal the Conservatives out of the game by cobbling together a coalition of Social Democrats, PS and the Centre (which like the Social Democrats had recorded their lowest-ever vote) but the Social Democrat leader got cold feet.[12] Still inexperienced, she would have become prime minister but at the expense of excluding the largest party. It is, in any event, highly doubtful that a Eurosceptic Social Democrat-PS-Centre combination would have survived for long.

In 2011, the PS became the first major 'winning party' in Finland ever to decline office and its decision to withdraw from the coalition negotiations led to another innovative governing combination – six parties from the post-communist Left Alliance to the Conservatives, all of which lost ground at the polls. It may seem paradoxical prima facie, but the greatest electoral triumph of Finnish populism – the PS' *jytky* '*victory*' in 2011 – did not affect the basic mechanics of the legislative party system, nor did it affect the logic of coalition formation, not least because this had long lacked a clear logic in spatial terms. There is certainly no evidence à la Bale (2003) that the rise of a middle-sized populist party has led to bipolar 'bloc politics'. The PS has been accommodated rather than ostracised; as ever, pragmatism has prevailed.

THE PS' IMPACT IN OFFICE

So far the analysis has proceeded on the basis of the widespread assumption that the PS has become an institutionalised party – a party system 'fixture' so to speak – and its entry into government in early summer 2015, which caused few raised eyebrows, seemed to confirm that assumption (Arter and Kestilä-Kekkonen 2014). The PS was, after all, the second-largest legislative party; it had pursued an expressly office-seeking course in the run-up to the election, polishing some of its rough populist edges in the process; and the PS had claimed four cabinet posts in the Centre-PS-Conservative coalition, the party leader, Timo Soini, taking the foreign secretaryship. But could history repeat itself? Barely five years after resigning from the Holkeri government in 1990, the forerunner SMP imploded amid internecine strife, a collapse in its vote and ultimately bankruptcy. Are there lessons to be learned from the history of the SMP?

Three general points are in order. First, if populist parties are created and led by a charismatic political entrepreneur, the threat of de-institutionalisation may derive from internal opposition to a personalised and autocratic leadership style. Soini's leadership style has been modelled on, and indeed compared to,[13] that of his mentor Veikko Vennamo and Vennamo's proclivity for unilateral decision taking and his abrasive – at times dismissive – approach towards colleagues undoubtedly contributed to the formation of an SMP splinter party, the Finnish People's Unity Party (*Suomen Kansan Yhtenäisyyden Puolue* [SKYP]) in autumn 1972. A member of the 1970–1972 SMP PPG described how under Veikko Vennamo's leadership the group was 'kept in secret and in handcuffs' (Poutianen 1972: 212). Ultimately, a majority – twelve out of the eighteen MPs – defected to the SKYP, almost certainly enticed to do so by an amendment to the party funding law enabling a splinter party, if more than half defected, to receive a pro-rata share of the mother-party's original allocation (Borg: 2015b). The SKYP therefore got the lion's share of the monies assigned to the 18-strong SMP PPG following the January 1972 general election.[14] This left the SMP struggling financially and the 1975 general election represented what Pekka Vennamo described as 'a battle for the SMP's survival'.[15]

Second, for populist parties closely identified with a charismatic leader, destabilisation may be the consequence of a failure to have, or implement, an effective succession plan. Soini will have been at the helm for twenty years when he steps down in June 2017; he has repeatedly said he will not groom a successor although one of the two main leadership candidates, the MEP Sampo Terho, appears to have the backing of the outgoing leader and the party elite. The charge that Terho is a 'Soini puppet' has been exploited by the other serious leadership contender, Jussi Halla-aho, representing the hard line anti-immigrant wing of the party. At least the PS will have clear leadership whoever wins. Pekka Vennamo's succession plan – when he stood down as PS chair – involved dividing up the leadership roles so that the PPG chair, the party chair and the party's one ministerial post would be held by separate individuals. Vennamo has subsequently conceded that this *troika* arrangement did not work but instead led to an internal power struggle.[16] He has described it as his greatest political failure.[17] Of the seven SMP MPs elected in 1991, four had defected by the following general election in 1995. According to the (then) party secretary, all the defections were calculated steps designed to cause the SMP maximum damage (Soini 2008: 66). In 1995, the SMP managed a paltry 1.3 per cent of the national poll and elected only a single parliamentarian. In autumn of that year, the party was wound up.

Third, for governing populist parties in particular the spectre of de-institutionalisation may well derive from the challenge of balancing the demands of *external coalition* (the need for compromise politics and yet profile maintenance in cabinet) with those of a disparate *internal coalition* (voters, members and parliamentarians expecting the delivery of manifesto promises) in such a way as to avoid electoral decline and party fragmentation. In the parliamentary arena, there may be simmering individual frustration that a ministerial portfolio was not forthcoming; factionalisation in the organisational arena may reflect an overall sense of loss of party direction and prompt the defection of active members; in the electoral arena, a perception that the party has sacrificed its radical credentials on the altar of power politics may prompt wholesale desertions. Within one year of entering government, the PS experienced the competing demands of external coalition and internal coalition in all three arenas, as voters, members and rank-and-file parliamentarians reacted against what Heinisch (2003: 101) describes as the 'filtration effect' – for example, filtering out the more radical aspects of its programme as a ruling party.

In the legislative arena, internal unrest has largely come from representatives of the younger, anti-immigrant wing of the party concerned that the PS in government has not done enough to stem the tide of refugees and asylum-seekers. In July 2015, the MP Olli Immonen made a Facebook entry in which he wrote in English, 'I'm dreaming of a strong, brave nation that will defeat this nightmare called multiculturalism. We will fight until the end for our homeland and one true Finnish nation'. There was some sympathy for his sentiments at both the PPG and district levels,[18] although the former SMP chair, Pekka Vennamo, compared the Immonen text to the Norwegian Anders Behring Breivik's 'call to arms'.[19] Immonen was expelled from the PPG for two months but has continued his hard-line, anti-immigrant stance.[20] In October 2015, another PS parliamentarian, Vesa-Matti Saarakkala, announced that he would resign from the PPG if a meeting of the party's decision-making organs was not convened to discuss the PS' status in the governing coalition (something mooted by the chair of the 'Young PS' organisation). According to Saarakkala, the government was not delivering on its programme which he claimed was committed to controlling the influx of immigrants. The Soini-led party executive voted eleven and two against convening a crisis meeting; Saarakkala withdrew his threat to leave the PPG and subsequently received a warning about his behaviour.[21] Soini stated simply that he would not be pressurised or threatened.[22] However, the tabloid *Iltalehti* contacted fifteen out of the sixteen PS district chairs, and seven thought a crisis meeting was necessary, with the Lapland chair ready to see the party shift into opposition.[23]

Turning to the internal arena, the goal of office and policy influence helped to cohere a diverse membership while the goal of vote-maximisation justified a leadership strategy of accommodating the disparate elements within the party. The PS had a clear *issue identity* sharpened by opposition to the EU (euro),[24] immigration and bailouts for ailing Eurozone members. As an opposition party, moreover, the PS provided a protest channel for those disaffected with 'old party politics'. Access to office, however, meant forfeiting *issue ownership* and the party's protest credentials – the PS acquiesced in a third Greek bailout and economic austerity measures – and prompted vocal criticism from the 'party in the country'. The complaints included 'a toothless immigration policy'; 'the party has turned its back on the working population'; the party has been privy to 'inequitable cuts that affect the poor disproportionately'; the party is characterised by nepotistic practices and 'there is a lack of openness and internal democracy'.[25]

Since the Immonen and Saarakkala episode the PPG has appeared relatively cohesive[26] and reports of activist unrest have been only intermittent, but the PS' standing in the polls has plummeted. In other words, it has been in the electoral arena where the demands of office have taken their greatest toll. Within three months of going into government, the PS' support had fallen by fully 7 percentage points compared with the 2015 general election performance – it had not been so low since April 2010 – and it was the fifth largest electoral party behind the Centre, Social Democrats, Conservatives and Greens (table 6.4).[27] By March 2017, the PS' support had been halved – down from 17.7 per cent in April 2015 to 9.0 per cent while, hardly coincidentally, the Social Democrats had risen to become the largest party. On

Table 6.4 Party Support

Social Democrats	22.9
Centre	20.7
Conservatives	16.9
Greens	10.7
PS	9.0
Leftist Alliance	8.9
Swedish People's Party	4.5
Christian Democrats	3.9
Others	2.5
N	2,895

A telephone poll conducted between 3 February and 1 March.

Source: Ylen kysely: 'Hallituspuolueiden suosio laskee, Sdp jatkaa kasvuaan' *Helsingin Sanomat* 3 March 2016.

the eve of the leadership ballot – and every paid-up member who attends the party conference has the vote – grassroots unrest ran deep and was reflected in Halla-aho's (hardly veiled) critique of Soini when announcing his decision to stand: 'What we need is a more democratic and decentralised party, with more internal debate in which a wide range of views are expressed'.[28] Halla-aho, for example, has expressed support for Finland's membership of NATO.[29]

For many active PS members, the party had sold out on its core principles. For the former editor of the party newspaper, Harri Lindell, PS was no longer a Christian social party,[30] while for a veteran activist from the SMP years, Jaana Siukola, the PS in government had neglected important social policy questions such as care for the elderly and support for mental health initiatives.[31] Significantly, 70 per cent of PS supporters currently place themselves to the right on the political spectrum, whereas, at the time of the 2011 and 2015 general elections, they placed themselves at the political centre.[32] Equally, to draw on Soini's earlier analogy, the PS ideologically has had a bazaar-like character. When members of the eighteen-member party executive in the Häme district were asked what the essence of 'true Finnishness' (*perussuomalaisuus*) was, the diversity of the responses was striking: a critical stance on immigration; patriotism; the cause of the less privileged (*pienen ihmisen asia*); nationalism; honesty; incorruptibility; Christian socialism; independence and freedom.[33]

It is important not to jump to hasty conclusions and assume the PS' electoral 'freefall' will continue. In the very nature of a populist party, the PS has depended on a substantial volatile vote to achieve its best results. It was significant that the party won the most votes on the election day itself in April 2015 and ended up three percentage points higher than its performance in the two-week period for advance (postal) balloting. The PS in short has been able to mobilise the floaters, waverers and serial abstainers. Whether the PS will continue to do so under new leadership must remain an open question. However, all things considered, the evidence suggests a core PS support in the region of 9–10 per cent of the active electorate. Significantly, at the 2015 general election, just over half (55 per cent) of PS supporters had voted for the party four years earlier (Borg 2015a: 24, 26).

CONCLUSION: THE 'SO WHAT?' QUESTION

This is the first study to view half a century of Finnish populism as a 'family business party', the first to make the case for viewing the SMP and PS as a single party and the first to seek to analyse the impact of half a century of populism on the party system in the electoral and legislative arenas. But has the existence of an intermittently sizeable populist party contributed to party system change?

In the electoral arena, the persistence and resilience of a populist party – and the periodic surges in its support – have heightened the historic (Agrarian-Liberal-Conservative-Swedish People's Party) fragmentation on the centre-right of Finnish politics and intensified the competition between the non-socialist parties in particular. The existence of a populist party has given voters an extra option and despite volatility in their support – the SMP and PS have been par excellence 'up-and-down' parties – there is evidence of a realignment on the part of a core PS electorate. Moreover, the scale of the PS' support in the last two general elections has meant that the largest party has barely managed to exceed 20 per cent of the active electorate.

The populist party (first the SMP and then the PS) may be said to have mobilised support along the lines of traditional class-based cleavages – small entrepreneurs (including farmers) and industrial workers – but also appealed as a value-based and not simply structure-based party. From a structural standpoint, the SMP and PS have targeted the 'left behind' people, namely those marginalised by societal modernisation – whether the accelerated rural de-population and urbanisation of the 1960s and 1970s or the impact of post-industrialisation in the new millennium. In the first case, families were 'left behind' by the flight of young people from the land, and in the second, workers were 'left behind' by the closure of traditional textile, paper, shipbuilding and steel plants. From a value-based perspective, the SMP and PS have mobilised along a TAN-based cleavage, for example, a nationalist dimension. Put simply, in the 1960s, there was opposition to the management of Finland's *Ostpolitik*; in more recent years, it has been opposition to the management of Finland's *Westpolitik*. Importantly, the PS has politicised a potentially new ethno-centric cleavage, which has pitted the (Finnish) nation against the European 'superstate' and Finnishness – the native language, culture and traditions – against the insidious inroads of an immigrant-accommodating, multi-cultural societal blueprint.

Populist mobilisation has been at the expense of all the older parties (except the minority language-based Swedish People's Party) but particularly the historic 'class parties' – the Centre (1970 and 2011) and Social Democrats (2011 and 2015). However, the mobilisation of the 'left behind' would not have occurred without charismatic leadership – the two Vennamos and Soini. Significantly, following the deepest recession in Finnish history in the early 1990s – and with the SMP on its knees and close to bankruptcy – it was the opposition-based Social Democrats who profited from a volatile protest vote and polled their best post-war result of over 28 per cent.

In the legislative party arena, the SMP evolved from pariah party (1970–1983) to a coalition party (1983–1990) and the PS from a marginal party

(1995–2010) to a mainstream party (2011–2015) and party of government (2015 onwards). Indeed, it might be difficult today to make a persuasive case for PS as a populist party. While in 2011, it was precisely as a populist party that the PS made unprecedented gains, the PS' rise has, if anything, reinforced rather than reduced the 'anything goes' dynamics of coalition-building. Put another way, there has been no fundamental realignment of the legislative party system; rather, the PS has been simply absorbed into the predominant office-seeking culture of the legislative parties and into a government-formation process that has defied conventional spatial logic. In 2011, the PS chose not to enter government when expected to do so; in 2015, it did so having made it clear that was its overriding goal. Briefly stated, while the PS has averaged 18.4 per cent of the vote over the last two general elections (2011 and 2015), it has had at best a minimal impact on the structure of legislative party competition. Only the GAL-based Greens have refused to consider a coalition with PS. On the eve of the accession of a new party leader, the loss of issue identity in government and a perception that the PS in office has had minimal policy impact (not entirely fair) has been reflected in voter desertions and a promise from both main leadership contestants to stage a referendum on Finland's membership of both the Eurozone and the EU itself. To that extent, Brexit has had an impact on PS policy and its search for renewed identity.

All in all, despite the 'ups and downs', it seems legitimate to speak of an institutionalised populist party lineage in Finnish politics marked by persistence and resilience. Equally, our analysis of the Finnish case does little to seriously challenge Mudde's (2014) conclusion that populist radical right parties have not fundamentally challenged the party systems in Western Europe. Indeed, even the case for new cleavage mobilisation must be viewed with caution. In the opinion polls in March 2017, support for the governing PS had fallen over 8 percentage points compared with the April 2015 general election – a reminder of the volatility of much of the populist party vote.[34]

POSTSCRIPT

It would probably take another chapter to do justice to the bizarre sequence of events that followed Jussi Halla-aho's victory in the PS leadership contest in June 2017. In brief, there were three stages. First, there was a government crisis. In addition to Halla-aho the party conference elected anti-immigrant hardliners to all three deputy-chair posts and, in response, the prime minister Juha Sipilä (Centre) and the finance minister, Petteri Orpo (Conservatives), having first met Halla-aho, refused any longer to work with the PS in government. At stage 2 a group of those parliamentarians and ministers on the losing side, including Soini, conspired and orchestrated a split in the PS' parliamentary group and a narrow breakaway majority of 20 rebels formed the 'New Alternative' (*Uusi Vaihtoehto*) just before the prime minister met the president Sauli Niinistö to tender the government's resignation.

At stage 3 the 'government crisis was cancelled' (in Sipilä's words) – digitally! The prime minister had piloted a light aircraft to meet the president at his summer residence in Naantali but on the car journey from Turku airport he received the 'written' confirmation he required of the formation of the new parliamentary group on his mobile phone which carried a photograph of the group's founding document[35] – a curious digital dénouement in a Nokia-renowned country to perhaps the strangest 'government crisis' in Finnish political history. Remarkably, moreover, although barely half the size of the original PS' PPG, the New Alternative nonetheless retained all five of the ministerial portfolios the PS gained after the 2015 general election.

Since its creation the breakaway group has collected (albeit not without some difficulty) the 5,000 signatures necessary to register as a political party under the name of 'The Blue Future' (*Sininen tulevaisuus*). The PS' PPG is 17 strong, but it appears to have retained a core base of support (around 9 per cent), whereas in an October 2017 opinion poll, commissioned by the state broadcasting company YLE, the Blue Future was at a meagre 1.5 per cent.[36] Not surprisingly, perhaps, the rebels have been viewed as turncoats and their perceived deceit attacked not only via social media but on the street too. The MP Pentti Oinonen, a PS member since 2000 but now a defector, reported that he had been confronted in the street by a man who threatened to take him behind the sauna and shoot him!

NOTES

1 Interview with Pekka Vennamo 22 November 2004.

2 The SMP's election campaign in 1970 was a shoestring operation based on word-of-mouth, house-to-house campaigning and Vennamo's populist rhetoric was invaluable. Bertta Vaittinen, the SMP's district secretary in Etelä-Häme, had a tape-recorder with her, and at each port of call, she asked whether she could play some short speeches from Vennamo. She played them in the village square too! Interview with Rainer Lemström 7 August 1992.

3 In the leader's column of the SMP organ *Suomen Uutiset*, Vennamo defined the party's three main tasks as (i) defending the people, (ii) ensuring the will of the people is realised and (iii) telling the people the truth.

4 Väisanen, Pekka 'Puheenjohtaja Vistbacka: Uusi puolue voisi olla ulospääsy SMP:kriisistä' *Helsingin Sanomat*.

5 'Menestyksen salaisuutena pitkäjänteinen työ' *PerusSuomalainen* 14/2008.

6 Männistö, Mika 'Toivo Mäkelän työ jatkuu' *PerusSuomalainen* 19 October 2009.

7 'Perussuomalaiset pyrkivät eduskuntaan köyhien oikeistopuolueena' *Helsingin Sanomat* 13 December 1999.

8 'EU-Suomen virallinen populisti' *Helsingin Sanomat* 19 December 2000.

9 'SMP ei ole suinkaan rasistinen puolue' *Helsingin Sanomat* 2 February 1991.

10 Yle: Ykkösaamu 30 April 2011.

11 Timo Soini, 'Why I don't support Europe's bailouts' *The Wall Street Journal* 9 May 2011.

12 Interview with Timo Soini 23 November 2012.

13 Vento, Heikki, 'Timo Soini on yksinvaltias – johtaa puoluettaan kuin Veikko Vennamo' *Suomen Kuvalehti* 44, 29 October 2015; Nieminen, Martta, 'Ystävällisiä neuvoja perussuomalaisille' *Helsingin Sanomat* 2 November 2015.

14 Called early by president Kekkonen in no small measure with a view to undermining the SMP.

15 Interview with Pekka Vennamo 22 November 2004.

16 Interview with Pekka Vennamo 22 November 2004.

17 'Tämän päivän politiikka näyttää vastenmieliseltä' *Iltalehti* 8 November 2014.

18 'Pirkanmaan perussuomalaiset tukevat Olli Immosta – "Isänmaallisuus ei ole rikos"' *Yle* 27 July 2015.

19 'SMP:n entinen puheenjohtaja vertaa Immosen tekstiä Breivikin manifestin' *Yle kotimaa* 26 July 2015.

20 'Immonen: Turvapaikanhakijoiden liikkumista rajoitettava' *Iltalehti* 3 February 2016.

21 'Saarakkala peruu eronsa ryhmästä' *Helsingin Sanomat* 13 October 2015; 'Saarakkala sai ryhmältä varoituksen' *Helsingin Sanomat* 22 October 2015.

22 'Timo Soini: Minua ei voi painosta eikä uhkailla' *Helsingin Sanomat* 10 October 2015.

23 Waris, Olli 'Rajua kritiikkiä: Rintamakarkuri!' *Iltalehti* 7 October 2015.

24 Savolainen, Jaana, 'Perussuomalainen porilainen' *Helsingin Sanomat* 3 January 2016.

25 'Ovi käy nyt tiuhaan perussuomalaisissa' *Iltalehti* 4 December 2015; 'Perussuomalaiset erottaisi lautakunnan' *Helsingin Sanomat* 21 February 2016.

26 'Kannatusalho piinaa perussuomalaisia' *Iltalehti* 4 March 2016.

27 'Politiikan mannerlaatat siirtyivät: Perussuomalaisten suosio romahti, SDP pomppasi kakkoseksi' *Yle* 8 October 2015.

28 'Jussi Halla-aho lyttäisi nykyisen puoluejohdon' *Helsingin Sanomat* 14 March 2017.

29 'Halla-aho haluaisi Suomen liittyvän Natoon' *Iltalehti* 17 February 2017.

30 'Valtuutettu pahoitteli maahanmuuttokritiikkiä' *Iltalehti* 18 November 2016.

31 'Soinin puolue painuu taas' *Helsingin Sanomat* 21 January 2017.

32 'Perussuomalaisten arvot harpanneet oikealle' *Helsingin Sanomat* 8 November 2016.

33 Jaakko Lyytinen and Tommi Nieminen, 'Nuiva tai tosinuiva' *Helsingin Sanomat* 12 March 2017.

34 'Sdp on nyt selvä ykkönen' *Helsingin Sanomat* 22 January 2016.

35 'Näin kapinallisten perussuomalaisten loikkaus junailtiin' *Helsingin Sanomat* 15 June 2007.

36 'Loikkareita syytettiin poliittisesta valtapelistä' *Helsingin Sanomat* 6 October 2017.

BIBLIOGRAPHY

Arter, D. (1999) 'Finland', in Robert Elgie (ed.) *Semi-presidentialism in Europe*, Oxford: Oxford University Press pp. 48–66.

—— (2010) 'The breakthrough of another West European populist radical right party? The case of the true Finns' *Government and Opposition*, 45(4): 484–504.

—— (2013) 'The "hows", not the "whys" or the "wherefores": The role of intra-party competition in the 2011 breakthrough of the True Finns', *Scandinavian Political Studies*, 36(2): 99–120.

—— (2016) 'When new party X has the 'X factor': On resilient entrepreneurial parties', *Party Politics*, 22(1): 15–26.

Arter, D. and Kestilä-Kekkonen, E. (2014) 'Measuring the extent of party institutionalisation: The case of a Populist Entrepreneur Party', *West European Politics*, 37(5): 932–956.

Bale, T. (2003) 'Cinderella and her ugly sisters: The mainstream and extreme right in Europe's bipolarising party systems', *West European Politics*, 26(3): 67–90.

Bardi, L. and Mair P. (2008) 'The parameters of party systems', *Party Politics*, 14(2): 147–166.

Borg, S. (2012) 'Perussuomalaiset', in Sami Borg (ed.) *Muutosvaalit 2011*, Helsinki: Oikeusministeriö pp. 13–38.

Borg, S. (2015a) 'Tulos, kannatusmuutokset ja äänestyspäätösten taustoja' in Sami Borg, Elina Kestilä-Kekkonen and Jussi Westinen (eds.) *Demokratiaindikaattorit 2015*, Helsinki: Oikeusministeriö pp. 13–38.

Borg, O. (2015b) *Valtio-Oppinut Vallan Kamareissa*, Tallinna: Tallinna-kustannus.

De Lange, S. L. (2012) 'New alliances: Why mainstream parties govern with radical right-ring populist parties', *Political Studies*, 60(4): 899–918.

Ford, R. and Goodwin, M. (2014) *Revolt on the right: Explaining support for the radical right in Britain*, London: Routledge.

Harmel, R. and Svåsand L. (1993) 'Party leadership and party institutionalisation: Three phases of development', *West European Politics*, 16(2): 67–88.

Harmel, R. and Janda, K. (1994) 'An integrated theory of party goals and party change', *Journal of Theoretical Politics*, 6(3): 259–287.

Hokkanen, K. (2002) *Kekkosen Maalaisliitto 1950–1962*, Helsinki: Otava.

Isohookana-Asunmaa, T. (2006) *Virolaisen aika – Maalaisliitosta Keskustapuolue 1963–1981 Maalaisliitto keskustan historia 5*, Porvoo: WSOY.

Kääriäinen, S. (2002) *Sitä Niittää Mitä Kylvää*, Jyväskylä: Gummerus.

Kittilä, U. (1958) 'Välähdyksiä maalaisliitontyön 40-vuotis taipaleelta', in *Maalaisliiton Varsinais-Suomen piirijärjestön 40-vuotisjuhlajulkaisu*, Turku: Maalaisliiton Varsinais-Suomen piiri.

Kriesi, H. (2014) 'The populist challenge', *West European Politics*, 37(2): 361–378.

Laver, M. (1989) 'Party competition and party system change', *Journal of Theoretical Politics*, 1: 301–324.

Lucardie, P. (2000) 'Prophets, purifiers and prolocutors: Towards a theory on the emergence of new parties', *Party Politics*, 6(2): 175–185.

Mair, P. (2006) 'Party system change', in R. Katz and W. Crotty (eds.) *Handbook of Party Politics*, London: Sage pp. 63–73.

——— (2008) 'Electoral volatility and the Dutch Party system: A comparative perspective', *Acta Politica*, 43: 235–253.

Mudde, C. (2007) *Populist radical right parties in Europe*, Cambridge: Cambridge University Press.

——— (2010) 'The populist radical right: A pathological normalcy', *West European Politics*, 33(6): 1167–1186.

——— (2013) 'Three decades of populist radical right parties in Western Europe: So what?', *European Journal of Political Research*, 52: 1–19.

——— (2014) 'Fighting the system? Populist radical right parties and party system change', *Party Politics*, 20(2): 217–226.

Poutiainen, E. (1972) *Melkoisen kovaa leikkiä*, Helsinki: Tammi.

Sartori, G. (1966) 'European political parties: The case of polarized pluralism', in J. LaPalombara and M. Weiner (eds.) *Political parties and political development*, Princeton: Princeton University Press pp. 137–176.

Sartori, G. (1976) *Parties and party systems: A framework for analysis*, Colchester: ECPR Press.

Soini, T. (2008) *Maisterisjätkä*, Helsinki: Tammi.

——— (2014) *Peruspomo*, Helsinki: WSOY.

Sorsa, K. (1974) *Kansanvallan kysymyksiä*, Helsinki: Tammi.

Strøm, K. and Müller, W. C. (1999) 'Political parties and hard choices', in K. Strøm and W. C. Müller (eds.) *Policy, office or votes?*, Cambridge: Cambridge University Press pp. 1–35.

Suhonen, P. (1972) 'Äänestäjien siirtymävirrat', in Pertti Pesonen (ed,) *Protestivaalit nuorisovaalit*, Helsinki-Tampere: Ylioppilastuki pp. 369–395.

Suomi, J. (1996) *Taistelu puolueettomuudesta Urho Kekkonen 1968–1972*, Helsinki: Otava.

——— (2005) *Pysähtyneisyyden vuodet 1981–1986*, Helsinki: Otava.

Sänkiaho, R. (1971) 'A model of the rise of populism and support for the Finnish Rural Party', *Scandinavian Political Studies*, 6: 27–47.

Tikkala, H. (2013) *Sydänkohtausvaalit SMP: N vuoden 1970 vaaliretoriikka ja oululaislehtien suhtautuminen nousevaan populistipuolueeseen*, Oulun yliopisto: Pro-gradu tutkielma.

Vennamo, V. (1987) *Kulissien takana*, Jyväskylä: Gummerus.

——— (1989) *Kekkos-diktatuurin vankina*, Jyväskylä-Helsinki: Gummerus.

Virolainen, J. (1997) 'Suomen keskustan kannatuksen lisääminen uudenmaan ja muiden etelän vaalipiirien suurissa kaupungeissa', in Matti Vanhanen (ed.) *Vihertyvä Uusimaa IV*, Helsinki: Tammi pp. 156–166.

Westinen, J. (2014) 'True Finns: A shock for stability? Testing the persistence of electoral geography in volatile elections', *Scandinavian Political Studies*, 37(2): 123–148.

Westinen, J. (2015) *Cleavages in contemporary Finland*, Åbo: Åbo Akademis förlag.

Wolinetz, S. (2002) 'Beyond the catch-all party approaches to the study of parties and party organisations in contemporary democracies', in J. Linz, J. R. Matero and R. Gunther (eds.) *The future of political parties*, Oxford: Oxford University Press pp. 135–165.

Part III

BIPOLAR AND POST-COMMUNIST PARTY SYSTEMS

Chapter 7

No Longer a Pariah? The Front National and the French Party System

Gilles Ivaldi

INTRODUCTION

The Front National (FN) is one of the oldest populist radical right parties in Europe. It epitomises the nativist and authoritarian mobilisation strategy of the populist radical right (Mudde 2007: 41). The FN was a marginal extreme-right formation outside the core of the French party system until it won 11 per cent in the 1984 European elections. Since then, it has received 9–18 per cent of the vote in most presidential and legislative elections, and it has established itself as major player in the French political system, recently winning a quarter of the vote in the 2014 European elections and the 2015 local elections (*see* table 7.1).

Competing in local, regional, national and European elections, the FN occupies a paradoxical position in the French party system. Although the majoritarian electoral laws used for most national elections usually prevent the FN from winning more than one or two seats in legislative elections, its electoral strength is a problem not only for the right, with which it is in direct competition, but also the left. Mainstream parties have generally refused to ally with the FN, preferring to erect a *cordon sanitaire* around it instead. Reflecting its pariah status, the FN has never shared power in national politics and has rarely shared power in local or regional governments.

However, the FN is strong enough to influence the outcome of national elections. The FN also influences the agenda of French politics and the parties with which it competes. As Meguid (2008) argues, mainstream parties must decide whether to dismiss, accommodate or attack populist challengers. Reflecting their ideological heritage, parties on the left find maintaining the *cordon sanitaire* easier than do their counterparts on the right. In the latter

172 *Chapter 7*

Table 7.1 The FN's National Electoral Results Since 1973

Year	Election	% valid	Year	Election	% valid
1973	Legislative	0.5	1998	Regional	15.0
1974	Presidential	0.7	1999	European	5.7
1978	Legislative	0.8	2002	Presidential	16.9
1979	European	1.3	2002	Presidential[a]	17.8
1981	Presidential	–	2002	Legislative	11.3
1981	Legislative	0.3	2004	Regional	14.7
1984	European	11.0	2004	European	9.8
1986	Legislative	9.6	2007	Presidential	10.4
1986	Regional	9.6	2007	Legislative	4.3
1988	Presidential	14.4	2009	European	6.3
1988	Legislative	9.7	2010	Regional	11.4
1989	European	11.7	2012	Presidential	17.9
1992	Regional	13.7	2012	Legislative	13.6
1993	Legislative	12.4	2014	European	24.9
1994	European	10.5	2015	Departmental[b]	25.2
1995	Presidential	15.0	2015	Regional	27.7
1997	Legislative	14.9			

[a] Second-round runoff.
[b] Local elections with FN presence in nearly all the cantons.

group, individual politicians and factions at different levels of government are tempted to ally with the FN in their battle with the left. Because it usually lacks sufficient support to tip the party balance, the FN has typically been little more than a nuisance for the mainstream right. Nevertheless, some nuisance factors are more important than others. For example, the FN has played an important agenda-setting role. The mainstream right has incorporated some of the FN's positions on immigration, assimilation and law enforcement. The FN has also reinforced the bipolar character of France's multiparty system, which lends support to Mudde's argument that populist radical right parties 'have not been a major factor in party system change in Western Europe' (2014: 223).

Further in the text, we examine the impact of the FN on both its competitors and the party system in which they compete. Therefore, we must consider multiple factors, including France's semi-presidential system, its electoral laws, the party system that they have shaped, and the opportunity structures and incentives that they generate. These factors have produced a clustered multiparty system in which competition takes place not only between but also within party blocs. Both are dominated by sprawling umbrella-like parties – the Socialist Party (Parti Socialiste, PS) on the left and, since 2002, the Union for a Popular Movement (Union pour un Mouvement Populaire, UMP) on the right – that encompass factions and tendencies on both sides of the spectrum.

The Fifth Republic party system emerged in the 1960s and 1970s. Although typically more fluid than many of its counterparts elsewhere in Europe – parties on the left and the right periodically reconfigure themselves – the divide between the left and the right is deeply institutionalised. Each constitutes a separate party subsystem whose shape and composition varies over time.

We begin by examining how the FN has affected the competition for votes during the successive stages of its development in the French party system. We assess the impact that the FN has had on the dimensionality of the political space and consider the strategic responses fashioned by mainstream parties. To do so, we examine policy convergence, campaign narratives and the use of institutional engineering as a means of reducing the influence of the FN. We then observe the dynamics of inter-party competition, focusing on recent strategic shifts under Marine Le Pen and investigating whether the *désenclavement* of the FN will create opportunities for new coalitions and alignments, thereby altering the competition for government. Finally, we consider changes in key parameters of the French party system.

COMPETITION FOR VOTES

The FN's political maturation has not been monotonic. According to Harmel and Svåsand (1993), the development of the French populist radical right can be divided into three stages that are characterised by the electoral performance, organisational complexity and strategic positions that the radical right has assumed.[1]

In the entry phase, the period of identity formation (1984–1989), the FN strove to establish its distinctive mobilising appeal among French voters, politicising and exploiting immigration and law-and-order issues. The latter were embedded in the party's nationalist, authoritarian and populist ideology, which fostered xenophobia and anti-Semitism (Shields 2007). This political launch was followed by a second phase from the 1990s to early 2000s, in which the party consolidated itself organisationally and electorally. The FN stabilised its electoral support and achieved relevance at the sub-national level. It also exhibited greater organisational strength and complexity as well as substantial membership growth (Ivaldi 1998). The third and current stage is the FN's entrenchment within the French party system. Since the mid-2000s, the party has attempted to address crucial issues such as credibility, identity and strategy. Its evolution is consistent with Harmel and Svåsand's (1993) proposition that the final stage of populist party institutionalisation involves establishing credibility and cooperation potential. In 2011, Marine Le Pen succeeded her father as leader of the FN. Occurring after four decades of unlimited rule, her succession supports the assertion that complete integration requires a more pragmatic and 'power-seeking' leader. The FN has been modernising in hopes of shedding its pariah status, while simultaneously preserving its populist radical right potential for voter mobilisation (Ivaldi 2016). Whether it will succeed remains to be seen, but the prospect opens up alternate alliances and coalitions.

Since the mid-1980s, the established parties in France, particularly the moderate right, have adjusted their responses to the FN's political challenges. The moderate right's spatial proximity to the FN makes them more susceptible to competition for voters. A sizeable share of the mainstream right vote began swinging to the populist radical right during the FN's launch (Martin 2000). Parties on the left have also been affected. The mobilisation by the FN of working- and lower-middle-class voters who previously supported the Socialists and the Communists has drained support from leftist parties in France (Gougou and Mayer 2013).

Parties can adapt in different ways to external stimuli generated by the emergence and persistence of new competitors. This adaptation can take the form of changes to parties' policies or emphases, their organisation or their strategy (Harmel and Janda 1994). This section examines the tools employed by mainstream parties to respond to the FN's presence and growth. We examine programmatic and policy moves as well as changes in political style and then turn to institutional strategies to which the established actors have sometimes resorted.

New Dimensions of Conflict

Across Western European party systems, the electoral development of the populist radical right has been associated with the 'niche' mobilisation of a specific set of issues alongside a new 'cultural' dimension (Rydgren 2005). Despite its pariah status, the FN has gained considerable influence over the political agenda by politicising alternate cultural issues. In addition to immigration (Schain 2006), other salient issues include law and order, moral values such as the family and opposition to European integration. Populist radical right voters have been galvanised via three issues: immigration, crime and unemployment (Perrineau 1998). In her longitudinal analysis of FN support, Mayer (2013: 165) shows that high scores on ethnocentrism and authoritarianism have been the primary attitudinal features of the populist radical right's electorate since the late 1980s (2013: 165).

The Comparative Manifesto Project (CMP) data for France can be used to examine the extent to which the FN has played a role in redefining the French policy agenda. CMP data provide party-specific measures of the relative salience of political issues in party platforms over time (Budge et al. 2001). Table 7.2 illustrates changes in the weighted mean party subsystem salience

Table 7.2 Mean Party Subsystem[a] and the FN's Salience in Socio-Economic and Socio-Cultural Issues

	Left[b]		Right[c]		FN	
FN Phase	% Eco.	% Cult.	% Eco.	% Cult.	% Eco.	% Cult.
Pre-FN emergence (1972–1983)	30.8	7.5	41.6	6.4	–	–
Identification (1984–1989)	33.0	9.3	50.2	8.2	14.6	28.5
Consolidation (1990–2002)	31.3	5.5	38.7	10.5	19.2	36.3
Stabilisation (2003–2012)	41.8	6.5	43.8	12.3	33.4	27.6

[a] Weighted by party vote in legislative elections.
[b] Socialists, Communists, Left-Wing Radicals and Greens.
[c] Conservatives, Centrists and Gaullists.

Source: CMP data.

of the socio-economic and socio-cultural policy domains across the main phases of FN development.[2] The data reveal a significant increase in cultural salience in the party subsystem on the right – from 6 per cent in the 1970s to 12 per cent since the early 2000s – which contrasts with the relative stability of the parties on the left (an average 7 per cent) and with the persistence of the FN's distinctive niche status.

Party Positions and Strategies

The way in which the other actors realign themselves on the cultural dimension in response to new questions raised by populist radical challengers is crucial to the electoral fortunes of populist radical right parties and their ability to entrench themselves in the party system. Analysing party competition in France, Meguid (2008) highlights the diverging strategies of the mainstream actors. The right has adopted weak accommodative tactics, co-opting the FN's positions on particular issues. Emphasising their principled opposition to the FN, the Socialists and their allies use strong adversarial strategies. Meguid concludes the following:

> The Socialists' timely and decisive adversarial tactics kept the immigration issue in the limelight and reinforced the niche party's claim to issue ownership, thereby encouraging the further defection of (mostly RPR) anti-immigrant voters to the Front National. (Meguid 2008: 190)

Similarly, Bornschier (2012) identifies the cultural positions of the mainstream left as a crucial factor in explaining the populist radical right's success in France. His findings suggest that the Socialists' adoption of libertarian-universalistic positions has simultaneously increased the salience of the cultural dimension *in toto* and obstructed the mainstream right's efforts to crowd out the radical right (Bornschier 2012: 140).

Findings from a systematic analysis of legislative policymaking since the early 1970s are consistent with studies of parties' competitive positions (Ivaldi 2011). The 'hard evidence' from legislation confirms that the legislative salience of cultural issues has been significantly heightened since the FN's emergence in 1984. The parties of the moderate right have been prompted to take up the policy platform of the populist radical right, but no evidence substantiates the left's use of dismissive strategies in relation to immigration policies. Ideological differences are more striking in terms of law and order and cultural liberalisation. During the 1974–2012 period, right-wing governments advanced twice as many security laws as their left-wing counterparts. By contrast, the periods of left-wing incumbency have been characterised by culturally liberal legislation emphasising equal rights and anti-discrimination policies that counter the populist radical right's exclusionist and illiberal agenda.

We see a different pattern in immigration. Although the French left has maintained more expansive immigrant integration policies since the early 1980s, electoral pressure from the FN has played a role in the Socialists' tightening of immigration control policies after 1984 (Ivaldi 2011). By contrast, the moderate right has consistently put forward restrictive immigration policies since the mid-1970s. Their framework has evolved from 'zero immigration' in the late 1980s to the 'chosen immigration' popularised by Sarkozy in 2007, which represents a more pragmatic approach to labour migration (Marthaler 2008). However, as public debate has shifted from immigration to the integration of foreigners, the moderate right has endorsed the FN's assimilationist preferences. The last two years of Sarkozy's presidency were characterised not only by a shift towards more restrictive integration measures but also by the mainstream right's arrogation of anti-Islam attitudes, a clear attempt to woo voters when the FN was gaining momentum in local elections.

Additionally, mainstream right politicians have repeatedly imitated the FN's xenophobic rhetoric and populist style (Schain 1999), which, at the organisational level, has often been entrusted to hardliners because of their personal or ideological proximity to the populist radical right. The mid-1980s saw the first opportunistic attempts of the UDF/RPR cartel[3] to exploit political themes publicised by the FN. Although toned down in the early stages of Sarkozy's presidency, the political exploitation of xenophobia was re-instilled in his 2010 Grenoble speech that endorsed the FN's longstanding assertion that immigration led to crime.

The FN's electoral stability demonstrates that the mainstream right's accommodative strategies have failed to challenge the populist radical right's ownership of key issues. The 2007 elections marked the principal exception to this trend. The effectiveness of the UMP's tactics to capture substantial FN support depended on changes in party competition. Consistent with Meguid's propositions, a key aspect was the radicalisation of the moderate right on national identity and criminality issues. This radicalisation was combined with a strong anti-establishment appeal that was embodied in Sarkozy's notion of 'rupture'. More important, the 2007 presidential race also saw the attenuation of the Socialists' adversarial strategy, which flowed from Ségolène Royal's shift to the right on the cultural dimension (Dupoirier 2008) and the FN's ideological and behavioural moderation. Le Pen's 2007 presidential campaign was notable for the low salience of the party's traditional ethno-cultural platform, its endorsement of a timid Republican agenda and the claim that it occupied the 'centre-right'. This disorientating tactical re-positioning helped estrange former FN voters. Lastly, the traumatic experience of 2002 incentivised voters to support mainstream candidates.

The issue structure in the 2012 elections returned to earlier patterns of competition on the cultural axis. Amid economic crisis and rising unemployment, memories of the 2002 political tremor gave way to political discontent with the UMP majority. The 2012 elections were characterised by a higher degree of 'cultural polarisation' in the presidential arena because of the increasing level of UMP-FN competition on the right and the PS' return to the libertarian pole of the cultural divide (Evans and Ivaldi 2013). The UMP continued to emulate the 'hard right' national identity strategy, which had been central to Sarkozy's successful 2007 presidential bid. The party pushed a new religious agenda alleging 'communitarian (*communautariste*) pressures' by Muslims while reaffirming France's 'Christian roots'. More important, the 2012 campaign showed Sarkozy's partial yet noticeable endorsement of the FN's differential nativism regarding immigration and social welfare issues. The UMP's adoption of the populist radical right's ethno-pluralist agenda, which was then integrated into the mainstream, continued in the 2012 leadership election: Jean-François Copé adopted the FN's concept of 'anti-white racism' and mimicked Marine Le Pen by demanding the elimination of universal medical assistance for migrants.

In 2012, Sarkozy pushed for an even more restrictive immigration agenda. Reaffirming his opposition to voting rights for foreigners in local elections and a PS plan for 'massive regularisation' of immigrants, Sarkozy proposed a referendum on the repatriation of illegal migrants. He also pledged to cut immigration by half over five years, impose stricter control on family reunions, limit social benefits for legal migrants, and force a revision of the Schengen agreement. During the campaign, the UMP adopted a provisional law reinstating the 'double sentence' that allowed for the deportation of foreign criminals after they served their jail term. Immediately after the first round, the UMP candidate re-emphasised key populist radical right issues while calling for the support of all 'patriotic' voters who were 'concerned with preserving their way of life' (*Le Monde*, 23 April 2012).[4] In relation to law and order, the UMP's zero-tolerance programme included yet another legislative reform for young offenders, the suppression of family allowances for school absentees, the generalisation of lay juries, the extension of the scope for minimum sentencing, life sentences for sexual crimes and a right of appeal for victims and their families during parole proceedings. In the runoff campaign, Sarkozy publicly endorsed Le Pen's proposal to create a 'presumption of self-defence' for police officers in their line of duty. During the 2014 leadership election, Sarkozy reiterated his rightist platform, calling for the abolition of same-sex marriage, an exit from Schengen, the end of medical assistance for migrants and the restoration of minimum sentences, simultaneously stigmatising 'immigration as a major problem which threatens our way of life' (*Le Monde*, 3 November 2014). In March 2015, Sarkozy endorsed FN themes by calling for a ban on Islamic veils in universities and on substitution menus for Muslim children in school canteens (TF1, 17 March 2015).

In 2012, the Socialists returned to their agenda of cultural modernisation, consistent with the left's polarising strategy since the early 1980s. At party and mass levels, this agenda reflected both the Socialists' alliance with the Greens and the changing composition of their electoral support both through the development of a more urban younger educated middle-class clientele and its decreasing appeal with working-class voters. The cultural liberalisation platform of the Socialists included same-sex marriage and adoption and a number of gender equality policy proposals. By contrast, the PS' immigration and security policies demonstrated the persistence of the balanced approach, which has been characteristic of the Socialists since the mid-1980s. Hollande advocated a reduction in the number of legal admissions and immigration quotas for foreign workers but adhered to the left's core ideological integrationist preferences, revealed in his pledge to grant voting rights to foreigners, to establish more transparent criteria for regularisation and to ban the detention of minors in transit zones. Emphasising dissuasion and prevention, Hollande's platform pledged to reinstate community-based policing (*police de proximité*) and to create new Priority Security Zones. It also advocated cancelling mandatory minimum sentences, increasing the number of educational juvenile detention centres and fighting racial profiling in police ID checks.

While successful in polarising the cultural vote, the left confronts new challenges on the socio-economic front. The transformation of the French policy space in the 2012 elections could signal a more fundamental change in the existing patterns of competition. Since the mid-1990s, the FN has fashioned electoral appeals to 'modernisation losers' across sections of the electorate that have been most affected by economic globalisation, fostering political discontent with the EU as well. Mayer (2013) found that negative feelings about the EU constituted the strongest predictor of the FN vote in 2012.

Catering to production and service workers' demands for cultural and social protection, the post-2007 populist radical right's agenda of welfare-chauvinism, economic nationalism and more redistributive egalitarian policies has increased the FN's attractiveness to lower social strata voters (Ivaldi 2015). This increased appeal has accentuated the electoral pressure on left-wing parties, a de-alignment process that might accelerate as disgruntled PS supporters in the lower and most vulnerable classes become increasingly dissatisfied with the socio-economic policies of the Socialist majority. In the context of the economic crisis and rising unemployment in France, the 2014 European election showed strong discontent with the governing Socialists. The FN topped the ballot with 25 per cent of the vote, further consolidating its appeal among blue-collar and lower-salaried voters who had been traditionally attached to left-wing parties.

Institutional Factors and Responses

The ways in which mainstream parties have responded to the electoral success of the populist radical right in France depend on the incentives generated by the institutions of the Fifth Republic. The constraints imposed by France's two-ballot majoritarian electoral formula play a significant role in shaping the behaviours of parties and voters (Elgie 2006). The French single-member, double ballot-runoff system manufactures parliamentary majorities in ways that have been primarily detrimental to newer smaller political competitors. These systemic properties explain the FN's inability to win enough seats to achieve coalition potential or to influence competition through its inclusion in a viable governing coalition (Sartori 1976).

Constitutional engineering is an overlooked dimension of party competition. As Benoit (2007) suggests, parties might have an interest in modifying institutions through electoral reform. The Socialist government's introduction of a proportional system before the 1986 legislative elections has been criticised as an attempt to gain political advantage by weakening the UDF/RPR cartel. Conversely, the Chirac government's restoration of the majoritarian system two years later has been regarded as a move to deprive the FN of its newly acquired power and to re-establish Gaullist domination over the right.

Manipulating the rules of the game has been one of the adaptive strategies that the established parties have used to reduce the impact of new competitors since the mid-1980s. Three facets of constitutional engineering should be mentioned here. The first concerns the changes that the dominant parties have made to the more permissive proportional electoral systems used in regional, municipal and European ballots. In the regional arena, the UMP's 2004 introduction of a new first-past-the-post (FPTP) bonus for the largest party resulted in a substantial increase in disproportionality and a marked decline in the seats won by the FN. The new rule deprived the populist radical right of the coalition potential that it had achieved in 1986 and 1998, when moderate right regional leaders had been forced to enter into coalitions with their FN counterparts.

Second, the most significant example of constitutional engineering was the reduction of the presidential term to five years (*quinquennat*), along with the decision to reverse the electoral calendar so that National Assembly elections took place immediately after the presidential elections. Although the main objective was to prevent a divided government (cohabitation), the constitutional reform also reflected a common interest shared by major parties. It reinforced the psychological effect of *vote utile* – that is, the tendency of voters to vote strategically to avoid wasting votes on parties with little chance of getting seats, particularly populist radical parties with little coalition potential (Dolez and Laurent 2010; Gschwend and Leuffen 2005).

Finally, we should also note the role played by anti-racist legislation. The 1990 Gayssot law that banned Holocaust denial complemented provisions of the 1972 cornerstone legislation. Although anti-racist laws are not solely a reaction to the FN's electoral success, they are regarded as a protection against anti-Semitism and historical revisionism and thus as a part of containment strategies.

COMPETITION FOR GOVERNMENT

A second set of questions concerns the impact of the populist radical right's parties on party competition for government. Shifts in the distribution of the vote can affect the party system by altering the patterns of coalition formation and the competition for government. In this section, we focus on how the interaction of institutions, parties and voters shape the party system, beginning with the FN's role in narrowing available government alternatives.

The FN's Role as Nuisance

The FN has grown sufficiently large to exert blackmailing power. For Sartori (1976: 123), a party can be considered politically relevant when it is able to affect the tactics of party competition. Blackmail potential usually refers to a party's ability to block other actors' attempts to form coalitions, but it can also include a party's ability to threaten other parties with electoral losses. This power of nuisance is defined as instances in which the electoral pressure from the FN significantly altered the balance between the two predominant blocs, thus affecting the final result.

Since the mid-1980s, the influence of the populist radical right has been limited in most national elections, which have been characterised by the predominance of either the left or the moderate right. Three cases of the FN's impact are discernible. The first case occurred during the 1997 legislative election, when the FN exerted blackmail power against the moderate right. A swing of at least half of the far-right vote would have tipped the balance to the right, resulting in victory for the RPR/UDF cartel and the unified control of the French executive. The second case concerns the 2002 presidential election, when the FN's leader and founder, Jean-Marie Le Pen, won 16.9 per cent of the first ballot. This percentage was sufficient to exclude PS leader Lionel Jospin from the second ballot and to force the PS to support incumbent President Jacques Chirac in his bid for re-election. This case stands out as the most pronounced incidence of nuisance vis-à-vis the left.

The last case occurred during the 2012 presidential ballot, when the FN had a significant impact, depriving Nicolas Sarkozy of the votes needed to defeat François Hollande. Le Pen's anti-Sarkozy campaign helped unite left-wing and populist radical right voters behind a common goal – ousting Sarkozy. Hoping to precipitate the conservative right's defeat in the legislative elections, Le Pen concentrated her attacks on Sarkozy. Polls indicated that only half of FN voters supported Sarkozy, thus handing the election to Hollande.

The Structure of Party Competition

Mair (1996) suggests that the structure of party competition distinguishes different party systems. Similarly, Wolinetz (2006) emphasises the need not only to isolate different patterns of party competition but also to consider the presence or absence of clustering, which can affect the system as a whole. In France, mainstream parties not only have clustered with neighbouring parties in permanent and semi-permanent electoral cartels but also have attempted to contain the populist radical right. The FN's relegation to the margins of the political system has been mostly achieved through two strategies: The first and most frequently used strategy is a *cordon sanitaire* with which mainstream parties agreed implicitly or explicitly not to ally or coalesce with the FN. The second and more episodic strategy is a Republican Front (*Front républicain*) consisting of ad hoc local alliances of parties across the spectrum wherever and whenever a populist radical right candidate was likely to win a decisive round. The use of these strategies has varied over time and with the FN's development and parties' positions on the left-right spectrum (*see* table 7.3).

Table 7.3 The Structure of Party Competition during the Main Phases of FN Development, 1972–2012

Phase	Period	FN	Competitive Positions Assumed by Political Actors		
			Right	Left	Republican Front
Pre-FN emergence	1972–1983	Irrelevant[a]	Fragmentation, UDF versus RPR competition	Union of the Left PS, PC govern. 1981	–
Identification	1984–1989	Coalescent,[b] seeking alliances with the right	Accommodation, tactical cooperation with the FN at the local level, UDF/RPR cartel	Exclusion and moral condemnation of the FN, PS versus PC competition	Emergent
Organisation Consolidation	1990–2002	Competitive[b] radicalisation, 'neither left, nor right' third-bloc strategy	Exclusion, moral condemnation, UDF/RPR cartel	Exclusion and moral condemnation of the FN, plural left in 1997 (PS, PC, Greens), fragmentation in 2002	Variable
Stabilisation	2003–2011	Competitive,[b] moderation (2007), policy credibility	Exclusion, party aggregation (UMP)	Exclusion and moral condemnation of the FN, party clustering, PC's decline and radicalisation	Localised
	2012–	Convergent,[b] policy credibility, tactical detoxication	Exclusion but more conciliatory attitude at the local level, party fragmentation (UMP vs. UDI)	Exclusion and moral condemnation of the FN, party fragmentation: FG's strategy of radical autonomy Emancipation of the Greens since April 2014	Unilateral (abandoned by the right, upheld by the left)

[a] Less than 1 per cent of the national vote in legislative and presidential elections.
[b] Dahl (1966).

In France, the clustering of parties on the left and the right reflects the incentives generated by the double ballot system. Parties need tactical electoral pacts with smaller allies to enhance their competitiveness. Cooperation typically involves candidates dropping out between ballots in favour of the strongest first-round candidate. *Désistement républicain* is a well-established practice. Cooperation in the Fifth Republic first occurred on the right in the mid-1960s. The early 1970s saw the formation of the Union of the Left by the Socialists and the Communists (Parti communiste, PC).

Coherent patterns of bloc competition emerged in the 1970s and consolidated in the 1990s and early 2000s. Absorbing elements of the right and the centre, the Gaullists had established a hegemonic position in the 1960s. In the 1970s, Gaullist hegemony ebbed. Under Mitterrand's leadership, the Socialists reorganised and created a presidential party. By the end of the decade, almost all political forces had been absorbed into blocs on the left and on the right, and the dominant one-party system had given way to a 'bipolar quadrille'. This new system featured four parties of nearly equal strength (PC, PS, UDF and RPR) in the electoral and parliamentary arenas. The 1978 elections epitomised this new formation: the effective number of electoral parties (ENEP) was 4.4, and the effective number of parliamentary parties (ENPP) was 3.8.

As table 7.4 demonstrates, party system fractionalisation began to increase between 1990 and 2002. The ENEP averaged 6.8 in presidential and legislative elections. Increased fragmentation reflected not only the consolidation of the Greens (Verts) and the FN but also the entry of new parties that altered both the distribution of the vote and the dimensions through which competition took place. European elections and national debates over EU treaties also provided opportunities for several Eurosceptic splinter groups to join party subsystems on the left and the right. The disintegration of the party system peaked in the 2002 'earthquake' presidential election. Reflecting splits on the left, the persistence of Eurosceptic actors and dissident parties that had formed in the late 1990s, the effective number of first-round candidates rose to 8.8. These candidates included the free-market liberals of Liberal Democracy (Démocratie Libérale, DL) who left the UDF in 1998, the presidential emancipation of the Radical Party of the Left (Parti Radical de Gauche, PRG) and Jean-Pierre Chevènement's Citizens Movement (Mouvement des Citoyens, MDC/MRC) from their traditional socialist allies, and Mégret's National Republican Movement (Mouvement National Républicain, MNR), which split from the FN in 1999. Although it was unusual, the 2002 presidential election had a considerable psychological and political impact on party elites from both ends of the spectrum. For instance, existing cooperative strategies were emphasised. By the late 2000s, party fragmentation had declined to 4.8 relevant parties. This value approximated the effective number of parties

during the FN's launch phase in the 1980s, and it was slightly higher than that
of the pre-FN party system (4.4 between 1972 and 1983 or 4.5 if all national
elections since 1958 are included).

The dynamics of political competition not only vary over time but also
differ within each cluster or bloc. Since the early 1980s, party strategies on
the right have been characterised by a disparity between presidential competition and co-operation in the legislative arena. Despite ideological differences and struggles regarding presidential leadership, relations between the
moderate components of the French right have been closer than those on the
left (Knapp 2004). On the right, organisational responses were set in motion
when the left took power in 1981. These responses continued as a way of
minimising the FN's electoral impact after 1986. The number of first-ballot
contests between the UDF and the RPR dropped from more than two-thirds in
1978 to less than a quarter after the left took power in 1981. Further consolidation took place between 1988 and 2002; parties on the right fielded single
candidates in nine out of ten constituencies.

Loose electoral alliances gave way to organisational mergers in 2002. The
parties realised that the FN could temporarily dislodge the two-bloc polity.
The Gaullist RPR dissolved and formed the UMP with other centre-right parties. In 2007 and 2012, the organisational hegemony of the UMP on the right,
particularly its blackmail potential in legislative elections, gave Sarkozy the
necessary resources to not only bring most of the former UDF parties into his
fold but also deter dissident presidential hopefuls.

On the left, greater variation existed in the patterns of competition between
the dominant PS and its rivals, the Communists and the Greens. Collaborative strategies were key to the Union of the Left after the 1972 *Programme
Commun* between the Socialists and the Communists, which led to the PS/
PC government of 1981. Reflecting competition from both the Greens and the
Communists, the left was subsequently fragmented. In the 1990s, the discussions that included new potential leftist and ecologist partners resulted in a
Socialist-led bloc, the *Gauche Plurielle* ('Plural Left'), which won the 1997
elections. The consolidation of the *Gauche Plurielle* reflected two strategic
shifts: the centripetal repositioning of the Communists under Robert Hue
and the Greens' decision to abandon their credo, 'neither left nor right', by
embracing the left.

Following five years of cohabitation, presidential elections took place in
2002 under the newly introduced *quinquennat*. The PS nominated Lionel
Jospin as their candidate. However, the ruling centre-left coalition had disintegrated, and the fragmentation of the left helped Le Pen advance to the
second ballot. The 2002 election was a powerful catalyst that encouraged
clustering on the left. The lessons learned helped the PS build more stable
clusters in the 2007 and 2012 elections, a strategic imperative central to the

theory of 'concentric circles' expounded by Hollande after 2002. In the lead up to the 2007 presidential election, the PS signed pre-election agreements with leftist radicals from the PRG and with Chevènement's MRC. The Socialists agreed to endorse candidates from minor partners in exchange for their support in the first round of the presidential contest. This agreement was extended to the Greens in 2012.

Although retaining most of the previous features of party competition, the 2012 elections saw a notable increase in polarisation on both ends of the spectrum. On the left, reconfiguration began when the Communists moved towards the anti-liberal sector in the 2005 referendum on the European Constitution. This shift not only moved the Communists further from the PS but also led to their participation in the anti-liberal Left Front (Front de Gauche, FG) with Jean-Luc Mélenchon's Left Party (Parti de gauche, PG) in 2009. The radicalisation of the PCF contrasted both with the cartelisation of the Greens, who became regular partners of the Socialists, and the satellite status that characterised the MRC's and PRG's relationships with the PS.

Shifts were also evident on the right. Although the UMP moved towards the centre in the early years of Sarkozy's presidency, it veered right in 2010. This turn led to the marginalisation and eventual exit of disgruntled liberals and Christian Democrats from the presidential party. Prominent centrist figures, such as former Ministers Jean-Louis Borloo and Hervé Morin, left the UMP, forming the Confederation of the Centres in May 2011 to assemble the centrist components of the moderate right. Moves towards greater autonomy heralded the creation of the Union of Democrats and Independents (Union des démocrates et indépendants, UDI) after the 2012 legislative elections and the formation of an independent parliamentary group with thirty deputies. More important, their separation from the UMP, along with other changes that we have described, produced a pattern of competition resembling that which had existed between Gaullist and non-Gaullist elements before the creation of the UMP in 2002. Since 2014, however, the Centrists in both MODEM and the UDI have returned to political co-operation with the UMP.

From Nuisance to Partner?

A second feature of party competition in France is the *cordon sanitaire* that the left and, to a lesser extent, the right have attempted to maintain vis-à-vis the populist radical right. This feature reflects diverse factors. On the left, a strong anti-fascist legacy shapes the ways in which parties respond to the FN. Parties on the left have led the way in morally condemning and politically ostracising the populist radical right, unambiguously rejecting accommodation in local and national politics. In the PS, the anti-FN stance was reinforced in the 1980s when the PS established links with anti-racist organisations, such as *SOS Racisme*, and endorsed multiculturalism, anti-discrimination policies and the integration of immigrants. The left fostered a range of anti-FN initiatives and campaigns, including SCALP (*Sections carrément anti-Le Pen*) in 1984, *REFLEXes*, *Ras l'Front* (1990), *No Pasaran* (1993) and the *Manifeste contre le Front national* (1990). Political containment culminated in the left's reluctant but unequivocal endorsement of Chirac's candidacy against Le Pen in the 2002 presidential runoff election.

By contrast, the mainstream right has been more ambivalent about how the FN should be treated. The RPR and UDF responses not only have varied over time but also have displayed conflicting views among leaders and divergent national and local opportunity structures. In the highly polarised context that followed the 1981 presidential and legislative elections, which not only brought the PS and the left to power but also resulted in the Communists' inclusion in Mitterrand's government, parties on the right emphasised incorporation. Given the looming threat of 'red fascists', the FN was considered the lesser of two evils. However, anti-Communism was not the only factor; cooperation with the populist radical right was also facilitated by convergence on economic issues and the FN's strategy to open itself up to collaboration with the mainstream right.

An important shift occurred in the early 1990s. The mainstream right abandoned political accommodation and assumed a more competitive posture vis-à-vis the populist radical right. This reflected not only a critical reassessment of the limited benefits of cooperating with their populist radical challenger but also Le Pen's continuing anti-Semitic and revisionist agenda, which made justifying electoral pacts more difficult. In 1990, the RPR/UDF cartel condemned the FN as 'racist and xenophobic', closing the door to future alliances. As a consequence, the FN underwent a process of relational and behavioural radicalisation, endorsing a 'neither left nor right' approach. Ostracism persisted while the populist radical right was consolidating. This core principle of the constitutive act that established the UMP in 2002 has been endorsed by all its leaders and repeatedly reiterated by Sarkozy and other leaders of the UMP. These leaders included Copé, Juppé and Fillon in the 2011 and 2012 elections and Sarkozy, again, after he won the UMP leadership race in November 2014.

The recent electoral rejuvenation of the FN and the more conciliatory posture adopted by Marine Le Pen highlight shortcomings in the moderate right's exclusionary stance. Its determination to not coalesce with the populist radical right has been tested by changes in the party balance. In the 2012 presidential campaign, Sarkozy acknowledged the 'democratic nature' of Marine Le Pen's party and its 'compatibility with Republican values'. This abrupt departure from the right's moral stance under Chirac took the FN one step closer to political legitimacy. In addition, the UMP's November 2012 party congress altered the balance of power within the party. Campaigning on a rightist platform that emulated the populist radical right's nationalist and authoritarian agenda, the Strong Right (Droite Forte) became the largest faction in the membership vote. In September 2013, a senior centrist, former Prime Minister François Fillon, stirred controversy by demanding that his party combat 'sectarianism' and abandon its ostracism of the FN. Although a tactical move, Fillon's tacit support of Le Pen reflected the mainstream right's increasing difficulty in maintaining a clear demarcation with the populist radical right and the need of all UMP primary candidates to consolidate support from the right if they hoped to win the 2016 presidential nomination.

As Mudde (2014: 224) suggests, 'studying sub-national party systems can also be useful for the prediction of possible future scenarios of party interaction' (2014: 224). Regionalised patterns of competition create different political opportunity structures for the moderate right. Growing FN support in the south of France in 2012 reopened a space for tactical pacts at the local level, revealing strong inter-regional variation. This variation increases the likelihood of more autonomous co-operation in the Mediterranean belt in which the FN and the UMP compete for the same electorate. In 2012, the FN reactivated the 'two-tier' competitive strategy that the mégrétistes briefly put in place in the late 1990s. This strategy combined the party's long-established anti-system orientation at the national level with a more conciliatory approach at the local level. The risk of collusion was exemplified in the 2015 regional election campaign, in which former local UMP leaders, such as Olivier Bettati, joined the FN list led by Marion Maréchal-Le Pen in the South.

This process resembles the vertical differentiation in political opportunity structures that fostered tactical deals between the FN and the mainstream right in the 1998 regional elections (Ivaldi 2007). Despite their moral stance at the national level, UDF and RPR leaders were unable to prevent local alliances, confirming the endurance of well-entrenched and self-sufficient local notables who often hold multiple offices and operate independently from national parties. Similar tensions persist between the centre and local party organisations. Although formal alliances did not materialise in the 2012 elections, a number of right-wing hardliners – mostly from the People's Right (*Droite Populaire*) – openly disagreed with their national leaders' uncompromising line and called for collaboration with a 'new' and more 'respectable' FN.

Both the deterioration of the *cordon sanitaire* and the populist radical right's increasing legitimacy have become more perceptible, while an earlier strategy, bringing together a 'Republican Front', has waned. The concept of a unified Republican Front, similar to the major parties' alliance against the

Poujadists in the 1956 elections, was first advanced in 1987. A number of local Gaullist leaders urged the withdrawal of their candidates and/or their support of the left if the threat of FN victories was deemed serious. This strategy was endorsed by the Socialists during the emblematic 1989 Dreux and Marseille legislative by-elections. Increased electoral pressure by the populist radical right also led to the presence of the Republican Front in local elections.

Although efficient electorally, the Republican Front posed problems for mainstream actors. The most important problem concerned the potential 'victimisation' of the FN and the de facto justification of its populist argument that alleged 'collusion' by political elites. As table 7.3 shows, the positions of mainstream parties have varied over time. In the 1997 elections – the peak of the FN's presence in legislative runoffs – both the PS and the RPR/UDF cartel criticised the viability of firewall strategies and refused to withdraw candidates in constituencies under the threat from the FN. Reinvigorated only sporadically in critical elections, the Republican Front was the exception rather than the rule after the mid-1990s. One highly symbolic example was the 2009 municipal by-election in Hénin-Beaumont, a northern city in which the FN was set to take control of its first city council since 1995.

Reflecting the dilemmas posed by the recourse of the Republican Front, the moderate right has adopted a 'neither/nor' strategy in which the UMP maintains its candidates in three-way contests, urging voters to reject both the FN and the left. Despite reservations from the party's moderate sectors, 'neither/nor' strategies were inaugurated in the 2011 cantonal elections and reintroduced in the 2012 legislative elections, even though polls showed increased public support for cooperation on the right. In 2012, the electoral impact of the UMP's new strategic line was visible in the departments of Gard and Vaucluse. The FN won two parliamentary seats in three-way contests with the left and the conservative right. By contrast, the local UMP's decision to perpetuate the Republican Front in Hénin-Beaumont was crucial to the Socialist candidate's defeat of Marine Le Pen in an extremely tight second-round race. The legislative and cantonal by-elections held in 2013 demonstrated the mainstream left's unilateral endorsement of the Republican Front strategy. In three local elections in which the FN defeated them and advanced to the second round, the PS urged its supporters to vote for the UMP. In the 2015 departmental elections, the right's 'neither/nor' strategy produced no less than 273 three-way runoffs with the FN, a substantial increase since 2011. In the 2015 regional elections, the Socialist's decision to withdraw their lists to support Republican candidates helped keep the FN away from regional power in the northern and southern regions.

PARTY SYSTEM IMPACT

One final set of questions concerns the FN's impact on the national party system. According to Knapp and Wright (2006: 259), the French party system is characterised by a balance between forces tending towards multi-polarisation and forces tending towards party system simplification (2006: 259). 'Bipolar multipartyism' describes the variation that exists in party configurations. In the 1970s and 1980s, the party system could be regarded as a bipolar quadrille in which relatively equal pairs of parties squared off against each other. The presence of a strong populist radical right party over the past thirty years has strengthened rather than weakened France's bipolar multipartyism. Cohabitation increased electoral instability. The 'proportionalisation' of voter behaviour and new competitors on both the left and the right weakened the bipolar format, putting pressure on majoritarianism in the second phase of the FN's development. Both the diversification of electoral systems and the proliferation of second-order elections fought under proportional representation opened a more favourable opportunity structure for parties outside the mainstream. This opportunity created political momentum that affected subsequent national elections (Parodi 1997).

Although centrifugal dynamics continue, the current stage, characterised by the hegemony of the UMP and the PS, involves a stabilised two-pole system that takes the form of 'imperfect bi-partyism' (Brouard et al. 2009; Grunberg and Haegel 2007). In 2007, this system showed centripetal tendencies that were heightened by François Bayrou's independent bid from the centre and the decline of protest parties on the fringes, but it became more centrifugal during the 2012 elections. However, it did so without significantly affecting its overall dualism.

To what extent has the French party system become more polarised? According to Sartori, polarised pluralism is defined by 'the enfeeblement of the centre [and] a persistent loss of votes to one of the extreme ends (or both)' (Sartori 1976: 136). Party system polarisation can be conceptualised and measured in various ways. It can be estimated according to the relative strength of actors at the extremes of the party system compared with those at the centre (Pelizzo and Babones 2007). Party manifestos can also provide estimates of party positions on a left-right spectrum, reflecting the degree of ideological differentiation among parties. Both alternatives are considered in table 7.4.

As the data indicate, the levels of polarisation in the French party system have been relatively stable since the early 1970s. Although the relative strength of the parties at the extremes increased in the 1990s and early 2000s (−43.2), in more recent years, polarisation has returned to its pre-FN average

Chapter 7

Table 7.4 The French Party System during the Main Phases of FN Development, 1972–2012

Phase	Period	Eff. Number of Parties: Electoral [Parliament][a]	Aggregate Volatility[b]: Total [Bloc]	Polarisation I Size of the Extreme Vote[c]	Polarisation II Left-Right Dimension[d]
		Party System Indicators			
Pre-FN emergence	1972–1983	4.4 [3.8]	13.9 [6.8]	−56.5	220.9
Identification	1984–1989	4.9 [3.5]	15.2 [5.9]	−56.1	212.5
Organisation Consolidation	1990–2002	6.8 [2.9]	16.7 [7.7]	−43.2	195.2
Stabilisation	2003–2012	4.8 [2.7]	18.5 [5.9]	−55.9	148.8

[a] Effective number of parties in elections and parliament (Laakso and Taagepera 1979), ENEP (electoral) = average of effective number of parties in presidential and legislative elections for each period; ENPP (parliament) = average of effective number of parliamentary parties in the National Assembly for each period.
[b] Total and bloc volatility (Bartolini and Mair 1990: 311–312), average of presidential and legislative elections for each period.
[c] Index of polarisation = [total extremes]-centre (Pelizzo and Babones 2007).
[d] Weighted average party polarisation from the RILE index.

Source: CMP data, author's calculations.

(−55.9 after 2003 and −56.5 from 1972 to 1983). Moreover, the current levels of polarisation are significantly lower than those of the Fourth Republic (Bartolini 1984). Turning to the distribution of parties along the left-right continuum, the weighted index of dispersion obtained from manifesto data shows that the French party system has become less ideologically polarised since the early 1970s, from 220.9 in the period that preceded the FN's electoral breakthrough to 148.8 in its current stage of stabilisation.

Similarly, the rates of aggregate electoral volatility reported in table 7.4 illustrate the stability of mass electoral behaviour and the bipolarity of the party system. Although aggregate electoral volatility increased moderately, from an average of 13.9 per cent for legislative and presidential elections during the pre-FN period to 18.5 per cent during the stabilisation phase, electoral shifts have been localised. Continuously low levels of block volatility (an average of 6 per cent) suggest both the durability of the traditional left-right cleavage and voters' continued propensity to stay within the boundaries of the two blocs that define French politics.

The French case shows the persistence of a moderately 'closed system of competition' that is characterised by wholesale alternation between the blocs on the left and the right, which restricts government access to a limited number of core parties. Cooperative strategies within each of the two mainstream blocs, enhanced by institutional features, maintain the fundamental bipolarity of the national party system (Cole 2003). As table 7.4 demonstrates, party system fragmentation increased from 4.8 electoral parties in the pre-emergence phase to 6.8 electoral parties during the FN consolidation phase in the 1990s. However, since the early 2000s, the system has had an average of 4.8 parties. In the National Assembly, the declining ENPP – nearly 3.8 during the bipolar quadrille in the 1970s and early 1980s but averaging 2.7 from the beginning of the FN stabilisation phase in 2003 – shows that the formal party system is now simpler.

The radicalisation of the mainstream right since 2007 has further decreased the division and attitudinal distance between the core support of both the conservative UMP and the FN. This narrowing gap lends additional support to the long-term stability of this two-bloc pattern (Andersen and Evans 2005). In particular, the repositioning of traditional right-wing voters on immigration and national identity issues has led to the formation of a large ethno-conservative bloc within the electorate that encompasses Gaullist and FN voters (Gougou and Labouret 2013). Fourquet and Gariazzo (2013) show that both the UMP and the FN electorates underwent a marked attitudinal shift in their positions on the cultural axis during the 2012 elections. Moreover, support for electoral pacts between the moderate right and the populist radical right has increased over time in both rightist factions.

CONCLUSION

For many years, the FN has been a political pariah. Despite its successes in elections since the mid-1980s, the French populist radical right has not achieved coalition potential. Instead, FN has been a recurrent but episodic nuisance for both the left and the right. Its current attempts at rapprochement are a departure from its previous posture. Marine Le Pen's leadership has been characterised by more pragmatic and collaborative shifts embedded in the notion of 'de-demonisation'. It is too early to assess the magnitude and durability of this transformation. As suggested by Ivaldi (2016), the current FN attempts to maximise votes by retaining the core features of a populist radical right party, maintaining an anti-establishment profile on issues such as immigration and law enforcement, while toning down its rhetoric to remove suggestions of anti-Semitism and racism. In doing so, the party seeks to maintain a strategic equilibrium, balancing radical postures on some issues with 'normalisation' on others. However, this transformation has consequences: de-demonisation clearly affects the FN's interaction with other actors and the public's perception of the FN as a 'far-right' party.[5]

Despite consolidated electoral returns, the FN has not altered the core bipolarity of the French political system, nor has it changed typical interactions in party competition. In numerical terms, changes have also been limited, and the formal party system has become less complex over time. Analyses of the 2012 elections suggest that the main patterns of party competition that were observable during the preceding phases of the FN's development have become even more pronounced. The conservative right has readjusted its agenda and moved closer to the FN, and it shows strong convergence in policy and voter preferences on cultural issues. As a result, the 2012 party system has seen the consolidation of a more cohesive ethnocentric-authoritarian bloc in French politics, with distinct moderate and radical components represented by the UMP and the FN, respectively.

The French left has preserved its libertarian and culturally progressive agenda. This agenda not only helps the Socialists achieve a high degree of bloc cohesion on the left but also exposes the profound division regarding toying with the FN in the mainstream right. The splitting off of the centrist wing of the UMP in 2011 further revealed the strategic gridlock in which the UMP finds itself. In the 2014 elections, Bayrou's Democratic Movement (Mouvement Démocrate, MODEM) travelled back to the centre-right and joined forces with Borloo's UDI. This reconfiguration could split the right among independent centrist, conservative and populist radical poles in future national elections, although the 2015 local and regional elections showed a strategic rapprochement between the newly formed *Républicains* (the former UMP) and their centrist allies.

The recent past has also witnessed the weakening of the *cordon sanitaire*. The UMP no longer supports the *Front Républicain*, leaving the mainstream left to continue a firewall strategy against the FN, even though many Socialist leaders have expressed doubts about the efficacy of a *Front Républicain* that is limited to the left. Further hesitation is likely while moderates and leaders on the right adjust to this pattern. Little doubt remains that the decision to renounce the Republican Front, increasing the political legitimacy of the FN, will have an impact on competition in a more fragmented right. The local elections of March 2015 have seen the proliferation of three-way runoffs and an increase in the number of seats won by the FN. Regionalised patterns of support for the populist radical right create clearer opportunity structures for cooperation in the south because the sociological, ideological and organisational convergence between the conservative and radical poles of the right is higher there. In Provence-Alpes-Côte d'Azur, the new Republicans/FN makeup of the regional council will provide opportunities for tactical alliances at the local level, putting mainstream containment strategies under greater strain and possibly heralding a substantial reconfiguration of the French right.

The current economic and political context is very propitious for the FN, which is enjoying bright electoral prospects. Polls suggest that Marine Le Pen could reach the second-round runoff in 2017. Should she manage to do so, she will demonstrate that the FN can be a considerable nuisance for what is likely to be a dramatically weakened PS. In 2014, the drop in electoral support for the left in the European elections indicated a three-bloc structure of party competition that was dominated by the FN and the mainstream right. Legislative polls show a significant rise in support for the FN, which has garnered approximately a quarter of the national vote. In the 2015 regional elections, the FN won 27.7 per cent of the vote nationally and made dramatric electoral breakthrough in the North and the South with over 40 per cent.

Despite this favourable context, the systemic impact of the FN continues to be limited by the constraints posed by the dynamics of France's majoritarian system. Competing under the two-ballot electoral formula, the FN can only be a localised nuisance across a relatively small number of constituencies, although the 2015 balance of forces between the left, the right and the FN could potentially give the FN a larger number of seats in the National Assembly in 2017, possibly depriving the mainstream right from a majority.

Finally, other obstacles might force the FN to reconsider its current strategies and postures. The first is the permanence of its core illiberal cultural agenda. The new leadership has managed to fine-tune the party's language, but little evidence shows more substantial changes to its radical ideology beyond this softer 'packaging' (Ivaldi 2016). The persistence of this radical agenda will continue to alienate the moderate sectors of the French electorate. Were the FN to de-radicalise in ways that might convince others, it risks losing its appeal to disenfranchised protest voters. In addition, more orthodox factions would not necessarily stay in the party. A second obstacle is that the FN's shift to the left on the economic dimension increases its ideological distance from the UMP on the state-market axis, making a 'black-blue' coalition less likely. Finally, the FN will have to confront the lack of credibility that its economic platform arouses. Both this platform and its plan to abolish the Euro evoke strong scepticism from the electorate, undermining the claim that the FN is moving from opposition to power.

NOTES

1   We omit the earlier period when the FN was politically irrelevant.

2   The salience of socio-economic issues is calculated by adding up categories per401 to per416 as well as categories per504 to per507. The salience of socio-cultural issues is calculated by adding up issues per601 to per608.

3   The main parties of the French right at the time were the centre-right Union for French Democracy (Union pour la Démocratie Française, UDF) and the Gaullist

Rally for the Republic (Rassemblement pour la République, RPR). A newly merged party, the Union for a Popular Movement (Union pour Mouvement Populaire, UMP), was created by President Jacques Chirac in 2002, which absorbed the RPR and most of the UDF.

4 In addition, Sarkozy's partisans went so far as to claim that 700 mosques across the country had called for a vote in favour of the Socialist candidate.

5 Public opinion data show that levels of acceptability have increased in recent years. In February 2015, 54 per cent of the French said that 'the FN was a threat to democracy' compared with 75 per cent in the mid-1990s (TNS-SOFRES surveys).

BIBLIOGRAPHY

Andersen, R. and Evans, J. (2005) 'The stability of French political space, 1988/2002', *French Politics*, 3(3): 282–301.

Bartolini, S. (1984) 'Institutional constraints and party competition in the French party system', *West European Politics*, 7(4): 103–127.

Bartolini, S. and Mair, P. (1990) *Identity, competition, and electoral availability: The stabilisation of European electorates 1885–1985*, Cambridge: Cambridge University Press.

Benoit, K. (2007) 'Electoral laws as political consequences: Explaining the origins and change of electoral institutions', *Annual Review of Political Science*, 10(1): 363–390.

Bornschier, S. (2012) 'Why a right-wing populist party emerged in France but not in Germany: Cleavages and actors in the formation of a new cultural divide', *European Political Science Review*, 4(1): 121–145.

Brouard, S., Appleton, A. and Mazur, A. (eds.) (2009) *The French Fifth Republic at fifty beyond stereotypes*, Basingstoke: Palgrave Macmillan.

Budge, I., Klingemann, H.-D., Volkens, A. and Bara J. (2001) *Mapping policy preferences: Estimates for parties, electors and governments 1945–1998*, Oxford: Oxford University Press.

Cole, A. (2003) 'Stress, strain and stability in the French party system', in J. A. Evans (ed.) *The French party system*, Manchester: Manchester University Press pp. 11–26.

Dahl, R. A. (1966) 'Patterns of opposition', in R. A. Dahl (ed.) *Political oppositions in Western democracies*, New Haven, CT and London: Yale University Press pp. 332–347.

Dolez, B. and Laurent, A. (2010) 'Strategic voting in a semi-presidential system with a two-ballot electoral system: The 2007 French legislative election, French', *Politics*, 8: 1–20.

Dupoirier, E. (2008) 'Le parti socialiste et la gauche: L'implacable spirale de l'échec', in P. Perrineau (ed.) *Le vote de rupture: Les élections présidentielle et législatives d'Avril–Juin 2007*, Paris: Presses de Sciences-Po pp.145–174.

Elgie, R. (2006) 'France: Stacking the deck', in M. Gallagher and P. Mitchell (eds.) *The politics of electoral systems*, Oxford: Oxford University Press pp. 70–87.

Evans, J. and Ivaldi, G. (2013) *The 2012 French presidential elections: The inevitable alternation*, London: Palgrave Macmillan.

Fourquet, J. and Gariazzo, M. (2013) *FN et UMP: Électorats en Fusion?*, Paris: Fondation Jean Jaurès, Collection Essais.

Gschwend, T. and Leuffen, D. (2005) 'Divided we stand – unified we govern? Cohabitation and regime voting in the 2002 French elections', *British Journal of Political Science*, 35(4): 691–712.

Gougou, F. and Labouret, S. (2013) 'La fin de la tripartition? Les recompositions de la droite et la transformation du système partisan', *Revue Française de Science Politique*, 63(2): 279–302.

Gougou, F. and Mayer, N. (2013) 'The class basis of extreme right voting in France: Generational replacement and the rise of new cultural issues (1984–2007)', in J. Rydgren (ed.) *Class politics and the radical right*, London: Routledge pp. 156–172.

Grunberg, G. and Haegel, F. (2007) *La France vers le bipartisme? La présidentialisation du PS et de l'UMP*, Paris: Presses de Sciences Po.

Harmel, R. and Janda, K. (1994) 'An integrated theory of party goals and party change', *Journal of Theoretical Politics*, 6(3): 259–287.

Harmel, R. and Svåsand, L. (1993) 'Party leadership and party institutionalisation: Three phases of development', *West European Politics*, 16(2): 67–88.

Ivaldi, G. (1998) 'The national front: The making of an authoritarian party', in P. Ignazi and C. Ysmal (eds.) *The organization of political parties in Southern Europe*, Westport, Greenwood: Praeger pp. 43–69.

———— (2007) 'The front national vis-à-vis power in France: Factors of political isolation and performance assessment of the extreme right in municipal office', in D. Pascal and P. Philippe (eds.) *The extreme right parties and power in Europe,* Bruxelles: Editions de l'Université de Bruxelles pp. 167–186.

———— (2011) 'Evaluating the populist challenge: Partisanship and the making of immigration policy in France (1974–2011)', paper prepared for the Mini-Symposium on 'New Right Populist Parties and Their Impact on European Parties and Party Systems', Council for European Studies (CES) Conference, Barcelona, June 2011.

———— (2015) 'Towards the median economic crisis voter? The new leftist economic agenda of the front National in France', *French Politics*, 13(4): 346–369.

———— (2016) 'A new course for the French radical-right? The Front National and "de-demonization"', in T. Akkerman, S. de Lange and M. Rooduijn (eds.) *Radical right-wing populist parties in Western Europe: Into the mainstream?*, London: Routledge.

Knapp, A. (2004) *Parties and the party system in France*, London: Palgrave.

Knapp, A. and Wright, V. (2006) *The government and politics of France*, London: Routledge.

Laakso, M. and Taagepera, R. (1979) 'Effective number of parties: A measure with application to West Europe', *Comparative Political Studies*, 12(1): 3–27.

Mair, P. (1996) 'Party systems and structures of competition', in L. LeDuc, R. G. Niemi and P. Norris (eds.) *Comparing democracies: Elections and voting in global perspective*, Thousand Oaks and London: Sage pp. 83–106.

Marthaler, S. (2008) 'Nicolas Sarkozy and the politics of French immigration policy', *Journal of European Public Policy*, 15(3): 382–397.

Martin, P. (2000) *Comprendre les évolutions électorales la théorie des réalignements revisitée*, Paris: Presses de Sciences Po.

Mayer, N. (2013) 'From Jean-Marie to Marine le Pen: Electoral change on the far right', *Parliamentary Affairs*, 66(1): 160–178.

Meguid, B. (2008) *Competition between unequals: Strategies and electoral fortunes in Western Europe*, Cambridge: Cambridge University Press.

Mudde, C. (2007) *Populist radical right parties in Europe*, Cambridge: Cambridge University Press.

——— (2014) 'Fighting the system? Populist radical right parties and party system change', *Party Politics*, 20(2): 217–226.

Parodi, J. L. (1997) 'Proportionnalisation périodique, cohabitation, atomisation partisane: Un triple défi pour le régime semi-présidentiel de la Cinquième République', *Revue Française de Science Politique*, 47(3–4): 292–312.

Pelizzo, R. and Babones, S. (2007) 'The political economy of polarized pluralism', *Party Politics*, 13(1): 53–67.

Perrineau, P. (1998) *Le Symptôme le Pen: Radiographie des électeurs du Front National*, Paris: Fayard.

Rydgren, J. (2005) 'Is extreme right-wing populism contagious? Explaining the emergence of a new party family', *European Journal of Political Research*, 44(3): 413–437.

Sartori, G. (1976) *Parties and party systems: A framework for analysis*, Cambridge: Cambridge University Press.

Schain, M. A. (1999) 'The National front and the legislative elections of 1997', in M. S. Lewis-Beck (ed.) *How France votes*, New York: Chatham House Publishers pp. 69–86.

——— (2006) 'The extreme-right and immigration policy-making: Measuring direct and indirect effects', *West European Politics*, 29(2): 270–289.

Shields, J. (2007) *The extreme right in France: From Pétain to le Pen*, London and New York: Routledge.

Wolinetz, S. B. (2006) 'Party systems and party system types', in R. Katz and W. Crotty (eds.) *Handbook on political parties*, London: Sage pp. 51–62.

Chapter 8

Italian Populism: Toppling and Re-building the Party System Twice

Bertjan Verbeek, Andrej Zaslove
and Matthijs Rooduijn[1]

When investigating the effect of populism on Italy's political system, putting the party system into the context of Italy's post-war political development is essential. This contextualisation requires distinguishing between the party system in its day-to-day operations and the larger political system in which it operates. In its day-to-day operations, the party system is part of a complicated amalgam of political institutions, which operate in careful shifting balances. This amalgam consists of at least two elements: First is the party system proper (the structure generated by the number of significant political parties). Second, and much less visible, the overarching structure that the constitution and the quasi-constitutional electoral laws generate affects the ways in which the options of actors in the more visible amalgam are limited or enhanced. Observers of Italian politics usually distinguish between the so-called First Republic (1946–1994) and Second Republic (1994–present). Despite the frequency with which electoral laws have been amended since 1992, the Second Republic partly differs because its electoral laws were designed to create a system in which Italian citizens had a clear choice between at least two alternatives. The hope was that creating a system of contestation (Dahl 1971) would liberate Italy from a polarised and 'blocked' party system, which had been the product of a political system in which genuine contestation seemed impossible, as the same parties seemed destined to continue their rule.

In this chapter, we trace the impact of populist forces on the Italian party system. In doing so, we present the following claims: First, populism helped catalyse the collapse of the First Republic. Populism initially emerged with the *Lega Nord* (Northern League, LN). The LN presented itself as an unpolluted alternative to the corrupt political system. We also contend that the

Movimento Cinque Stelle (Five Star Movement, M5S) played a similar role in the 2013 elections. Second, populism played a crucial role in changing the political agenda, particularly in the case of the LN and *Forza Italia* (Go Italy, FI). Third, populism was crucial in transforming the Italian party system, especially the ways in which parties compete for governing power. It contributed to the move from polarised pluralism to a fragmented bipolar party system. The parties in the Second Republic's new party system promoted a Manichean view of politics, as evidenced by the increased polarisation, measured by the ideological distance between the parties in the party system. As noted, the most recent influence of populism emerged with the advent of the M5S in the 2013 elections. The party system was toppled again, forcing the Renzi government (2013–2016) to change the balance of power between the Chamber and the Senate to prevent yet another type of gridlock, different from that of the First Republic, but potentially just as problematic. Fourth, the end of the Cold War was crucial in establishing the context for the end of the First Republic. Because communism was no longer a threat, disgruntled and dissatisfied voters, who had been afraid that the Italian Communist Party (*Partito comunista italiano*, PCI) would grow too large and even take office, were less inclined to continue supporting the Christian Democrats (*Democrazia cristiana*, DC). Finally, the constraints due to the electoral laws of the Second Republic were important in forcing the right-wing populists to give their support to the centre-right, thus contributing to the acceptance of the previously frowned upon radical right.

Further in the chapter, we will trace the impact of populism on Italy's party system by first examining the parameters of the party system, including electoral volatility, the effective number of parties and polarisation. Second, we examine the competition for voters via policies, that is, how parties compete over political issues. Third, we focus on how parties compete for government power. We distinguish among the demise of Italy's First Republic, the transition to the Second Republic, and the institutionalisation of the Second Republic.

POPULISM: ITALIAN STYLE

In this chapter, we refer to populism as defined in the introduction to this volume. Thus, populism is a thin-centred ideology consisting of several crucial components: it centres on the people, clearly distinguishing between the pure people and corrupt elites; it is Manichean, drawing on an antagonistic distinction, that is, between good and evil; and it argues that the voice of the pure people can be represented in what is often referred to as the general will

(Akkerman et al. 2014; Mudde 2004; Mudde and Kaltwasser 2013; Rooduijn 2014). Because populism is a thin-centred ideology, it must attach itself to other ideologies: it is unable to stand on its own (Mudde and Kaltwasser 2013; Stanley 2008). In the case of Italy, we see a variety of populist actors. We categorise the LN in the 1980s and early 1990s as a populist regionalist party; in the late 1990s, it becomes a regionalist and populist radical right party (Albertazzi and McDonnell 2005; Gallagher 1994; Ruzza and Fella 2009; Zaslove 2011). FI is a populist liberal party, fusing the thin-centred populist ideology with support for market liberalisation, lower taxes and less bureaucracy (Ruzza and Fella 2009; Fella and Ruzza 2013; Zaslove 2008). Finally, what began as a populist left-wing libertarian movement (but which has evolved into a political movement that is difficult to define) of Beppe Grillo, the M5S juxtaposes the 'pure' people vis-à-vis the corrupt elites and champions left libertarian values (e.g. environmental protection) and social issues (e.g. support for education) (Tronconi 2015; Verbeek and Zaslove 2016).

THE DEMISE OF THE FIRST REPUBLIC

The birth of the modern Italian political system is usually attributed to the 1946 referendum on the monarchy and the 1948 Constitution. This referendum marked the end of a turbulent period in which Italy, after the civil war between the *Repubblica di Salò* and the resistance ended, attempted to reboot its democracy through a government of national unity (Candeloro 1986; Mammarella 2012). As we will see, the specific institutional choices and the legacy of the fascist past would shape the parameters of the party system under the First Republic (1946–1994).

Meta-Structure

The meta-structure of the Italian party system was defined by two essential components: its electoral system and political culture during the post-war period. The designers of Italy's post-war democracy decided that an almost perfect system of proportional representation (PR) would work in Italy. They were motivated by the fear that another system might produce one dominant party (see further in the chapter). These developments resulted in a proliferation of parliamentary parties (Ginsborg 1989: 130–131). The Italian 1948 constitution allowed for abrogative referenda, which only became effective in the 1970s (Bartolini 1982: 212–213). This instrument, which allowed the repeal of existing laws, would prove important in helping bring about the end of the First Republic (see further in the chapter). Importantly, this arrangement coincided with the emergence of a political culture that effectively denied extreme right-wing and extreme left-wing parties' acceptance as potential governing parties, meaning that both the large Italian Communist Party and the smaller heir to the fascist era, the *Movimento sociale italiano* (Italian Social Movement, MSI), were excluded from the government. This exclusion lasted throughout most of the First Republic, meaning that between 30 and 40 per cent of the Italian electorate voted for a party that had little hope of becoming a governing party (cf. Barnes 1966). The Italian party system at this time consisted of two anti-system parties at the fringes that forced the centrist parties to hold together (Sartori 1976). Given the dominance of the Christian Democrats in the centre, they were able to dominate every single government in the First Republic. This system remained blocked because of the Cold War, which allowed a number of players to discredit the PCI by linking it to Soviet communism. Similarly, Italy's fascist past effectively made identification with the political right a sensitive issue (Pridham 1981: 197).

Populist Forces

During the First Republic, several political forces could be associated with populism. However, for the purposes of this volume, which defines populism in terms of a thin-centred ideology, the main populist force was the LN. Nevertheless, recognising the importance of populism in the immediate post-war era (1943–1948) is vital. Indeed, the foundation of post-war Italy was partly grounded in a debate about the nature of the sovereign people: On the one hand, some believed that the genuine Italian people were represented by the Italian resistance movement, which had fought and defeated Italian fascism and German occupation (1943–1945). For some resistance fighters, this idea was distinctly based on anti-elitism, in the sense that the elites, including the monarchy, had condoned – and even contributed to – the centralised fascist state. The resistance stood for morally impeccable, virtuous democrats (Serneri 1995). A weak political translation of this idea was the short-lived *Partito d'azione*. On the other hand, the early post-war years saw the rise of an anti-party party, the *Uomo Qualunque* (UQ), which rejected the ideal that Italy envisaged through the resistance. It distrusted central government and argued that cleansing Italian society of fascism, as advocated by the mainstream parties, had resulted in the punishment of the common person but had left former fascists in higher places. The movement gained thirty seats in the 1946 national elections and performed reasonably well in the 1946 local elections. However, its lack of a party structure contributed to its demise (Setta 1975; Tarchi 2003). These forerunners of populism are important in understanding the First Republic: united, although in different ways, in their juxtaposition of the people vis-à-vis the political elites, the values embodied by non-communist resistance and the UQ reflect an undercurrent in Italian society that seems to emerge in times of crisis and transition. Despite their successes in the 1945–1948 period, they did not become institutionalised due to internal dissent and the DC's success (cf. Cotta and Verzichelli 2007: 42–43).

Parameters of the Party System

Ironically, the unstable immediate post-war years produced a situation in which the party system remained blocked (Galli 1966; Sartori 1976; Daniels 1999) until the late 1990s. Italy's fascist past made it impossible, even illegal, for political parties to position themselves on the extreme right of the political spectrum. The parties that came closest (the UQ and the MSI) either disappeared quickly (in the case of the UQ) or were treated as political pariahs. On the left, the Cold War enabled other parties to portray the PCI as untrustworthy. In 1947, the grand coalition of the socialists, the communists, the Christian Democrats and the liberals dissolved, effectively exiling the PCI from political office at the national level. By the 1948 elections, the dominant discourse had thus significantly reduced the range of parties eligible to govern (Cotta and Verzichelli 2007: 42–43).

Steadily Increasing Volatility

A remarkable feature of Italian politics in the First Republic was that political parties did not register major changes in electoral support (Agnew 1996), as reflected in Italy's relative lack of electoral volatility for most of the First Republic (*see* figure 8.3). Interestingly, these marginal changes still resulted in changes in the government and in the relative weight of parties within the government (as expressed by governmental positions). In a certain way, this situation was only logical: although the PR electoral system produced a multiparty system, it effectively (because of the exclusion of the alleged anti-system parties on the left and the right) centred on coalitions that were dominated by one large party (the DC) (Cotta and Verzichelli 2007: 36–48). Given the likely continuation of this situation, individual voters tended to stand by regionally or locally based politicians who tended to develop clientelist structures (cf. Kopecký and Scherlis 2008). Anti-system sentiments were expressed through spoiled or blank votes. Voters' dissatisfaction with the PCI's lack of success in playing the game according to the rules would prove fertile ground for the extra-parliamentary movements of the 1960s and 1970s and, eventually, the terrorism of the 1970s and 1980s (cf. Pešta 2014).

The battle between the *Partito socialista italiano* (Italian Socialist Party, PSI) (sometimes combined with the *Partito socialista democratico italiano* [Italian Social Democratic Party, PSDI]) and the PCI for the left-wing vote was a clear exception to this general lack of electoral volatility. The growth of the PCI at the expense of the PSI (and, to a lesser degree, PSDI) in the 1950s indicated that the socialists had an opportunity to strengthen their position vis-à-vis the DC by winning over voters from the PCI. In the 1980s, PSI leader Bettino Craxi made surpassing the PCI and rising to power his explicit goal. Although the *sorpasso* never happened – at its narrowest in 1987, the gap between the two was 12 per cent – Craxi's PSI expanded enough to make the DC nervous and to win him the position of prime minister in 1983 (Pasquino 1986). Interestingly, Craxi has been described as a populist, although this label refers more to his political style: as a party, the PSI always remained a party of the establishment, as it was soon to discover (Urbinati 1998: 124, endnote 29).

However, on another front, a different kind of volatility had begun to emerge: starting in a series of local and regional elections in northern Italy in the late 1980s, different regional movements, known as leagues, or *Leghe*, demonstrated that breaking the dominance of the traditional parties (the DC, the PCI, and the PSI) was possible (cf. Agnew 1995; Gallagher 1994; Natale 1991). The *Lega Lombarda*'s smashing success in the 1990 regional elections in Lombardy (coming in second with 18.9 per cent of the vote)[2] was a watershed moment in Italian politics, indicating that switching political parties, even ideological camps, might actually make sense.

Effective Number of Parties

We must be careful in determining the parties that really mattered in the Italian party system. Although the actual number of parties in the First Republic is relatively high, the exclusion of the MSI and the PCI from the dominant political spectrum essentially reduced the number of parties that could participate in the government to five: the PSI, the PSDI, the Italian Liberal Party (PLI), the Italian Republican Party (PRI) and the DC (Cotta and Verzichelli 2007). If we use the Laakso and Taagepera (1979) measure, the effective number of parties between 1946 and 1992 is just above 4 – ENEP – and just below 4, measured by ENPP (*see* figure 8.1).

Polarisation without Alternation

Determining the degree of polarisation partly depends on how polarisation is measured. Following Sartori (1976), we find that the party system was polarised – with the DC in the centre and the anti-system communist party and the MSI at the poles. Because of the anti-system nature of the latter, the

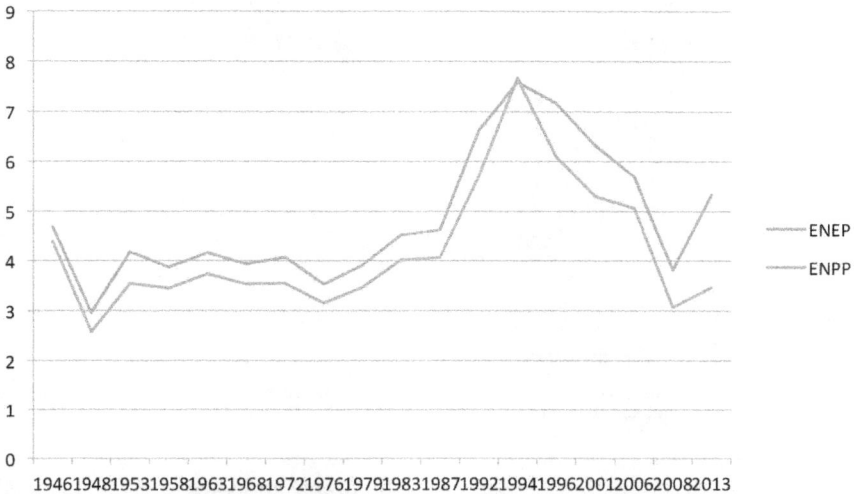

Figure 8.1 Effective Number of Parties (Votes and Seats)

Source: Based on the Laakso and Taagepera (1979) measure of the effective number of parties; http://www.tcd.ie/Political_Science/staff/michael_gallagher/ElSystems/Docts/ElectionIndices.pdf.

system was blocked. This situation could not produce a clear alternation in government. Much has been made of the number of Italian cabinets in the First Republic (52 governments between 1946 and 1991) (Hellman 1992); the DC was the dominant party, mostly alternating between centre-left and centre-right coalitions. The balance of power between the different DC factions (*correnti*) often affected the choice of a coalition partner, seeking to balance a more progressive DC prime minister with more right-wing coalition partners. Therefore, a moderate form of alternation existed, though it never excluded the DC from governing (cf. Mershon 2001). However, according to other polarisation indicators – for instance, the average distance between parties based on the Dalton (2008) measure of polarisation using data from the Comparative Manifesto Project – moderate depolarisation occurred after the mid-1970s, as the PCI moved closer to the political centre and the government, allowing for the DC-PCI alliance in the 1976–1979 *compromesso storico* (*see* figure 8.2).

Competition for Voters

Under the First Republic, Italy's elections were held according to a relatively pure PR system. Although it facilitated a new party's easy entry, electoral upheaval did not occur. The exclusion of the political left and right from the political game contributed to this stability, along with the development of a system of locally and regionally based clientelist politics, which helped fix the

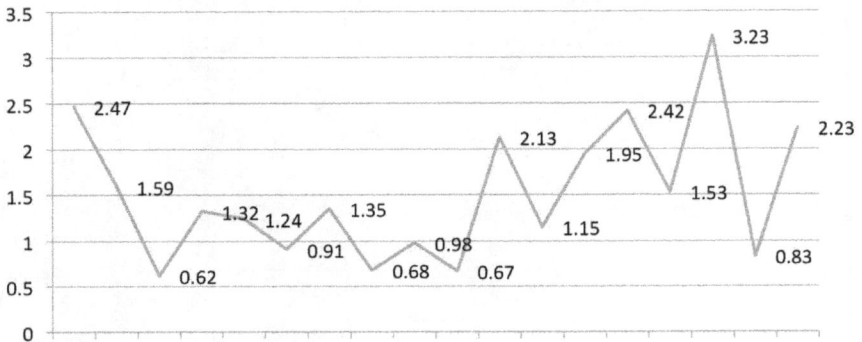

Figure 8.2 Ideological Polarisation

Source: Comparative Manifesto Project Polarisation Index. The measure is based on the Dalton measure (2008). The scale is from 0 to 10: 0 indicates no polarisation, while 10 indicates full polarisation.

political system: politicians ran their own fiefdoms, and various parties gained strength in different areas (the PSDI around Alessandria, the PSI around Milan and in parts of Tuscany and the DC in the Veneto and the south). Therefore, as long as parties served their clients, they did not have to worry about major electoral shifts in national elections, which occurred regularly every four to five years. Nevertheless, they altered the makeup of the coalitions to respond to minor electoral shifts in local and regional elections and sometimes in polls.

Competition for Government

Within this context, Italy increasingly resembled a country in which a limited number of political parties would continue to divide the spoils. In that sense, no traditional kind of competition for government existed; an orderly alternation of coalitions among five political parties was the norm. Unsurprisingly, in those days, Italy was described as a *partitocrazia* rather than a parliamentary democracy (Cotta and Verzichelli 2007). It thus planted the seeds for a transition that would arrive in the early 1990s (Massari 1996: 136), as cracks were beginning to show (see further in the chapter). The growing number of spoiled and blank votes also reflected this growing discontent (Bardi 1996: 354). The political consequences of subsequent events set the stage for the emergence of populist forces and the transition into the so-called Second Republic.

THE TRANSITION (1992–1994)

The LN was able to build its success on the fundamental frustration of the Italian public with the dominant political class and the state as provider of public goods. This frustration originated in many domains: the unprecedented increase in mafia violence with the brutal killing of judges Giovanni Falcone and Paolo Borsellino; outrage over state secrets (the downing of a commercial airplane near Ustica in 1980 and the revelation of Operation Gladio); the numerous political scandals revealed by independent prosecutors, such as Antonio Di Pietro, in their operation *Mani pulite*, which led to the arrest of numerous politicians; and the inability of the Italian economy to adhere to the norms required for the creation of an internal market, as evidenced by the expulsion of the Italian lira from the European Monetary System in 1992. The 1992–1994 period can be characterised as a transitional period in which the Amato (1992–1993) and Ciampi (1993–1994) governments sought to ride out the storm (McCarthy and Pasquino 1993; Newell 2000).

Meta-Structure

The early 1990s witnessed important cracks in the meta-structure of the Italian party system. First, the referendum instrument allowed challengers of the status quo to mobilise dissent and put pressure on the dominant political class to establish different electoral rules. In 1991, the movement led by former Christian Democrat Mario Segni introduced a successful referendum that reduced the number of preferential votes, a system that had become an instrument for clientelism. Two years later, the Radical Party, led by the flamboyant Marco Pannella, presented a successful referendum to abolish PR in Senate elections. The referendum instrument thus proved an effective catalyst of change that forced the existing political class to issue a new electoral law (Donovan 1995). This law was a mixture of PR (one-third) and majoritarian (two-thirds) elements for both the Senate and the Chamber, and it was used in 1994 for the first time. Meanwhile, the dominant political culture changed because of the end of the Cold War and the demise of the Soviet Union. These dramatic events signalled the bankruptcy of communism as a viable ideology. Although these events created huge problems for the PCI, it also robbed the mainstream parties of their historical foe, thus changing the discourse of political antagonism and acting as an impetus for electoral volatility (see further in the chapter). Overall, during the transition period, the blocked Italian system had started opening up (Baldini 2011).

Populist Forces

Populism is integral in explaining the downfall of the First Republic, especially since it was seen as a manner in which to provide a solution to corruption and the aftermath of *Tangentopoli* and *Mani pulite*. The LN's success proved that becoming a relevant new player in the Italian party system was possible. The LN originated from the various regionalist movements that began appearing in the early 1980s, particularly in Veneto, Lombardy and Piedmont, and it had success in local and regional elections (Agnew 1995; Biorcio 1997; Diamanti 1996a; Natale 1991; Zaslove 2011). These regions, with their small- and medium-sized family enterprises, held the secret to Italy's acclaimed economic success in the 1980s, but they felt trapped in a political-administrative system that was run mainly by Christian Democrats, who were perceived to be rent seeking on their success (Cento Bull and Gilbert 2001; Diamanti 1996b, 2003; Locke 1997). After the *Lega Lombarda* started dominating the leagues' movement, the leagues merged into a national party (the LN) in 1991, and its charismatic leader, Umberto Bossi, guided the regionalist movement towards becoming a regionalist-populist party (Biorcio 1997; Diamanti 1996a; Gallagher 1994; Schmidtke 1993). Adopting a Manichean view of the corrupt elites versus the pure people, that is, the hardworking, northern Italians versus southern Italians and their political representatives in Rome, the LN's thin-centred populist ideology was combined with regionalism and support for a free market economy (Biorcio 1997; Zaslove 2011). The LN proved increasingly successful in the 1980s, reaching new heights in the 1990 regional elections and the 1992 national elections; it was one of the major political forces in northern Italy and became a true alternative to the existing parties in the process, challenging the post-war party system (Diamanti 1996a, 2003).

Parameters of the Party System

Around 1992, the dominant forces in Italian politics were increasingly under attack for corruption, but they still expected to prevail. Indeed, discrediting communism after the Cold War had caused the PCI to fall into disarray, seemingly reinforcing the position of the five mainstream parties. In the 1992 elections, the PSI had crept closer to the PCI's successor, the Democratic Party of the Left (*Partito democratico della sinistra*, PDS), while the DC, despite suffering what was considered a rather crushing defeat (losing 5 per cent of the vote), remained the largest party. These parties could not foresee the major changes taking place in the Italian landscape: the end of communism had robbed the mainstream parties of their main adversary; the corruption scandals that involved numerous Christian Democrats, socialists and social democrats were eating away their legitimacy (McCarthy and Pasquino 1993); and the rise of the LN was a warning signal. The political system was slowly changing; voters began voting for new political forces such as the LN, as reflected in the dramatically increasing levels of volatility.

Italian voters increasingly displayed a tendency to change parties. Whereas volatility under the First Republic was generally low, Italian voters became more volatile in the early 1990s (*see* figure 8.3). Perhaps most surprising, the number of Italian voters switching between blocs increased from 1.3 in 1987 to 7.5 in 1992 (Bardi 2007: 720). This increased volatility occurred at the same time as the rise of new parties, of which the populist LN proved the main beneficiary, obtaining 8.6 per cent of the national vote in the Chamber of Deputies in the 1992 elections, making them the fourth largest party in the Chamber of Deputies.[3] According to the Laakso and Taagepera (1979) measure, the effective number of parties hovers around 4.0 under the First Republic (between 1946 and 1992) but increases to around 7.5 (ENEP and ENPP), in 1994 (*see* figure 8.1). As a consequence, the cosy alliance among the five mainstream governing parties was not only under attack from the outside (*Mani pulite*, the investigations into corruption that took place in the early 1990s) but also in the electoral arena. In particular, the rise of populism, which managed to pose as a viable, non-corrupt alternative, contributed to this attack. The results of local, regional and national elections in the early 1990s, leading up to the 1992 and 1994 national elections, suggested that the mainstream ruling parties had been increasingly discredited; the left's attempts to reinvent itself (as the PDS) had not yet taken hold; and the LN's populist message proved appealing to voters who were seeking change. These conditions would set the stage for the launch of FI in 1993, which was rein-forced by the contours of the new electoral laws (see further in the text). With the reduced weight of the anti-system parties, the party system became less blocked and thus less polarised. This is the case not only in Sartorian terms, but also if we examine the polarisation as measured the ideological distance between parties (*see* figure 8.2).

Competition for Voters and for Government

During the 1992–1994 transition period, the competition for voters centred on the de-legitimisation of the traditional political class and, in turn, the entire political system. The growing number of politicians implicated in corruption scandals ensured that parties attempted to present themselves as incorruptible. Not only traditional ruling parties found this task increas-ingly difficult, as epitomised by Bettino Craxi's flight to Tunisia in 1994 after being convicted for corruption, but also the former communists, who were immersed in their own problems of ideological transformation. Thus, the battleground was left to the populist LN, and, less so, to the MSI, which had always had anti-elitist credentials and had started its transformation from a neo-fascist party into a post-fascist right-wing party. Obviously, the desire for a new, untainted political class dominated the public debate. In the wake of the LN's appeal, its agenda of institutional reform started to strike a chord in discussions about the need to reinvent Italian democracy. With the collapse of the government of Giuliano Amato and the success of the referendum movement, the competition for the government was post-poned until the technocratic government of Carlo Azeglio Ciampi (1993–1994), partly due to the referendum, prepared new electoral laws. Once the outlines of the new electoral system became known over the course of 1993, Italian political parties started to anticipate the consequences of the new rules; they were aware of the ire of Italian voters, the former commu-nists' failure to fill the voids and the LN's success. Enter Silvio Berlusconi (McCarthy 1996).

CONSOLIDATING THE PARTY SYSTEM UNDER THE SECOND REPUBLIC (1994–2008)

The technocratic Ciampi government planned the changes that would hope-fully revitalise Italian democracy. These plans were laid in the context of increased instability near Italy's borders (the former Yugoslavia), the increased pressure from Europe to prepare the Italian economy for the Eco-nomic and Monetary Union (EMU), and ongoing domestic political scandals.

Meta-Structure

The meta-structure of the party system changed because of two alterations to the electoral rules of the Second Republic. First, the 1993 law produced a mixture of PR and majoritarian systems. It sought to create a bipolar system, in which alternation would be finally possible between elections. This struc-tural condition forced parties to present themselves in pre-electoral alliances that had a chance of dominating parliament but that had to respect the posi-tion of smaller parties within the coalition. In 2005, a new law introduced a PR system which guaranteed a minimum of 55 per cent of the seats to the largest single party or coalition. The bonus reinforced the importance of organising pre-electoral coalitions that had a chance of winning. The major cultural shift was the disappearance of anti-system parties from the Italian political system. On the right side of the political spectrum, Berlusconi's repeated success since 1994 (see further in the text) made the centre-right a legitimate political alternative and accommodated the transformation of the ostracised MSI into the acceptable centre-right *Alleanza nazionale* (National Alliance, AN) (Ruzza and Schmitke 1996). On the left side, the transformation of the former communist party into a moderate, social democratic party left room for a radical left-wing party that the other parties did not consider an anti-system party: *Rifondazione comunista* (Communist Refoundation, RC) (Bertolino 2004). Consequently, parties under the Second Republic needed to form coalitions that were large enough to win elections. These chances depended partly on the parties on the ideological fringe, which meant that smaller parties within the electoral coalitions reinforced their positions. Italy's party system moved from a centrifugal system to a centripetal system. The new meta-structure prevented the DC from playing its traditional role as centrist broker. Indeed, the DC split into several minor left and right manifestations, often joining the respective and centre-left and centre-right coalitions (cf. Diamanti and Ceccarini 2007: 43–46).

Populist Forces

In the late autumn of 1993, Silvio Berlusconi grasped that the fractures of the First Republic and the rise of the LN offered an opportunity to build a new centre-right political force. Overnight, he founded and built FI, which would prove highly successful in the 1994 elections. Berlusconi relied, in part, on a populist platform, as he juxtaposed the corrupt political class vis-à-vis the honest and hardworking entrepreneur, whom he represented. FI's populism combined with a liberal market ideology, calling for lower taxes and less bureaucracy. Although Berlusconi's populism was similar to that of the LN, he neatly distinguished his brand of populism from the LN's regionalist populism (McCarthy 1996; Verbeek and Zaslove 2016).

Parameters of the Party System

Unsurprisingly, the 1994 elections represented a major break from past elections. The electoral laws and the demise of the parties clearly indicated that Italian voters now had a chance to effectively change allegiances, as reflected in the further increase in electoral volatility, the increase in the effective number of parties and the emerging competition between centre-right and centre-left coalitions. Total volatility increased to 36.7 per cent in 1994 (*see* figure 8.3). The 1994 elections were the most volatile elections to date. Of course, tracing the causes of the high levels of volatility is difficult; however, it very likely emanated from a combination of demand and supply side considerations. Volatility had already increased in the early 1990s, and the supply of new parties, including the populists, created opportunities for voters to switch parties.

Although the 1994 elections were highly volatile, volatility decreased, for the most part, in the 1990s and the 2000s. This decrease resulted from the consolidation of the new party system and, most importantly, the emergence of a fragmented but bipolar party system. Figure 8.3 shows that total volatility decreased to approximately 13.0 per cent in 1996 and to 22.4 per cent in 2001, before decreasing further to approximately 10 per cent in 2006 and in 2008. These developments correspond with a lower number of effective parties (*see* figure 8.1). These figures reflect the institutionalisation of a bipolar Italian party system. Nevertheless, given that neither FI nor the PDS were able to win a majority on their own, they had to rely on and compromise with smaller parties, such as RC (for the PDS) and the LN (for FI) (after 2000) (Albertazzi et al. 2011; Bartolini et al. 2004).

Assessing the polarisation of the party system has become increasingly complex since 1996; depending on how one measures polarisation, two conclusions seem warranted. First, as noted, the demise of the anti-system parties and the advent of the populist parties precipitated the gradual emergence of a bipolar party system, thus indicating a break with what Sartori referred to as polarised pluralism. Second, if we measure polarisation as the ideological difference between political parties (based on Dalton's measure using Comparative Manifesto Project coding of party programs), we see that the Italian party system becomes increasingly polarised. Ironically, the Italian party system thus faces a contradictory situation. Since 1996, party competition has moved towards a bipolar system, while ideological polarisation has increased, reaching its peak in 2006 (*see* figure 8.3).

Competition for Voters

Populism and populist parties profoundly influenced how parties competed for voters during this period. Populist actors – primarily the LN and, to a lesser extent, FI – tabled some of the most important issues and debates. The most important concerns were institutional reform, immigration, market reform and EU integration.

Institutional Reform. The Italian state has undergone profound changes since the early years of the First Republic. Initially, Italy was modelled after a unitary state, with power emanating from Rome (Ziblatt 2006). Although the constitution contained provisions for regional government, they were not enacted until the 1970s (Cotta and Verzichelli 2007). Thus, when the regionalist leagues in the 1980s and the LN in the 1990s demanded the transformation of the Italian state, their demands were considered a challenge to the existing Italian state (Gallagher 1992; Giordano 2000). Throughout the years, the LN had changed its positions regarding institutional reform, at times advocating federalism, while at other times advocating the breakup of the Italian state.

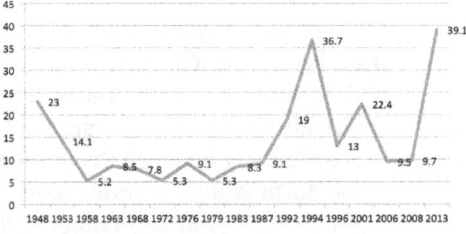

Figure 8.3 Total Volatility (Measured by Percentage)

Source: Total volatility from Chiaramonte and Emanuele (2013: 68).

For example, in the early 1990s, the LN advocated dividing Italy into three macro regions, roughly based on the north, the centre, and the south (Cento Bull and Gilbert 2001; Zaslove 2011). The LN's notion of institutional reform was predicated on economic and cultural considerations. The LN argued that the cultural differences among the regions, particularly between the north and the south, were too pronounced, and that the north would be more economically solvent without the south (Biorcio 1997; Cento Bull and Gilbert 2001; Zaslove 2011). In the period after the 1994 elections, in part, seeking to distinguish itself from FI, the LN advocated outright secession, arguing that the north would benefit from leaving Italy and noting that the north should perhaps join the EU and the EMU as an independent entity. During this period, the party intensified its attempts to forge a so-called *Padanian* identity, while attempting to create parallel institutions, such as its own parliament (Giordano 1999; Cento Bull and Gilbert 2001; Zaslove 2011). Partly because of its declining electoral success and an apparent lack of support for its separatism, the LN moderated its position, moving to advocate devolution. Importantly, this moderation allowed the LN to re-join the centre-right coalition with FI and the AN (Biorcio 2000; Giordano 2003; Zaslove 2011).

The LN's position on institutional reform had tangible implications for the Italian party system. Over time, almost all Italian parties changed their positions regarding the nature of the Italian state, in most cases advocating (or supporting) some form of devolution. For example, in 2001, the centre-left government led by Giuliano Amato, partly to combat the centre-right (especially in the north), introduced what amounted to far-reaching reforms, moving the Italian state in the direction of a federal state (Cento Bull 2001; Keating and Wilson 2010; Zaslove 2011).

Immigration. By the mid-1990s, Italy had changed from a country of emigration to a country of immigration (Einaudi 2007). These transformations caused Italian law regarding migration to change. In 1998, the centre-left passed the so-called Turco-Napolitano law. This was an important attempt to regulate migration and to begin the process of integrating migrants into Italian society, particularly via residence permits (Zincone 2006). Within this context, immigration played an increasingly important role in the LN's discourse. In the process, the party began to oppose not only the influx of migrants but also the policies of the government (Zincone 2006; Andall 2007; Zaslove 2011). The radicalisation of the LN's position regarding immigration had an impact on the party system and eventually on immigration policy. In part, because the LN did not have to contend with a fascist past, as the AN did, the party was able to successfully radicalise the discourse on the centre-right (Andall 2007; Zaslove 2011). The LN joined the centre-right coalition in the 2000s, which had two consequences: First, it influenced its coalition partners' stances on immigration, particularly that of FI. Second, it produced the Bossi-Fini immigration law of 2002. This law was the first in a series of more restrictive immigration laws (Zincone 2006; Andall 2007; Zaslove 2011; Ambrosini 2013).

Market Reform. Market reform has played an important role for both populist parties, FI and the LN. In the early years of the LN's development, it articulated a strong discourse against the state, the bureaucracy and taxation (Giordano 2000; Zaslove 2011). Similar themes were present in FI's discourse: the party called for lower taxes, less bureaucracy and the transformation of social services and pensions through a series of privatisations and a system of coupons so that, for example, hospitals would more resemble private companies (McCarthy 1996: 136). Both parties played an important role in transforming the economic policies of the centre-right. However, in the late 1990s, both parties, but particularly the LN, started to display less consistent positions on economic issues. The LN became increasingly critical of globalisation, and hence supported the protection of the welfare state and domestic producers who were challenged by international competition (Woods 2009; Huysseune 2010; Zaslove 2011). FI coupled its demand for tax cuts with its support of infrastructure projects, particularly in the south. In addition to its success in the north, FI had gained significant support in the south, which explains its support of infrastructure development in the latter (Diamanti and Lello 2005).

European Integration. European integration is another domain in which populism has influenced the Italian party system. Again, an evolution regarding the positions of the different populist parties has occurred. The LN began as a party that supported the EU and the integration process. In fact, throughout the mid-1990s, the LN was pro-EU, seeing the integration process as an institutional structure through which to further its federalism and perhaps its separatist project (Zaslove 2011). However, with the deepening and widening of integration, the party became increasingly Eurosceptical (Conti 2006; Huysseune 2010). Although the LN does not reject European integration outright, it has undoubtedly become increasingly sceptical of the integration process, arguing that integration centralises power in Brussels. As one of the founding EU countries, Italy has always been a pro-EU country (Verbeek and Zaslove 2015). However, the LN's evolving position is mirrored in the other parties; since the early 2000s, many Italian parties have become increasingly wary of European integration, as is the case with FI. Partly influenced by its coalition with the LN, FI has become critical of European integration. For example, in 2002, Berlusconi was not overly enthusiastic about the introduction of the Euro, nor was he supportive of other initiatives, such as Airbus. However, when push came to shove, the Italian government under Berlusconi's leadership did support landmark developments, such as the EU's Constitutional Treaty (Zaslove 2011; Verbeek and Zaslove 2015).

Competition for Government

The emergence of populism within Italy coincides with the consolidation of the Italian party system in the Second Republic. As we saw earlier in the chapter, volatility decreases. More importantly, for the first time in Italy's democratic history, alternation is occurring between the left and the right. Based on Sartori's notion of party competition (1976), Italy has moved from centrifugal competition to centripetal competition and from a polarised pluralist system to a fragmented bipolar system (cf. Bartolini et al. 2004). The party system clearly remains fragmented, that is, the number of parties remains high. However, because the anti-system parties have disappeared and a new voting system has emerged, alternation now exists between two coalitions. We refer to this system as a fragmented bipolar system (Verbeek and Zaslove 2015).

The rise of populism has influenced this process. First, the most important party on the centre-right is FI. FI became the focal point of the centre-right, that is, the key party around which the other centre-right parties organised (Diamanti and Lello 2005). In addition, the LN, during this period, became an important FI ally, especially in the north. Although the LN's electoral support declined to approximately 5 per cent, it remained an important party within its northern strongholds. As a result, its pre-electoral coalitions with the centre-right parties became important to its political survival and influence and, in turn, the centre-right coalition's chances (cf. Bartolini et al. 2004; Biorcio 2000). The centre-right coalition was partly held together by its opposition to the left, which often resembled a Manichean division between the left and the right. Interestingly, despite the end of the Cold War and the conversion of the PCI into a social democratic party, Berlusconi was able to continue using anti-communist tropes (Allum 2011; Fella and Ruzza 2013). Importantly, populist parties, by forming the backbone of the centre-right governments in this era, became part and parcel of the new system. Ironically, they thus became part of the establishment, thus setting the stage for the next populist wave.

(DE)-CONSOLIDATING THE SECOND REPUBLIC
(2008–PRESENT)

The experience of the Second Republic with alternation between centre-right (1994–1995; 2001–2006; 2008–2011 [until the technical government of Mario Monti]) and centre-left coalition governments (1996–2001; 2006–2008) proved that political contestation in Italy is possible after all. However, at the meta level, this situation effectively turned both alliances into established elites, which created an opportunity for a new populist movement to present itself as a viable alternative: the M5S of Beppe Grillo. These events would challenge the party system established under the Second Republic, especially after the results of the 2013 elections (Verbeek and Zaslove 2016).

Meta-Structure

Ironically, instead of solving the problem, populist parties contributed to the growing disillusionment with the political class. Large segments of the population, particularly younger voters, increasingly did not feel represented by mainstream political parties. On the centre-right, the scandals surrounding Berlusconi – and later on the LN – discredited the former populist champions of anti-elitism (Fella and Ruzza 2013); the internal divisions within the centre-left made it appear powerless against Berlusconi. The tendency to portray the political battlefield as a battle of good versus evil, which was effectively reduced to Berlusconi versus the left-coalition, seemed to no longer allow for alternative political actors. However, an increasing number of voters believed that the former heroes of the people now resembled the traditional political class that seemed interested in gaining power for its own interests, often referred to as the rise of the *anti-politica*. These perceptions provided fertile ground for Grillo's movement (Bordignon and Ceccarini 2013).

Populist Forces

In the new millennium, founded by the comedian Beppe Grillo, the M5S emerged as a new populist force. Grillo had been critical of the governing parties and the political class for some time, using them as material for his comedy shows. In the 2000s, Grillo created his own political movement, creating a blog site in 2005 and an official political party in 2009 (Biorcio and Natale 2013; Bordignon and Ceccarini 2013). Combining populism with the active use of the internet and a series of high-profile political gatherings, Grillo's party emerged as the largest single political party in the 2013 elections (D'Alimonte 2013). In another context, we have referred to this process as mutating populism (Verbeek and Zaslove 2016), by which we mean that, in the Italian situation, populism often reacts to populism; in this case, Grillo began to build his movement in opposition to the existing parties, generally the established populist parties, that is, FI and the LN.

Parameters of the Party System

As in the two previous periods of transition (post–Second World World and in the early 1990s), the parameters of the party system were affected, most clearly in terms of volatility: the 2013 elections were the most volatile ever at 39.1 per cent, while the effective number of parties increased, although not dramatically. This limited increase partly resulted from a political landscape that was dominated by three large parties: the M5S, the newly formed *Partito Democratico* (Democratic Party, PD) and the *Popolo della Libertà* (People of Freedom, PDL). However, we also witness inter-bloc volatility. For example, research demonstrates that M5S support comes from voters from the left and the right: De Sio and Paparo estimate that 24 per cent had voted for the PD, 31 per cent had voted for the PDL, and 10 per cent had voted for the LN (De Sio and Paparo 2014: 132). They estimate that 40 per cent of M5S voters had previously voted for the centre-left, while some 45 per cent had supported the centre-right (De Sio and Paparo 2014: 131–132).[4]

Competition for Voters and for Government

After a period of austerity under the Monti technical government (2011–2013) (Di Virgilio and Giannetti 2014), unsurprisingly, the role of the EU and economic policy were the issues that dominated the 2013 election campaign (Di Virgilio et al. 2015). Partly because of its ability to exploit these issues, the M5S became a key player in the 2013 elections. Using this newly found influence, it began to restructure party competition. A study of the election campaign (using expert surveys) demonstrates that, unsurprisingly, the parties on the left (including M5S) were very similar when it comes to socio-economic issues. However, if we consider the EU dimension, we find that the PD was pro-Europe; the M5S opposed EU integration; and FI sat somewhere in the middle (Di Virgilio et al. 2015). Importantly, with the advent of the M5S, parties now compete over issues that cover numerous dimensions instead of a neat left-right division: consequently, the party system has no core, that is, no party can act as a coalitional linchpin or an axis through which these issues can be channelled (Di Virgilio et al. 2015). M5S' challenge to the left-right axis is partly responsible for this coreless party system, which has affected coalition and government formation.

The M5S' influence can also be observed in the changing nature of the competition for the government. Grillo's party was the single largest party in the Chamber of Deputies, although it did not belong to the largest coalition. Still, M5S was large enough to act as a spoiler. Given that Italy has a perfect bicameral system, the Senate created an additional complication, partly due to the 2005 electoral law that provided different electoral systems for the Senate and the Chamber of Deputies. The result was a stalemate; in other words, neither the left nor the right could form a government on its own, which was further exacerbated by the M5S' refusal to form an alliance with either the left or the right. As such, the bipolar nature of the party system under the Second Republic was challenged: achieving left-right alternation became more difficult, effectively forcing previous antagonists to strike a deal to form a government. Initially, Gianni Letta and then Matteo Renzi negotiated what amounts to a grand coalition between the centre-left and centre-right.

CONCLUSION: POPULISM AND THE ITALIAN PARTY SYSTEM

In terms of the research question that guides this volume, populism has clearly had far-reaching effects on the Italian party system. Italian populism has twice catalysed the transformation of the Italian political system: First, in the late 1980s and early 1990s, the LN's populism gained credibility as a viable alternative in a fixed political landscape, which eventually contributed to the creation of a bipolar party system; later, the M5S' populism reflected the extent to which the populism of FI and the LN had been institutionalised into mainstream Italian parties, allowing the M5S to cast itself as a true alternative and, in turn, shake the bipolar nature of the party system of the Second Republic. Second, populist parties can fulfil several functions: they can serve to topple the system, that is, as a catalyst for the transformation of party systems. However, they are not limited to this destructive function: in the cases of both FI and the LN, we see that populists are able to govern and that they can even become institutionalised. Third, the influence of populism on party systems can take various forms. Mobilisation seems to be the key: populists can serve to facilitate volatility. Finally, moving beyond the thin-centred ideology of populism, the attached ideology that a populist party adopts may also have implications for party system change, particularly changing policy positions which this volume refers to as the competition for voters. In the case of Italy, populist parties attached to regionalist, radical right, liberal and, for a short period, left-libertarian ideologies have influenced the position of other parties on issues such as immigration, European integration, institutional reform and protection of the welfare state and of Italian domestic producers.

The present chapter offers some interesting insights into populism in general. First, populism can be both functional and dysfunctional to a democracy. The debate surrounding populism often suggests that populist parties are distant from, or even a threat to, liberal democracy. However, the LN's role in the 1980s and early 1990s demonstrates that populist parties can galvanise democratic opposition to a blocked, gridlocked and corrupt system that is dominated by one party, as it helped topple the First Republic and usher in the Second Republic. The jury is still out on the M5S' role in transforming the Italian party system anew. Second, as described earlier in the chapter, populist parties can be integrated in the political system. Through their governing coalitions, FI and the LN proved that populist parties could be accepted governing parties. Third, the Italian context suggests that several viable populist parties may be accommodated within a party system. The thin-centred ideology of populist parties allows them to carve out specific niches and to respond to one another. Finally, the transformations of the Italian party system since the late 1980s cannot be understood without considered international changes, particularly the end of the Cold War. The Cold War contributed to the stalemate that governed the First Republic by excluding the so-called anti-system parties. The end of communism, robbing the DC of its traditional opponent and wreaking havoc in the centre-left, created a political space for new parties and legitimised former anti-system parties, such as the MSI/AN, thus changing the ground rules of Italian politics.

NOTES

1   We would like to thank Davide Vittori (LUISS Guido Carli) and Stephen Hellman (York University) for their valuable suggestions.
2   The Ministry of the Interior (*see* http://elezionistorico.interno.it/).
3   The Ministry of the Interior (*see* http://elezionistorico.interno.it/).
4   These estimates are based on aggregate electoral data, using the Goodman method (*see* De Sio and Paparo 2014).

BIBLIOGRAPHY

Agnew, J. (1995) 'The rhetoric of regionalism: The Northern League in Italian politics, 1983–94', *Transactions of the Institute of British Geographers*, 20(2): 156–172.
———— (1996) 'Mapping politics: How context counts in electoral geography', *Political Geography*, 15(2): 129–146.
Agnew, J. A. (2002) *Place and politics in modern Italy*, Chicago, IL: University of Chicago Press.
Akkerman, A., Mudde, C. and Zaslove, A. (2013) 'How populist are the people? Measuring populist attitudes in voters', *Comparative Political Studies*, 47(9): 1324–1353.
Albertazzi, D. and McDonnell, D. (2005) 'The Lega Nord in the second Berlusconi government: In a league of its own', *West European Politics*, 28(5): 952–972.
Albertazzi, D., McDonnell, D. and Newell, J. L. (2011) 'Di lotta e di governo: The Lega Nord and Rifondazione Comunista in office', *Party Politics*, 17(4): 471–487.
Allum, F. (2011) 'Silvio Berlusconi and his "toxic" touch', *Representation*, 47(3): 281–294.
Ambrosini, M. (2013) 'Immigration in Italy: Between economic acceptance and political rejection', *Journal of International Migration and Integration*, 14(1): 175–194.

Andall, J. (2007) 'Immigration and the Italian left democrats in government (1996–2001)', *Patterns of Prejudice*, 41(2): 131–153.

Baldini, G. (2011) 'The different trajectories of Italian electoral reforms', *West European Politics*, 34(3): 644–663.

Bardi, L. (1996) 'Anti-party sentiment and party system change in Italy', *European Journal of Political Research*, 29(3): 345–363.

Bardi, L. (2007). 'Electoral change and its impact on the party system in Italy', *West European Politics*, 30(4): 711–732.

Barnes, S. H. (1966) 'Italy: Oppositions on left, right, and center', in R. A. Dahl (ed.) *Political oppositions in Western democracies*, New Haven, CT, and London: Yale University Press pp. 303–331.

Bartolini, S. (1982) 'The politics of institutional reform in Italy', *West European Politics*, 5(3): 203–221.

Bartolini, S., Chiaramonte, A. and D'Alimonte, R. (2004) 'The Italian party system between parties and coalitions', *West European Politics*, 27(1): 1–19.

Bertolino, S. (2004) *Rifondazione Comunista: Storia e organizzazione*, Bologna: Il Mulino.

Biorcio, R. (1997) *La Padania promessa*, Milan: Saggiatore.

—— (2000) 'Bossi – Berlusconi, la nuova alleanza', *Il Mulino*, 49(2): 253–264.

Biorcio, R. and Natale, P. (2013) *Politica a 5 stelle: Idee, storia e strategie del movimento di Grillo*, Milan: Feltrinelli Editore.

Bordignon, F. and Ceccarini, L. (2013) 'Five stars and a cricket: Beppe Grillo shakes Italian politics', *South European Society and Politics*, 18(4): 427–449.

Candeloro, G. (1986) *Storia dell'Italia moderna*, vol. 11, *La fondazione della repubblica e la ricostruzione. Considerazioni finali*, Milan: Feltrinelli.

Cento Bull, A. (2001) 'Towards a federal state? Competing proposals for constitutional revision', *Italian Politics*, 17(1): 185–202.

Cento Bull, A. and Gilbert, M. (2001) *The Lega Nord and the northern question in Italian politics*, Basingstoke and New York: Palgrave.

Chiaramonte, A. and Emanuele, V. (2013) 'Volatile and tripolar: The new Italian party system', in L. De Sio, V. Emanuele, N. Maggini and A. Paparo (eds.) *The Italian general election of 2013: A dangerous stalemate?*, Rome: Centro Italiano Studi Elettorali pp. 63–68.

—— (2014) 'Bipolarismo addio? Il sistema partitico tra cambiamento e de-istituzionalizzazione', in A. Chiaramonte and L. De Sio (eds.) *Terremoto elettorale: Le elezioni politiche del 2013*, Bologna: Il Mulino pp. 233–262.

Conti, N. (2006). 'Party conflict over European integration in Italy: A new dimension of party competition?', *Journal of Southern Europe and the Balkans*, 8(2): 217–233.

Cotta, M. and Verzichelli, L. (2007) *Political institutions in Italy*, Oxford: Oxford University Press.

D'Alimonte, R. (2013) 'The Italian elections of February 2013: The end of the second republic?', *Contemporary Italian Politics*, 5(2): 113–129.

Dahl, R. A. (1971) *Polyarchy: Participation and opposition*, New Haven, CT: Yale University Press.

Dalton, R. J. (2008) 'The quantity and the quality of party systems party system polarization, its measurement, and its consequences', *Comparative Political Studies*, 41(7): 899–920.

Daniels, P. (1999) 'Italy: Rupture and regeneration?', in D. Broughton and M. Donovan (eds.) *Changing party systems in Western Europe*, London and New York: Pinter pp. 72–95.

De Sio, L. and Paparo, A. (2014) 'Elettori alla deriva? I flussi di voto tra 2008 e 2013', in A. Chiaramonte and L. De Sio (eds.) *Terremoto elettorale: Le elezioni politiche del 2013*, Bologna: Il Mulino pp. 129–152.

Di Virgilio, A. and Giannetti, D. (2014) 'The general election in Italy, February 2013', *Electoral Studies*, 34: 369–372.

Di Virgilio, A., Giannetti, D., Pedrazzani, A. and Pinto, L. (2015) 'Party competition in the 2013 Italian elections: Evidence from an expert survey', *Government and Opposition*, 50(1): 65–89.

Diamanti, I. (1996a) 'The Northern League: From regional party to party of government', in S. Gundle and S. Parker (eds.) *The new Italian Republic: From the fall of the Berlin Wall to Berlusconi*, London and New York: Routledge pp. 113–129.

—— (1996b) *Il male del Nord: Lega, localismo, secessione*, vol. 33, Roma: Donzelli Editore.

—— (2003) *Mappe dell'Italia politica: Bianco, rosso, verde, azzurro . . . e tricolore*, Bologna: Il Mulino.

Diamanti, I. and Ceccarini, L. (2007) 'Catholics and politics after the Christian Democrats: The influential minority', *Journal of Modern Italian Studies*, 12(1): 37–59.

Diamanti, I. and Lello, E. (2005) 'The Casa delle Libertà: A house of cards?', *Modern Italy*, 10(1): 9–35.

Donovan, M. (1995) 'The referendum and the transformation of the party system', *Modern Italy*, 1(1): 53–69.

Einaudi, L. (2007) *Le politiche dell'immigrazione in Italia dal unità a oggi*, Bari: Laterza.

Fella, S. and Ruzza, C. (2013) 'Populism and the fall of the centre-right in Italy: The end of the Berlusconi model or a new beginning?', *Journal of Contemporary European Studies*, 21(1): 38–52.

Foot, J. M. (1996) 'The "left opposition" and the crisis: Rifondazione Comunista and La Rete', in S. Gundle and S. Parker (eds.) *The new Italian Republic: From the fall of the Berlin Wall to Berlusconi*, London and New York: Routledge pp. 173–188.

Gallagher, T. (1992) 'Rome at bay: The challenge of the Northern League to the Italian state', *Government and Opposition*, 27(4): 470–485.

—— (1994) 'The regional dimension in Italy's political upheaval: Role of the Northern League 1984–1993', *Parliamentary Affairs*, 47(3): 456–469.

Galli, G. (1966) *Il bipartitismo imperfetto: Comunisti e democristiani in Italia*, Bologna: Il Mulino.

Ginsborg, P. (1989) *Storia d'Italia da dopoguerra a oggi. Società e politica 1943–1988*, Turin: Einaudi.

Giordano, B. (1999) 'A place called Padania? The Lega Nord and the political representation of northern Italy', *European Urban and Regional Studies*, 6(3): 215–230.

———— (2000) 'Italian regionalism or "Padanian" nationalism: The political project of the Lega Nord in Italian politics', *Political Geography*, 19(4): 445–471.

———— (2003) 'The continuing transformation of Italian politics and the contradictory fortunes of the Lega Nord', *Journal of Modern Italian Studies*, 8(2): 216–230.

Hellman, S. (1992) 'Italy', in M. Kesselman and J. Krieger (eds.) *European politics in transition*, Lexington, MA: D. C. Heath pp. 327–423.

Huysseune, M. (2010) 'A Eurosceptic vision in a europhile country: The case of the Lega Nord', *Modern Italy*, 15(1): 63–75.

Kopecky, P. and Scherlis, G. (2008) 'Party patronage in contemporary Europe', *European Review*, 16(3): 355–371.

Laakso, M. and Taagepera, R. (1979) '"Effective" number of parties: A measure with application to West Europe', *Comparative Political Studies*, 12(1): 3–27.

Locke, R. M. (1997) *Remaking the Italian economy*, Ithaca, NY: Cornell University Press.

Mammarella, G. (2012) *L'Italia di oggi: Storia e cronaca di un Ventennio 1992–2012*, Bologna: Il Mulino.

Massari, O. (1996) 'Italy's postwar transition in contemporary perspective', in G. Pridham (ed.) *Stabilising fragile democracies: Comparing new party systems in Southern and Eastern Europe*, London and New York: Routledge pp. 126–145.

McCarthy, P. (1996) 'Forza Italia: The new politics and old values of a changing Italy', in S. Gundle and S. Parker (eds.) *The new Italian Republic: From the fall of the Berlin Wall to Berlusconi*, London and New York: Routledge pp. 130–146.

Mershon, C. (2001) 'Party factions and coalition government: Portfolio allocation in Italian Christian democracy', *Electoral Studies*, 20(4): 555–580.

Mudde, C. (2004) 'The populist zeitgeist', *Government and Opposition*, 39(4): 542–563.

Mudde, C. and Kaltwasser, C. R. (2013) 'Exclusionary vs. inclusionary populism: Comparing contemporary Europe and Latin America', *Government and Opposition*, 48(2): 147–174.

Natale, P. (1991) 'Lega Lombarda e insediamento territoriale: Un'analisi ecologica', in R. Mannheimer (ed.) *La Lega Lombarda*, Milan: Feltrinelli pp. 83–121.

Newell, J. L. (2000) *Parties and democracy in Italy*, Dartmouth: Dartmouth Publishing.

Pasquino, G. (1986) 'Modernity and reforms: The PSI between political entrepreneurs and gamblers', *West European Politics*, 9(1): 120–141.

Pasquino, G. and McCarthy, P. (eds.) (1993) *The end of post-war politics in Italy: The landmark 1992 elections*, Boulder, CO: Westview Press.

Pešta, M. (2014) 'The origins of the left-wing terrorism in Italy after 1968', *Dvacáté století (The Twentieth Century)*, 6(1): 61–73.

Pridham, G. (1981) *The nature of the Italian party system: A regional case study*, London: Croom Helm.

Rooduijn, M. (2014) 'The nucleus of populism: In search of the lowest common denominator', *Government and Opposition*, 49(4): 573–599.

Ruzza, C. and Fella, S. (2009) *Re-inventing the Italian right: Territorial politics, populism and 'post-fascism'*, London and New York: Routledge.

Ruzza, C. and Schmidtke, O. (1996) 'Towards a modern right: Alleanza Nazionale and the "Italian revolution"', in S. Gundle and S. Parker (eds.) *The new Italian Republic: From the fall of the Berlin Wall to Berlusconi*, London: Routledge pp. 147–158.

Sartori, G. (1976/2005) *Parties and party systems: A framework for analysis*, Cambridge: Cambridge University Press/Colchester: ECPR Press.

Serneri, S. N. (1995) 'A past to be thrown away? Politics and history in the Italian resistance', *Contemporary European History*, 4(3): 367–381.

Setta, S. (1975) *L'Uomo Qualunque 1944–1948*, Rome and Bari: Laterza.

Schmidtke, O. (1993). 'The populist challenge to the Italian nation-state: The Lega Lombarda/Nord', *Regional & Federal Studies*, 3(3): 140–162.

Stanley, B. (2008) 'The thin ideology of populism', *Journal of Political Ideologies*, 13(1): 95–110.

Tarchi, M. (2003) *L'Italia populista: Dal qualunquismo ai Girotondi*, Bologna: Il Mulino.

Tronconi, F. (ed.) (2015) *Beppe Grillo's Five Star Movement: Organisation, communication and ideology*, Surrey: Ashgate Publishing, Ltd.

Urbinati, N. (1998) 'Democracy and populism', *Constellations*, 5(1): 110–124.

Verbeek, B. and Zaslove, A. (2015) 'The impact of populist radical right parties on foreign policy: The Northern League as a junior coalition partner in the Berlusconi governments', *European Political Science Review*, 7(4): 525–546.

———— (2016) 'Italy: A case of mutating populism?', *Democratization*, 23(2): 304–323.

Woods, D. (2009) 'Pockets of resistance to globalization: The case of the Lega Nord', *Patterns of Prejudice*, 43(2): 161–177.

Zaslove, A. (2008) 'Here to stay? Populism as a new party type', *European Review*, 16(3): 319–336.

———— (2011) *The re-invention of the European radical right: Populism, regionalism, and the Italian Lega Nord*, Montreal: McGill-Queen's Press-MQUP.

Ziblatt, D. (2006) *Structuring the state: The formation of Italy and Germany and the puzzle of federalism*, Princeton, NJ: Princeton University Press.

Zincone, G. (2006) 'The making of policies: Immigration and immigrants in Italy', *Journal of Ethnic and Migration Studies*, 32(3): 347–375.

Chapter 9

Earthquake or Hurricane?[1]

The Rise and Fall of Populist Parties in Poland

Fernando Casal Bértoa and Simona Guerra

INTRODUCTION

In this chapter, we study the development of the Polish party system since the 1989 Round Table talks, examining the impact that populism might have had on the party system, especially given that populist forces have been present in Poland since its transition to democracy and that populism has always permeated its party system. Populism, encapsulated in the grass-roots of the Solidarity movement during the transition and Lech Wałęsa's presidency in the first half of the 1990s (see Kubik and Lynch 2006), finally found political opportunity structures in the democratic process at the turn of the twenty-first century during the EU accession process, its aftermath and beyond.

This chapter opens with a brief presentation of party politics in Poland. Before analysing the eventual effects that populist parties had on the development of the Polish party system – with a special focus on polarisation, competition, fragmentation and closure – this chapter introduces the concept of (Polish) populism, exploring its demand side and its role in the competition surrounding political issues. In our analysis, we stress the distinctive features of Poland's democratisation, which left individuals 'lost in a maze, baffled by the outcomes of the democratic process' (Jasiewicz 2008: 11). In particular, we argue that, while populism in the form of discourse and representation has always been present in Poland, populist parties' success has resulted from the confluence of different factors, including historical legacies, the social costs of economic reforms, the EU integration process and the recent economic and financial crisis. We also argue that populism per se has only had a limited (and indirect) effect on the Polish party system by consolidating

and amplifying what, otherwise, was and is a party system primarily characterised by weak party organisations, disloyal elites, volatile electorates and a
continuously open structure of competition.

THE POLISH PARTY SYSTEM: STILL AN
ALPHABET SOUP

Contrary to most Western European party systems (see other chapters in
this volume) and the Hungarian party system (Enyedi and Róna, chapter 10,
this volume), the Polish party system's history cannot be summarised with a
couple of names.[2] Since the first free and fair legislative elections took place
in 1991, no less than thirty-nine political parties have managed to obtain
representation in the Polish parliament (*Sejm*). Figure 9.1, which summarises
the history of party development in Poland between 1989 and 2015,[3] clearly
portrays the kind of alphabet soup that Polish voters have faced before almost
every election (the 2005 and the 2007 elections being perhaps the only
exceptions).

As figure 9.1 conveys, the history of party development in Poland over
the past twenty-five years of democratic politics can be summarised in

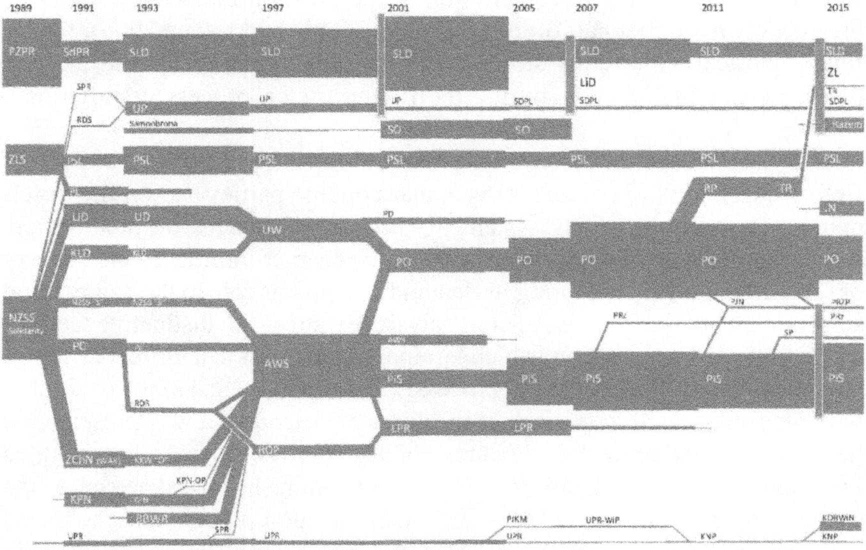

Figure 9.1 Polish Political Party Tree (1989–2015)

Note: The thickness of the lines closely corresponds with the party's electoral support. A complete list of
party acronyms and names can be found at the end of the chapter.

two words: constant change. Thus, parties not only have come and gone – with greater or lesser degrees of success – but also have been affected by numerous splits and mergers. The clearest proof of this constant change is that only one (i.e. Polish Peasant Party) of the aforementioned thirty-nine parties has managed to obtain parliamentary representation in every single election.

Such instability at the party level has had important effects, as explained elsewhere (Casal Bértoa 2012) at the systemic level. Thus, throughout its history, the Polish party system has been characterised by moderate fragmentation, high electoral instability and an open structure of competition, as we will have the opportunity to observe later in this chapter. However, the Polish party system should not necessarily be classified as a chaotic system or as a 'non-system' (Sanchez 2009). In fact, notwithstanding the system's aforementioned inchoate character, Polish politics have been characterised by a cross-cutting multidimensional space of inter-party competition that revolves around two cleavages (i.e. economy and history/culture) that divide the political spectrum into four different politico-ideological fields (Casal Bértoa 2014):

(a) Social democratic (strong support for state interventionism and cosmopolitanism)
(b) Agrarian (support for state interventionism combined with traditionalism)
(c) Conservative (a combination of pro-market attitudes and traditionalism, usually in a Christian Democratic version)
(d) Liberal (strong support for free-market/enterprise and modern values)

Throughout its twenty-five-year democratic history, these four fields have been represented by different parties, especially on the right side (i.e. conservative and liberal) of the political spectrum. Thus, the conservative field had Solidarity (S), the Christian National Union (ZChN) and the Centre Accord (PC) as its principal representatives between 1991 and 1996, before converging into Solidarity Electoral Action (AWS) in 1997, which was soon replaced by the short-lived League of Polish Families (LPR) and Law and Justice (PiS) in 2001. Between 1994 and 2001, the liberal field was represented by the Freedom Union (UW), a merger of the Democratic Union (UD) and the Liberal Democratic Congress (KLD) (Szczerbiak, 2001). Since 2001, the liberal field's principal representative has been the Civic Platform (PO), a splinter party of the UW, which then became the Democratic Party (PD). By contrast, and with the brief interlude of Self-Defence (SRP) between 2001 and 2007, the Democratic Left Alliance (SLD), a merger of various former Communist parties, trade unions and associations in 1999, and the Polish Peasant Party (PSL) have always been the major players in the social democratic and agrarian fields.

As we will see later in this chapter, a second constant in the Polish party system has been its bipolar structure of competition. This structure pitted post-communist parties, combining the social democrats with the agrarians, against post-Solidarity parties, combining the conservatives and the liberals, between 1991 and 2004; however, since 2005, with the demise of the SLD and the disappearance of the so-called post-communist cleavage, it has pitted the two parties within the post-Solidarity camp – namely, the liberal PO and the conservative PiS – against one another.

In order to understand the extent to which populist parties have influenced this already rather open party system, particularly given the changes that took place in 2005, we will first define populism and examine why it exists in the Polish context.

POPULISM IN POLAND: EMERGENCE AND PERSISTENCE

This chapter suggests that Polish populism, as a discourse and representative doctrine within the party system, has emerged and been present from the very beginning of the democratisation process (see also Kubik and Lynch 2006). However, its success is a consequence and confluence of varying factors, where agency – understood as the specific coalitional strategies that party leaders adopt at particular points in time – is significant. We use 'populism', as defined in this volume, as a thin-centred ideology consisting of three main factors: It seeks to represent the people and speaks for them, it adopts the divide between the people and the corrupt elites and it develops a Manichean antagonistic view (Mudde 2004; Mudde and Kaltwasser 2013).

Polish society resisted the communist regime and maintained a de facto degree of societal pluralism despite attempts to impose a totalitarian system. Totalitarianism was rejected by most Poles (Linz and Stepan 1996). During the communist regime, the Catholic Church represented the cradle of resistance and autonomy, legitimising organised protest and opposition. The arrest of Cardinal Stefan Wyszyński (1952–1956) was one of several attempts to weaken the Church's resistance, but it further reinforced the dichotomy between 'we, the people' and 'they, the communists'. This dichotomy was strengthened by the unity of the Polish state, partly due to the partitions (1764–1795) and Poland's ethnic homogeneity, following the absorption of Byelorussian and Ukrainian minorities after Second World War, the extermination of most of the Jewish population and the expulsion of the German minority.

The Catholic Church maintained its vital role across society and supported the Polish 'Solidarity' 'refolution'.[4] In Kubik's words, Solidarity 'was never simply a trade union or a movement, but a cultural class in *statu nascendi*. . . subjected to tremendous internal centrifugal tensions . . . held' together by 'a polarized vision of "we/the people/Solidarity" versus "them/authorities/communists"' (in Kubik and Lynch 2006: 11), which became a political force. This dichotomy persisted and created a clear distinction between opponents of the regime (the Solidarity Republic) and the governing elites (the Polish People's Republic).

When Lech Wałęsa was elected as president of Poland (1990–1995), he described himself as the leader of Polish civil society rather than emphasising his institutional role as president of the Polish Republic (see De Lange and Guerra 2009). Wałęsa represented 'the people' and called attention to the division between politics and the people, politically recognising its existence. He was the former leader of Solidarity, the Polish trade union, and was acting as the spokesperson for civil society. His opponent, Stanisław Tymiński, who was defeated in the presidential electoral race, used 'us *vs.* them' rhetoric and spoke in the language of the people (Wysocka 2009). The 'us *vs.* them' dichotomy endured as the dominant cleavage in the 1990s, as a historical legacy and religiosity represented the most important explanatory factors underpinning citizens' behaviours (Jasiewicz 2009; Markowski 1999).

Table 9.1 displays the percentage of votes (and seats) obtained by populist parties in both presidential and legislative elections[5] as well as the level of populism observed in political discourse according to political parties' stances in 'election manifestos, speeches of the party leader during and immediately after the election campaign, and the parliamentary debate that takes place prior to the vote of confidence for a new government' (Stanley 2015a: 247–248).

After Tymiński's surprising performance in 1990, during the first decade of Polish politics (1991–2001), populism had a rather moderate presence, as shown in table 9.1. In fact, no other populist parties managed to enter parliament, with the exception of Tymiński's political platform (Party X) in 1991

Table 9.1 Level of Populism in the Polish Party System (1991–2015)

Elections	1990–1991	1993–1995	1997	2000–2001	2005	2007	2010–2011	2015
Presidential	23.1	8.2		3.6	15.5		2.4	25.1
Legislative[a]	0.6	8.3	5.7 (1.3)	18.1	21.1	2.8	0.6	13.6
	(0.7)			(19.8)	(19.6)			(9.1)
Discourse[b]	0.44	0.44	0.46	0.64	0.64	0.46	0.49	n/a

[a] The percentage of seats is shown in brackets.
[b] The index ranks from 0 (lack of populist stances) to 1 (full-flesh populist discourse).

(three seats) and the Movement for the Reconstruction of Poland (ROP) in 1997 (six seats), which took advantage of former premier Jan Olszewski's reasonable performance in the presidential elections in 1996 (*see* tables 9.1A and 9.2A).

Indeed, populism had not increased at all levels until the run-up to EU membership in 2004 and the emergence of two Eurosceptic parties: namely, the LPR, a radical right-wing party, and the populist agrarian SRP. When, later in 2007, Poland held pre-term elections, the LRP and the SRP did not secure enough votes to obtain a parliamentary seat, showing that, despite its persistence, populism could not emerge at a time of perceived economic and/or social crisis. However, the populists did not have to wait long. Only seven years after the electoral extinction of both the SRP and the LPR, a new populist party (Kukiz'15), led by former rock star Paweł Kukiz, won 8.8 per cent of the vote (forty-two seats) (*see* table 9.1A). Its electoral success in the October 2015 legislative elections should not have come as a surprise, especially if we consider that young people's disappointment and disillusionment had already brought Kukiz more than 20 per cent of the vote in the May 2015 presidential elections, making him the third most popular candidate with just ten fewer points than the sitting president, Bronisław Komorowski (the PO's candidate), and the ultimate winner, Andrzej Duda (PiS).

In the 2015 October elections, characterised by both low (roughly 50 per cent) turnout – a constant in Polish politics – and youth discontent/protest, Kukiz'15 made the threshold by coming third with 8.8 per cent of the votes. In addition, both KORWiN (21.20 per cent) – led by Janusz Korwin Mikke, a seventy-two-year-old politician advocating a radical right and Eurosceptic programme – and Kukiz'15 (20.90 per cent) received most of the student vote (see Guerra and Casal Bértoa 2015).

EXPLAINING POPULISM IN POLAND: DEMAND AND PARTY COMPETITION

In the late 1990s, Poland was close to securing membership in both NATO and the EU. The social and economic costs of the democratisation process materialised at this time. The public's support for EU membership suddenly dropped (to 55 per cent in May 1999), while the percentage of those opposed to EU membership rose (to 26 per cent in May 1999) (CBOS data). According to Centrum Badanii Opinii Społecznej (CBOS, a public opinion research centre[6] in Warsaw), farmers were more strongly opposed to membership,[7] and scepticism and anxiety had an impact on the changing patterns of attitudes towards the EU.[8] Growing scepticism could be detected in the surveys on the pace of Poland's accession: the option of joining 'as soon as possible' (50 per cent in April 1998; 42 per cent in May 1999) increasingly lost support, while citizens perceived that accession 'as late as possible' could benefit Poland (23 per cent in April 1998; 32 per cent in May 1999) (CBOS 1999, 07/99). This shift may be explained by the domestic politics of EU integration: the AWS government introduced new policies for healthcare, education, administration systems and social insurance (Guerra 2013). Conditionality and the social costs linked to the reforms could have affected public attitudes towards the EU and the pace at which Poland was moving towards membership. Levels of support for EU membership dropped from 80 per cent in 1996 to 55 per cent in 2001 (Guerra 2013).

In the 2001 parliamentary elections, stronger opposition – mobilised by the LPR, a fundamentalist extreme right-wing party – came to the fore (see De Lange and Guerra 2009). In November 2001, two-thirds of the LPR's potential electorate opposed EU membership (CBOS 2001, BS/155/2001). As Aleks Szczerbiak and Paul Taggart stress in the case of the 2003 accession referendum (2004: 575), the presence of more Eurosceptic parties brought more contestation to political debates, and people's preferences became more strongly defined. In Poland, concerns regarding the impact of EU integration were salient issues on voters' minds after the negotiation process began.

Dissatisfaction with the government persisted. The reforms implemented by the new post-Solidarity minority government, in office since February 1999, were considered unsatisfactory.[9] In January 2001, discontent was widespread: 62 per cent, 37 per cent and 28 per cent thought that the situation was getting worse with regard to healthcare, education and the pension system and local administration, respectively (CBOS 2001 02/2001). Government policy was thought to be affecting the economic situation; fewer citizens believed that policy was creating opportunities (approximately 30 per cent); and more citizens felt it did not create any kind of prospects (approximately 60 per cent) (CBOS 1999 02/99). Reflecting decreased government employment, the unemployment rate rose from 10.6 per cent in 1999 to 16.1 per cent in 2000 and 18.2 per cent in 2001.[10] However, the inflation rate decreased from the 11.8 per cent annual average in 1998 to 5.3 per cent in 2001, as a result of tight monetary policy (Guerra 2013).

The LPR and the SRP were the two political parties that were able to capitalise not only on the discontent that had been emerging since the late 1990s but also on nationalist issues, conservative values, economic concerns about closing accounts with the communist past and Polish policy towards the EU. Although this analysis suggests and stresses that Poland actually does not show much higher levels of polarisation compared with the average polarisation of party systems in Europe, these parties emerged and were electorally successful between 1997 and 2011, and the levels of polarisation increased (*see* table 9.3). This success and consequent increase in polarisation was not only linked to a shared sense of national belonging that went hand by hand with the democratisation process but also reflected widespread discontent with the social and economic costs of reforms (see also De Lange and Guerra 2009). This polarised environment was also reflected at the presidential level by the Solidarity President Lech Wałęsa (1990–1995) and the heir of the rebranded former communist party (SLD), Aleksander Kwaśniewski, who was minister of sport in the communist government in the 1980s and president of Poland from 1995 to 2005.

According to Andrea Pirro (2015: 17), populist parties on the radical right are 'capable of shaping their own fortune as far as their proclaimed *and* actual stands over certain issues are concerned'. These stands can be not only mobilised at the domestic level but also externally determined, as in this case with the process of EU integration. As documented in the literature (De Lange and Guerra 2009; Guerra 2012) and supported by this analysis, the LPR's success can be explained by historical legacies and opportunity structures that are shaped both internally and externally. The interplay between party agency and policy competition increases the salience of issue ownership in ways that can determine the success of political parties and reshape party competition. Historical legacies were linked to three core ideological traits of the League, 'Catholic conservatism, nationalism, and populism', while domestic and external dimensions influenced another two omnibus issues, 'anticommunism and Euroscepticism' (De Lange and Guerra 2009). The age of discontent (2001–2005) that witnessed the emergence of successful populist parties, including the LPR, a populist radical right party, produced an electorate that was mainly concerned with protecting Poland through social conservative values (in 2005, higher-priority issues included 'abortion', 'low birth and decreasing population', and the 'role of the Church'), grappling with Poland's communist past and addressing the possible settlement of foreigners in Poland (*see* table 9.2).

As table 9.2 shows, the SRP, the populist agrarian party that became electorally successful between 2001 and 2005, was the defender of farmers and citizens who believed Poland was moving in the wrong direction with regard to EU membership, and privatisation was one of the main concerns in 2001 among its voters (*see* table 9.2). Andrzej Lepper, the leader of the SRP and a farmer from the north-east and west of the country, was a son of these regions in Poland, where the Balcerowicz (shock therapy) plan and other reforms had a considerable impact on the social costs of democratisation. Lepper could understand the distress of 'his people' because he was one of them. His economic ruin due to the growing interest on the loans that he had taken out due to the economic reforms also initiated his political career, and his protests and illegal blockades received widespread popular support

Table 9.2 Salient Issues in the 2001 and 2005 General Elections

Issue	2001			2005		
Party	PL	LPR	SRP	PL	LPR	SRP
Crime	8.92	9.08	8.79	8.89	8.77	**4.16**
Privatisation	4.94	5.38	4.02	5.84	6.34	5.42
Unemployment	9.69	9.86	9.65	9.64	9.78	9.81
Tax policy	8.25	8.49	8.64	8.27	8.26	**4.60**
State subsidies for agriculture	7.48	8.25	7.89	7.04	7.82	**8.36**
State social responsibility	7.78	8.33	7.84	8.15	8.37	8.45
Polish policy towards the EU	6.10	**4.96**	5.35	7.30	7.25	**6.79**
Closing accounts with Poland's communist past	3.29	**4.75**	3.23	5.16	**6.43**	5.15
Foreign capital in Poland	5.35	4.95	5.01	6.48	6.62	6.43
Settlement of foreigners	n/a	n/a	n/a	4.50	**5.50**	4.06

Note: Table adapted from De Lange and Guerra (2009) and Fitzgibbon and Guerra (2009).

Source: 2001 and 2005 PNES. The values appear in **bold** when LPR and SRP voter scores higher or lower (–0.50/1 or +0.50/1) than those of the average Polish voter (PL). Values range between 0 (marginal) and 10 (priority).

(Szczerbiak 2002: 12). When the relationship between Poland and the EU became more intense because of the opening of the negotiation process, the idea that the political elite was going to sell Poland and the concrete fear that foreigners would occupy Polish lands won votes for the SRP. The widespread fear of an alleged international conspiracy set on buying Polish lands and destroying the Polish nation characterised this period (see Fitzgibbon and Guerra 2009). Lepper promised to fight corruption, and crime, economic issues and EU integration became salient for the SRP electorate between 2001 and 2005 (*see* table 9.2).

PiS, the main party in the coalition in 2006 and 2007, 'stole' most of these issues, increasing its economic and conservative agenda and shifting its position from a typical right-wing conservative party 'with noticeable though weak nationalist and populist leanings, into a radical nationalist, and visibly populist-socialist one' (Markowski 2006: 820), and the LPR and the SRP subsequently lost many voters. A focus on EU integration was beneficial in the short term (Guerra 2013), and PiS absorbed the populist vote.

The big turn in partisan competition was apparent during the 2005 presidential and general elections, and it will be examined in the following sections. The polarisation that accompanied the emergence of a populism based on an 'us *vs.* them' cleavage changed into a 'social *vs.* liberal' dichotomy, which was absorbed by the two post-Solidarity political parties, the PO and PiS, because of the lack of any alternative on the centre-left.

THE POLISH PARTY SYSTEM: FROM ATOMISATION TO NEVER-ENDING STABILISATION

As has been already mentioned, the Polish party system can be considered one of the most inchoate in the post-communist region and, in turn, across Europe (Casal Bértoa 2013). Indeed, as shown in figure 9.1, which captures the most important party splits and mergers in Poland, and table 9.3, which presents some of the most important dimensions[11] of the Polish party system, the Polish party system has always been characterised by high electoral volatility and party turnover, moderate fragmentation and polarisation, and a bipolar structure of competition, initially pitting 'post-communist' parties against 'post-Solidarity' parties first (1991–2004) and 'liberal' parties against 'social' parties later on (2005–2015).

However, despite this flux in electoral preferences (even at the inter-bloc level) and political formations, the constant (if any) in the history of the Polish party system is its multidimensional *space of competition*, which, as most scholars have noted, revolves around two primary axes: historical-cultural and economic axes (Grzybowski and Mikuli 2004; Jasiewicz 2007; Markowski 2007).[12] The historical-cultural axis is characterised by two overlapping cleavages and/or divides, religious and post-communist, but the second axis focuses solely on economic issues. The religious cleavage pits those advocating a stronger role for the Catholic Church in public life and education against those preferring the state to be neutral; the 'post-communist cleavage' (Grabowska 2004) distinguishes between those who are favourably disposed to the previous communist regime and those who oppose it and call for a purge of previous communist party members or collaborators.

Table 9.3   Polish Party System Indicators (1991–2015)

Year	Polarisation (Dalton's Index)	Effective number of electoral parties (ENEP)	Effective number of legislative parties (ENPP)	Electoral disproportionty	Number of new parties (≥ 0.5% votes)	Electoral (and bloc) volatility	% seats of the two biggest parties
1991	0.25	13.8	10.9	3.6	–	–	26.5
1993	0.3	9.8	3.9	17.8	4	28.9 (19.1)	65.9
1997	0.4	4.6	3	10.6	4	19.3 (6.7)	79.3
2001	0.44	4.5	3.6	6.3	4	35.2 (18.5)	61.1
2005	0.45	5.9	4.3	7	3	34 (25.7)	62.6
2007	0.44	3.3	2.8	4.7	0	23.7 (11.8)	81.5
2011	0.34	3.7	3	6	4	7.7 (2.4)	79.1
2015	n/a	4.4	2.7	13.6	4	31.9 (18.2)	81.1

Source: Casal Bértoa (2016), Casal Bértoa and Walecki (2014: 314), Döring and Manow (2012) and Gwiazda (2016: 101).

By contrast, the economic cleavage distinguishes between citizens with strong statist and egalitarian orientations and those who identify with more market-orientated and economically liberal beliefs (Castle and Taras 2002; Szczerbiak 2006a).

Contrary to some expectations, between 1991 and 2004, the historical-cultural axis, rather than the economic axis, defined the logic of competition and coalition formation in Poland. As a result, 'left' and 'right' referred to attitudes towards the social role of the Church and de-communisation (*Vergangenheitsbewältigung*) rather than the role of the state (Jasiewicz 2002; Kitschelt et al. 1999). As figure 9.2 demonstrates, this historical-cultural focus led to what Sielski (2004: 18) called 'a two-bloc stabilised multiparty system', which pitted the post-communist parties, primarily the social-democratic SLD and the agrarian PSL, against the post-Solidarity parties. The latter party bloc consisted of the liberal UW and PO and a diverse group of Christian Democratic parties, particularly the AWS and PiS.

As figure 9.2 shows, the previous logic of partisan competition ended in October 2005 when the 'communist *vs*. anti-communist' opposition (Brier 2009) gave way to what Szczerbiak (2006b) has defined as a confrontation between 'social and liberal Poland'. While a CBOS poll earlier that year (April–May 2005) had already suggested a wane in the historical-cultural opposition among Polish voters, only after the first round of the presidential elections held on 9 October 2005 did the economic axis replace the historical-cultural axis as the main structural factor underlying the process of partisan interaction and coalition formation. In particular, because candidates from the two main post-Solidarity parties (Donald Tusk from the PO and Lech

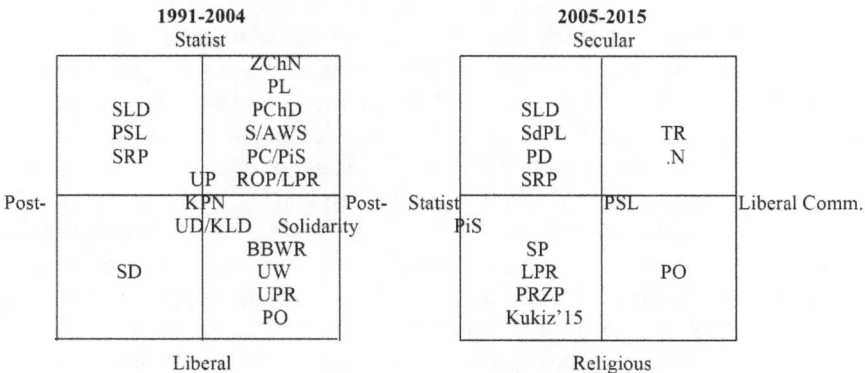

Figure 9.2 Polish Political Parties and Ideological Orientations during Two Different Periods

Source: Casal Bértoa (2014: 28).

Kaczyński from PiS) made it to the second round, to the detriment of the main post-communist candidate (Włodzimierz Cimoszewicz from the SLD),[13] both Tusk and Kaczyński were forced to emphasise their ideological differences. Because the PO and PiS were both post-Solidarity and pro-Catholic Church parties,[14] the candidates and their parties turned to economic issues to differentiate their platforms. The PO was more pro-market, while the PiS was more interventionist.[15] In turn, they started portraying themselves as representatives of 'transition winners' and 'transition losers' (Słomczyński et al. 2007).

A ninety-degree turn in the two-dimensional cross-cut space of competition (*see* figure 9.2) not only constituted a shock to the mechanics of the party system but also opened the door for a rapprochement between PiS and the two main populist parties, the LPR and the SRP. The SRP's candidate and party leader, Andrzej Lepper, had come in third with 15 per cent of the vote during the first round of the presidential elections. A simply mathematical calculation clearly showed not only Lech Kaczyński but also Tusk that the candidate who received Lepper's endorsement in the second round would become president.[16]

Conscious of his pivotal role, the SRP leader sent a letter to both presidential candidates, promising to support their presidential aspirations in exchange for his participation in the future government.[17] Although Tusk explicitly refused to collaborate with Lepper's party during the final debate of the campaign, Kaczyński's position was ambiguous. With the support of Lepper's electorate, Kaczyński defeated Tusk in the 2005 presidential election. Soon afterwards, coalition talks began between PiS, the LPR – which had withdrawn its own presidential candidate[18] – and the SRP. Three weeks later, PiS formed a minority cabinet with parliamentary votes from the LPR, the SRP and, eventually, the PSL.

This ad hoc solution proved temporary, and a proper coalition was subsequently formed, first at the parliamentary level (the so-called stabilisation pact) in February 2006 and then at the government level three months later (Stanley 2015b). With the formation of this coalition and the establishment of the PO as the main opposition party, the so-called post-communist cleavage in Poland lost its hold on party politics, and the economic (i.e. liberal-statist) cleavage became the main division between 'left and right' and the main axis of competition and coalition formation. This shift was confirmed by the coalition between the PO and the PSL in 2007, two years after the appointment of Kazimierz Marcinkiewicz as prime minister with the support of PiS, the LPR and the SRP (Casal Bértoa 2012: 462–463). This coalition endured until 2015 when a new 'social' coalition was formed between PiS, its splinter party United Poland (SP) and Poland Together (PRPZ), a splinter party of the most conservative faction of PO (*see* figure 9.1).

THE IMPACT OF POPULIST PARTIES
IN A MUDDY CONTEXT

As shown in table 9.1, populist discourses in general and populist parties in particular have been a constant in Poland since the first free and fair elections in November 1990. However, the SRP and the LPR did not gain parliamentary seats until 2001; in fact, populism and populist parties lacked the opportunity to exert any impact on party system development in Poland until 2006, when the 'populist coalition government' was formed (Stanley 2015b). Therefore, we focus our analysis on the six years from 2001 to 2007.

Competition

Considering the discussion thus far and the electoral, parliamentary and governmental irrelevance of Party X and the ROP, the only two populist parties with parliamentary representation during the first ten years of the Polish democracy, the impact of populist parties on the logic of partisan competition (i.e. the post-communist left vs. the post-Solidarity right) that structured the Polish party system at the end of the twentieth century (Bakke and Sitter 2005: 249) can arguably be considered non-existent. The same can be said about the LPR or the SRP between 2001 and 2005, even if the SLD had considered the latter a potential government partner in September 2001.[19]

However, both the SRP and the LPR had an impact on the change from a historical-cultural (i.e. religious) logic to an economic logic of competition in October 2005, even if this effect was only indirect. In fact, neither the rise of these two populist parties, which already existed in 2001, nor the increase in polarisation (see the section on polarisation in further section), which was certainly fostered by the political discourse and ideological claims of both the SRP and the LPR, necessarily caused the change in the logic of competition and coalition formation; instead, as explained earlier, the 2005 presidential campaign and the internally driven collapse of the main post-communist party (the SLD) as the principal element (or party) on the party system's second pole contributed to this shift. Indeed, the collapse of the SLD caused a 'core' change (Smith's 1989) and transformed the logic of subsequent inter-party competition. In other words, the 2005–2007 'populist coalition' (Stanley 2015a) helped consolidate the current confrontation between PiS, representative of 'transition losers' or 'social Poland', and the PO, representative of 'transition winners' or 'liberal Poland', but it did not cause this confrontation. Even after the demise of both the SRP and the LRP, 'social and liberal Poland' are still the only two alternatives for voters, which clearly proves the populist coalition's indirect influence on the Polish party system.

Polarisation

As shown in figure 9.1, Poland's ideological spectrum has ranged from the extreme right, which has tended to be fragmented and unstable (Kasprowicz 2015; Pankowski 2010), to the social democratic SLD, the successor of the communist party, on the left (Millard 2010). However, from a comparative perspective, the Polish party system has been characterised by an average level of ideological polarisation. Further, in contrast to other Eastern and Western European democracies, Poland's level of polarisation is not only close to the average European level but also occupies sixteenth place in terms of polarisation (Casal Bértoa 2013: 409), closer to moderately polarised Germany or the United Kingdom than to the more extreme cases of Cyprus (in Western Europe) and the Czech Republic (in Eastern Europe).

As the first column in table 9.3 shows, the 1991 and 1993 elections did not display a high level of ideological polarisation, which cannot be said of the subsequent four elections. Indeed, Poland experienced a major increase in the level of polarisation in 1997. Polarisation would remain high between 2001 and 2007, peaking in 2005, before falling to more moderate levels in 2011. Should the Polish populist parties be considered responsible for this increase? A first glance at table 9.3 would suggest these parties are somewhat responsible: the increase in polarisation coincides with the entry of the ROP, the first populist party to form a parliamentary group, into parliament, and the subsequent decrease coincides with the electoral demise of the SRP and the LPR, the only other populist parties to gain parliamentary seats. However, an in-depth study of the 1997 elections shows that the change observed in the levels of ideological polarisation was not due to the rise of populism (*see* table 9.1) or the ROP's breakthrough (*see* table 9.1A) because their electoral and/or parliamentary leverage was weak; instead, the increased polarisation stems from the increased confrontation between post-communist (i.e. the SLD and the PSL) and post-Solidarity (i.e. the AWS and the UW) parties (Castle and Taras 2002).

With the exception of ad hoc episodes of collaboration between post-communist and post-Solidarity forces at the time of the so-called contract parliament (the ZSL and Solidarity), Waldemar Pawlak's unsuccessful cabinet in 1992 (UD, ZChN and PSL), or the constitutional process of 1996–1997 (SLD and UW), these two types of parties had always been at odds. However, the polarisation between these two camps did not reach its peak until the unsuccessful re-election of Lech Wałęsa in 1995, the right's subsequent failure to win the 1997 constitutional referendum and the unification of all the major post-Solidarity conservative parties under the AWS banner. At this point, scholars (Grabowska 2004; Szczerbiak 2001) began talking about the emergence of a post-communist 'cleavage' that was driving the Polish political competition (both in terms of voters and parties) into two inimical camps.

The split of AWS, which had previously taken conservatives under its wing, Christian Democrats and radicals, the appearance of the LPR in 2001, and the SRP's electoral surge (from 2.8 in 1993 to 10.2 in 2001) contributed to the increased level of polarisation. In 2005, polarisation increased again when both the LPR and the SRP got their hands on the Polish government, as explained in more detail further in the text.

Still, the level of polarisation in the Polish party system did not change much after the electoral disappearance of both the SRP and the LPR (only 2.8 per cent of the overall vote and no seats) in 2007 (*see* table 9.3). However, we should not forget that such lack of change in terms of polarisation was due to PiS' initial attempt to take over the populist electorate. The polarisation in Poland neared the low levels of 1993 only after the moderation of PiS' discourse and the substitution of historical-cultural for economic issues in the 2011 electoral campaign. Despite the success of populist parties in 2001 and the formation of the 'populist coalition' in 2005 (Stanley 2015b), which increased ideological polarisation, the Polish party system had already become more polarised (since 1997) and retained the same level of polarisation until 2011.

Fragmentation (Newness) and Volatility

Although Poland was the first East European country to rid itself of communism, its process of party development was 'tortuous' and suffered from 'extreme fragmentation and instability' (Szczerbiak 2001: 12). The first legislative elections in October 1991, with 111 electoral lists and 29 political groupings with at least one parliamentary seat, stand out in the Polish party system, which has always been fragmented – with, on average, between five and six[20] 'effective electoral' parties (*see* table 9.3) and no less than seven political parties obtaining at least 0.5 per cent of the vote (Casal Bértoa and Walecki 2014: 340).

In a way, the 1991 elections, which certainly had 'all the makings of what Giovanni Sartori called extreme multipartism' (Grzybowski 1994: 69), set the pattern for subsequent elections. However, the introduction of a 5 per cent electoral threshold in 1993 reduced the number of parties in parliament by more than 70 per cent. As table 9.3 demonstrates, electoral disproportionality increased from 3.6 per cent in 1991 to 17.8 per cent in 1993. With an electoral coalition of 33 right-wing parties under the AWS umbrella in 1997 (Szczerbiak 2001), electoral disproportionality dropped to 10.6 per cent, and it has remained at a rather high average of 7.5 per cent ever since.

Further in the text, we examine the extent to which populist parties have affected the format of the Polish party system by increasing the level of fragmentation, provoking change in terms of the type of party system (e.g. from limited to extreme pluralism), or both. The second column in table 9.3 demonstrates that the effective number of 'legislative' parties has always oscillated between three (1997, 2007 and 2011) and four (1993, 2001 and 2005). With the exception of the 1991 elections, the Polish party system has always been a 'limited pluralist' (Sartori 1976) system. Even if 'more or less populist newcomers still keep popping up' (Bakke and Sitter 2005: 249), the total number of new parties with more than 0.5 per cent of the vote per election has been, on average, around three (*see* table 9.3) – a rather low number compared with those of other party systems in the region. This number did not even increase during the October 2015 parliamentary elections (*see* table 9.1A), which introduced two new populist forces (i.e. Kukiz'15 and KORWiN).

If we employ Sartori's 1976 typology and consider the extent to which populist parties have contributed to change in the party system, we see that populist parties had an impact on the party system by increasing the level of fragmentation and polarisation, but the rise of these parties did not lead to real change in terms of the type of the party system, as the effective number of parties continued to be over four and the level of polarisation has been more than 0.4 (*see* table 9.3).[21] Especially considering its 'bipolar' structure throughout its history (*see* section 1 and the last column in table 9.3), the Polish party system certainly continues to be – as it was in 1991 – an extremely fragmented but moderately polarised party system.[22]

Both fragmentation and polarisation (especially of the elites) contributed to the instability of voters' preferences in Poland, making the party system one of the most electorally unstable in Europe (Casal Bértoa 2013: 417). Indeed, as the last column in table 9.3 demonstrates, electoral volatility scores remained quite high before and after 2011. In 2001, the rise of populist parties and the peak of volatility coincide. However, the latter was not so much due to the former but rather due to the organisational collapse of the AWS and the electoral revival of the SLD, which was in a coalition with the UP in 2001 (Markowski and Cześnik 2002). In a similar vein, the high volatility scores in 2005 reflected the electoral collapse (from 41 per cent to 11 per cent) of the SLD[23] coalition rather than the rise of the SRP and the

LPR (Szczerbiak 2006b). The same can be said of the 2015 parliamentary elections, in which the swing from the PO to PiS and .N, from the SLD to Razem and from TR to .N – rather than the surge of Kukiz'15 and the swing from the KNP to KORWiN – contributed to three-quarters of the net electoral volatility.

Moreover, electoral volatility scores only reached the single digits in 2011, well after the collapse of populist parties in 2007 and the changes in the structure of competition that were reflected in the highest level of bloc volatility in 2005. In Poland, high volatility (both inter- and within-bloc) levels can be explained by the lack of organisational loyalty among the elites, which has prompted continuous splits and *short-lived* mergers and thereby hindered the process of party institutionalisation (*see* figure 9.1), rather than by changes in voters' electoral preferences or the success of populist alternatives (Powell and Tucker 2014).

PARTY SYSTEM CLOSURE: POPULIST PARTIES IN GOVERNMENT

As we have seen, with the possible exception of the 2011 elections, when populist parties received less than 1 per cent of the popular vote and captured no seats, populist parties have been a constant presence in the Polish party system in both the electoral and parliamentary arenas (*see* tables 9.1, 9.1A and 9.2A). However, the same cannot be said for their presence in the governmental arena. Between 1991 and 2006, populist parties were deliberately excluded from government, even in instances in which they had 'coalition' potential (e.g. SRP in 2001). Therefore, to what extent did the inclusion of the SRP and the LPR in May 2006 alter the structure of inter-party competition at the time of government formation?

Following Mair (1997), we examine the degree to which the patterns of inter-party competition for government remain closed or have changed over time (Enyedi and Casal Bértoa 2011; Linz and Montero 2001; Toole 2000). As table 9.4 shows, government alternations in Poland have occurred after elections (seven times) and between elections (six times). However, while the former were wholesale (i.e. when the new cabinet includes none – or all – of the previous government parties), the latter have all been partial (i.e. the new cabinet includes some of the parties present in the previous cabinet). Moreover, with just two exceptions (in 2007 and in 2011), innovative coalition governments have always been the norm. Finally, in terms of access to power, the Polish party system can also be considered particularly open. If we consider all seventeen parties with parliamentary

Table 9.4 Chronology of Polish Governments (1991–2014)

1991 (PC-ZChN-PL-PSL/S)	1992 (UD-ZChN-KLD-Others)	1993 (SLD-PSL)
Elections	*Government Falls*	*Elections*
4 government parties	Partial alternation	Wholesale alternation
	Innovative formula	Innovative formula
	Open access	Open access

1997 (AWS-UW)	2000 (AWS)	2001 (SLD-UP-PSL)
Elections	*Government Reorganisation*	*Elections*
Wholesale alternation	Partial alternation	Wholesale alternation
Innovative formula	Innovative formula	Innovative formula
Open access	Closed access	Open access

2003 (SLD-UP)	2004 (SLD-UP-SdPL)	2005 (PiS)
Government Reorganisation	*Government Reorganisation*	*Elections*
Partial alternation	Partial alternation	Wholesale alternation
Innovative formula	Innovative formula	Innovative formula
Closed access	Open access	Open access

2006 (PiS-SRP-LPR)	2007 (PiS)	2007 (PO-PSL)
Government Reorganisation	*Government Reorganisation*	*Elections*
Partial alternation	Partial alternation	Wholesale alternation
Innovative formula	Familiar formula	Innovative formula
Open access	Closed access	Open access

2011 (PO-PSL)	2015 (PiS-SP-PRZP)	
Elections	*Elections*	
No alternation	Wholesale alternation	
Familiar formula	Innovative formula	
Closed access	Open access	

Source: Adapted and updated from O'Dwyer (2006: 46–47).

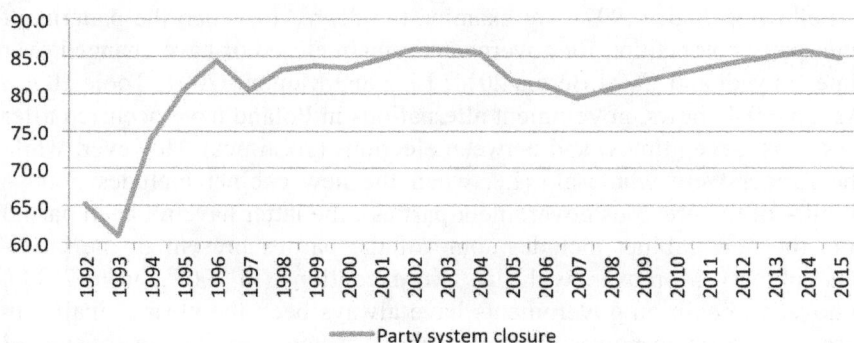

Party system closure

Figure 9.3 Party System Closure in Poland (1992–2015)

Source: Casal Bértoa (2016).

representation between 1993 and 2015,[24] only five (i.e. the KPN, the ROP, TR, Kukiz'15 and .N) have not formed part of the government at least once (Casal Bértoa 2012).

In such an open context, in which the structure of partisan competition for government was predominantly characterised by partial alternation, innovative formulae and open access, the formation of the 'populist coalition' in May 2006 cannot be considered a change in an already unstable and volatile Polish party system; its formation is instead a manifestation of one of the party system's characteristics (O'Dwyer 2006; Toole 2000).

Figure 9.3, which uses Casal Bértoa and Enyedi's (2016) new index to show the degree of closure *per annum* of the Polish party system, clarifies this relationship. A rather open party system exists,[25] and, with the exception of 2011, it has always suffered an important shock after every election. Moreover, although the 2006 'populist coalition' certainly helped increase the instability/openness of the party system, it can be regarded as another rock cast into what was already a sinking ship.

DISCUSSION: AN EARTHQUAKE OR A HURRICANE?

The analysis shows that populism, as a discourse and representative doctrine within the Polish party system, has been present in the electoral and parliamentary arenas since the fall of communism. The pathway to government opened only in 2006, when populist parties gained additional support in the run-up to EU integration (2004). The Polish party system has always been one of the more fragmented systems in Europe, but populist parties have only affected the system indirectly. Polarisation increased in those years because of the confrontation between post-Solidarity and post-communist ideologies, with the former falling under the AWS umbrella and the latter waving the rebranded social democratic banner. The presidencies of Lech Wałęsa (1990–1995), former leader of the Solidarity movement, and Aleksander Kwaśniewski (1995–2005), former minister of sport under the communist regime, reinforced this polarisation. This two-bloc competition (i.e. post-communist *vs.* post-Solidarity) continued to characterise the Polish party system until 2005, when the political confrontation between the presidential candidates of PiS and the PO gave rise to a new but nevertheless bipolar (i.e. social versus liberal) structure of party competition. Regardless, populist parties did play a role in (1) bringing about the consolidation of the current two-bloc competition (social versus liberal) and (2) reinforcing its open character.

Table 9.5 The Impact of Populist Parties on Party System Development in Poland: A Summary

Competition	Polarisation	Fragmentation	Volatility	Closure	Overall
2	1	1	1	2	7/15 (46.7%)

Note: 0 = none; 1 = low; 2 = medium; 3 = high.

However, as table 9.5 shows, the impact of these parties is quite limited. The system was quite open before and after the changes in 1993, 1997, 2005 and 2007 (*see* figure 9.2), which were not directly linked to the emergence and success of populist parties. On the contrary, populism was absorbed into this very open system and helped sustain what was already a fertile breeding ground for political parties in general. In this sense, the recurrent populism in Polish politics has seemingly been more like a hurricane than an earthquake. Our review of populist parties and the Polish party system since democratisation has revealed the following:

1. Populism has been always present, but it was not significant until 2005 and then again between 2007 and 2014.
2. Volatility and fragmentation are mostly due to party elites and voters' discontent with government policies.
3. Competition has been influenced by presidential elections, especially in 2005.
4. Polarisation has stemmed from the weight of the past, particularly the historical confrontation between post-communist and post-Solidarity parties.

The rise and fall of populist parties in Poland between 2001 and 2007 wreaked havoc on the Polish party system, but parties (the PO, PiS, the SLD, and the PSL) with strong foundations (i.e. social democratic, agrarian, liberal and conservative) endured. Unlike an earthquake, these parties did not produce 'sudden, unpredictable and massive disruption' (Deegan-Krause and Haughton 2015: 61); instead, they forced the two main post-Solidarity parties (i.e. the PO and PiS) to adapt to the new political environment. The entry of these parties led to a ninety-degree turn, rather than a rupture, in the logic of competition.[26]

Although historical legacies were very influential before 2006, the shift towards a 'social versus liberal' Poland has also changed the types of populist discourse that are likely to succeed. The discontent emerging from the financial and economic crisis, although not hitting a low point in Poland, was channelled in controversial debates that had already emerged in the pre-accession years. Lepper gave voice to the fight against crime and to the Polish peasantry, but his electorate was more concerned with the costs of the economic transition and market economy. 'Generation Y', frustrated by the economic and political situation, can provide a stronger impetus for populist success. In 2015, young people's disappointment and disillusionment delivered more than 20 per cent of the student vote to PiS, Kukiz'15 and KORWiN, led by Janusz Korwin Mikke, a seventy-two-year-old politician advocating a radical right and hard Eurosceptic programme. The main legacy of populism is the persistence of a fertile breeding ground and populism's survival in a very open (and crippled) party system, characterised by disloyal political elites, continuous electoral discontent and the lack of a credible alternative on the left end of the political spectrum. The illiberal turn of the new PiS-led government, with the appointment of various controversial ministers (e.g. Antoni Macierewicz and Zbigniew Ziobro) and the speedy adoption of various legislative reforms (i.e. Constitutional Court, media, civil service), shows a rather exclusive concept of 'law and justice', confirming the worst fears of the 2006–2007 'populist coalition' (see Guerra and Casal Bértoa 2016). If, as Deegan-Krause and Haughton (2015) have maintained, hurricanes are more predictable than earthquakes, then the next populist windstorm will likely come soon.

ACKNOWLEDGEMENTS

We would like to thank Tim Haughton (University of Birmingham), Andrea L. P. Pirro (Scuola Normale Superiore, Florence) and Aleks Szczerbiak (University of Sussex) for their valuable comments on a previous version of this chapter. We are also thankful to Kevin Deegan-Krause (Wayne State University) for his assistance with the graphic design of figure 9.1.

The authors also gratefully acknowledge Dr Clare McManus, School of Social and Political Sciences, University of Glasgow, and Professor Radosław Markowski and Professor Mikołaj Cześnik, Polish Academy of Sciences and Warsaw School of Social Psychology for the PNES data. The 2001 and 2005 Polish National Election Studies are part of a long-running series in the field of political sociology and political science. The 2001 Polish National Election Study, affiliated with the Institute of Political Studies, Polish Academy of Science, is sponsored by the Polish State Committee for Scientific Research (KBN), grant No. 5 H02E 02120; and co-sponsored by the Economic and Social Research Council (ESRC) and Warsaw School of Social Psychology (SWPS). The 2005 Polish National Election Study 2005 is a study affiliated with the Institute of Political Studies, Polish Academy of Sciences, and sponsored by the Polish Ministry of Science and Information, grant No. 5 1 H02E 060 28, co-sponsored by the Stefan Batory Foundation, Public Opinion Research Centre (CBOS), Institute of Philosophy and Sociology, Polish Academy of Sciences and University of Glasgow (Department of Politics & Department of Central and East European Studies).

APPENDIX

Table 9.1A Electoral and Parliamentary Support for Populist Parties in Polish Legislative Elections (1991–2015)

Party	1991	1993	1997	2001	2005	2007	2011	2015
PWN	0.1	0.1	0.1	0	–	–	–	–
X	0.5 (0.7)	2.7	–	–	–	–	–	–
SRP	–	2.8	0	10.2 (11.5)	11.4 (12.2)	1.5	–	–
RdR	–	2.7	–	–	–	–	–	–
PFN	–	0	–	–	–	–	–	–
ROP	–	–	5.6 (1.3)	–	–	–	–	–
LPR	–	–	–	7.9 (8.3)	8 (7.4)	1.3	–	–
RP	–	–	–	–	1.1	–	–	–
PPN	–	–	–	–	0.3	–	–	–
DO	–	–	–	–	0.3	–	–	–
IRP	–	–	–	–	0	–	–	–
NOP	–	–	–	–	0	–	–	–
SP	–	–	–	–	–	0	–	–
KNP	–	–	–	–	–	–	0.5	0
PR	–	–	–	–	–	–	0.1	–
NDP	–	–	–	–	–	–	0	0
Kukiz'15	–	–	–	–	–	–	–	8.8 (9.1)
KORWiN	–	–	–	–	–	–	–	4.8

Note: The percentage of legislative seats appears in brackets.

Table 9.2A Electoral support for populist parties/candidates in Polish presidential elections (1990–2015)

Candidates (Party)	1990	1995	2000	2005	2010	2015
Stanisław Tymiński (Independent)	23.1*			0.2[a]		
Andrzej Lepper (SRP)		1.3	3.1	15.1	1.3	
Jan Olszewski (RdR)		6.9				
Jan Łopuszański (PP)			0.5			
Leszek Bubel (PPN)				0.1		
Jan Pyszko (ONP-LP)				0.1		
Marek Jurek (PR)				–	1.1	
Pawel Kukiz (Independent)				–	–	20.8
Janusz Korwin-Mikke (KORWiN)				–	–	3.3
Marian Kowalski (RN)				–	–	0.5
Jacek Wilk (KNP)				–	–	0.5

[a] Supported by *Ogólnopolska Koalicja Obywatelska* (OKO, the All-Polish Citizens' Coalition).

Note: Candidates continuing on to the second round are marked with an asterisk (*).

LIST OF PARTY ACRONYMS

Populist Parties

DO = Ancestral Home; IRP = Initiative for the Republic of Poland; KNP = Congress of the New Right; KORWiN = Coalition for the Renewal of the Republic – Freedom and Hope; Kukiz'15 = Kukiz 2015; LPR = League of Polish Families; NDP = Our Home Poland; NOP = National Revival of Poland; ONP-LP = Organisation of the Polish Nation-Polish League; PFN = Polish National Front; PP = Polish Agreement; PPN = Polish National Party; PR = Right of the Republic; PWN = National Polish Society; RdR = Movement for the Republic; RN = National Movement; ROP = Movement for the Reconstruction of Poland; RP = Patriotic Movement; SP = Patriotic Self-Defence; SRP = Self-Defence of the Republic of Poland; X = Party X.

Other (Non-Populist) Parties

AWS = Solidarity Electoral Action; BBWR = Non-Partisan Bloc for Support of Reforms; KLD = Liberal Democratic Congress; .N = Modern; PC = Centre Agreement; PChD = Christian Democratic Party; PD = Democratic Party; PiS = Law and Justice; PL = Peasant Alliance; PO = Civic Platform; PRZP = Poland Together United Right; PSL = Polish People's Party; TR = Your Movement; S = Solidarity; SD = Alliance of Democrats; SdPL = Social Democracy of Poland; SLD = Left Democratic Alliance; SP = United Poland; UD = Democratic Union; UPR = Real Union Politics; UW = Freedom Union; ZChN = Christian National Union; ZSL = United People's Party.

NOTES

1 See Haughton and Deegan-Krause (2015).

2 For a more in-depth study of Polish party systems, please see Szczerbiak (2001), Millard (2010) and Gwiazda (2015).

3 Given the extremely fragmented character of the 1991–1993 legislature, figure 9.1 displays all parliamentary parties between 1993 and 2015, along with the most successful (i.e. ≥ 4 seats) ones in 1991.

4 The term 'refolution' refers to the process of political, social and economic change that took place in Central and Eastern Europe. It was similar to a revolution but relied on the old political system without major purges; in most cases, it was half reform, half revolution (Ash 1989).

5 For a detailed list of populist parties, presidential candidates, and the parties that supported them, please see tables 9.1A and 9.2A in the appendix. In contrast to some scholars (Bakke and Sitter 2005: 248; Van Kessel 2015), though similar to Enyedi and Rona (in this volume), we consider PiS to be a social national conservative party rather than a populist party (Buzalka 2008: 757; De Lange and Guerra 2009; Szczerbiak 2007).

6   Centrum Public Opinion Research Centre is the actual translation of Badanii Opinii Społecznej, and it is the research centre for public opinion in Poland.

7   In 1998, nearly half (45 per cent) of the respondents, among them farmers, declared their opposition to EU membership (CBOS 1998, 06/98); 74 per cent of them had concerns about their future in the EU (CBOS 1998, 05/98).

8   After the beginning of the negotiations, 45 per cent of Poles felt 'hopeful', while 36 per cent felt 'anxious' (CBOS 1998, 05/98).

9   Fifty-nine per cent considered the actions on public health service unsatisfactory, and 74 per cent felt this way about agrarian policies (CBOS 1999, 02/99).

10   GUS, Głowny Urząd Statyczny (undated).

11   Ranging from 0 (non-polarised) to 1 (polarised), Dalton's polarisation index is calculated using the formula $\{[\Sigma(vi)*([xi-x]/5)^2]\}^{1/2}$, where vi is the proportion of votes of the ith party, xi refers to its left-right score, and x represents the *average* party system score on the left-right scale (2008: 9). Both ENEP and ENPP are calculated according to Laakso and Taagepera's (1979) well-known formulae: $1/\Sigma v(s)i$, where vi and si are the proportion of votes and seats, respectively, of the ith party. Electoral volatility is measured by the formula provided by Pedersen (1979): $V=\Sigma|Ci,t-1- Ci,t|/2$, where V is volatility, Ci,t is the vote share for a ith party at a given election (t) and Ci,t-1is the vote share of the same ith party at the previous elections (t-1).

12   For a comparison with other East-Central European countries, please see Casal Bértoa (2012, 2014).

13   Amid (never proved) corruption allegations, he resigned just three weeks before the first round of elections.

14   However, they differed in their religious intensity, with PiS being much more clerical than the PO (Casal Bértoa 2014: 27–29).

15   On the one hand, the PO was a splinter party of the UW, which was founded through a merger of the UD and the extremely neoliberal KLD, whose leader was Donald Tusk. On the other hand, PiS was founded by the Kaczyński twins as a splinter party of the AWS; it is thus open to the social teachings of the Catholic Church.

16   The difference between Tusk and Kaczyński during the first round was barely three percentage points in favour of the former.

17   Notably, on 25 September 2005, PiS won legislative elections by a small margin (27 per cent against the PO's 24 per cent). The SRP came in third again with 11.4 per cent of the vote. Any eventual cabinet, excluding a PO-PiS grand-coalition, now prevented by its two leaders' presidential ambitions, would certainly have to obtain Lepper's endorsement.

18   Maciej Giertych, father of Roman Giertych (LPR's leader at the time).

19   This idea was immediately rejected due to the SRP's 'image as an organisation too radical for the taste of the mainstream public in Poland and too unpredictable for the smooth conduct of Poland´s foreign relations' (Jasiewicz and Jasiewicz-Betkiewicz 2002: 1066).

20   Depending on whether the 'exceptionally fragmented' elections of 1991 are excluded or included.

21   As mentioned in a previous work (Casal Bértoa 2013: 401), party systems 'with an ENPP of 4.0 of higher . . . correspond to [Sartori's] category of extreme pluralism' (see also Mainwaring and Scully 1995: 32).

22   According to Sartori (1976), even an extremely fragmented party system might be 'bipolar', provided that it revolves around two – moderately distanced – ideological poles.

23   In 2005, the SLD also suffered its first major split due to the formation of *Socjaldemokracja Polska* (SdPL, Social Democracy of Poland).

24   Minorities, to which a 5 per cent electoral threshold does not apply, are excluded.

25   As Casal Bértoa (2013: 413) demonstrates, the Polish party system is one of the most open in Europe.

26   While an electoral earthquake would have changed the dimensions of competition, the latter did not change; it instead rotated, driven (though only indirectly) by the populist cyclone.

BIBLIOGRAPHY

Ash, T. G. (1989) 'Revolution in Hungary and Poland', *New York Review of Books*, 36(13): 9–15.

Bakke, E. and Sitter, N. (2005) 'Patterns of stability: Party competition and strategy in Central Europe since 1989', *Party Politics*, 11(2): 243–263.

Brier, R. (2009) 'The roots of the "fourth Republic": Solidarity's cultural legacy to Polish politics', *East European Politics and Societies*, 23(1): 63–85.

Buzalka, J. (2008) 'Europeanisation and post-peasant populism in Eastern Europe', *Europe-Asia Studies*, 60(5): 757–771.

Casal Bértoa, F. (2012) 'Parties, regime and cleavages: Explaining party system institutionalization in East Central Europe', *East European Politics*, 28(4): 452–472.

——— (2013) 'Post-communist politics: On the divergence (and/or convergence) of east and west', *Government and Opposition*, 48(3): 398–433.

——— (2014) 'Party systems and cleavage structures revisited: A sociological explanation of party system institutionalization in East Central Europe', *Party Politics*, 20(1): 16–36.

——— (2016) *Database on Who GOVERNS in Europe and beyond, PSGo.* whogoverns.eu (accessed 8 January 2016).

Casal Bértoa, F. and Enyedi, Z. (2016) 'Party system closure and openness: Conceptualization, operationalization and validation', *Party Politics*, 22(3): 265–277.

Casal Bértoa, F. and Walecki, M. (2014) 'Regulating Polish politics: "Cartel" parties in a non-collusive party system', *East European Politics*, 30(3): 330–350.

Castle, M. and Taras, R. (2002) *Democracy in Poland*, Boulder, CO: Westview Press.

CBOS (2001) 'BS/155/2001 Komunikat z badań, Społeczne poparcie dla integracji z Unią Europejską', Warsaw: November.

CBOS bulletin (2001) '*Opinia*'. www.cbos.org.pl (accessed 30 June 2015).

Dalton, R. J. (2008) 'The quantity and the quality of party Systems', *Comparative Political Studies*, 20(10): 1–22.

Deegan-Krause, K. and Haughton, T. (2015) 'Hurricane season: Systems of instability in Central and East European party politics', *East European Politics and Societies*, 29(1): 61–80.

De Lange, S. L. and Guerra, S. (2009) 'The league of Polish families between east and west, past and present', *Journal of Communist and Post-Communist Studies*, 42(4): 527–549.

248 Chapter 9

Döring, H. and Manow, P. (2012) 'Parliament and government composition database (ParlGov): An infrastructure for empirical information on parties, elections and governments in modern democracies', *Version*, 10(11): 6.

Enyedi, Z. and Casal Bértoa, F. (2011) 'Patterns of inter-party competition (1990–2009)', in P. G. Lewis and R. Markowski (eds.) *Europeanizing party politics? Comparative perspectives on Central and Eastern Europe*, Manchester: Manchester University Press.

Fitzgibbon, J. and Guerra, S. (2010) 'Not just Europeanization, not necessarily populism: Potential factors underlying the mobilization of populism in Ireland and Poland', *Perspectives on European Politics and Society*, 11(3): 273–291.

Grabowska, M. (2004) *Podział postkomunistyczny: Społeczne podstawy polityki w Polsce po 1989 roku*, Warsaw: Scholar.

Grzybowski, M. (1994) 'Poland: Towards overdeveloped pluralism', in S. Berglund and J. A. Dellenbrant (eds.) *Party systems and political cleavages*, Cheltenham: Edward Elgar Publishing House.

Grzybowski, M. and Migulik, P. (2004) 'Poland', in S. Berglund, J. Ekman and F. H. Aarebrot (eds.) *The handbook of political change in Eastern Europe*, Cheltenham: Edward Elgar Publishing House.

Guerra, S. (2012) 'Eurosceptic allies or Euroenthusiast friends? The political discourse of the Roman Catholic Church in Poland', in L. Leustan (ed.) *Does God matter? Representing religion in the European Union*, London: Routledge Series on Religion and Politics.

——— (2013) *Central and Eastern European attitudes in the face of union*, Basingstoke: Palgrave Macmillan.

Guerra, S. and Casal Bértoa, F. (2015) 'How Poland's political landscape was redrawn overnight', *The Conversation*, 27 October. Available at: https://theconver sation.com/how-polands-political-landscape-was-redrawn-overnight-49697.

——— (2016) 'Poland: Right turn', 2015 elections round-up, *The Conversation*, 2 January. Available at: https://theconversation.com/2015-the-year-in-elections-51642.

Gwiazda, A. (2015) *Democracy in Poland: Representation, participation, competition and accountability since 1989*, New York: Abingdon: Routledge.

Głowny Urząd Statystyczny (undated) (accessed 30 June 2015).

Jasiewicz, K. (2002) 'Portfel czy Różaniec? Wzory Zachowań Wyborczych Polaków w Latach 1995–2001', in R. Markowski (ed.) *System Partyjny i Zachowania Wyborcze. Dekada Polskich Doświadczeń*, Warsaw: Elbert Foundation/ISP PAN.

——— (2007) 'Poland', in P. Webb and S. White (eds.) *Party politics in new democracies*, Oxford: Oxford University Press.

——— (2008) 'The new populism in Poland. The usual suspects?', *Problems of Post-Communism*, 55(3): 7–25.

Jasiewicz, K. and Jasiewicz-Betkiewicz, A. (2002) 'Poland', *European Journal of Political Research*, 41(7–8): 1057–1067.

Kasprowicz, D. (2015) 'The radical right in Poland – from the mainstream to the margins: A case of interconnectivity', in M. Mikenberg (ed.) *Transforming the transformation? The East European radical right in the political process*, Abingdon: Routledge.

Kitschelt, H., Mansfeldova, Z., Markowski, R. and Tóka, G. (1999) *Post-communist party systems: Competition, representation and inter-party cooperation*, Cambridge: Cambridge University Press.

Kubik, J. and Lynch, A. (2006) 'The original sin of Poland's third Republic: Discounting "Solidarity" and its consequences for political reconciliation', *Polish Sociological Review*, 1(153): 9–38.

Laakso, M., and Taagepera, R. (1979) ' "Effective" number of parties: A measure with application to West Europe', *Comparative Political Studies*, 12(1): 3–27.

Linz, J. J. and Montero, J. R. (2001) 'The party systems of Spain: Old cleavages and new challenges', in L. Karvonen and S. Kuhnle (eds.) *Party systems and voter alignments revisited*, London: Routledge.

Linz, J. J. and Stepan, A. (1996) *Problems of democratic transition and consolidation: Southern Europe, South America, and post-communist Europe*, Baltimore, MD: The Johns Hopkins University Press.

Mainwaring, S., and Scully, T. (1995) *Building democratic institutions: Party systems in Latin America*, Stanford, CA: Stanford University Press.

Mair, P. (1997) *Party system change: Approaches and interpretations*, Oxford: Clarendon Press.

Markowski, R. (1999) 'Polish party system: Institutionalization – political representation – issue structuring', Draft paper prepared for presentation at the ECPR Joint Sessions Mannheim, 26–31 March.

——— (2006) 'The Polish elections of 2005: Pure chaos or a restructuring of the party system?', *West European Politics*, 29(4): 814–832.

——— (2007) 'System Partyjny', in L. Kolarska-Bobińska, J. Kucharczyk and J. Zbieranek (eds.) *Demokracja w Polsce 2005–2007*. Warzawa: Instytut Spraw Publicznych.

Markowski, R. and Cześnik, M. (2002) 'Polski system Partyjny: Dekada Instytucjonalnych i ich Konsekwencje', in R. Markowski (ed.) *System Partyjny i Zachowania Wyborcze: Dekada Polskich Doświadczeń*, Warsaw: Elbert Foundation/ISP PAN.

Millard, F. (2006) 'Poland's politics and the travails of transition after 2001: The 2005 elections', *Europe-Asia Studies*, 58(7): 1007–1031.

——— (2010) *Democratic Elections in Poland, 1991–2007*, Abingdon: Routledge.

Mudde, C. (2004) 'The populist zeitgeist', *Government and Opposition*, 39(4): 542–563.

——— (2014) 'Fighting the system? Populist Radical Right Parties and Party system change', *Party Politics*, 20(2): 217–226.

Mudde, C. & Rovira Kaltwasser, C. (2013) 'Exclusionary vs. inclusionary populism: Comparing contemporary Europe and Latin America', *Government and Opposition*, 48(2): 147–174.

O'Dwyer, C. (2006) *Runaway state-building: Patronage politics and democratic development*, Baltimore, MD: Johns Hopkins University Press.

Pankowski, R. (2010) *The populist radical right in Poland*, Abingdon: Routledge.

Pedersen, M. N. (1979) 'The dynamics of European party systems: Changing patterns of electoral volatility', *European Journal of Political Research*, 7(1): 1–26.

Pirro, A. L. P. (2015) *The populist radical-right in Central and Eastern Europe: Ideology, impact, and electoral performance*, Abingdon: Routledge.

Powell, E. N. and Tucker, J. A. (2014) 'Revisiting electoral volatility in post- communist countries: New data, new results and new approaches', *British Journal of Political Science*, 44(1): 123–147.

Sartori, G. (1976) *Parties and party systems: A framework for analysis, vol. 1*, Cambridge: Cambridge University Press.

Sielski, J. (2004) 'Polski system Partyjny', in K. Kowalczyk and J. Sielski (eds.) *Polskie Partie i Ugrupowanie Parlamentarne*, Wydawnictwo: Adam Marszałek pp. 9–26.

Słomczyński, K. M., Janicka, K., Shabad, G. and Tomescu-Dubrow, I. (2007) 'Changes in class structure in Poland, 1988–2003: Crystallization of the winners-losers' divide', *Polish Sociological Review*, 1(157): 45–64.

Smith, G. (1989) 'A system perspective on party system change', *Journal of Theoretical Politics*, 1(3): 349–363.

Stanley, B. (2015a) 'The post-populist non-crisis in Poland', in H. Kriesi and T. S. Pappas (eds.) *European populism in the shadow of the Great Recession*, Colchester: ECPR Press.

———— (2015b) 'Confrontation by default and confrontation by design: Strategic and institutional responses to Poland's populist coalition government', *Democratization*, 23(2): 1–20.

Szczerbiak, A. (2001) *Poles together? The emergence and development of political parties in post-communist Poland*, Budapest: Central Publishing House European University Press.

———— (2002) 'After the election, nearing the endgame: The Polish euro-debate in the run up to the 2003 EU accession referendum', in *Opposing Europe Research Network Working Paper No. 7/Sussex European Institute Working Paper No. 53, Famer*, Brighton: Sussex European Institute, University of Sussex.

———— (2006a) 'Power without love: Patterns of party politics in post-communist Poland', in S. Jungerstam-Mulders (ed.) *Post-communist EU member states: Parties and party systems*, Aldershot: Ashgate.

———— (2006b) ' "Social Poland" defeats "liberal Poland"? The September–October 2005 Polish parliamentary and presidential elections', SEI Working Paper No. 86, Falmer, Brighton: Sussex European Institute, University of Sussex.

———— (2007) ' "Social Poland" defeats "liberal Poland"? The September–October 2005 Polish parliamentary and presidential elections', *Journal of Communist Studies and Transition Politics*, 23(2): 203–232.

———— (2014) 'Making sense of Poland's Congress of the New Right', polishpolitics-blog.wordpress.com/2014/06/11/making-sense-of-polands-congress-of-the-new-right/ (accessed 4 August 2014).

Szczerbiak, A. and Taggart, P. (2004) 'The politics of European referendum outcomes and turnout: Two models', *West European Politics*, 27(4): 557–583.

Toole, J. (2000) 'Government formation and party system stabilization in East Central Europe', *Party Politics*, 6(4): 441–461.

Van Kessel, S. (2015) *Populist parties in Europe: Agents of discontent?*, Basingstoke: Palgrave Macmillan.

Wysocka, O. (2009) 'Populism in Poland: in/visible exclusion', in L. Freeman (ed.) *In/Visibility: Perspectives on inclusion and exclusion*, Vienna: IWM Junior Visiting Fellows' Conferences, Volume 26.

Chapter 10

Governmental and Oppositional Populism: Competition and Division of Labour

Zsolt Enyedi and Dániel Róna

INTRODUCTION

The central question of the current volume is how European party systems cope with the populist challenge and whether the recent successes of populist parties have upset the nature of party relations in European nation-states. The Hungarian case reminds us that these seemingly straightforward questions imply a number of assumptions and simplifications: that parties can be categorised as populist and non-populist, that populist parties are not identical with the core parties and that party relations used to be characterised by a set of conventions that have been recently challenged by the arrival of newcomers. In the Hungarian case, these assumptions only partially apply; therefore, the dynamics of the Hungarian case significantly deviate from the European 'master narrative'. Accordingly, a number of caveats are in order.

The first caveat concerns the ideological profile of the analysed parties, Jobbik (the Movement for a Better Hungary) and Fidesz (originally the Alliance of Young Democrats). Although the populist elements of these parties' ideologies, discourses and strategies justify their inclusion in studies on populism (Bozóki 2008, 2015), both have relevant elitist features, and populism usually plays a secondary role behind conservative nationalism (Enyedi 2015, 2016). Additionally, Fidesz is one of the founding parties of Hungarian democracy. Unlike most populist parties, it is a large party. It is so large that asking whether it has influenced the Hungarian party system makes limited sense. After all, this party controlled more than two-thirds of the representatives in the Parliament between 2010 and 2015. Fidesz essentially *is* the Hungarian party system. Jobbik also uneasily fits the stereotype of a small populist challenger as it has commanded the support of one-fifth of Hungarian voters since 2009. Together, the two parties obtained approximately 70 per cent of the vote in 2010 and in 2014. If both of them are classified as populist, few parties remain for the non-populist category.

Additionally, even a superficial knowledge of post-communist politics indicates that the temporal frame of many of the cases discussed in this volume, that is, a sequence of decades-long stability followed by recent turbulence, will not perfectly fit our case. Although almost three decades have passed since the collapse of communism, the stability that character-ises Western electorates has not been achieved in Hungary (Tóka and Popa 2013; Van der Brug et al 2009). The Hungarian party system is one of the most stable systems in Eastern Europe, yet the average electoral volatility during the 1990s and early 2000s was three times greater than that in estab-lished Western democracies. Under such conditions, there was no room for the development of cleavage-based core parties. Party identifications, albeit stronger than in most neighbouring countries, remained fragile.

Finally, one of the central categories of the current volume, 'reaction to populism', also needs to be contextualised. The focus must be not only on the reactions to the rise of radical Jobbik but also on the implications of the gradual transformation of Fidesz, that is, a mainstream party. Even more importantly, in the analysed case, the parties that needed to 'respond' to the populist challenge included the populist parties themselves, which had to react to one another.

THE HUNGARIAN PARTY SYSTEM: FIDESZ, JOBBIK AND THE REST

The consensus among observers is that populist tendencies started to play a central role in the politics of Fidesz after they lost the 2002 election (Körö-sényi 2007). Jobbik was also established after that election; therefore, 2002 will be the starting point of the subsequent analysis. The analysis will focus on the 2010–2014 period, as Jobbik became a significant force only in 2009 and a parliamentary party only in 2010.

Over the past decade, the Hungarian party system has consisted of relatively few relevant parties. Only the Hungarian Socialist Party (MSZP), Fidesz, the Alliance of Free Democrats (SZDSZ) and Jobbik unequivo-cally qualify. Jobbik has never been in government, but it is relevant as an 'anti-system party'; it has as an elaborate radical right-wing, anti-regime ideology. The MSZP is the successor of the Hungarian Socialist Workers Party and has been the dominant left-wing party since the early 1990s. For about one-half of the entire post-communist period, a Socialist has served as prime minister. The Socialists governed together with the liberal SZDSZ and formed the so-called left-liberal alliance, a secular, pro-Western and internationalist bloc.

Fidesz, the leading right-wing party since 1996, used to be a member of the liberal party family, but it joined the alliance of European Christian Democratic and Conservative parties (EPP) in 2000. Fidesz's move to the right was closely related to, and largely followed, the implosion of the Hungarian Democratic Forum (MDF), the Christian Democratic People's Party (KDNP) and the Independent Smallholders' Party (FKGP), which were the conservative parties that governed the country during the first years of post-communist transition (Enyedi 2006). Of these three parties, only the KDNP survived, though only as a satellite party of Fidesz.

The issue content of the Hungarian party competition has always been different from that of the classical Western patterns. Cultural issues, including national identity, sovereignty, historical grievances (especially the treaties that ended the two world wars and the character of the Horthy and Kádár regimes), the role of churches, the regulation of the public media and the extent to which governing parties can colonise state institutions, overshadowed issues related to welfare, taxes and equality (Karácsony 2005, Tóka 2006). Given the focus on cultural issues, it is customary to divide the parties into nationalist and cosmopolitan camps – the former dominated by Fidesz since the mid-1990s, and the latter led by the MSZP and (until 2010) by the SZDSZ.

As table 10.1 indicates, the Hungarian party system is one of the more concentrated party systems in Europe. Between 2002 and 2010, approximately 90 per cent of the MPs and 80 per cent of voters belonged to either Fidesz or the MSZP. The disproportionality figures in table 10.1 show that the electoral

Table 10.1 Fragmentation, Volatility and Disproportionality of the Hungarian Party System, 1990–2014

	1990	*1994*	*1998*	*2002*	*2006*	*2010*	*2014*
Vote share of parliamentary parties	84.2	87.6	88.5	88.7	96.8	96.2	96.3
Vote share of the two largest parties	46.1	52.7	62.3	83.1	85.2	72.3	70.7
Effective number of parties	5.9	5.3	4.5	2.8	2.7	2.9	3.2
Effective number of parliamentary parties	3.7	2.9	3.1	2.2	2.4	2	2
Aggregate volatility		25.8	31.7	18.3	9	32.7	10
Change in the vote share of the government		−25.8	−12.2	−3.6	2.1	−30.4	−8
Loosemore-Hanby index[1]	20.3	22.9	16.5	11.7	6.4	15.4	22

[1] The Loosemore-Hanby index measures the proportionality of elections. The index is the sum of the absolute differences between the vote percentages and the seat percentages, divided by two. The smaller the value is, the more proportionate the result is. The 2006 Hungarian national election was quite proportionate from a European perspective, whereas the 2014 result was highly disproportionate.

Source: www.valasztas.hu.

system, which has a robust majoritarian component, contributes significantly to the low fragmentation of the party system.

The first two decades of the party system were characterised by increasing electoral stability. By 2006, the net electoral volatility (as indicated by the Pedersen index) had declined to 9 per cent. According to the fragmentation and volatility data, the Hungarian party system appeared as consolidated as any established Western party system. However, after the 2006 election, a major realignment occurred (*see* figure 10.1). Due to the economic downturn and a leaked speech[1] of the prime minister, Hungarian voters deserted the governing Socialist Party in mass. For the next decade, Fidesz was left without a rival. During the subsequent election in 2010, the government parties suffered a worse defeat than any government in post-communist Hungarian history. The margin between Fidesz and the MSZP widened to more than 30 per cent. Many of the 'traditional' parties, including the SZDSZ, the FKGP and the MDF, disappeared from the electoral arena, and the hitherto marginal Jobbik received almost as many votes as the MSZP. In subsequent years, the MSZP's popularity declined even further, and Jobbik became the second-largest Hungarian party.

The electoral rules further amplified the electoral landslide of Fidesz. With 53 per cent of the vote, the party obtained two-thirds of the seats. Having won this supermajority, Fidesz introduced an even more disproportional electoral system. In 2014, the party won 'only' 45 per cent of the vote share, but the same percentage of seats as in 2010.

After 2010, numerous left-wing initiatives were launched, but none of them became relevant in Sartori's sense, while the MSZP continued to

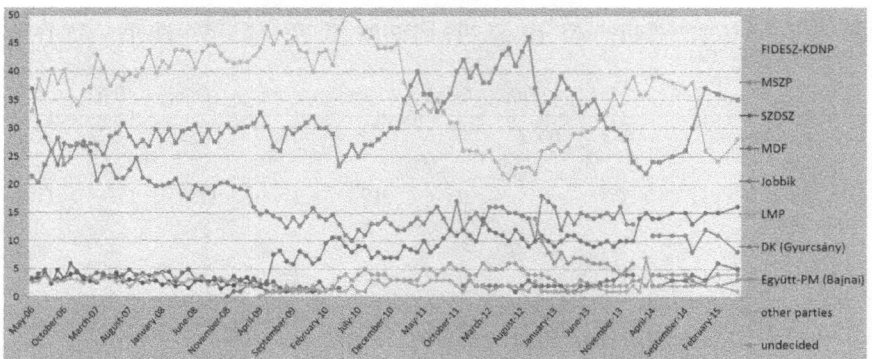

Figure 10.1 The Popularity of Parties between 2006 and 2014 in Hungary (percentages)

Source: Authors' own collection, based on data from Medián polling company.

stagnate around 10 per cent. More importantly, given the thrust of the current chapter, the popularity of Jobbik, a party established in 2003, skyrocketed in the wake of a series of crimes involving Roma perpetrators (Karácsony and Róna 2011). The party received 17 per cent of the votes in 2010 and 20 per cent in 2014. After 2014, thanks to the further decline of MSZP, Jobbik captured the second-party position.

This brief summary of the party system's parameters and its most relevant changes during the 2000s show that, despite the post-communist particularities mentioned earlier in the text, the Hungarian dynamics resemble the typical Western pattern in some crucial respects. Although the electorate has never been as anchored as in established democracies, the party system used to have a relatively simple, 'consolidated' structure. This structure was bipolar and symmetric. In 2006, major changes rocked the extra-parliamentary arena. These changes, as will be discussed further in the text in more detail, related to the ascendency of populist strategies. At the same time, the party system remained concentrated, and in 2014, following the upheaval of the 2010 election, electoral volatility declined to its earlier, relatively low, levels. In other words, the standard party system parameters changed only modestly, and the principal consequences of populism lie elsewhere.

COMPETITION FOR VOTERS

The first question that needs answering concerns whether Fidesz's policy shifts and Jobbik's appearance induced changes in party competition. According to the European 'master narrative', populist parties disturb the traditional, class-based, left-right competition by politicising topics such as multiculturalism, citizenship and European integration. The Hungarian trajectory differs from the European pattern because, first, as described earlier, cultural issues and democracy-related questions have always played a larger role than economic issues in defining parties' ideological profiles; second, the populist wave started with Fidesz's shift towards economic populism, well before the rise of the Jobbik.

Fidesz started building a new economic profile after its 2002 election loss, demanding an active state that protects citizens against the vagaries of the market. The party's economic populism included a robust anti-establishment rhetoric and efforts to mobilise citizens via referendums, demonstrations and petitions. The new strategy opened the door to lower-class voters to join the party (Knutsen 2011). In subsequent years, Fidesz became a genuine cross-class organisation. Its ideological foundations remained unaltered, but it added to its conservative nationalist profile a set of 'socialistic' demands – for example, free education, free health care, low utility prices and high pensions –

and a discourse that emphasised the interests of the 'people' against the interests of the elites and the 'rule of institutions'.

Prior to 2002, welfare issues were 'owned' by the MSZP. Between 2002 and 2006, the MSZP-led government lived up to its reputation as a 'caring' party, as evidenced by its re-election in 2006 – the first re-election in the history of post-communist Hungary. However, while the MSZP's generous policies were popular, its concomitant reckless spending put the country on the brink of bankruptcy. In 2006, the public deficit exceeded 10 per cent. The national debt reached 65.9 per cent of the GDP in 2006, and increased further to 79.8 per cent in 2009 (compared with 52.7 per cent in 2001). The ensuing economic crisis rapidly transformed into the MSZP's crisis, whereby the Socialists lost two-thirds of their supporters.

The parties that filled the void created by the collapse of the MSZP were Fidesz and Jobbik. The latter differs from the former primarily in terms of its outsider status and its appeal to anti-elite, anti-Roma and anti-Semitic voters. Particularly the emphasis on the Roma issue constituted a major innovation, as none of the mainstream parties had previously focused on this issue. The foreign policy orientation of the two parties also differs: Fidesz supports membership in EU and NATO, while Jobbik would support a new referendum on these issues and calls for some form of institutionalised alliances with Eastern powers. Consequently, Fidesz often attacks Jobbik as an agent of Russian interests, while Jobbik depicts Fidesz as a sometimes reluctant but ultimately obedient lackey of Brussels, the United States and Israel. The two parties also differentiate themselves along the moderate-radical spectrum: according to Fidesz, Jobbik is irresponsible and violent, while Jobbik considers Fidesz clientelistic and corrupt. However, the competition between the two parties is ultimately more about valence, credibility and competence than about rival ideologies or policy positions. They both see themselves as part of the nationalist camp. According to both parties, the elections are largely about the conflict between domestic and foreign interests, and the left serves the interests of the latter.

During the 2000s, the growing popularity of 'us *vs.* them' rhetoric increased the perceived stakes of elections. The right portrayed the elections as a struggle for national sovereignty, while the left projected a conflict over the fundamental values of democracy – a choice between authoritarianism and antifascism. The stakes also increased because both Jobbik and Fidesz advocated a majoritarian conception of democracy and an active state that could override the logic of the private economy. Fidesz and Jobbik agree that the government must protect the interests of domestic producers and consumers; therefore, the state is allowed to discriminate against foreigners, regulate prices, support specific enterprises, nationalise certain properties and industries, and exempt citizens from the burdens of unfair bank loans.

The attitudinal similarities between the government and one of the major opposition parties facilitated the centralisation of the state in Hungary, the contraction of multinational companies, primarily in the financial and service sectors, and provided support for an increasingly hostile public attitude towards banks and foreign landowners. However, this logic has not stayed within the boundaries of the economy: international human rights organisations, internationally owned media outlets and liberal intellectual centres have also experienced the separate but converging hostility of the two parties.[2]

Until 2014, the media and most political actors framed the elections as a left-right struggle. However, since 2014, the growth in Jobbik's public support and the gradual decline of Fidesz's popularity have changed the electoral context. By 2016, the fragmented left, Jobbik and Fidesz constituted three roughly equally strong political camps. Fidesz continues to be the most prominent actor, and its status as one of the principal alternatives in the party system has not been threatened. However, the challenger's identity is the object of political debate. For those who see the left as the provider of the principal contender for prime minister, the traditional pattern of the Hungarian party system remains unaltered, and the competition continues to relate to the issues of nationalism, anti-communism and clericalism. However, if Jobbik is considered Fidesz's main rival, the stakes have more to do with clean government and the rate of change in the illiberal direction.

In many regions of the country, particularly in small towns and villages, the left has ceased to be a credible force and competition has narrowed to a choice between Fidesz and Jobbik – that is, between two versions of populist politics. This unusual configuration is not fully reflected by the mass media, partly because Jobbik lacks support from the elites and thus continues to argue its cause from a marginalised position and partly because Jobbik is still not considered capable of forming a government on its own. Similarly, in the rhetoric of both Fidesz and the left, Jobbik appears simply as a transient aberration, a symptom of the crisis, and not a political rival. A more direct confrontation between traditional parties and Jobbik is lacking also because one such strategy produced poor results. In 2009, during the EP elections, the left-liberal SZDSZ campaigned by focusing directly on Jobbik. The party posters featured photos of smart-looking citizens, representing the SZDSZ electorate, and skinheads. Citizens were asked to choose. They did: the SZDSZ lost virtually all of its voters, while Jobbik celebrated its first breakthrough victory. Many observers concluded that the SZDSZ actually helped Jobbik attract media attention and was thus partly responsible for the radical right's success.[3]

In the subsequent 2009–2014 period, mainstream politicians tried to pretend that Jobbik did not exist and refused to enter into direct debates with the representatives of Jobbik. Many media outlets, especially on the left, refused to interview Jobbik politicians, lending support to this mainstream strategy. The 2014 electoral results demonstrated that the boycott was ineffective. As a result, both the media and the left changed their strategies, and Jobbik politicians became regular guests on talk shows and at political debates. However, most pundits continue to expect a left-right competition for the premiership in 2018.

JOBBIK'S INFLUENCE ON THE FIDESZ GOVERNMENT

Opposition parties can shape and frame the political agenda both directly – by organising demonstrations, submitting legislative proposals, calling press conferences and giving speeches and interpellations in the Parliament – and indirectly – by using mass media, especially friendly media outlets. Accordingly, in order to gauge the influence of Jobbik on Hungarian party politics in general and on the Fidesz government in particular, we present a thematic review of the speeches given in the Hungarian Parliament, the cover pages of the party's weekly (*Barikád*) and the largest demonstrations organised by the party during the first three years of the Fidesz government. As far as the parliamentary interventions are concerned, we examined so-called speeches before the orders of the day and the instantaneous questions of the party president, Gábor Vona (table 10.2).

   Table 10.2 reveals that Jobbik's agenda was dominated by law-and-order and Roma issues between 2010 and 2013. The attacks on the EU, the IMF, multinational companies and banks were also an important part of this agenda. Interestingly, corruption was not a leading issue. In the party president's parliamentary speeches, conspiracy theories, criticism of Israel and irredentism were only marginally present. On the other hand, the demonstrations and particularly the party magazine's cover pages show different emphases. As far as the latter is concerned, anti-Semitism appears as a central topic for the respective period.[4]

   Studies examining backbenchers' 'after the orders of the day' speeches substantiate the existence of an extremist discourse. In this category, the Treaty of Versailles (Trianon) and nationalism (26 per cent), Hungarian ancient history (25 per cent), anti-communism (25 per cent) and anti-Semitism (10 per cent) were the most popular topics.[5] For example, one Jobbik MP commemorated the anniversary of a famous blood libel case that triggered anti-Semitic hysteria at the end of the nineteenth century, reminding the audience that the perpetrators had never been punished. Another MP expressed the happiness of 'all football fans, irrespective of club sympathies' that a team with a Jewish background fell out of the Hungarian league's first division, as it was a 'foreign body' in Hungarian football.

Table 10.2 Jobbik's Principal Initiatives to Set the Political Agenda, 2010–2013

	Vona Gábor's Parliamentary Questions and Speeches		Barikád's Cover Pages		Main Demonstrations Organised by Jobbik	
	n	%	n	%	n	%
Roma issues and law-and-order measures	12	29	7	12	8	44
Criticism of the EU and the IMF	7	17	3	5	3	17
Foreigners' landownership	5	12	3	5	2	11
Accountability of the previous Socialist-Liberal government	5	12	2	4	3	17
Criticism of banks, multinational companies, and foreign currency-based bank loans	5	12	1	2	2	11
Criticism of austerity measures	3	7			2	11
Criticism of Jews and Israel	2	5	9	15	2	11
Commemoration of the Versailles Treaty and protest against the conditions of Hungarians living in the lost territories	1	2	5	8	1	6
Anti-communism	1	2	4	7	2	11
Corruption	1	2	–	–	1	6%
Conspiracy theories	0	0	3	5	–	–
Total	42	100	60	63	18	144

Note: Particular demonstrations can touch on more than one topic; therefore, the sum is more than 100 per cent. The sum for cover pages is less than 100 per cent because a large proportion of cover pages concern idiosyncratic issues that are not represented in the table.

Source: Authors' own collection.

The established parties are not in a position to mimic this rather extremist agenda, and they have particularly rejected Jobbik's anti-Roma and anti-Semitic rhetoric; however, on a number of topics, they did shift their emphases and, in some instances, their positions.

The adjustments in the MSZP's profile were minor but significant. The pre-2010 Socialist government supported tough criminal legislation and submitted four laws to the Parliament that can be associated with the growing tensions surrounding the Roma (*see* table 10.3).[6] The Road-to-Work programme that the Socialist government accepted in 2009 channelled some welfare benefits through the so-called Social Cards, a format that allows the recipients to spend the benefits only on a limited number of goods, such as food and clothing. This programme seemed to work with the assumption that the poor spend their social benefits on harmful goods or habits (e.g. alcohol, cigarettes and gambling) and that they cannot be trusted with cash. In 2010, the party used the poster 'Tax allowances instead of family benefits' to appeal to concerns about the amount of family benefits received by large, non-tax-paying families (Policy Solutions 2011). The 2010 MSZP programme, contrary to all previous programmes, explicitly mentioned the conflicts between the Roma and non-Roma and called for respect for the norms of the majority (Bíró-Nagy and Róna 2013). According to expert surveys, between 2010 and 2012, the MSZP became more reluctant about granting rights to ethnic minorities (Pirro 2015).

Fidesz proved even more responsive to the changing political climate, despite its comfortable lead in the polls. Between 2010 and 2012, the Fidesz-led government accepted twelve bills that introduced stricter regulations and harsher punishments for criminal actions[7] and lowered the age of criminal responsibility to twelve years old. The new regulations allowed property owners to use disproportionate violence against intruders. Fidesz also introduced 'three-strikes' laws, which doubled the penalties of those who committed three violent criminal acts (Penal Code Act 2012/C.) and constrained the power of judges to release prisoners who received life sentences.

Table 10.3 contrasts the entire 2006–2010 legislative period of the leftist government with the first thirty-five months of the subsequent Fidesz government. The table shows a sharp increase in law-and-order measures, but it also indicates that some of these measures were actually used against the Hungarian Guard, Jobbik's uniformed, paramilitary wing.

Jobbik and Fidesz politicians tend to agree that the rights of citizens should be matched by corresponding obligations. Accordingly, under the Fidesz government, the unemployed who rejected participating in public works and parents who failed to send their children to school were deprived of their social benefits. The use of Social Cards was extended. Local authorities were given the power to deny subsidies to undeserving citizens (2011/CLXXXIX act), including those who failed to keep order in their houses[8] or who exhibited anti-communitarian behaviour (the Constitutional Court rejected the latter provision).[9] All these policies enacted by Fidesz were part of Jobbik's

Table 10.3   Bills Increasing Criminal Penalties between 2006 and 2012

	2006–2010 (48 months)	2010–2012 (31 months)
Legal initiatives aiming to increase penalties	4	12.5
Legal initiatives threatening Jobbik and its paramilitary organisation, the Hungarian Guard	4	2.5

Note: Some bills fit the categories only partially, thus the fractions in the table.

Source: Authors' own collection, parlament.hu.

programme[10] (Jobbik 2010: 35, 38–41) or existed in the practices of towns governed by Jobbik politicians.

Fidesz's education policies also converged on Jobbik's ideas on the subject. Contrary to pre-existing legal conventions, Fidesz decided to support the possibility of segregated Roma classes. Schools regained their earlier right to fail pupils in elementary classes. Law enforcement officials were assigned to schools. The educational system was centralised, the production of school books was nationalised and an obligatory moral/religious component was introduced into the school curricula. Schools were required to organise excursions to the territories that were lost at the end of the First World War. Again, all these measures were in some way part of Jobbik's programme (see Jobbik programme's 2010: 49–51).

The radical party seemed particularly influential regarding issues of a symbolic nature. Jobbik's 2010 manifesto urged the Parliament to write a new constitution and to include references to God and to the Holy Crown in this constitution, to remove prominent leftist politicians' statutes, to introduce a memorial day to commemorate the Treaty of Versailles, to give citizenship to Hungarians living in the neighbouring countries and to include the work of extreme-right writers in national textbooks. All these demands were endorsed and implemented by Fidesz in subsequent years (see also in Bíró-Nagy et al. 2013).

Fidesz introduced some other original ideas of Jobbik with a twist. For example, Jobbik demanded that citizens without elementary education be excluded from the electorate. Fidesz rejected this proposal but initiated the voluntary registration of voters. This bill was ultimately vetoed by the Constitutional Court. Had it been implemented, the bill would have had consequences similar to those of the rejected Jobbik initiative; it would have disproportionately excluded the poor and the Roma from voting in elections. Although these initiatives failed, the government (supported by Jobbik) has managed to reshape the boundaries of the Hungarian electorate through the extension of citizenship and suffrage to half a million ethnic Hungarians who were living in neighbouring countries.

In line with Jobbik's demands, the government nationalised private pensions, forbade banks from evicting non-paying debtors, forced the banks to forego portions of loans, and introduced extra taxes on banks and multinational companies. The governing party also developed increasingly vehement anti-EU and anti-globalisation rhetoric. Brussels and Washington were targeted for supporting the colonisation of Hungary. On immigration, an issue that used to have relatively little practical relevance in Hungary, Prime Minister Viktor Orbán's discourse echoed the standard populist radical right programme ('Economic immigration is a bad thing in Europe; it should not be seen as having any benefits because it only brings trouble and danger to the peoples of Europe. . . . We don't want to see large groups of minorities with different cultural characteristics and backgrounds among us').[11]

Furthermore, in early 2015, the government launched a high-profile anti-immigrant campaign; it initiated a public 'consultation' about immigration and terrorism, suggesting that the two phenomena go hand in hand. As part of this campaign, the government flooded the country with posters that informed immigrants that they could not take Hungarians' jobs (even though virtually no immigrants wanted to stay and work in Hungary). This hard-line rhetoric was employed well before the Syrian migration crisis. When the first large wave of asylum seekers arrived in Hungary in August 2015, the government swiftly employed a set of legislative and executive decisions that would have satisfied any far-right party in Europe.[12] Punishments for human trafficking were tightened; penal procedures were shortened; illegal entry into the country was made punishable by a prison sentence; a fence along the Serbian border was erected; and the army was mobilised to guard the borders. The prime minister announced that Europe's Christian roots were under threat and criticised Western countries for their overly generous immigration policies. The government filed a lawsuit at the European Court of Justice against the EU quotas concerning the relocation of asylum seekers and launched a petition against it entitled 'Let's defend the country!' collecting more than a million signatures. While Jobbik demanded even more aggressive means against non-compliant immigrants (including the use of teargas and rubber bullets), the two parties converged on the idea of placing national interests above humanitarian concerns.

Fidesz also followed Jobbik's lead in foreign policy. The former loosened its close ties with the United States and the EU (Viktor Orbán was once the vice president of the EPP and was responsible for transatlantic relations) and developed cosy relations with various Eastern powers, such as Russia, China, Central Asian states and Turkey (Policy Solutions 2012: 23). Again, given that Jobbik introduced the idea of 'opening [Hungary] to the East' years prior to this major change in Fidesz's foreign policy orientation, the latter party ended up implementing Jobbik's programme rather than its own (table 10.4). Bipartisan support for the contract with Russia concerning the nuclear plant at Paks indicates not only the similarity of the two parties in terms of foreign relations but also their common pro-nuclear energy policy.

Jobbik and Fidesz are similarly ready to use moralistic arguments against phenomena that they consider dangerous side effects of modernisation. Both parties supported the prohibition of supermarket operations on Sundays and the media act as part of a traditional Christian narrative: Sunday is for family activities, not for shopping, and a central media authority is necessary to protect the public against content that could harm children (Bíró-Nagy et al. 2013: 246).

Table 10.4 Areas of Convergence between Fidesz and Jobbik

Issue	Who Publicly Initiated It First?
Restrictions on immigration	Jobbik[a]
Building a new nuclear reactor block in Paks	Jobbik (2009 manifesto)
Prohibition of open shops and commercial facilities on Sundays	Jobbik[b]
Eurosceptical rhetoric and opening to the East (especially Russia)	Jobbik (2009 manifesto)
Media act (media authority is empowered to impose severe sanctions to preserve traditional values)	Jobbik (2010 manifesto)
Government-enforced price cuts on utilities	Fidesz
Windfall taxes on banks and telecommunication companies	Fidesz[c]
Bailout of foreign currency borrowers	Jobbik (2010 manifesto)
Nationalisation of private pension funds	Jobbik (2010 manifesto)
Public works for the unemployed	Jobbik (2010 manifesto)
Exclusion of problematic citizens (the unemployed, those whose children do not attend kindergarten or school, and those who pursue 'anti-community' behaviour) from welfare benefits	Jobbik (2010 manifesto)
Increased legal penalties for criminals and capital punishment	Fidesz[d]
Centralisation of education, incorporation of nationalist authors into school curricula, mandatory student excursions to neighbouring countries, potential for segregated classes, and reduced age for mandatory school attendance	Jobbik (2010 manifesto), partially
Components of the new constitution: reference to the Holy Crown, reference to Christian roots, memorial day of the Versailles Treaty, citizenship to Hungarians living in the neighbouring countries	mostly Jobbik (2010 manifesto)
Re-evaluation of the 1990–2010 political system as a product of a 'stolen, incomplete transition'	MIÉP

[a] In February 2015, Jobbik initiated a referendum regarding four issues, including restrictions on immigration.
[b] http://www.hirado.hu/2015/03/28/gogos-szerint-a-jobbik-a-fidesznel-is-erosebben-korlatozna; http://www.parlament.hu/irom39/01793/01793.pdf.
[c] In its 2010 manifesto, Jobbik pushed to eliminate the tax allowances of multinational companies and promised allowances to small- and medium-sized domestic enterprises instead. Thus, even if the windfall taxes on multinational companies were not directly initiated by Jobbik, they fit very well the agenda of the party.
[d] In 2002, after a brutal massacre in village Mór, Orbán said that he would seriously consider the reintroduction of capital punishment (http://index.hu/belfold/ovhalalbunt/). However, Jobbik was the first to adopt the idea as an official party position.

Finally, the two parties developed a very similar interpretation of the 1989 regime change. Jobbik considers the 1989 changes a sham, a 'stolen transition' (see Krekó and Mayer 2015). According to Orbán, the transition was incomplete, as it did not eliminate post-communist forces.[13] Anti-communism is considered by both parties to be fundamental to their identity and ideology.

Table 10.5   Areas of Divergence between Fidesz and Jobbik

Vision of democracy	Some in Fidesz support the vision of the 'illiberal state', though within the confines of the EU. Jobbik argues for 'value-based democracy', but many of its leaders reject democracy entirely.
Human rights	Both argue for the primacy of community interests, but Jobbik is more radical in disregarding the rights of problematic groups, for example criminals. Both parties criticise human watchdog organisations for their allegedly leftist-liberal political leanings.
EU and foreign policy	Both criticise the EU and gesture towards Russia, Iran and Central Asian states, but Fidesz has an 'Atlanticist' wing.
Views on the pre-war Horthy era	Fidesz is ambivalent, while Jobbik is entirely positive.
Minority rights	Fidesz rejects Jobbik's openly anti-Roma, anti-Semitic and anti-gay stance, but both parties are opposed to multiculturalism and marriage equality.
Tax system	Fidesz supports a flat tax, while Jobbik prefers a progressive tax.

As table 10.5 indicates, the two parties preserved different profiles on a number of issues. For instance, Jobbik is particularly supportive of employees' rights, while Fidesz tends to side with the employers.

Even more importantly, throughout the examined period, Fidesz remained part of the EPP, while Jobbik remained marginalised on the European scene, shunned even by the European radical parties, either because of its anti-Semitism or because of its links to paramilitary organisations. However, the difference between the two parties in terms of their ideological profiles and political agendas gradually narrowed. This narrowing resulted not only from the radicalisation of Fidesz but also from the moderation of Jobbik, especially after 2014. On the eve of the 2014 election campaign, Gábor Vona, the party leader, announced a new 'people's party' strategy. He promised that the party's representatives would no longer burn the EU flag, make offensive statements about minorities or campaign for an exit from the EU. These changes resembled patterns of reforms within the French Front National (FN), including a growing emphasis on the state's active role in supporting pensioners and youths. However, as opposed to the FN, no major clashes within the leadership occurred, and no wave of expulsions followed the EU announcement of the new strategy.

INTERPRETING THE CONVERGENCE

The convergence between Fidesz's actions and Jobbik's ideas is not entirely a result of the latter's impact on the former. One must acknowledge that many of the surveyed policies had multiple triggers, and Fidesz was experiencing an internal transformation, as indicated by the gradual marginalisation of some of its moderate politicians. For example, the change in its foreign policy orientation also stemmed from Fidesz's conflicts both with Brussels and with Washington and with the declining appeal of the West's orientation due to the EU's economic problems. The abrupt introduction of windfall taxes on banks in 2010 and the nationalisation of private pension funds resulted from the need to balance the budget at a time when the EU and the IMF showed no flexibility regarding the budget deficit. The anti-immigration campaign and Orbán's support of capital punishment were probably more informed by public opinion polls and focus groups than by Jobbik.

However, in other instances, Jobbik's role as a cause, or at least a trigger, is less disputable. For example, in September 2011, Fidesz introduced a law to help those indebted to banks due to foreign currency loans – immediately after Jobbik started its petition campaign on the same topic.[14] In another instance, Fidesz politicians and the Fidesz-related media attacked the Bilderberg group[15] immediately after Jobbik's weekly devoted its cover to the issue on 13 June 2013.[16]

However, we need to ask the question: Why would a relatively minor party such as Jobbik have such a large impact on Fidesz, a party that could easily govern alone? One explanation could be that in the wake of the 2006 riots and the subsequent political crisis Fidesz considered the growth potential on the radical right to be particularly large. In this framework, the policy concessions to Jobbik can be interpreted as preventive measures that aimed to keep the latter out of government. This defensive strategy makes sense, as Fidesz's electoral dominance took shape during a period of declining turnout, making its electoral dominance potentially fragile. Moreover, a considerable portion of Fidesz voters also sympathise with Jobbik (Róna and Sós 2011, Republikon 2013);[17] the overlap between the two parties is more pronounced than the overlap between any other pair of Hungarian parties. Radical gestures can keep wavering voters within the orbit of Fidesz. In the long run, the Jobbik electorate is the only constituency from which Fidesz can hope to gain a significant number of new voters.

However, this explanation is not entirely convincing. Jobbik is still an unlikely challenger in competition for office, as the international community is very unlikely to tolerate a Jobbik government. Moreover, the left constitutes a force that is as large as Jobbik, and its prospects to govern are probably better. However, Fidesz has not attempted to implement proposals emanating from the left.

The hypothesis of a direct impact, running from Jobbik's success to Fidesz's policy changes, is, therefore, not entirely plausible. Without any doubt, Jobbik advocated many of the surveyed legislative changes earlier than Fidesz did. Therefore, the correct sequence for a causal influence is present. But in the absence of a robust causal mechanism, we need to consider alternative explanations, which do not rely on direct causation.

According to the first such alternative explanation, Fidesz gradually manoeuvred itself into a radical position, motivated originally by short-term considerations to consolidate its grip on power. Its violations of the written and unwritten rules of liberal democracies may have been designed to be temporary measures. However, in the midst of the ensuing conflicts with liberals, socialists and many Western governments and non-governmental organisations (NGOs), the core electorate and the party leadership gradually developed a more radical authoritarian right-wing identity.

According to a second narrative, the two parties' ideologies had already been close to each other for more than a decade, but this similarity had to be concealed. The fact that Fidesz needed to hide its actual ideological preferences prior to it landslide victory is well illustrated by the history of the citizenship law. In 2006, a second-tier Fidesz leader spoke about the possibility of granting voting rights to Hungarians living in neighbouring countries and thereby 'deciding the country's fate for twenty years'.[18] Immediately after the speech, the party distanced itself from this politician and from the idea of extending the electorate beyond Hungary's borders. For four years, Fidesz was silent on the issue, allowing Jobbik to champion the cause. However, immediately after the election, Fidesz implemented the appropriate legal changes, and the number of newly enfranchised ethnic Hungarians reached soon half a million. More than 95 per cent of those who voted in this group supported Fidesz in the 2014 parliamentary election.[19]

According to this second narrative, Jobbik functions as the avant-garde of Fidesz. Fidesz can test the waters by letting Jobbik introduce radical proposals (see also Krekó and Mayer 2015). Once these proposals have been part of the public discourse for a while, Fidesz then embraces and introduces them to the Parliament, with some changes. The changes usually make the proposals less radical, allowing Fidesz to appear as a moderating force. The symbolic separation of the two parties is carefully maintained: Fidesz never supports Jobbik's initiatives in the Parliament. However, on numerous occasions, the rejected proposals have been included in Fidesz's legislative or executive agenda at a later stage.

COMPETITION FOR GOVERNMENT

As described in the introduction, the Hungarian party system used to have a transparent bipolar pattern. Elections focused on the question of whether the country should be governed by a left-wing or a right-wing coalition. None of the parties ever moved from one governing bloc to another. Access to government was restricted to a relatively small circle of parties. The last time that a new party entered into the government was in 1998. Since then, the Fidesz-led right has alternated with the MSZP-led left. At the turn of the millennium, the Hungarian party system became closed in terms of alternation patterns, government access and coalition formulae (Enyedi and Casal Bértoa 2011). Given the fluidity of party politics elsewhere in the post-communist world, this development was rather remarkable.

In 2010, the logic of government formation changed. Because of its landslide victory, Fidesz could form a single-party majority government.[20] Although this outcome in itself does not relate to populism, the effectiveness of the populist propaganda according to which leftist parties serve the interests of (foreign) elites was crucial in perpetuating the collapse of the left and the hegemony of the right. Public opinion shifted so radically towards the right that the 'traditional' left-right alternation ceased to be viable.

The left's collapse and fragmentation, together with Jobbik's emergence and stabilisation, imply that only two options currently exist for government formation: either Fidesz keeps on winning elections, perpetuating the dominant party system, or major innovations must occur. These innovations would involve either some sort of cooperation between old and new left-wing and centrist parties or Jobbik's inclusion in the government. In terms of party competition, Jobbik's inclusion would constitute a significant change. However, the expected hostile international reactions make this scenario rather unlikely. A minority government with Jobbik support is somewhat more imaginable: MIÉP, Jobbik's radical right predecessor, occasionally supported the Fidesz government from the opposition benches during the 1998–2002 period.

Fidesz's middle-party status makes the continuation of its governmental role plausible. The electoral system, whose majoritarian aspects have been strengthened, provides additional support. Thanks to the redrawn (gerrymandered) electoral boundaries, Fidesz can preserve its grip on the government, even if it gains fewer votes than its principal opponents (Tóka 2014). The extensive patronage system, the government-sponsored NGOs and the alliance of historical churches further cement Fidesz's grip on power. If, however, Fidesz is eventually forced to choose between the left and the radical right, the dilemma may split the party. Debates concerning coalition preferences are the most common source of party fissures in Hungary.

The present configuration simultaneously exhibits the features of the (pre) dominant party system and polarised pluralism. The number of significant parties is low, but other features of polarised pluralism, such as bilateral opposition and the presence of anti-system parties, play a crucial role in maintaining the predominance of Fidesz. The high degree of polarisation is indicated not only by the high polarisation indices based on left-right identification data or on expert evaluations (Dalton 2008, http://www.parlgov.org)[21] but also by Fidesz's interpretation of its victory as a 'regime-changing revolution'. In addition, the current opposition parties demand a fundamental change in the political regime. The overwhelming victory of the opposition (whether right or left) would immediately lead to a new constitution and a new set of political and economic institutions, perhaps resulting in new state symbols[22] and in attempts to hold the present governing elite legally accountable.

To conclude the review of the changes in the competition of the governmental arena, the Hungarian party system has opened itself up somewhat on the margins after 2010; nevertheless, it has remained a relatively closed party system and continues to be one of the most closed systems in Eastern Europe (Casal Bértoa and Enyedi 2016). So far, Jobbik remains the only party that is able to challenge the politicians who founded Hungarian democracy in 1989. All other new actors hover around the 5 per cent threshold that is needed to enter the Parliament. Penetrating the governmental arena remains as difficult as ever for newcomers.

The party system changed from a bipolar system into a 'tri-polar', centre-based configuration in terms of social support and district-level competition. However, due to Jobbik's low governing potential, the traditional 'Fidesz *vs.* the left' rivalry still dominates the governmental arena, albeit currently resembling a struggle between a limping David and a still vigorous Goliath.

CONCLUSION

During the 2000s, the growing support for populist politics occurred alongside a number of consequential changes in Hungary. The degree of polarisation increased; the median positions of the voters and of the legislators shifted to the right; and a new political regime of illiberal democracy started to take shape. The right became divided; however, in terms of governmental politics, this division has thus far proved inconsequential because Fidesz has remained strong enough to govern alone.

Between Jobbik and Fidesz, a complex relationship developed. This relationship can be described as follows: (1) Jobbik questions the traditional left-right divide by attacking the entire corrupt establishment; (2) Fidesz boosts its governing and centrist credentials by highlighting Jobbik's extremism; (3) Jobbik advances ideas that aim to replace liberal democracy with nationalist democracy – and subsequently with autocracy; and (4) Fidesz modifies, moderates, streamlines and implements Jobbik's ideas. Even Fidesz's most radical initiatives (e.g. the abolition of state registration of voters) appear as moderate measures because a more radical proposition is always on the table (e.g. the disqualification of citizens who have no elementary education). This 'central' position has been instrumental in consolidating the rule of Fidesz: as Wolfgang Schüssel, the Austrian ex-chancellor, noted, 'Orbán is the only guarantee against the extreme right'.[23]

By highlighting the symbiotic relationship between the two parties and Jobbik's instrumental role in helping Fidesz to secure its dominant status within the party system, we imply no conspiracy. Our conclusion refers to Jobbik's systemic function, not to the intentions of its activists. Underlining the competitive nature of the relationship is also important. Even if Jobbik is unable to replace Fidesz as a government party, the former can reduce the latter's parliamentary majority. If it succeeds in undermining the authenticity of Fidesz as a right-wing force, it may even help the left to victory.

According to spatial theories, the rightward movement of a centre-right party decreases the market share of the radical right. Thus far, the Hungarian case provides more support for the claim that parties can create new electoral markets (Deegan-Krause and Enyedi 2010) and, more specifically, that a rightwards shift of centre-right parties can extend the political spectrum further to the right, thereby benefitting radical competitors of the centre-right parties (Ignazi 2003).

If Fidesz, not Jobbik, is regarded as the primary example of a populist party, the principal lesson learned from the Hungarian case is that populist parties are capable of governing. They are also able to profoundly alter the rules of the political game. Political buffoons are often populists, but populists are not necessarily buffoons. Given highly organised parties, disillusioned voters, imaginative leaders and the division of labour between two populist parties, populist political systems can be sustainable.

NOTES

1 Speaking to his fellow MPs, Ferenc Gyurcsány admitted that he had been lying about the state of the economy and claimed that his government's performance was the worst in Europe. A leak of this speech resulted in huge demonstrations and – partly violent – protest actions that lasted for several months.

2 Jobbik's 2010 manifesto clearly stated these claims. Viktor Orbán's famous 'illiberal state' speech is also a good example of this orientation. See https://hungarianspectrum. wordpress.com/2014/07/31/viktor-orbans-speech-at-the-xxv-balvanyos-free-summer-university-and-youth-camp-july-26-2014-baile-tusnad-tusnadfurdo/.

3 http://mandiner.blog.hu/2009/04/21/jobbik_szdsz_kampany.

4 When Hungary signed an international contract with Israel, *Barikád* appeared with a black cover with the subtitle 'I'm fed up with the Holocaust'. Another *Barikád*

cover pictured the statue of Bishop Gellért holding a Menorah in his hands, with the subtitle 'Wake up Budapest: Is this what you wanted?'

5 Republikon think tank: Jobbik Arcai (Faces of Jobbik). Budapest, 2011.

6 Those laws further empowered the police to ensure public safety and order. They allotted harder punishment for several types of crime (e.g. stealing metal), which occur frequently in the Roma community.

7 Already the previous Socialist government adjusted its policies to the new climate by submitting four laws to the Parliament that can be associated with the 'Roma-problem'.

8 http://index.hu/belfold/2011/03/08/tiszta_udvar_rendes_haz_utan_jar_csak_segely/.

9 Fidesz modified the earlier mentioned 2011/CLXXXIX. act to make possible for municipalities to sanction the 'anti-community behaviour'. Report of the HVG website: http://hvg.hu/itthon/20130304_Nem_eleg_az_ombudsmannak_az_onkormanyzati.

10 http://jobbik.hu/sites/default/files/jobbik-program2010gy.pdf.

11 https://euobserver.com/justice/127172.

12 http://www.kormany.hu/en/prime-minister-s-office/news/upcoming-new-legislation-to-protect-hungary-s-southern-border.

13 http://budapestbeacon.com/public-policy/full-text-of-viktor-orbans-speech-at-baile-tusnad-tusnadfurdo-of-26-july-2014/.

14 Jobbik's referendum-question proposal implied that, instead of the 240 Hungarian Forint-Swiss Franc exchange rate valid in 2011, the original 150–160 rate should be applied. The government implemented the idea in a somewhat more moderate form – at the exchange rate of 180.

15 http://index.hu/kulfold/2013/06/24/a_magyar_valasztok_ellen_tor_viviane_reding/.

16 http://barikad.irasai.hu/oldalak/barikad-201324-32133/.

17 http://republikon.hu/media/12152/20130419.pdf.

18 This speech was given by István Mikola: http://hu.wikiquote.org/wiki/Mikola_Istv%C3%A1n.

19 In fact, only 120,000 of them actually voted.

20 Nominally, the electoral list was a Fidesz-Christian Democrats list, but the Christian Democrats do not form an autonomous political unit; their candidates are selected by the Fidesz leadership.

21 After 2010, Dalton's index of polarisation shows a decline. However, this decline occurred because Fidesz, which is moderate on economic issues, grew considerably and the weight of the Socialists decreased radically.

22 Fidesz removed the word 'Republic' from the country's name, and the left-wing opposition would prefer to reverse this name change.

23 http://valasz.hu/uzlet/a-politikanak-beken-kell-hagynia-a-mediat-50042.

BIBLIOGRAPHY

Bíró-Nagy, A. and Róna, D. (2013) 'Rational radicalism: Jobbik's road to the Hungarian parliament', in G. Meseznikov, Olga Gyárfásova and Z. Butorova (eds.)

Alternative politics? The rise of new parties in Central Europe, Bratislava: Institute for Public Affairs, 149–185.

Bíró-Nagy, A., Tamás, B. and Vasali, Z. (2013) 'Hungary', in R. Melzer and S. Serafin (eds.) *Right-wing extremism in Europe: Country-analyses, counter-strategies and labour-market oriented exit strategies*, Berlin: Friedrich Ebert Foundation, 229–253.

Bozóki, A. (2008) 'Consolidation or second revolution? The emergence of the New Right in Hungary', *Journal of Communist Studies and Transition Politics*, 24(2): 191–231.

Bozóki, A. (2015) 'The illusion of inclusion: Configurations of populism in Hungary', in M. Kopecek and P. Wcislik (eds.) *Thinking through transition: Liberal democracy, authoritarian pasts, and intellectual history in East Central Europe after 1989*, Budapest-New York: Central European University Press.

Casal Bértoa, F. and Enyedi, Z. (2016) 'Party system closure: Conceptualization, operationalization, and validation', *Party Politics*, 22(3): 265–277.

Dalton, R. J. (2008) 'The quantity and the quality of party systems: Party system polarization, its measurement, and its consequences', *Comparative Political Studies*, 41(7): 899–920.

Deegan-Krause, K. and Enyedi, Z. (2010) 'Agency and the structure of party competition: Alignment, stability and the role of political elites', *West European Politics*, 33(3): 686–710.

Enyedi, Z. (2006) 'The survival of the fittest: Party system concentration in Hungary', in S. Jungerstan-Mulders (ed.) *Post-communist EU member states: Parties and party systems*, Aldershot: Ashgate, 177–202.

——— (2015) 'Plebeians, citoyens and aristocrats or where is the bottom of bottom-up? The case of Hungary', in H. Kriesi and T. Pappas (eds.) *Populism in the shadow of the Great Recession*, Colchester: ECPR Press, 229–244.

——— (2016) 'Paternalist populism and illiberal elitism in Central Europe', *Journal of Political Ideologies*, 21(1): 9–25.

Enyedi, Z. and Casal Bértoa, F. (2011) 'Patterns of inter-party competition (1990–2008)', in P. Lewis and R. Markowski (eds.) *Europeanizing party politics? Comparative perspectives on Central and Eastern Europe*, Manchester: Manchester University Press, 147–168.

Jobbik, Movement for a Better Hungary (2010) 'Radikális változás. A Jobbik országgyűlési választási programja a nemzeti önrendelkezésért és a társadalmi igazságosságért'. [Radical Change. Jobbik's Programme for National Sovereignty and Social Justice.]

Karácsony, G. (2005) 'A történelem fogságában. Generációk, életutak és politikai preferenciák Magyarországon', in R. Angelusz and R. Tardos (eds.) *Törések, hálók, hidak. Választói magatartás és politikai tagolódás Magyarországon, 2005*, Budapest: Demokrácia Kutatások Magyar Központja Alapítvány, pp. 161–206. [In the Captivity of History: Generations, Life Paths and Political Preferences in Hungary.]

Karácsony, G. and Róna, D. (2011) 'The secret of Jobbik (Hungarian extreme right party)', *Journal of East-European and Asian Studies*, 2(1): 61–92.

Knutsen, O. (2011) 'Strukturális hatások, társadalmi koalíciók és pártválasztás Magyarországon', in R. Tardos, Z. Enyedi and A. Szabó (eds.) *Részvétel, képviselet, politikai változás*, Budapest: Demokrácia Kutatások Magyar Központja Alapítvány pp. 119–157. [Structural Impacts, Social Coalitions and Party Choice in Hungary.]

Krekó, P. and Mayer, G. (2015) 'Transforming Hungary – together? An analysis of Fidesz-Jobbik relationship', in M. Minkenberg (ed.) *Transforming the transformation? The East European radical right in the political process*, London: Routledge, 183–205.

Körösényi, A. (2007) 'A jobboldal elhúzódó válsága', *Kommentár*, 4. [The Ongoing Crisis of the Right in Hungary.]

Ignazi, P. (2003) *Extreme right parties in Western Europe*, Oxford: Oxford University Press.

Pirro, A. L. P. (2015) 'The populist radical right in the political process: Assessing party impact in Central and Eastern Europe', in M. Minkenberg (ed.) *Transforming the transformation? The East European radical right in the political process*, London: Routledge, 80–104.

Republikon (2013) 'Pártok egy évvel a választások előtt', Budapest: Republikon Think-thank. [Parties a Year Ahead of the Election.]

Róna, D. and Sós, I. (2011) 'A térmodellen túl: Másodlagos preferenciák a 2010-es országgyűlési választáson', *Politikatudományi Szemle*, 20(4): 113–140. [Beyond the Downsian Spatial Model. Secondary Party Preferences in the 2010 National Election.]

Tóka, G. (2006) 'Vezérek csodálói: a Magyar választói magatartás nemzetközi összehasonlításban [Leaders' Admirers: Hungarian Voting Behaviour in Cross-national Comparison]', in G. Karácsony (ed.) *Parlamenti választás 2006: Elemzések és Adatok [Parliamentary elections 2006: Analyses and data]*, Budapest: DKMKA pp. 17–58.

———— (2014) 'Constitutional principles and electoral democracy in Hungary', in E. Bos and K. Pócza (eds.) *Constitution building in consolidated democracies: A new beginning or decay of a political system?*, Baden-Baden: Nomos Verlag, 1–14.

Tóka, G. and Popa, S. (2013). 'Hungary', in S. Berglund, J. Ekman, K. Deegan-Krause and O. Knutsen (eds.) *Handbook of political change in Eastern Europe*, Cheltenham: Edgar Elgar, 291–338.

Van der Brug, W., Franklin, M., Popescu, M. and Tóka, G. (2009) 'Towards a European electorate: One electorate or many?', in J. Thomassen (ed.) *The legitimacy of the European Union after enlargement*, Oxford: Oxford University Press pp. 66–93.

Part IV

CONCLUSION

Part V

CONCLUSION

Chapter 11

Populist Parties and the Changing Contours of European Party Systems

Steven Wolinetz

Consider two sets of snapshots: The first depicts Western European party systems in the 1950s and 1960s, and in the 1990s and 2000s; the second, Central and Eastern European party systems in the latter two periods. The earliest photos in the first set are sharp – insofar as change was occurring, it was on the margins – while the later ones are fuzzier because newer parties are crowding in and party strengths changing. Depicting party systems in Central and Eastern Europe, the second set is different: the earlier photos are blurred – parties come and go in rapid succession. However, the later ones are sharper: we have a better idea of who is who and where they stand.

These images omit more than they include. We evoke them because they provide a backdrop for the analysis that follows. This chapter examines the impact that populist parties have had on nine Western European and two Central European party systems and considers how they 'absorb the blow'. Doing so is a challenge. Our contributors have produced rich analyses, but the parties and the party systems they analyse are sufficiently different that we must take care comparing them. Complicating our task, party systems are no longer as static as Lipset and Rokkan (1967) indicated. Nor are they the product of a single actor or party family but rather the interaction of many. Among the parties considered, only Fidesz has been able to use its majority to reshape the Hungarian party system (Enyedi and Róna, chapter 10, this volume). However, even here, as in other party systems, populist parties are one determinant among many. Our premise is that populist parties in many countries have grown large enough to affect competition for votes and competition for government and the pattern of interactions that define their party systems (Sartori 1976, p. 41). As table 11.1 demonstrates, parties like the Danish People's Party (DF), the Norwegian Progress Party (FrP), and the Dutch Freedom Party (PVV) ranked as the second or third largest party, and the Swiss People's Party (SVP), initially the smallest of the four major parties, is now the largest. This reflects not only the growth of populist parties but also the diminishing share won by older established parties.

Table 11.1 indicates the average support that populist parties received in parliamentary elections from 1990 through 2015 in the countries considered in this volume. Populist party strength has not only increased in many

Table 11.1   Populist Party Strength in Europe, 1990–2015

	Party or Parties	Ideological Orientation	Range of Support 1990–2015	Mean Support 1990–2015	Rank in Elections since 2000 & Share of the Vote
Austria	FPÖ	Populist radical right (PRRP)	10–26.9%	18.4%	2002 3rd (10.0%) 2006 4th (11.0%) 2008 3th (17.5%) 2013 3rd (20.5%)
	BZÖ (2006–2015)	Populist right	3.5–10.7%	4.6%	2006 5th (4.1%) 2008 4th (10.7%)
Netherlands	CD (1990–1998)	PRRP	0.6–2.5%	1.6%	——
	LPF (2002–6)	Populist liberal	5.7–17.0% (2002–6)	11.4%	2002 2nd (17.0%) 2003 5th (5.7%)
	PVV (2006–2015)	PRRP	5.9–15.5%	10.5%	2006 5th (5.9%) 2010 3rd (15.5%) 2012 3rd (10.1%)
	SP	Populist left	1.3–16.6%	7.6%	2002 6th (5.9%) 2003 4th (6.3%) 2006 3rd (16.7%) 2010 5th (9.8%) 2012 4th (9.7%)
Switzerland	SVP	PRRP	11.9–29.4%	23%	2003 1st (26.7%) 2007 1st (28.9%) 2011 1st (26.6%) 2015 1st (29.4%)
Denmark	FrPd (1990–2001)	Populist liberal	0.6–6.4%	8.0%	2001 11th (0.6%)
	DF (1998–2015)	PRPP	7.4–20.6%	13.3%	2001 3rd (12.4%) 2005 3rd (13.3%) 2007 3rd (13.9%) 2011 3rd (12.2%) 2015 2nd (20.6%)
Norway	FrP	PRRP	6.3–22.9%	16.3%	2001 3rd (14.7%) 2005 2nd (22.1%) 2009 2nd (22.9%) 2013 3rd (16.3%)

(Continued)

Table 11.1 (Continued)

	Party or Parties	Ideological Orientation	Range of Support 1990–2015	Mean Support 1990–2015	Rank in Elections since 2000 & Share of the Vote
Sweden	ND (1991–94)	PRRP	1.2–6.7%	3.9% 5.3%	1991 6th (6.7%) 1994 8th (1.2%)
	SD (2010–15)	PRRP	1.4–12.9%	5.7%	2002 8th (1.4%) 2006 8th (2.9%) 2010 6th (5.7%) 2014 3rd (12.9%)
Finland	SMP/PS	PRRP	1.0–19.1%	7.1%	2003 8th (1.6%) 2007 8th (4.1%) 2011 3rd (19.1%) 2015 2nd (17.7%)
France (legislative-1st ballot)	FN (1993–2012)	PRRP	4.3–15.3%	11.4%	2002 3rd (11.3%) 2007 4th (4.3%) 2012 3rd (13.6%)
Italy	LN[a]	PRRP	4.1%–10.1%	7.1% 35.3% 25.6%	2006 5th (4.5%) 2008 3rd (8.3%) 2013 5th (4.1%)
	FI/PdL[b]	Populist liberal	21.6–46.4%	36.3%	2001 1st (45.6%) 2006 2nd (23.6%) 2008 1st (32.8%) 2013 3rd (21.6%)
	M5S (2013)	Left populist	25.6%		2013 1st (25.6%)
Poland	SRP (Self Defense)	PRRP	1.5–11.4%	3.3%	2005 3rd (10.2%) 2007 5th (1.5%)
	LPR (League of Polish Families)	PRRP	1.3–8.0%	5.7%	2001 6th (7.9%) 2005 5th (8.0%) 2007 5th (1.3%)
	Korwin (2015)	Conservative/PRR	4.8%	4.8%	2015 7th (4.8%)
	Kukiz'15 (2015)	PRRP	8.8%	8.8%	2015 3rd (8.8%)
Hungary	Fidesz[c]	National conservative	9–44.9%	32.4%	2002 2nd (41.1%) 2006 2nd (42.5%) 2010 1st (52.7%) 2014 1st (44.9%)
	Jobbik (2003–)	PRRP Extreme right	16.7–20.2%	18.5%	2010 3rd (16.7%) 2014 3rd (20.2%)

[a] Excludes the 1994 and 2001 elections because LN participated in the Polo delle Libertà.
[b] FI contested most elections in alliance with the National Alliance (AN) and, on two occasions, LN. Data indicate the percentage won by the Polo delle Libertà or Case delle Libertà).
[c] In alliance with Christian Democratic People's Party.

Source: ParlGov database (Döring and Manow 2016).

instances but, contrary to Mudde (2013; 2014), is large enough to 'matter' and affect party systems. Mooted in his 2012 Stein Rokkan Lecture, Mudde's assertion that populist parties were not large enough to matter was based on data only through 2011. Parties like the Austrian Freedom Party (FPÖ), with 20.5 per cent of the popular vote in 2013, and the Danish People's Party (DF), with 20.6 per cent in 2015 have grown stronger in elections since then. Based on European averages, his data included systems in which populist parties were negligible as well as others in which they were stronger. However, parties in electoral competition do not base their strategies and tactics on European-wide averages, but rather on what their opponents are saying and doing in the arenas in which they find themselves. Despite broad similarities, each party system is a distinct arena. If we want to investigate the impact that populist parties have had, we have to consider their strength relative to competitors and examine how their presence affects the ways they interact. Our contributors have focused on stronger rather than weaker parties. In the sections that follow, we compare their impact on competition for government and competition for votes. We begin with older party systems and extend the discussion to newer ones. Our first step is to review what has and has not been changing.

CHANGING PARAMETERS

Populist parties are one of several sources of change: the share of votes won by mainstream parties – the principal competitors or 'insiders' that anchor party systems and define what competition is about – has been declining and the effective numbers of parties contesting elections and winning seats have increased. So have rates of electoral volatility and the frequency of high volatility elections (Dassoneville and Hooghe 2017; Chiaramonte and Emanuele 2017; Mair 2008, 2013). Reflecting the emergence of Green and left libertarian and populist parties, the proportions of party systems that are 'new' have also increased (Emanuele and Chiaramonte 2016). Chiaramonte and Emanuele (2017) examine electoral volatility and party system regeneration in Western Europe since 1945. Figure 11.1 uses their data to graph mean total volatility in elections from 1945 to 1968, from 1969 to 1991 and from 1992 to 2015 in the Western European party systems we consider. Figure 11.2 shows the mean effective number of parties winning seats in parliament in these periods. Along with data on the increasing frequency of high volatility elections (Mair 2008; 2013; Chiaramonte and Emanuele 2017), they provide a view of Western European party systems that are more 'fluid' and less frozen than they once were and are also more similar to less firmly anchored Central and Eastern European systems than before. Nevertheless,

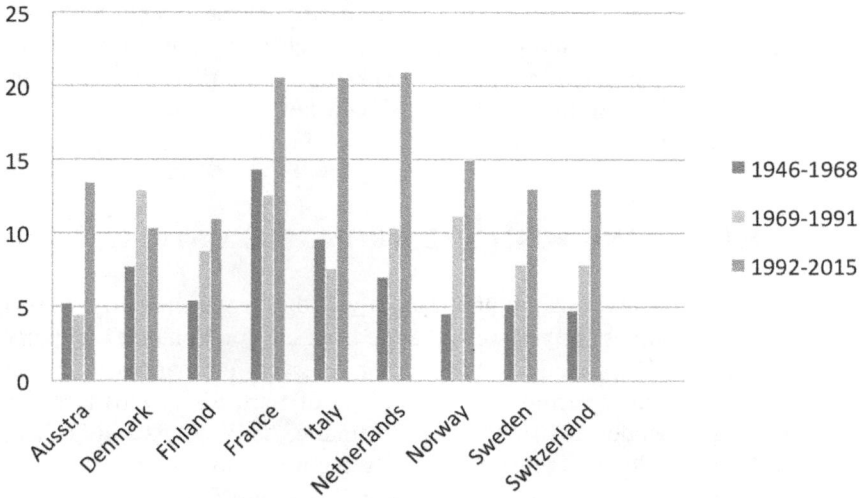

Figure 11.1 Mean Value of Total Volatility

Source: Emanuele (2015).

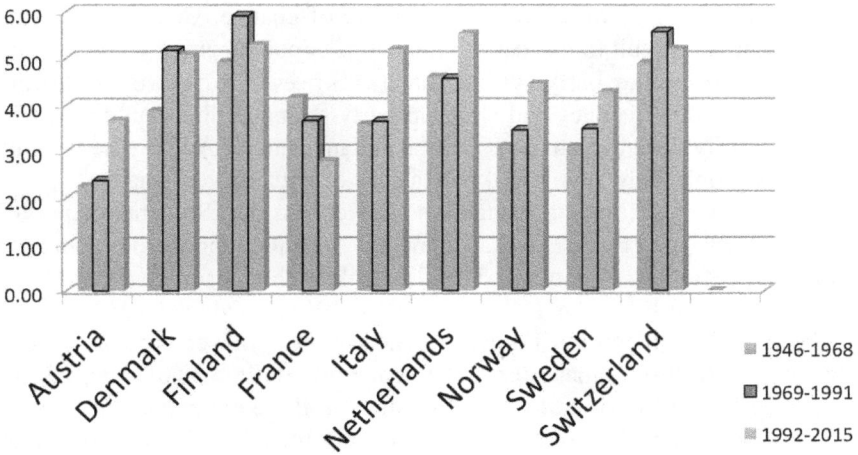

Figure 11.2 Mean Effective Number of Parliamentary Parties 1945–2015

Source: Dassoneville and Hooghe (2017); ParlGov database (Döring and Manow 2016).

we should neither overstate the degree of similarity nor the extent of change: There is still variation in the dimensions on which party competition takes place (Rohrschneider and Whitefield 2012) and, in older party systems, parties rooted in earlier conflicts not only remain but also continue to be the principal competitors.

MEASURING WITH THE WRONG YARDSTICK?

Discussing impacts takes us into the fraught world of assessing party system change. Differentiating party system change from electoral change and party change, Mair (1997) insisted that the term be reserved for changes in format and mechanics resulting from shifts from one of Sartori's (1976) types to another (see also Mudde 2014). This is problematic. As Wolinetz and Zaslove (chapter 1, this volume) indicate, Sartori's typology no longer differentiates as well as it once did: Two of its four cells contain few cases and most party systems are instances of moderate pluralism although they have more than five or six relevant parties (Mair 1997, 2006; Wolinetz 2006).[1] Instead, students of party systems use measures such as Laakso and Taagepera's effective number of parties (Mair 2006; Wolinetz 2006) or resort to distinctions that are more implicit than explicit, such as differentiating systems that have bipolar competition from those that do not, as Mair (2001) and Bale (2003) do. Adequate for many purposes, this leaves us without classificatory schemes allowing us to assess the incidence of change. Compounding the problem, it is difficult to discuss the impact of populist parties without using language that implies party system change. However, what we are dealing with are electoral changes and shifts in party strengths that could, but will not necessarily, lead to changes in format and mechanics. Among the systems considered, only Italy is unmistakably a case of party system change.

Nor is this only form of change we should consider. Students of parties have been intrigued by E. E. Schattschneider's (1960) suppositions about the scope and definition of conflict. This dovetails with theories of generational realignment (see Burnham 1970; Key 1955, 1964; Sundquist 1983) unique to the American literature. Equivalent theories have never been developed for Europe: Instead, debate about the scope and definition of conflict was precluded by the freezing of party alignments and the entrenchment of mass parties (Lipset and Rokkan 1967). This reinforced the 'fundamental bias toward stability' that Bartolini and Mair (2007: 70) detected: parties could change but party systems did not. It is no surprise that our principal theories of change focus on parties and party ideology (Kirchheimer 1966; Katz and Mair 1995; 2002) rather than party systems. The principal exception is the literature on dealignment (Dalton, Flanagan, and Beck 1984; Dalton and Wattenberg 2000; Dalton 2004; Dalton and Anderson 2011). Meshing with

Inglehart's (1971; 1977) work on value change, as well as the emergence of Green and left libertarian parties, this raised questions about the durability of older cleavages. However, the emphasis has been on dealignment rather than realignment. This is changing. Scholars like Kriesi (2008; 2012), Bornschier (2010) and Kitschelt and Rehm (2015) maintain that changes in the dimensions on which party competition takes place have been occurring. The emergence of new dimensions is one of the principal explanations for the emergence of populist parties (Kitschelt and McGann 1995). We ask whether this opens the way for further change.

THE ARGUMENT IN BRIEF

Our premise is that populist parties not only affect competition for government but also influence the dimensions on which competition takes place. How they do so depends on the positions they occupy and the degree to which they are excluded from or incorporated into pre-existing structures of competition. In some instances, populist parties have been incorporated in ways that leave older structures intact or, failing that, subtly changed. Nor has there been the shift towards bipolarity that Bale (2003) predicted: systems that were bipolar continue be bipolar. Those that were not are not.

The picture changes when we look at competition for votes. Mobilising around issues like immigration and loss of national autonomy, populist parties give greater definition to the socio-cultural dimension initially articulated by Green and left-libertarian parties. Doing so, they increase the likelihood of arguments about the scope and definition of conflict (Schattschneider 1960).

Treating the party systems we do requires caution and dexterity. Our arguments about competition for government apply more to older democracies. Poland and Hungary are newer democracies that differ in key respects. In Hungary, populist rhetoric and appeals are used both by the governing party, Fidesz, and by Jobbik, its opponent on the right. Populist leaders and parties have been a recurring force in Poland but none have managed to entrench themselves. Advancing an illiberal view of democracy, Law and Justice (PiS) uses populist rhetoric. Where appropriate, we formulate arguments applicable to all eleven, but comment separately if that cannot be done. Our first step is to clarify the terms of analysis.

Insiders and Outsiders

Political scientists pay more attention to some parties than others. In the past, we concentrated on major parties, mentioning minor parties in passing. The literature on populist parties differentiates populist from mainstream parties. Neither distinction serves our purposes: The populist parties considered

Table 11.2 Populist Insiders and Outsiders

	Populist Insiders	Populist Outsiders	Ambiguous or Mixed
Austria		Freedom Party (FPÖ)	
Netherlands		List Pim Fortuyn (LPF) Freedom Party (PVV) Socialist Party (SP)	
Switzerland	Swiss People's Party (SVP)		
Denmark		Progress Party (FrPd) Danish People's Party (DF)	
Norway		Progress Party (FrP)	
Sweden		New Democracy (ND) Sweden Democrats (SD)	
Finland		Finnish Rural Party (SMP) Finns Party (PS)	
France		Front National (FN)	
Italy (Second Republic)	Forza Italia/People of Freedom (FI/PdL)		Lega Nord (LN): self-defined outsider, but dominant in the north; shares power as part of coalition with FI/PdL
Poland		Self Defense (SRP) League of Polish Families (LPR) Korwin Kukiz'15	Law and Justice (PiS): Conservative nationalist party that uses same kind of populist rhetoric
Hungary	Fidesz: self-defined outsider; but governing and increasingly dominant party	Jobbik	

include smaller parties that challenge larger ones and larger parties that are major parties and one of the principal competitors. Evoking a Manichean division between uncaring elites and an undifferentiated people, populist parties should be consummate outsiders. However, some are insiders that use populist rhetoric to advance vis-à-vis parties whom they associate, if not with the establishment, then with outside forces or, in former Communist countries, the previous regime. Parties like the Swiss People's Party (SVP), Fidesz, and Forza Italia (FI, later People of Freedom, PdL) are 'populist insiders' whose impact is likely to be different from 'populist outsiders' like the Front National (FN) in France, the Danish People's Party (DF) and or the Austrian Freedom Party (FPÖ), a self-defined outsider that briefly served as a governing party before Jörg Haider recast it as a populist party. Table 11.2 indicates which parties are populist insiders or outsiders.

It is also common to differentiate government and opposition parties. In the past, political scientists distinguished between pro-system and anti-system parties. More recently, Mair (2013) differentiated parties that govern from parties that represent. In next section, we use Gordon Smith's notion of the party system core (Smith 1989a, 1989b) to examine the impact that outsiders, some of which are populist parties, have on insiders, the principal competitors that rotate in and out of power.

DEFINING THE CORE

Looking for ways to assess party system change, Gordon Smith (1989a, 1989b) proposed focusing on the party system core. Doing so, he evoked distinctions we commonly make. Although its composition could not be determined by a specific formula, the core referred:

> to those features that have been essential for the way in which the system has functioned and, as a corollary, which appear most resistant to change. (Smith 1989b: 162)

Often overlapping, these included:

1 the party or parties that over a substantial period have been in leading positions;
2 those parties that have been especially influential for the functioning of the system;
3 the particular pattern of party alignments, especially the coalitional line-up, that has evolved. (Smith 1989b: 162)

According to Smith (1989b), a party system's core includes the principal catch-all parties, along with others that fit his second criterion. In practical terms, this includes most relevant parties: parties that have coalition or blackmail potential and use it are part of the core, but parties that lack coalition or blackmail potential are not. However, the core is defined not only by the parties that comprise it but also by the relational features – the pattern of sympathies and antipathies – that make a party system what it is. Here, we see elements of Sartori's insistence on 'systemness' (1976, pp. 43–44) and Mair's (1989; 1997) emphasis on competition for government.

There is no formula determining whether parties are part of the core. As Smith (1989b) indicates, simple cores are easier to discern than complex ones. Included are parties that support or join coalitions, as well as others that affect competition for government. Because parties can move in and out, the composition of the core at one interval, T_1, is not necessarily the same as its composition at another, T_2. If parties move in and out in rapid succession, we are dealing with a weakly institutionalised party system. Among the party systems we consider, none fit this description, but Poland comes closest. Although 'disloyal elites' have sometimes abandoned one label for another, Casal Bértoa and Guerra (chapter 9, this volume) indicate that there is a durable structure of competition, which fits Smith's third criterion.

Smith (1989a, 1989b) advanced the core as a way of assessing change in individual party systems, but indicated that it would also be possible to compare 'core structures' in different ones. We follow his lead, examining the impact that populist parties have had on the core structures of older party systems as well as the roles they play in newer party systems. Doing so, we take advantage of the fact that older Western European party systems were not only relatively static but also had well-defined and readily discernable cores in the 1950s and 1960s. These consisted of 'insiders' who, rotating in and out of office, governed or opposed. Figure 11.3 provides a schematic representation of the party system core. Drawing on Daalder (1966) and Sartori (1966), we have added two

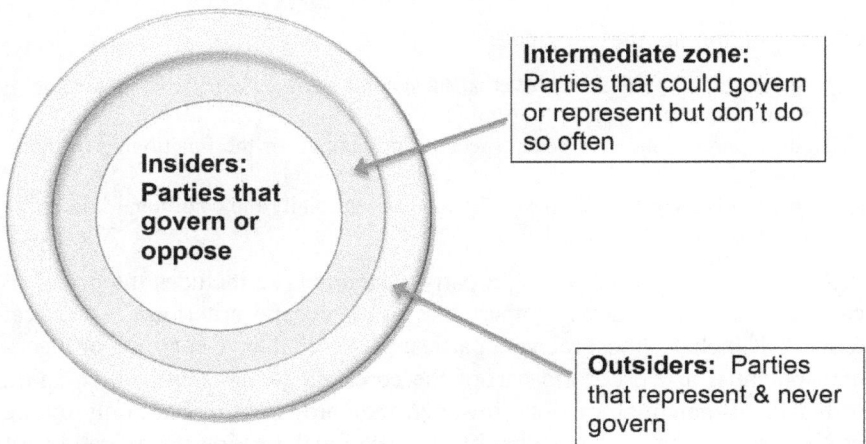

Insiders: Parties that govern or oppose

Intermediate zone: Parties that could govern or represent but don't do so often

Outsiders: Parties that represent & never govern

Figure 11.3 The Party System Core

concentric circles. The outer ring contains 'outsiders' – parties that represent but never govern. In between is an 'intermediate zone' with parties that could govern or represent but rarely do so. We use the earliest systematic analyses of party systems – in many instances, the chapters in Dahl (1966) or, failing that, other sources – to determine which parties belong in the core.

Table 11.3 indicates the mean aggregate strength of the parties that made up the cores of older Western European party systems. The data are for 1945–1968, 1969–1991 and 1992–2015, the intervals that Chiarmonte and Emanuele (2017) use in their analyses of change, which we also used in our discussion of electoral volatility and changes in the effective number of parties. The data confirm Emanuele and Chiaramonte's (2016) finding that newer parties are winning an increasing share of the vote. In several instances, the aggregate strength of the parties that made up the core in the first period (T_1) was relatively stable in the second period (T_2) but declined sharply in the third (T_3). In many countries, Green and left-libertarian and more recently populist parties have been among those attracting parts of the electorate that mainstream parties once counted as part of their loyal support. This has led to shifts in the party balance and the growth of populist parties. Important for our purposes is whether their presence creates challenges for the mainstream parties that make up the core – we will refer to them as 'insiders' – if they want to maintain their position as one of the principal competitors. Drawing on Mair (2013), we noted a division of labour between parties that govern and parties that represent. The former are the government and opposition parties that anchor and define most party

Table 11.3 The Party System Core: Aggregate Support Won by Parties in the Post-war Core (Means)

	T_1	T_2	T_3	*Difference*
	1945–1968	*1969–1991*	*1992–2015*	$T_1–T_3$
	%	%	%	%
Austria	88.4	88.9	63.7	24.7
Denmark	86.6	68.2	69.9	16.8
Finland	91.3	82.9	77.1	14.2
France – from 1945	75.4	45.0	30.9	44.5
France from 1958	68.0	48.1	30.9	37.1
Italy (First Republic Core)	86.6	87.1	0.0	86.6
Netherlands	88.4	78.8	66.9	21.5
Norway	81.9	76.2	61.8	20.1
Sweden	93.9	89.4	73.7	20.2
Switzerland	82.6	76.3	77.2	5.4

Note: Calculated according to definitions in the text; see appendix 11.1 for sources and parties included.

Source: ParlGov database (Döring and Manow 2016).

systems. Making distinctions like these are common practice: introducing polarised pluralism, Sartori (1966: 148–49, charts 3 and 4) sketched a 'pro-system' core surrounded by 'half-way anti-system parties' and 'anti-system parties'. Writing about the reach of party systems, Daalder (1966: 65) differentiated government and opposition parties (the core) as well as 'isolationist parties' and 'anti-system parties'. The parties surrounding today's cores are not anti-system parties but outsiders of different stripes. These include parties that only represent, present if electoral laws permit, as well as parties that would share power if they could do so on terms they could accept. The same is true of insiders who rotate in and out of power, but the terms on which they would compromise differ.

Thinking about party systems in this way provides us with a means to examine the impact of populist parties on party systems. Assume for the moment that we are dealing solely with multiparty politics in parliamentary systems: If a cabinet is to survive, it must have the confidence of a majority. Parties forming governments are typically insiders. If they are to govern, they must (a) enlist other insiders as coalition partners or support parties or (b) reach out to parties that are outside the core. Presumably, parties doing so prefer parties that are (a) ideologically kindred, providing a basis for connected coalitions, as well as (b) reliable and willing to keep their part of any bargain. Populist insiders are more likely to fit one or both criteria; populist outsiders are less likely to fit either. If we are dealing with outsiders, then the question is whether they remain outsiders who neither desire to govern nor are sought as coalition partners or support parties, or are drawn into the intermediate zone – parties that could govern but rarely do so – or become part of the core because they have become governing parties that rotate in and out of office.

Situations like the latter are rare. A different scenario comes into play if insiders, their share of the vote and seats diminished, can no longer build majorities from parties with which they can comfortably ally. Here we assume not that parties necessarily build minimum-winning or minimum-connected coalitions, but rather that insiders work more readily with some parties than others. Faced with diminishing shares of the vote and caucuses smaller than they once were, insiders can either form coalitions with parties with which they are less comfortable – for example, less connected coalitions – or enlist parties outside the core. A key question is whether the presence of populist outsiders (a) allows mainstream parties to form coalitions that would not otherwise be possible or (b) makes it difficult or impossible for mainstream parties to form coalitions they would otherwise prefer. Figure 11.4 provides a graphic representation of the choices involved.

Positing this, we have assumed the populist parties are outsiders. That is often but not always the case. If a populist party is an insider, then we ask

allow formation of coalitions previously impossible

Populist outsider: has sufficient seats to

prevent mainstream party from forming preferred coalition

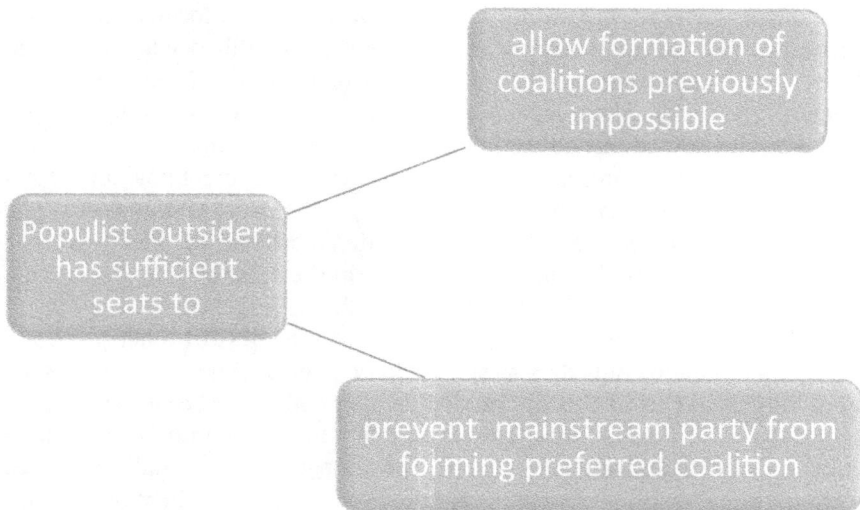

Figure 11.4 Populist Outsiders and Competition for Government

different questions – for example, how its populism affects election outcomes and whether and how populism affects its function as a governing party. Inclusion or exclusion matters: In the next section, we consider the extent to which both insiders and outsiders exclude themselves of their own volition or are excluded because of a formal or informal *cordon sanitaire*.

INCLUSION AND EXCLUSION

Contemporary populist parties are different from the anti-system parties that roiled interwar democracies (Cappocia 2002). Although many are illiberal, none oppose liberal democracy (Mudde 2014). Nor are they necessarily outsiders or anti-system forces that are beyond the pale. As we shall see, many were initially outsiders that either excluded themselves and/or were excluded by mainstream parties. However, these choices were not carved in stone and changed when parties reassessed their situation. Many populist parties were initially outsiders that excluded themselves or were excluded by the mainstream parties that neither needed nor desired their support. The latter was particularly true of parties like FN in France or the Freedom Party (FPÖ) in Austria that could be associated with an older extreme right or Nazism. FN was excluded by France's majoritarian electoral system and by a *cordon sanitaire* in which the mainstream left and right agreed to cooperate to keep FN candidates from advancing to second ballot or, failing that, strategies of 'republican' defense that produced similar arrangements locally rather than nationally. Nor was their support in the National Assembly needed. However, Jean-Marie Le Pen advanced to the second ballot in the 2002 presidential election, and his daughter, leading a more sanitised party, ostensibly stripped of its earlier inclinations, did so in the 2017 presidential election. Competing under proportional representation, the FPÖ was in a different position, represented not only in federal but also in länder parliaments. Although the ÖVP and the SPÖ excluded the FPÖ from the national cabinet, the FPÖ governed in Jörg Haider's Carinthia and shared power in the other nine länder (Ivaldi, chapter 7, and Falland and Heinisch, chapter 2, this volume).

Over time, there has been a change in the willingness of other parties to incorporate populist outsiders as support parties or coalition partners. Many were initially excluded either through their own volition or because they were subject to a *cordon sanitaire*. However, maintaining a cordon can be difficult: sooner or later someone defects. Nor are parties that initially excluded themselves necessarily content to remain on the sidelines. Situations change either because populists want to govern or mainstream parties seek them out. Austria provides one example: as Falland and Heinisch (chapter 2, this volume) point out, coalition between the FPÖ and Jörg Haider in 2000 was possible because Jörg Haider was anxious to govern, and the ÖVP was unhappy in its role as junior partner in coalitions with the SPÖ. In Denmark, the mainstream right sought out support from the Danish People's Party (DF). Like Denmark, populist parties in Norway and Finland were excluded but eventually included. Only in Sweden have populists not served as support parties or coalition partners. As Jupskås (chapter 5, this volume) points out, in Denmark and Norway, first generation populist radical right parties were excluded but second generation parties were included. The same is true in the Netherlands.

POPULIST INSIDERS

The situation of populist insiders is different. Both the Swiss People's Party (SVP) and Fidesz in Hungary were governing parties that took on a populist mantle. The SVP was the smallest of the four parties that share power in the Federal Council. Although it divided the party – as Mazzoleni (chapter 4, this volume) indicates, populism was advanced by Blocher and the Zurich wing of the party and eventually led to a split – the SVP has flourished: Growing through the 1990s, it has been the largest party since 2003. Initially a liberal party, Fidesz used populism to become the principal party of the right in Hungary (Enyedi and Róna, chapter 10, this volume). In Italy, the collapse of the First Republic's party system made new political formations not only possible but also necessary. Forza Italia used populism to build a party that,

Table 11.4   Patterns of Inclusion and Exclusion

	Party	Cordon Sanitaire *or* Self-Exclusion
Austria	Freedom Party (FPÖ)	1986–1999 2006–2017
Netherlands	Centre Democrats (CD, CN)	Yes
	List Pim Fortuyn (LPF)	None
	Freedom Party (PVV)	Initially none; yes from 2015
	Socialist Party (SP)	Self-excludes
Switzerland	Swiss People's Party (SVP)	None (insider)
Denmark	Progress Party (FrPd)	De facto
	Danish People's Party (DF)	None
Norway	Progress Party (FrP)	De facto (first generation) Gradual incorporation (second generation)
Sweden	New Democracy (ND)	Yes
	Sweden Democrats (SD)	Yes
Finland	Finnish Rural Party (SMP)	None
	Finns Party (PS)	None
France	Front National (FN)	*Cordon sanitaire* or 'republican' defense
Italy (First & Second Republic)	Italian Communist Party (PCI)	Yes (national level)
	Forza Italia	None (insider)
	Lega Nord	None
	Five Star Movement (M5S)	None but M5S self-excludes
Poland	Law and Justice (PiS)	None (insider)
Hungary	Fidesz	None (insider)
	Jobbik	Yes

after the collapse of the First Republic's party system, emerged as the principal party on the right in Italy's Second Republic party system.

Table 11.4 summarises patterns of inclusion and exclusion. Both have implications for competition for government and competition for votes.

Competition for Government

In this section, we consider whether populist parties have triggered changes in competition for government. Of particular interest are situations in which the presence of a populist party precludes mainstream parties from form-ing coalitions that they might have preferred or, alternatively, allows them to form coalitions that would not otherwise have been possible. Our cases include instances of both. However, populist parties are only one source of change. As de Lange (chapter 3, this volume) indicates, the Dutch have had a succession of novel coalitions since 1994 and, from 2002 to 2012, a series of short-lived governments, of which two included populist parties as coalition partners or support parties. However, these changes pre-dated the growth of populist parties and reflected the weakening of mainstream parties and par-ticularly the Christian Democratic Appeal (CDA).

As table 11.5 indicates, there is considerable variation in the degree to which changes in competition for government have occurred. There are only a few instances in which pronounced changes have occurred but several in which smaller changes are apparent. Among the party systems displaying greater change are Italy, where the polarised pluralism of the First Republic gave way to the bipolar competition of the Second, the Netherlands and Aus-tria. In France, few changes in competition for government occurred through 2016. Majoritarian electoral laws prevented the FN from capturing the presi-dency or translating its electoral strength into seats in the National Assembly. Ivaldi (chapter 7, this volume) argues that this limited the role of FN to a nuisance – albeit a very important one – able to affect competition for govern-ment only if it mobilised sufficient support to advance to the second ballot in presidential or National Assembly elections. Use of either a *cordon sanitaire* or, more recently, 'republican defense' prevented this from happening in all but a few districts. However, in 2002, Jean-Marie Le Pen accumulated more votes than the Socialist candidate, Lionel Jospin, forcing PS leaders to urge supporters to vote for Jacques Chirac. Had other circumstances not led to the collapse of both the PS and the Republicans (before 2015, the Union for a Popular Movement, UMP), a variant of this scenario might have unfolded in the May 2017 presidential elections. Instead, Marine Le Pen, leading a newly sanitised FN, and Emmanuel Macron, leading the newly founded En Marche, advanced from a hotly contested first ballot to the second, which Macron won with 66.1 per cent to Le Pen's 33.9 per cent. Winning 21.3 per cent of the first ballot of the 2017 presidential election and advancing to the second ballot, and 13.2 per cent on the first ballot of the National Assembly election a month later, FN was more than a nuisance but not the cause of collapse of PS, of the Republicans and, with them, of the bipolar structure of competition that had characterised the Fifth Republic since the 1980s.

In Switzerland, the transformation of the Swiss People's party from a smaller farmers party to a populist radical right party has produced subtle changes in competition for government. Among the remaining Western

Table 11.5 Competition for Government

	Alternation in Government	Novel Coalitions	Outsiders' Access to Government	Overall Pattern	Incidence of Change
Austria	Minimal	Rare: FPÖ in 2000, BZÖ in 2005	Limited	**Closed:** Reversion to grand coalition for long periods	**Minimal:** Earlier pattern repeats – Reduced competition & reduced voice for factions in order to maintain SPÖ-ÖVP coalition
Netherlands	Partial	Frequent	High	**Open:**	**High:** – Shorter duration of cabinets – Unanimous legislative coalitions less frequent – Frequent use of innovative formulas including minority government – From 2002 to 2012, formation of cabinets via logrolling
Switzerland	None	None	None	**Closed:** Power sharing in Federal Council continues	**Some:** Subtle changes – Magic formula abandoned – Increased recourse to referenda
Denmark	Full	Some	High	**Partially closed:** Frequent recourse to minority government to exclude FrPd (1980s) & incorporate DF as support party (2000a)	**Some:** – Some in response to FrPd – Minority government used to avoid working with FrPd & later to incorporate DF – Eventual return to bipolar competition – Mainstream parties (insiders) use minority government to maintain position as principal competitors
Norway	Full	Some	Some	**Relatively closed:** Frequent recourse to minority government Eventually bipolar	**Some:** – Initially closed, then more open – Eventual reassertion of bipolar competition – Mainstream parties (insiders) use minority government to maintain position as principal competitors

(Continued)

Table 11.5 (Continued)

	Alternation in Government	Novel Coalitions	Outsiders' Access to Government	Overall Pattern	Incidence of Change
Sweden	Full	Some	Some	**Relatively closed:** Bipolar	**Some:** – More frequent recourse to minority government – Occasional cooperation across blocs to limit SD influence – Mainstream parties (insiders) use minority government to maintain position as principal competitors
Finland	Partial	Frequent	High	**Open:** 'Anything goes'	**None:** Open pattern unchanged
France	Full	None	None until 2017	**Closed:** Bipolar competition until 2017	**Minimal:** Until 2017, but left and right periodically reconfigure
Italy (Second Republic)	Full from 1994–2013	Some	Some	**Open:** Some changes in electoral vehicles Bipolar competition	**Substantial:** Change from polarised pluralism of First Republic Some cross-bloc cooperation since 2013
Poland	Full	Yes because of fluid party system	High because of fluid party system	**Open:** Changes in electoral vehicles used Bipolar competition	**Some:** – 90° change in axes of competition after 2005
Hungary	Full	None	None	**Closed:** Bipolar competition	**Some:** Shift towards one-party dominance

European party systems, the most pronounced changes are in Austria and the Netherlands. In contrast, in the three Scandinavian countries and Finland, populist parties have been absorbed into existing patterns with relatively small changes in previous structures of competition. However, mainstream parties have had to depend more on parties on their flanks in order to maintain their position. In the next section, we explore what happened in consensual, consociational and adversarial democracies.

CONSENSUAL DEMOCRACIES: THE NORDIC COUNTRIES

There are reasons why change has occurred in some instances but not in others. Finland's 'anything goes' pattern of coalition formation is so open that most combinations fit within it (Arter, chapter 6, this volume). That is not the case in Denmark, Norway and Sweden. All have party systems that after an earlier period of Social Democratic dominance (weaker in Denmark than in the rest) ended up with bipolar competition (Arter 1999; Einhorn and Logue 2003). Recourse to minority government made it possible to form governments without the Danish and Norwegian Progress parties when they appeared in the early 1970s, and more recently, to include 'second generation' populist parties as support parties for governments of the right. As Jupskås (chapter 5, this volume) indicates, in Denmark, this initially led to an eclectic range of governments, including one in which Socialists and Liberals shared power. From 2001 to 2011, Denmark had a series of minority governments in which the mainstream right relied on the Danish People's Party (DF) for support. After this, Social Democrats (SD), Social Liberals (RV) and through 2014 the Socialist People's Party (SF) governed until the 2015 election. Winning 20.7 per cent of the vote, DF emerged as the largest party on the right, but chose to support a minority Liberal (V) government. A similar process is underway in Norway. There the Progress Party (FrP) became a support party from 2001 to 2005 and in 2013 a partner in a minority government led by the Conservative Party (H).

The pattern in Sweden has been different. Like Denmark and Norway, Sweden has a bipolar party system in which majority coalitions or minority governments have been the norm, but Sweden has yet to incorporate either New Democracy (ND) or its successor, the Sweden Democrats (SD). Neither was (or is) considered a suitable coalition partner and the latter has been subject to a *cordon sanitaire*. Neither the left nor the right had a majority in the parliament elected in 2014. A minority Social Democratic government assumed power. Rather than allow the SD to hold the balance of power, the two blocs agreed that the largest bloc – in this case, the right – should determine the budget. However, as Jupskås (chapter 5, this volume) points out, this arrangement was showing signs of strain a year after it was put in place; parties on the right were tempted to defect.

CONSOCIATIONAL DEMOCRACIES

The three consociational or former consociational democracies exhibit different patterns. In Switzerland, the SVP's transformation and subsequent growth resulted in subtle changes in the rules of the game. Power sharing in the Federal Council persists, but neither the 'magic formula' that allocated seats in fixed ratios to the four largest parties nor the unwritten rule that members of the Federal Council who sought re-election would be automatically returned have survived. However, as Mazzoleni (chapter 4, this volume) indicates, mainstream parties continued to work with the SVP despite its populist bent and frequent use of referenda to oppose policies to which the Federal Council had agreed. Doing so was within the bounds of the acceptable. More important, other parties had more to lose from excluding the SVP than acquiescing to changes in the rules of the game. Nevertheless, there were limits to what the other mainstream parties would accept: as Mazzoleni points out, in 2008, SVP leader Blocher was not re-elected to the seat he had previously won on the party's behalf. In the ensuing machinations, this went to a splinter party and came back to the SVP only in 2015.

Austria and the Netherlands display greater changes in competition for government. As Fallend and Heinisch (chapter 2, this volume) indicate, the Social Democrats (SPÖ) and the People's Party (ÖVP) shared power in Austria from 1945–1966 in all-inclusive grand coalitions, but from 1966 to 1983 they engaged in bipolar competition in which each attempted to win a majority. The only obstacle was the FPÖ. Initially a small nationalist party, it had evolved into a liberal party that from 1983 to 1986 held the balance between the two larger parties. Its transformation into a populist radical right party and subsequent growth prompted the SPÖ and ÖVP to renew their coalition. This persisted through 1999. A coalition of the ÖVP and FPÖ took office in 2000 but collapsed when the FPÖ imploded, plummeted in the 2002 elections and subsequently split. Although the ÖVP governed with the rump of the FPÖ and the Alliance for the Future of Austria (BZÖ) after it broke away, the ÖVP and the SPÖ came back together in 2007. However, their coalitions have been based on increasingly narrow majorities.

Several observations are in order: The SPÖ-ÖVP coalitions after 1986 and 2005 were put in place for different reasons than the post-war grand coalitions. Then the two parties – rivals in a country that had fought a civil war prior to annexation by Germany – formed a grand coalition to defuse conflicts while sharing power and patronage (Fallend and Heinisch, chapter 2, this volume; Engelmann 1966). Similar coalitions were formed after 1986 because neither the SPÖ nor the ÖPV regarded the FPÖ as a suitable partner. Neither had sufficient seats to form a majority without the FPÖ, nor was minority government an option. The situation changed when the ÖPV and FPÖ formed a coalition of the right. Each had reasons for doing so. As Fallend and Heinisch (chapter 2, this volume) indicate, Jörg Haider was anxious to govern and the ÖPV was unhappy with its role as the junior partner in SPÖ-led coalitions. Once the FPÖ, the larger of the two wings into which the party divided, resumed its radical posture, the SPÖ and the ÖPV found themselves forced to govern together. No alternate majority was possible.

The pattern has been different in the Netherlands, a former consociational democracy that retains vestiges of power sharing. Since 1994, the Dutch have had a succession of novel coalitions and from 2002 through 2012, short-lived cabinets punctuated by early elections. This was different from the pattern of partial alternation that characterised cabinet formation from 1946 to 1994. However, the driving force was not the presence of populist parties but rather depillarisation and the declining strength of mainstream parties. The CDA and its predecessors had been the pivot around which pre-1994 coalitions were built. As de Lange (chapter 3, this volume) indicates, the LPF and the PVV emerged later and neither has been subject to a *cordon sanitaire*. If Austria ended up with a dearth of alternative coalitions, the Dutch had a surfeit of them. With a large number of parties represented in parliament, they always did, but with 85–90 per cent of the vote and seats in parliament mainstream parties had sufficient strength to form cohesive centre-left or centre-right coalitions. That changed when the confessional vote dropped and rates of electoral volatility increased, ushering in a series of novel coalitions.

In power from 1994 to 2002, the Kok governments brought Social Democrats (PvdA), Democrats 66 (D66) and Liberals (VVD) together in two 'purple' coalitions that were novel because they included parties that had not previously governed together and excluded the CDA. Both governed in a period of relative harmony. That changed in the run-up to the 2002 elections. The Kok government came under attack not only from a populist liberal party, the List Pim Fortuyn (LPF), but also from the populist left Socialist Party (SP). From 2002, fluctuating party strengths, increased polarisation and the emergence of a socio-cultural dimension orthogonal to the state-market divide made forming coalitions difficult. Parties lacked sufficient seats to form two-party cabinets. Instead, they used logrolling to form coalitions that were less cohesive (de Lange, chapter 3, this volume).

ADVERSARIAL DEMOCRACIES

France, Italy, Poland and Hungary are adversarial democracies. All have or have had a bipolar structure of competition, but in the two Western European cases, this reflected party system changes spurred by a combination of regime change and changes in their electoral laws. Change occurred earlier in France. The shift from the assembly-dominated Fourth Republic to the semi-presidential Fifth Republic and the use of majoritarian systems for the election of the president and the National Assembly encouraged political forces to combine into two competing blocs able to cooperate in order to prevent opponents from capturing the presidency or winning additional seats. Italian reformers hoped that changing the electoral law would have similar effects. Their hand forced by a referendum repealing the proportional component of the law regulating Senate elections, Italian politicians passed an electoral law that facilitated the fragmented bipolar competition that has characterised Italy's Second Republic.

Although a populist party, the Lega Nord, helped trigger the collapse of Italy's First Republic party system, it is difficult to trace differences between the First and Second Republic party systems solely to the impact of populist parties. Instead, the ways in which populist forces were channelled reflects changes in institutions and electoral laws. In France, the double ballot electoral system ensured that FN was confined to the role of nuisance that Ivaldi (chapter 7, this volume) attributes to it. Only when PS manipulated the electoral law, introducing proportional representation to prevent the mainstream right from winning a majority, was FN able to win seats in proportion of it to its electoral strength. However, that has not prevented the party from growing into a potent political force that can be a threat to the mainstream right and left. As Ivaldi points out, in the 2002 presidential election, FN's founder and leader, Jean-Marie Le Pen, finished ahead of PS' leader and candidate, Lionel Jospin, forcing PS leaders to urge their followers to vote for the sitting president and candidate of the mainstream right, Jacques Chirac. A different version of this scenario unfolded in 2017.

In both Hungary and Poland parties of the right – each in their own way insiders – have embellished conservative nationalism with populist rhetoric that has been used to define the right and in doing so, maintain or advance their position. Although this has an impact on competition for government, it is better understood as part of our discussion of competition for votes. We return to it there.

Cordon Sanitaire, Self-exclusion, and Changing Opportunity Structures

Let us look at continuity and change. We begin with the nine Western European party systems and then consider Poland and Hungary. One thread running through several cases is the decreasing share of the vote and seats that mainstream parties command. One reason – but only one – has been the emergence and growth of populist parties, but this is only one facet of a broader series of changes. Populist parties are as much a consequence as a cause of these developments. Tracing them goes beyond the scope of this volume. Our concern is what happens when populist insiders shift the party balance or populist outsiders wedge themselves into already crowded party systems.

We focus initially on the impact that outsiders have had. Arguably, their emergence should narrow the range of alternate coalitions available to mainstream parties, forcing them together in the same way that bilateral oppositions did in Sartori's (1976) analyses of polarised pluralism. However, the only instances in which dynamics like that have operated are Austria, where the FPÖ's growth from 1986 to 1999 and 2006 onwards, forced the two mainstream parties to come together in cartel-like grand coalitions, and Second Republic Italy, where the recent growth of the Five Star Movement (M5S) and need for a majority in the Senate as well as the Chamber of Deputies forced the Renzi government to seek support from the New Centre-Right (a new party that split from Berlusconi's party). However, a situation like this unfolded in the Netherlands, where the reluctance of two mainstream right parties to ally with Geert Wilders' Freedom Party (PVV) forced them to enlist parties to their left in prospective coalitions in the aftermath of the 2017 elections, and could unfold in other party systems as well. However, situations like this need to be seen in context. The Dutch have a long history of 'difficult party relations' (Daalder 1955) and protracted cabinet formations are the norm. As they invariably do, Dutch politicians tried to build a majority government that could last a full four years instead of relying on minority governments, as politicians in Denmark, Norway and Sweden often do. This required a record 225 days.

Sharing power in Switzerland's Federal Council is the norm. Swiss parties manage to carry out business as usual – albeit with certain key qualifications – despite the transformation of the SVP. Dutch parties had, if anything, too many possible coalitions rather than too few. So do Finnish parties that carry out a very different version of business as usual – coalitions that vary so much that they defy efforts to classify them.

Of the remaining seven party systems, six are bipolar systems. So was Second Republic Italy until the growth of the M5S. Both Poland and Hungary display their own variants of bipolar competition organised around cultural and historical divides between political forces that either grew out of or opposed previous regimes. In Hungary, these are represented by a diminishing number of well-institutionalised parties. In Poland a similar divide has been represented by an array of parties more ephemeral than the disloyal elites who orchestrate and abandon them (Casal Bértoa and Guerra, chapter 9, this volume).

Until 2017, the Fifth Republic France displayed a fluid form of bipolar competition. The principal line of division was between the mainstream left and right. Political forces on both sides of the divide periodically split and recombined. However, this has been driven not by the FN, which for the most part has been unable to influence competition for government, but rather by the ways in which forces on the left and right responded to the logic of the electoral system (Ivaldi, chapter 7, this volume; Knapp 2004). The three remaining systems are Norway, Sweden and Denmark. All are consensual democracies that combine cooperation and consultation, varying mixes of minority and majority government as well as bipolar competition and occasional cooperation from parties from opposite sides of the spectrum.

ANALYSIS: INCORPORATION AND COMPETITION FOR GOVERNMENT

What explains differences and similarities? As table 11.6 indicates, there is no evidence that the type of political system – in this case, whether a country was a consociational or consensual democracy – matters. Nor does the structure of competition. There is no consistent variation among systems that were (or are) bipolar and those that are not. It could be argued that we have too few cases or that these party systems are too different to be usefully compared. Both are valid, but it is not clear that a larger subset of more similar cases would yield different results. Looking at the ways in which populist parties have been incorporated into pre-existing structures of competition does. As we shall see, exclusion or self-exclusion results in greater changes than incorporation.

These cases suggest that changes in competition for government are likely if the emergence of populist parties (or any new party) and shifts in the party balance make it difficult or impossible for mainstream parties to maintain previous coalitions and alliances, or, differently put, whether shares of the vote and the way which parties align allow populist parties to have blackmail potential. This was the case in the Netherlands and Austria, but not in Denmark and Norway. The Austrian case raises questions about whether using a *cordon sanitaire* to quarantine challengers will result in changes in competition for government. It suggests that it will if the challenger is large enough to prevent mainstream parties from forming coalitions they would otherwise prefer. In pre-2000 and post-2006 Austria, neither the ÖVP nor the SPÖ could form majority coalitions without joining together or enlisting the FPÖ.

Table 11.6 The Structure of Political Competition

	Type of Political System[a]	Type of Party System[b]	Structure of Political Competition	Incidence of Party System Change[b]
Austria	Former consociational democracy	Moderate pluralism	Coalescent from 1945 to 1966 Competitive from 1966 to 1986 Coalescent from 1986 to 1999 Competitive 2000 to 2005 Coalescent from 2006 to present	None
Netherlands	Former consociational democracy	Moderate pluralism	Multipolar/coalescent	None
Switzerland	Consociational	Moderate pluralism	Coalescent	None
Denmark	Consensual democracy	Moderate pluralism	Bipolar competition from the 1970s to present	None
Norway	Consensual	Moderate pluralism	Bipolar competition from the 1970s to present	None
Sweden	Consensual	Moderate pluralism	Bipolar competition from the 1970s to present	None
Finland	Consensual	Moderate pluralism (with a large number of parties)	Multipolar	None
France	Adversarial	Moderate pluralism	Bipolar	Earlier change from polarised pluralism to moderate pluralism Variation in form of bipolarity
Italy	Adversarial	Polarised pluralism through 1994 Moderate pluralism from 1994	Bipolar from 1994 to 2013	Collapse of First Republic party system and change in electoral law result in bipolar but fragmented cooperate
Poland	Adversarial	Moderate pluralism	Bipolar	90° rotation in axes of competition
Hungary	Adversarial	Moderate pluralism	Bipolar	From balanced competition to one-party dominance

[a] Based on Lijphart (1999).
[b] From Sartori (1976).

This contrasts with Denmark and Norway: in Denmark, parties on the mainstream right enlisted the Danish People's Party (DF) as a support party sustaining successive minority governments in power from 2001 to 2011 and more recently from 2015. However, this did not occur when populist parties first appeared but rather after DF, a populist radical right party, had replaced the anti-establishment and anti-tax Progress Party. By this time, public attitudes and mainstream party positions had changed. Jupskås (chapter 5, this volume) notes that the DF was offered 'substantive concessions' on immigration policy in exchange for its support. Norway is similar to but also different from Denmark. As Jupskås indicates, Norway was able to maintain bipolar competition in the 1970s and 1980s without relying on the Progress Party (FrP). However, this became more difficult in subsequent decades. The Norwegian Progress Party was a support party from 2001 to 2005 and has been a governing party since 2013.

Sweden also has a bipolar party system but neither the first generation ND nor its eventual successor, the SD, has been enlisted as a support party or coalition partner. Instead, parties of the left and right opted for 'cross-bloc collaboration'. This occurred during an economic crisis in the early 1990s and since 2010. As Jupskås (chapter 5, this volume) notes, neither the mainstream right nor the Social Democrats and their allies have had parliamentary majorities. Instead, a coalition of the right in office from 2010 to 2014 relied on support from the left.

Recourse to a *cordon sanitaire* had a greater impact in Austria because the bloc of seats that the FPÖ commanded was large enough to affect coalition formation. In France, the FN has also been subject to a *cordon sanitaire*, but this operated through electoral alliances that prevented the FN from advancing to the second ballot in most presidential and constituency level National Assembly elections. In Hungary, Jobbik has commanded an increasing share of the vote but lacks blackmail potential; the electoral system awards Fidesz an increasingly disproportionate share of seats in parliament. However, we can see the impact of exclusion and self-exclusion in First Republic Italy, where reluctance to include the Communists led to Christian Democratic dominance and polarised pluralism, and Second Republic Italy since 2013. Spain is not one of our cases, but the impact that a left populist party, Podemos (We Can), has had on the party system since it entered the Cortes has been considerable: Podemos excluded itself not only after the 2015 election but also after a 2016 election called to resolve the deadlock. Neither the Socialists (PSOE) nor the People's Party (PP) was willing to share power. Only when the PSOE changed leaders in 2016 was it possible to invest a minority People's Party government to replace the caretaker cabinet in place since the previous December.

ALTERNATE COALITIONS

Populist parties can also affect competition for government by making alternate coalitions possible. This occurred both in Austria in 2000, when the ÖVP joined with the FPÖ, and in Denmark, in 2001 when the mainstream right enlisted the Danish People's Party (DF) as a support party. In several instances, the initial response to the appearance of populist radical right and anti-establishment parties was to exclude them through a formal or informal *cordon sanitaire*. Whether this affected competition for government depended on whether they had sufficient seats to have blackmail potential. Even if they did, mainstream parties frequently resorted to well-established practices like minority government in Scandinavia to sustain cabinets without enlisting populist support. However, this has changed over time: Among the cases considered, there is a tendency towards greater inclusion not only of older parties but also newer ones like the List Pim Fortuyn (LPF) and the Dutch Freedom Party (PVV).[2]

Maintaining a *cordon sanitaire* can be difficult: one or more parties may want to defect in order to exploit alternate coalitions. This temptation should increase if mainstream parties find themselves in cross-bloc alliances they would normally avoid. However, this is not the only factor at work: as both Jupskås (chapter 5, this volume) and Ivaldi (chapter 7, this volume) indicate, some populist parties change and seek to end their isolation.[3] In Denmark and Norway, it was 'second generation' parties that were enlisted as support parties and coalition partners. Moreover, as de Lange (chapter 3, this volume) argues, mainstream parties may find it expedient to respond to electoral markets. Reservations about immigration and multiculturalism and the EU have become more prominent, encouraging some mainstream parties to modify positions and, if need be, incorporate populist parties as support parties or coalition partners. Motives for doing so could reflect electoral advantage – keeping voters from defecting to populist parties while attracting others – as well opportunities to pursue a different mix of policies. This would be especially true if the costs of forming such a coalition were, as Mudde (2014) argues, relatively 'cheap' – for example, the party being incorporated receives concessions in areas like immigration and integration but does not constrain mainstream parties in other areas (see also de Lange 2012).

LIBERAL AND LEFT POPULIST PARTIES

Thus far we have focused on the impact of populist radical right parties and, in one or two instances, populist liberal parties, but said little about populist left parties. This is unavoidable. The only two populist left parties among our cases are the PS in the Netherlands and the M5S in Italy. Drawing on Lucardie (2000), de Lange (chapter 3, this volume) characterises the SP as a purifier rather than a prophet and argues that its primary impact has been on the Dutch Social Democratic Party (PvdA), with which it competes. However, the PvdA has yet to enlist the SP as a prospective coalition partner, nor has the SP, with 16.6 per cent of the vote in 2006 and 9.7–9.8 per cent in recent elections, been able to provide the PvdA or Green Left (with which it could also ally) with an alternate majority. In contrast, M5S has had an impact on government formation in Italy. So has Podemos in Spain.

Taken together, these cases indicate that populist parties can affect competition for government, but whether they do or do not depends on the degree to which their presence affects the ability of parties to form preferred coalitions. This can occur if exclusion or self-exclusion makes it impossible to do so, but, as we have seen, the presence of populist parties may also open up opportunities not previously available. Nor is this the only reason why changes in competition for government occur. As the Dutch case indicates, the weakened position of mainstream parties also matters.

Competition for Votes

Competition for votes has multiple dimensions. Broadly construed, it includes how parties campaign and contest elections: with whom and how they compete; how they cast their appeals; the issues and themes they invoke; the underlying dimensions on which they compete; whether they target the entire electorate or selected groups within it; and the degree to which they manage to pry votes away from other parties. Further, we focus on their ability to set or reset agendas, and the impact of populist parties on the dimensions on which competition takes place.

There is variation in the degree to which populist parties have been able to shape what party competition is about. Typically, populist parties are one voice among many – the situation when populist parties are new parties as well as when an older party like the Swiss People's Party (SVP) transforms itself into populist party – but, in some instances, populist parties have had a greater impact on what party competition is about. This occurred in Italy and Hungary. As Verbeek, Zaslove and Rooduijn (chapter 8, this volume) point out, populist forces were confined to the margins until the final years of Italy's First Republic, when a populist radical right party, the Lega Nord, triggered its demise. The collapse of the First Republic party system created a vacuum that diverse elements scrambled to fill. Among them were not only the Lega Nord but also Silvio Berlusconi's Forza Italia (FI, later People of Freedom, PdL). Built on Berlusconi's media empire (Hopkin and Paolucci

1999), Forza Italia assembled elements of the centre right into a party that used populist appeals to propagate its message. In the process, he not only built a populist liberal party but, along with the Lega Nord and Alleanza nationale (AN), also defined the right in the fragmented bipolar party system that developed under a new electoral law.

Populist parties have also had considerable opportunity to define what party competition is about in Hungary. Initially a liberal party, Fidesz moved to the right and added populism to its repertoire after its defeat in 2002. Helped by reactions to a leaked speech by a Socialist prime minister, Fidesz assumed a dominant position not only on the right but also in Hungary. Although Enyedi and Róna (chapter 10, this volume) argue that Fidesz's populism was secondary to conservative nationalism, Fidesz and Jobbik, once it gained prominence, have been able to define what the right in Hungary stands for.

Both Ivaldi's chapter on France (chapter 7, this volume) and Enyedi and Róna's chapter on Hungary (chapter 10, this volume) sketch symbiotic relationships between populist radical right and mainstream parties. In France, FN stakes out positions that are sometimes taken over by the mainstream UMP. Fidesz is a mainstream party whose populist overtones are so pronounced that it can be considered a populist party. Enyedi and Róna argue that the relationship between Fidesz and Jobbik can be interpreted either as a case of agenda-setting in which Jobbik stakes out positions taken over by Fidesz or as a situation in which Jobbik acts as a vanguard that prepares the way for more radical positions that Fidesz eventually adopts and implements. Weighing the merits of both, Enyedi and Róna indicate the latter is closer to the truth.

In Italy, the Lega Nord placed immigration and integration and, after it changed its position, Euroscepticism on the agenda. In Switzerland, the SVP uses not only election campaigns but also referenda that it initiates to influence agendas. As Mazzoleni (chapter 4, this volume) indicates, positions on immigration, asylum and the welfare state advanced by the SVP in referenda were eventually taken up by centre-right parties and, in some instances, acknowledged by the PS as well.

Other chapters talk about changes in discourse or the underlying dimensions of conflict. Mazzoleni (chapter 4, this volume) maintains that the SVP politicised the issue of national independence versus supranational integration. Comparing the impact of populist parties in Denmark, Norway and Sweden, Jupskås (chapter 5, this volume) contrasts the effects of first- and second-generation parties. Particularly in Denmark and Norway, the first generation mobilised a protest vote, but the second generation challenged the dominant cleavage structure by focusing on immigration and national identity. Polarisation on socio-cultural issues increased, and positions on immigration are increasingly important in explaining voting behaviour. Similar changes are underway in Sweden. Writing about Finland, Arter (chapter 6, this volume) argues that the Finns Party (PS) and its predecessor, the Finnish Rural Party, mobilise the traditional-authoritarian-nationalist end of the socio-cultural dimension. Ivaldi (chapter 7, this volume) indicates that the mainstream right and left have responded differently to the nativist positions on immigration that FN espoused. The mainstream left tried to balance culturally liberal positions on law and order and integration with stricter controls on immigration. In contrast, the mainstream right promoted stricter law enforcement and restricted immigration. Table 11.7 summarises what each chapter has had to say about competition for votes.

Indicating that there have been changes in the issues discussed in election campaigns, the tone of political discourse or dimensions on which competition takes place does not mean that populist parties are the principal or only agent responsible for these changes. De Lange (chapter 3, this volume) notes that in the Netherlands, mainstream parties responding to the electoral market were the first to put immigration on the agenda. In a similar vein, Mudde (2007) argues that politicians from mainstream parties sometimes adopt more radical discourse before populist parties achieve significant growth.

Arguing that populist parties position on one pole of the socio-cultural dimension is consistent with an important stream in the literature (see Kitschelt and McGann 1995; Kriesi 2008, 2012; Bornschier 2010; Bornschier and Kriesi 2013; Häusermann and Kriesi 2015), but it does not mean that populist parties create it or that it will be salient in every election. Events such as the 2008 economic and financial crisis can refocus attention, temporarily or more durably, on economic issues (Hernandez and Kriesi 2016; Kriesi and Pappas 2015). In Western Europe, Green and left-libertarian parties were the first to address the socio-cultural dimension. Over time, social democratic parties took up some of their positions. Populist radical right parties take up positions on the opposite pole, but, in doing so, they take ownership of positions that in some instances were initially staked out by parties of the mainstream right, such as the Liberals (VVD) in the Netherlands.

There is debate about the degree to which populist parties set agendas that other parties follow. One strand focuses on who was first to raise the issue (Bale 2008; Mudde 2013; Rooduijn et al. 2014). This is important from an historical point of view, but may not matter if populist parties entrench themselves and take ownership of issues like opposition to immigration or the EU (Petrocik 1996; Petrocik et al. 2003; Goodliffe 2015). If this occurs, we can assume that populist parties ensure that these issues remain on the agenda.

A second strand concerns the extent to which other parties mimic populist parties. In some instances, they do, but this is not always the case (Akkerman 2012; Akkerman 2015). One of the earliest findings of the Comparative Manifesto Project was that parties addressed preferred issues (Budge and Farlie 1983). Moreover, as Meguid (2008) argues, parties have the option

Table 11.7 Competition for Votes

	Populist Party or Parties	Target Groups, Discourse	Issue Agenda/Dimensions of Conflict	Impact on Other Parties	Competition for Votes	Party Balance
Austria	FPÖ	Shifting: eventually working class, conservative Catholics	Shifting positions: Initially pro-EU, pro-market; eventually anti-EU, social populist; nativist, anti-immigrant Mobilises traditional authoritarian nativist end of GAL/TAN dimension	Some changes in SPÖ & ÖVP positions	Diminished competition between SPÖ & ÖVP; both turn inward, concentrate on mobilising core support	Pronounced shift
Netherlands	LPF & PVV	Changes in discourse & programmes	Emergence of immigration, integration as issues; increased polarisation Articulate socio-cultural dimension	Some, but mainstream parties raise issues first: 'Enforcing' role	Multi-faceted: Competition on two-dimensional orthogonal to each other	Frequent shifts; no clear direction; no longer large but several mid-sized parties
Switzerland	SVP		Uses referenda to advance positions; increased polarisation Raises question of national independence vs. supra-national institutions	Shifts in positions of centre-right parties	SVP vote-seeking; introduces more professional campaigning Others slow to follow; system on the whole more competitive	Pronounced shift
Denmark	FrPd	First generation taps protest vote	Anti-tax	None		Temporary shift
	DF	Growing working-class support	Immigration & integration Second-generation party taps socio-cultural dimension	Some	Challenges former cleavage structure	Important shift

(Continued)

Table 11.7 (Continued)

	Populist Party or Parties	Target Groups, Discourse	Issue Agenda/Dimensions of Conflict	Impact on Other Parties	Competition for Votes	Party Balance
Norway	FrP	More petty bourgeois, working class	Immigration becomes more important once EU question resolved. Emergence of liberal-authoritarian cleavage	Minimal	Challenges former cleavage structure	Shift
Sweden	ND & SD		Later emergence of immigration issues	Impact on issue agenda once in parliament	Challenges former cleavage structure	Shift
Finland	SMP PS	Displaced farmers Displaced workers	PS taps traditional-authoritarian-nationalist	Minimal	None	Temporary shift
France	FN	Increasingly targets working-class voters	Immigration & integration; anti-EU. Taps traditional-authoritarian nationalist social populist	Influences mainstream right	Injects cultural dimension into debate. Can influence outcomes	Shift
Italy	LN & FI/PdL		Federalism. Immigration. European integration	Shifts in discourse, LN influences FI/PdL positions	Increases competition for votes	Helps define Second Republic party system
Poland	SRP LPR	Those left behind	Minimal impact	Minimal	Indirect effect on logic of party competition; rotation in axes of competition	Fleeting impact: parties not present on sustained basis
Hungary	Fidesz & Jobbik		Nationalist; social populist; intensify socio-cultural dimension	Symbiotic relationship with each other	Intensify	Pronounced shift

of adopting dismissive, adversarial or accommodative stances. Fallend and Heinisch (chapter 2, this volume) show that both the SPÖ and the ÖPV initially responded dismissively to the FPÖ, but the ÖPV (and eventually the SPÖ) changed discourse and positions when the FPÖ grew strong enough to threaten them. A similar development was underway in France. As de Lange (chapter 3, this volume) indicates, mainstream Dutch parties began talking about immigration before populist parties appeared; only the Liberals rewrote their programme in response to the List Pim Fortuyn.

Populist parties use different issues to mobilise support. Many populist radical right parties combine opposition to immigration and the EU with a defence of welfare state entitlements, not for everyone, but rather for (native-born) citizens. This has enabled parties like the FPÖ and DF to gather support from a heterogeneous base of support that includes people in routine occupations who once would have supported parties of the left. Jupskås (chapter 5, this volume) argues that Scandinavian populist parties have become working-class parties.

We might expect mainstream parties to respond not only by trying to shore up their support but also by using more aggressive tactics to lure voters from other parties. Not all of our chapters comment on this, but Austria and Switzerland are interesting: In the former, the growth of the FPÖ at the expense of the ÖVP and (to a lesser extent) the SPÖ did not result in the early adoption of similar positions or the adoption of similar vote-seeking strategies. Anxious to maintain their coalition, both concentrated on mobilising core supporters, in effect limiting competition for votes and debate in parliament (Fallend and Heinisch, chapter 3, this volume). Nor was the SVP's electorally aggressive posture met with an equivalent response from other mainstream parties. Although election campaigning eventually became more professionalised, initially each absorbed their losses and carried on with business as usual. However, competition on issues increased because of the SVP's use of referenda. Although the SVP ruffled feathers and challenged the rules of the game, it did so using well-established, constitutionally legitimate procedures that other parties – principally the Socialists – had previously employed, making it difficult to challenge the SVP without challenging the system itself (Mazzoleni, chapter 4, this volume).

Taken together, the chapters suggest that populist parties influence the positions that other parties take as well as the dimensions of competition. Populist parties generate change both by affecting underlying dimensions and by bringing about changes in electoral alignments. Many attract a broad range of support, including the allegiance of parts of the former working class, altering the party balance, which can affect competition for government.

Populist Parties and Party Systems

Let us draw this to a conclusion. Our aim was to examine the impact of populist parties on European party systems. Populist parties are one of several factors that shape and reshape party systems but not necessarily the most important. If there is one single factor that has been driving the patterns of continuity and change, it is not populist parties, per se, but rather the diminishing ability of mainstream parties to dominate competition for government in the way that they once could. Nevertheless, populist parties have been vehicles through which an increasingly prominent socio-cultural cleavage has been given greater definition. Our cases also suggest that populist parties have had an impact on competition for votes because they – with other parties – frame what elections are about. Altering the alternatives voters confront, this can accelerate change because younger cohorts are exposed to different sets of choices than older ones. This is one of several ways in which parties and, *inter alia*, party systems exercise agency in cleavage formation (Deegan-Krause and Enyedi 2010; Enyedi 2005; Kalyvas 1996).

Populist parties also affect competition for government. However, this depends on the extent to which populist parties have been incorporated into previous structures of competition: in several instances, mainstream parties have incorporated populist parties in ways that leave key features intact, albeit in modified form. As indicated, their aggregate strength is weaker. In several instances, mainstream parties maintain their positions only by drawing other parties into party system cores that are more permeable than they once were. In contrast, exclusion or self-exclusion narrows the range of coalitions that mainstream parties can form.

Stating that populist parties have been vehicles through which new issues and concerns have been brought forward and socio-cultural cleavages have been given greater definition does not mean that they were the first to raise these concerns, nor that they initiated competition on the socio-cultural dimension. We are dealing with the emergence of a new dimension that has replaced religion and religiosity as a second dimension of conflict around which parties may organise. Variously called the 'socio-cultural dimension' (the term we have used), the (new) cultural dimension and GAL/TAN dimension, this pits cosmopolitans, who are favourably disposed to Green, alternative and libertarian values, against locals with traditional, authoritarian and nativist values (Bornschier 2010; Grande 2008; Kriesi 2008, 2012; Kitschelt and Rehm 2015; Kriesi and Häusermann 2015).[4] Its emergence does not reflect the actions of any party or party family, but rather social, economic and political changes that have been occurring in older Western democracies and, in different ways, newer ones as well. Underpinning them are changes in social and occupational structure that separate people in routine jobs – white- and blue-collar production workers – from socio-cultural professionals whose work is not routine (Kriesi 2008, 2012).

This divide first surfaced in the late 1960s and early 1970s. New social movements and Green and left-libertarian parties were the first to enter the fray. Both gave expression to demands different from than those on offer from mainstream parties. More recently, populist parties have given greater definition to this dimension. Positioning near the traditional, authoritarian and nationalist pole, populist parties and mainstream parties that share some of their perspectives complete this dimension. If populist parties have played a role, it is that of midwife or facilitator, advancing processes are already underway. How this unfolds depends on the ways in which party systems, or rather parties within them, respond. One response is to quarantine newer political forces using devices such as *cordon sanitaire* to limit their impact. An alternate response is to 'absorb the blow' by drawing populist parties into pre-existing structures of competition. Ironically, the first may have greater impact on competition for government than the latter. We examine this momentarily.

POLAND AND HUNGARY

Like the narrative that Wolinetz and Zaslove set out in the introductory chapter, this argument applies more to the nine Western European party systems we have considered than to Poland or Hungary. Populism is important in both countries but the ways in which it is channelled and its impact varies. The principal divisions in Poland and Hungary reflect historical grievances, questions about the role of churches and how transitions to democracy were managed, rather than the class and economic divisions prominent in the western democracies. This is a cultural division exploited primarily by mainstream parties rather than challengers. In Poland, it feeds into a party system that is less institutionalised than its counterparts elsewhere. Nor does populism necessarily take the same form. As Casal Bértoa and Guerra (chapter 9, this volume) indicate, populism is a recurring force in Poland, but thus far none of the parties and movements or leaders that have articulated it have managed to entrench themselves in the party system. In contrast, populism is deeply embedded in Hungary: both Fidesz and its principal competitor on the right, Jobbik, are populist parties. As Enyedi and Róna (chapter 10, this volume) indicate, it is difficult to talk about the impact of populism on the Hungarian party system because Fidesz, increasingly dominant in recent years, is, in some respects, the party system. Nevertheless, Law and Justice (PiS), a conservative nationalist party, cloaks its appeal in populist garb. It is instructive that neither set of authors, but particularly Casal Bértoa and Guerra, is willing to label Fidesz or Law and Justice populist parties. Their hesitation highlights a problem – the use of populist appeals to rally support by parties that are principal competitors – that could become common if mainstream parties, unable to rely on earlier patterns of mobilisation and allegiance, confronted with strong populist challengers, decide to mimic their discourse.

Absorbing the Blow: The Impact of Populist Parties on Party Systems

Let us return to the question posed in the introductory chapter. Investigating their impact on broader structures of competition and on competition for government, we found scant indication that populist parties have brought about substantial changes in either. Instead, in several instances, populist parties have been absorbed into previous structures of competition in ways that leave key features intact. However, this was not without costs: in several instances, mainstream parties 'absorbed the blow' by enlisting support from parties outside the core, including parties that did not normally govern but could (parties from the intermediate zone) or parties that would not normally be recruited nor necessarily want to share power (outsiders). The Western European populist parties whose impact we have been exploring have been shifting from the outer to the intermediate zone, but except in the cases of the Swiss People's Party (SVP), which was started out as an insider, and Berlusconi's People of Freedom (initially Forza Italia), which used populist appeals to establish itself as a key element of the right in Italy's Second Republic party system, they are not yet part of the core. Whether they will be in the future remains to be seen.

Denmark is an example of incorporation: there the mainstream right enlisted the Danish People's Party (DF) as a support party for minority governments in office from 2001 to 2011. Doing so, they reinforced a well-established bipolar structure of competition. This continued not only when governments of the left took power from 2011 to 2015 but also from 2015, when a Venstre (V) government supported by DF assumed office. Unusually, DF had grown larger than Venstre but opted to remain a support party rather than coalition partner. Other party systems, such as the Norwegian and, to a lesser extent, the Dutch and Finnish, absorbed the blow in similar fashion. However, this was not the only alternative: in contrast, Swedish parties preferred cross-bloc cooperation to the inclusion of the ND or the SD. Nevertheless, the archetype of exclusion is Austria. There, the reluctance of the SPÖ and the ÖVP to include the Freedom Party (FPÖ) forced them to come together in a series of coalitions resting on increasingly narrow bases of support. In order to maintain this cartel-like arrangement, the two parties shut down competition between them, limiting the influence not only of internal factions but also of parliament, producing a closed structure of competition.

Our analysis has shown that in most instances, populist parties have been incorporated not into the party system core but rather the intermediate zone – parties that could be called upon should their support be required. Whether this will continue is another matter. We have examined the impact of populist parties in elections through 2016. Regularly scheduled parliamentary elections are taking place in several countries: both the Netherlands and France held elections in the first half of 2017 and Germany and Austria follow in the fall. Although neither the PVV nor FN did as well as they might have, the PVV won 13.1 per cent (a gain of 3.0 per cent) and ended up as the second-largest party. The subsequent cabinet formation was difficult because the largest party, the Liberals (VVD), had only 21.3 per cent of the vote and, in contrast to earlier cabinet formations, none of the major parties was willing to consider the PVV as a coalition partner or draw on it for support. In France, the big story was not the advance of FN, whose candidate, Marine Le Pen, gained in the presidential election but lost 0.4 per cent in legislative elections, but rather the collapse of the PS and, to a lesser extent, the Republicans. In Austria, Germany and other countries, it is likely that at populist parties will do as well as, if not better than, in previous elections. Few of the issues that populist parties have exploited – the refugee crisis, immigration and integration, antipathy to the European Union and the impact of austerity in poorer member states – are likely to disappear in the near future. We can only guess at the implications that this will have for competition for government, but it could prove difficult for mainstream parties to incorporate populist parties on the same bases that they did before: Aware of their increased strength, stronger populist parties might demand more from mainstream parties than the latter are willing to concede. However, this is not the only consequence: if populist parties command larger blocs of seats, it will be more difficult to form coalitions without them.[5]

Whether and to what extent this will occur remains to be seen. We conclude by reflecting on what needs to be done if we want to study the changing contours of European party systems. Much of our thinking has been shaped by seminal analyses such as Lipset and Rokkan (1967) and Sartori (1966, 1976) and Mair (1997). The dominant view has been that party systems change rarely, if at all. However, many of the factors that underpinned their stability have been or are changing: the mass parties and the extended networks that parties of mass integration and kindred organisations used to mobilise and socialise successive generations of voters have all but disappeared, replaced initially by mass media and, more recently, social media. Detached from society, many parties are not well attuned to the sentiments of followers or the public (Katz and Mair 1995; Katz and Mair 2002; Mair 2013; van Biezen et al. 2012). In several instances, newer parties, including

Greens and left-libertarians, and more recently populist parties, have been better equipped to do so.

All of this suggests continued electoral volatility and fragmentation, as well as changes in competition for government and competition for votes and broader structures of competition. Studying what happens requires different toolkits than we now have. These have been shaped by presumptions of stability and the rarity of party system change. Lipset and Rokkan's (1967) observation that the party systems of the 1960s resembled the party systems of the 1920s not only intrigued a generation of scholars but also triggered ongoing debate about whether 'frozen' party systems might be thawing. Typically, the verdict has been no. Out of this came understandings that electoral change was not the same as party system change and that party system change occurs only if there is a change in relational features of party system. Assessed by a change from one of Sartori's (1976) types to another, such changes are rare (Mair 1997). Among the party systems we have examined, only Italy met the test.

Setting a high bar has prevented us from mistaking temporary variations for durable developments. However, this has made it difficult to examine changes in competition for votes and competition for government without tripping over language that struggles to differentiate changes in facets of party competition from party system change. Compounding the difficulty, the principal instrument used to assess change, Sartori's typology, no longer differentiates as effectively as it once did. As we already noted, one type, moderate pluralism, is overcrowded while polarised pluralism has emptied out. This leaves us straining to describe important trends. This volume provides an example: our contributors indicated that Austria, the Netherlands and Hungary were moving towards polarised pluralism. However, their reasons varied: in Austria and, to a lesser extent, Hungary, the principal factor was the absence of alternate coalitions; in the Netherlands, polarisation. Because typologies highlight key features that not all cases necessarily share, this is to be expected. However, it leaves us without the tools we need to compare changes when they occur: Moving towards polarised pluralism is not the same as getting there. If we want to preserve the meaning of polarised pluralism, then we need other categories to capture key facets without stretching what Sartori meant. One solution might be to develop intermediate categories, such as strained pluralism, that capture features, such as an absence of alternate coalitions or extreme polarisation, that our contributors have indicated.

Nor do we have a body of theory about how European party systems change. This contrasts with the literature on the American party system. Suppositions about periodic realignments have been part of its canon since Key (1955) first wrote about them (Burnham 1970; Sundquist 1983). Although there are doubts about the validity of its theoretical underpinnings (see Mayhew 2002), which, in some instances, took on a teleological aura (Burnham 1970),[6] and empirical validity, realignment helped scholars come to grips with the continuity of parties that sometimes repositioned themselves so substantially that change was readily discernable. This is the function of American institutions and winner-take-all competition for indivisible offices, such as the presidency, but indicating that institutions matter is only a start: we need tools to assess different variants of continuity and change, including changes in the scope and definition of conflict (Schattschneider 1960) and changes in competition for government and the ways parties interact. A first step is to bid farewell to the notion that party systems are frozen (Lipset and Rokkan 1967). A second could be developing some kind of periodisation to catalogue changes. A third is to build on efforts, such as Arter (1999; 2009), drawing on Smith (1989a; 1989b), that examine change in smaller clusters of party systems. Finally, we need to rebuild Sartori's typology, examining the larger range of competitive party systems now available to us, so that it becomes possible to talk about shifts from one type of party system to another or, failing that, from one classification to another. Here it is important to pay attention to not only his typology but also his method: Sartori (1976) stressed the need to examine the cases. He did so in depth: an earlier version of his typology (Sartori 1966) appeared ten years before the final iteration. Few scholars are allowed that luxury today, but we will need it if we are to isolate differences and similarities among a larger universe of competitive systems.

NOTES

1 Sartori (1976) argued that numbers mattered but how parties interacted mattered more. His most well-known exception was for consociational democracies, but his detailed explanations of moderate and pluralism contain several others.

2 Drawing on Lucardie and Voerman (2007), de Lange (chapter 3, this volume) argues that this reflected consociational practice. It is possible that other factors like a sense that something had to be done, came into play. Dutch parties responded in a similar way when new parties and dissident groups appeared in the late 1960s and early 1970s (Wolinetz 1973). Responses in both periods could reflect consociational practices, but self-interest might have been at work as well: parties and dissident groups in the earlier period did not win large percentages of the vote, but they mobilised elements of the electorate important to mainstream parties. Incorporation drew their supporters and activists into mainstream politics (Wolinetz 1973). In the 2000s, shares of the vote may have also dictated inclusion: In 2002, the LPF's 17 per cent made it the second-largest party. In 2010, the PVV's 15.5 per cent made it third largest, trailing only the Social Democrats (PvdA) with 20 per cent and the Liberals (VVD) with 20.7 per cent.

3 Meyer and Wagner (2013) argue that vote-seeking niche parties, a category that includes many populist parties, have a strong incentive to recast themselves as mainstream parties.

4 No one has agreed on a single name for this dimension. Interpretations of its nature vary. Kriesi (2008, 2012) argues that contemporary cultural divisions are an extension of older divisions on religion and religiosity. Because older divisions were often institutionalised around churches, correlated with religiosity and church attendance and mobilised very different groups, it is better to consider the socio-cultural divide as a new cleavage.

5 Another unknown is the impact of governing on populist parties. See Akkerman and de Lange (2012a, 2012b).

6 Burnham (1970) argued that generational realignments provided renewal and rejuvenation that was not only necessary but also worked to the benefit of all.

Appendix 11.1   Parties Making Up the Postwar Core (Western Europe)

Austria	People's Party and Socialist Party
Denmark	Social Democrats, Radical Liberals, Liberals, Conservatives
Finland	Finnish People's Democratic Union (Communists), Social Democrats, National Coalition Party, Centre
France	Communists, Socialists, Popular Republicans Radicals, Conservatives
Italy	Communists, Socialists, Social Democrats, Christian Democrats, Republicans, Liberals
Netherlands	Labour, Catholic People's Party Anti-Revolutionary Party, Christian Historical Union, Liberals
Norway	Labour, Centre (Agrarian), Liberals, Conservatives
Sweden	Social Democrats, Centre (Agrarian), Liberals, Conservatives
Switzerland	Social Democrats, Radical Democrats, Christian Democrats, Farmers, Traders & Citizens (from 1971, Swiss People's Party)

Source: Dahl (1966).

BIBLIOGRAPHY

Akkerman, T. (2012) 'Comparing radical right parties in government: Immigration and integration policies in nine countries (1996–2010)', *West European Politics*, 35(3): 511–529.

———— (2015) 'Immigration policy and electoral competition in Western Europe: A fine-grained analysis of party positions over the past two decades', *Party Politics*, 21(1): pp. 54–67.

Akkerman, T. and de Lange, S. L. (2012a) 'Pariahs or partners? Inclusion and exclusion of radical right parties and the effects on their policy positions', *Political Studies*, 63(5): 1140–1157.

———— (2012b) 'Radical right parties in office: Incumbency records and the electoral cost of governing', *Government and Opposition*, 47(4): 574–596.

Arter, D. (2009) 'From a contingent party system to party system convergence? Mapping party system change in postwar Finland', *Scandinavian Political Studies*, 32(2): 221–239.

———— (1999) 'Party system change in Scandinavia since 1970: "Restricted change" or "general change"?', *West European Politics*, 22(3): 139.

Bale, T. (2003) 'Cinderella and her ugly sisters: The mainstream and extreme right in Europe's bipolarising party systems', *West European Politics*, 26(3): 67–90.

———— (2008) 'Turning round the telescope: Centre-right parties and immigration and integration policy in Europe', *Journal of European Public Policy*, 15(3): 315–330.

Bartolini, S. and Mair, P. (2007) *Identity, competition, and electoral availability: the stabilization of European electorates 1885–1985*, Cambridge: Cambridge University Press; New York, 1990. Reprinted with a new introduction by the authors, ECPR Press.

Bornschier, S. (2010) *Cleavage politics and the populist right the new cultural conflict in Western Europe*, Philadelphia: Temple University Press.

Bornschier, S. and Kriesi, H. (2013) 'The populist right, the working class, and the changing face of class politics', in J. Rydgren (ed.) *Class politics and the radical right*, London: Routledge pp. 10–30.

Budge, I. and Farlie, D. (1983) 'Party competition – selective emphasis or direct confrontation? An alternative view with data', in H. Daalder and P. Mair (eds.) *Western European party systems: Continuity & change*, London and Beverly Hills, CA: Sage Publications pp. 267–305.

Burnham, W. D. (1970) *Critical elections and the mainsprings of American politics*, New York: Norton.

Canovan, M. (1999) 'Trust the people! Populism and the two faces of democracy', *Political Studies*, 47(1): 45–71.

Capoccia, G. (2002) 'Anti-system parties: A conceptual reassessment', *Journal of Theoretical Politics*, 4(1): 9–35.

Casal Bértoa, F. C. and Enyedi, Z. (2016) 'Party system closure and openness: Conceptualization, operationalization and validation', *Party Politics*, 22(3): 265.

Chiaramonte, A. and Emanuele, V. (2017) 'Party system volatility, regeneration and de-institutionalization in Western Europe (1945–2015)', *Party Politics*, 23(3): 376–88.

Daalder, H. (1955) 'Parties and politics in the Netherlands', *Political Studies*, 3: 1–16.

Daalder, H. (1966) 'Parties, elites, and political developments in Western Europe', in J. LaPalombara and M. Weiner (eds.) *Political parties and political development*, Princeton: Princeton University Press pp. 43–77.

Dahl, R. A. (1966) *Political oppositions in Western democracies*, New Haven: Yale University Press.

Dalton, R. J. (2004) *Democratic challenges, democratic choices: The erosion of political support in advanced industrial democracies*, Oxford, Toronto: Oxford University Press.

Dalton, R. J. and Anderson, C. (2011) *Citizens, context, and choice: How context shapes citizens' electoral choices*, Oxford, Toronto: Oxford University Press.

Dalton, R. J., Flanagan, S. C., Beck, P. A. and Alt, J. E. (1984) *Electoral change in advanced industrial democracies*, Princeton, NJ: Princeton University Press.

Dalton, R. J. and Wattenberg, M. P. (2000) *Parties without partisans: Political change in advanced industrial democracies*, New York: Oxford University Press.

Dassoneville, R. and Hooghe, M. (2017) 'Economic indicators and electoral volatility: Economic effects on electoral volatility in Western Europe, 1950–2013', *Comparative European Politics*, 15(6): 919–943.

De Lange, S. L. (2012) 'New alliances: Why mainstream parties govern with radical right-wing populist parties', *Political Studies*, 60(4): 899–918.

Deegan-Krause, K. and Enyedi, Z. (2010) 'Agency and the structure of party competition: Alignment, stability and the role of political elites', *West European Politics*, 33(3): 686–710.

Döring, H. and Manow, P. (2016) Parliaments and governments database (ParlGov): Information on parties, elections and cabinets in modern democracies, Development version.

Einhorn, E. S. and Logue, J. (2003) *Modern welfare states: Scandinavian politics and policy in the global age*, second ed., Westport, CO: Praeger.

Emanuele, V. (2015) Dataset of electoral volatility and its internal components in Western Europe (1945–2015), Version: 1, GESIS Data Archive, http://doi.org/10.7802/1112.

Emanuele, V. and Chiaramonte, A. (2016) 'A growing impact of new parties: Myth or reality? Party system innovation in Western Europe after 1945', *Party Politics*, Prepublished Nov. 21, 2016, doi: 10.1177/1354068816678887.

Engelmann, F. C. (1966) 'Austria: The pooling of opposition', in R. A. Dahl (ed.) *Political oppositions in Western democracies*, New Haven: Yale University Press pp. 260–283.

Enyedi, Z. (2005) 'The role of agency in cleavage formation', *European Journal of Political Research*, 44(5): 697–720.

Goodliffe, G. (2015) 'Europe's salience and "owning" Euroscepticism: Explaining the Front National's victory in the 2014 European elections in France', *French Politics*, 13(4): 324–345.

Grande, E. (2008) 'Globalizing Western European politics: The change of cleavage structures, parties and party systems in comparative perspective', in H. Kriesi, E. Grande Romain, M. Dolezal, S. Bornshier and T. Frey (eds.) *West European politics in the age of globalization*, Cambridge: Cambridge University Press pp. 320–344.

Häusermann, S. and Kriesi, H. (2015) 'What do voters want? Dimensions and configurations in individual-level preferences and party choice', in P. Beramendi, S. Hausermann, H. Kitschelt and H. Kriesi (eds.) *The politics of advanced capitalism*, New York: Cambridge University Press pp. 202–230.

Hernandez, E. and Kriesi, H. (2016) 'The electoral consequences of the financial and economic crisis in Europe', *European Journal of Political Research*, 55(2): 203–224.

Hopkin, J. and Paolucci, C. (1999) 'The business firm model of party organisation: cases from Spain and Italy', *European Journal of Political Research*, 35(3): 307.

Inglehart, R. (1971) 'The silent revolution in Europe: Intergenerational change in post-industrial societies', *American Political Science Review* 65(December): 991–1017.

———— (1977) *The silent revolution: Changing values and political styles among Western publics,* Princeton, NJ: Princeton University Press.

Kalyvas, S. N. (1996) *The rise of Christian Democracy in Europe,* Ithaca, NY: Cornell University Press.

Katz, R. S. and Mair, P. (1995) 'Changing models of party organization and party democracy: The emergence of the Cartel Party', *Party Politics* 1(1): 5–28.

———— (2002) 'The ascendancy of the party in public office: Party organizational change in twentieth-century democracies', in R. Guntner, J. Montero and J. Lin (eds.) *Political parties: Old concepts and new challenges,* Oxford: Oxford University Press pp. 113–135.

Key, V. O. (1955) 'A theory of critical elections', *The Journal of Politics,* 17(1): 3–18.

Kirchheimer, O. (1966) 'The transformation of Western European party systems', in J. LaPalombara and M. Weiner (eds.) *Political parties and political development,* Princeton, NJ: Princeton University Press pp. 177–200.

Kitschelt, H. and McGann, A. J. (1995) *The radical right in Western Europe: A comparative analysis,* Ann Arbor: University of Michigan.

Kitschelt, H. and Rehm, P. (2015) 'Party alignments: Continuity and change', in P. Beramendi, S. Hausermann, H. Kitschelt and H. Kriesi (eds.) *The politics of advanced capitalism,* New York: Cambridge University Press pp. 179–201.

Knapp, A. (2004) *Parties and the party system in France: A disconnected democracy?* New York: Palgrave Macmillan.

Kriesi, H. (2008) *West European politics in the age of globalization,* Cambridge: Cambridge University Press.

Kriesi, H. (2012) *Political conflict in western Europe,* Cambridge: Cambridge University Press.

Kriesi, H. and Pappas, T. S. (2015) *European populism in the shadow of the Great Recession,* Colchester, UK: ECPR Press.

Laakso, M. and Taagepera, R. (1979) ' "Effective" number of parties: A measure with application to West Europe', *Comparative Political Studies,* 12(1): 3–27.

Lijphart, A. (1999) *Patterns of democracy: Government forms and performance in thirty-six countries,* New Haven, CT: Yale University Press.

Lipset, S. M. and Rokkan. S. (1967) 'Cleavage structures, party systems, and voter alignments: An introduction', in S. M. Lipset and S. Rokkan (eds.) *Party systems and voter alignments: Cross-national perspectives,* New York: Free Press pp. 1–64.

Lucardie, P. (2000) 'Prophets, purifiers, and prolocutors: Towards a theory on the emergence of new parties', *Party Politics,* 6(2): 175.

Lucardie, P. and Voerman, G. (2007) 'The List Pim Fortuyn and the government: A love-hate relationship', in P. Delwit and P. Poirer (eds.) *The extreme right parties and power in Europe,* Brussels: l'Université de Bruxelles pp. 247–263.

Mair, P. (1989) 'The problem of party system change', *Journal of Theoretical Politics,* 1(3): 251.

———— (1997) *Party system change: Approaches and interpretations,* Oxford: Clarendon Press.

———— (2001) 'The green challenge and political competition: How typical is the German experience?', *German Politics,* 10(2): 99–116.

———— (2006) 'Party system change', in R. S. Katz and W. Crotty (eds.) *Handbook of party politics,* London: Sage pp. 63–74.

———— (2008) 'Electoral volatility and the Dutch party system: A comparative perspective', *Acta Politica*, 43(2–3): 235–253.

———— (2013) *Ruling the void: The hollowing of Western democracy*, London: Verso.

Mayhew, D. R. (2002) *Electoral realignments: A critique of an American genre*, New Haven, CT: Yale University Press.

Meguid, B. M. (2005) 'Competition between unequals: The role of mainstream party strategy in niche party success', *American Political Science Review*, 99(3): 347–359.

———— (2008) *Party competition between unequals: Strategies and electoral fortunes in Western Europe*, Cambridge: Cambridge University Press.

Meyer, T. M. and Wagner, M. (2013) 'Mainstream or niche? Vote-seeking incentives and the programmatic strategies of political parties', *Comparative Political Studies*, 46(10): 1246–1272.

Mudde, C. (2007) *Populist radical right parties in Europe*, Cambridge: Cambridge University Press.

———— (2013) 'Three decades of populist radical right parties in Western Europe: So what?', *European Journal of Political Research*, 52(1): 1–19.

———— (2014) 'Fighting the system? Populist radical right parties and party system change', *Party Politics*, 20(2): 217–226.

Müller, W. & Fallend, F. (2004) 'Changing patterns of party competition in Austria: From multipolar to bipolar system', *West European Politics*, 27(5): 801–835.

Oesch, D. (2015) 'Occupational structure and labor market change in Western Europe since 1990', in P. Beramendi, S. Hausermann, H. Kitschelt & H. Kriesi (eds.) *The politics of advanced capitalism*, Cambridge: Cambridge University Press pp. 112–132.

Petrocik, J. R. (1996) 'Issue ownership in presidential elections, with a 1980 case study', *American Journal of Political Science*, 40(3): 825.

Petrocik, J. R., Benoit, W. L. and Hansen, G. J. (2003) 'Issue ownership and presidential campaigning, 1952–2000', *Political Science Quarterly*, 118(4): 599–626.

Rohrschneider, R. and Whitefield, S. (2012) *The strain of representation: How parties represent diverse voters in Western and Eastern Europe*, Oxford: Oxford University Press.

Rooduijn, M., de Lange, S. L. and Van der Brug, W. (2014) 'A populist *Zeitgeist*? Programmatic contagion by populist parties in Western Europe', *Party Politics*, 20(4): 563–575.

Sartori, G. (1966) 'European political parties: The case of polarized pluralism', in J. LaPalombara and M. Weiner (eds.) *Political parties and political development*, Princeton, NJ: Princeton University Press pp. 137–176.

———— (1976) *Parties and party system: A framework for analysis*, Cambridge: Cambridge University Press.

Schattschneider, E. E. (1960) *The Semisovereign people: A realist's view of democracy in America*, New York: Holt, Rinehart, and Winston.

Smith, G. (1989a) 'A system perspective on party system change', *Journal of Theoretical Politics*, 1(3): 349–363.

———— (1989b) 'Core persistence: System change and the "people's party"', *West European Politics*, 12(4): 157–168.

Sundquist, J. L. (1983) *Dynamics of the party system: Alignment and realignment of political parties in the United States*, Revised edition, Washington, DC: Brookings Institution.

Wagner, M. (2012) 'Defining and measuring niche parties', *Party Politics*, 18(6): 845–864.

Wolinetz, S. B. (1973) *Party re-alignment in the Netherlands*, PhD diss., Yale University.

———— (2006) 'Party systems and party system types', in R. S. Katz and W. Crotty (eds.) *Handbook of party politics*, London, Thousand Oaks and New Delhi: Sage Publications pp. 51–62.

Van Biezen, I., Mair, P. and Poguntke, T. (2012) 'Going, going . . . gone? The decline of party membership in contemporary Europe', *European Journal of Political Research*, 51(1): 24–56.

Van Kessel, S. (2015). *Populist parties in Europe: Agents of discontent?* Houndmills, Basingstoke: Palgrave Macmillan.

Index

Italicized page numbers indicate references to figures; **bold** page numbers indicate references to tables.

About the Contributors

David Arter is an emeritus professor and currently a director of research in the Faculty of Management at the University of Tampere, Finland. He is editor-in-chief of the journal *Scandinavian Political Studies* and has written on aspects of Nordic politics over many years.

Fernando Casal Bértoa is an assistant professor in the School of Politics and International Relations at the University of Nottingham (United Kingdom). He is a member of the OSCE/ODIHR 'Core Group of Political Party Experts'. He is also co-chair of the Council for European Studies' Research Network on 'Political Parties, Party Systems and Elections', as well as co-director of REPRESENT: Research Centre for the Study of Parties and Democracy. His work has been published in the *Journal of Politics*, *European Journal of Political Research*, *Sociological Methods and Research*, *West European Politics*, *Party Politics* and *Democratization*, among others. He is currently co-writing a monograph titled *Party System Closure: Alliances and Innovations in Europe between 1848 and 2017*. Recently, he was awarded the 2017 Gordon Smith and Vincent Wright Memorial Prize as well as the 2017 AECPA Prize for 'Best Article'.

Zsolt Enyedi is professor at the Political Science Department of Central European University. He (co-)authored two and (co-)edited eight volumes and published a large number of articles and book chapters on the topics of party politics, comparative government, church and state relations and political psychology. His articles appeared in journals such as *European Journal of Political Research*, *Political Studies*, *Political Psychology*, *West European Politics*, *Party Politics*, *Europe-Asia Studies*, *Problems of Post-Communism*, *Journal of Political Ideologies* and *European Review*. Enyedi was the 2003 recipient of the Rudolf Wildenmann Prize and the 2004 winner of the Bibó Award. He held research fellowships at the Woodrow Wilson Center, Kellogg Institute (Notre Dame University), the Netherlands Institute for Advanced Studies, the European University Institute (Florence, Italy) and Johns Hopkins University.

Franz Fallend is senior scientist at the University of Salzburg, Department of Political Science. His research has focused on Austrian politics, political parties, federalism and regionalism. He has published articles in *Österreichische Zeitschrift für Politikwissenschaft* (Austrian Journal of Political Science) and *European Journal of Political Research*, *Democratization* and *Representation: The Journal of Representative Democracy*. In 1997, he co-edited, with Herbert Dachs and Elisabeth Wolfgruber, the book *Länderpolitik: Politische Strukturen und Entscheidungsprozesse in den österreichischen Bundesländern* (State Politics: Political Structures and Decision-Making Processes in the Austrian States).

Simona Guerra is associate professor of Politics, School of History Politics and International Relations, University of Leicester. Her main research interest is in attitudes towards the European Union, which was the focus of her first monograph, *Central and Eastern European Attitudes in the Face of Union* (2013). Simona has recently published a co-edited book (with Manuela Caiani), *Euroscepticism, Democracy and the Media: Communicating Europe, Contesting Europe* (2017), and she is working on her second monograph, *Religion and Euroscepticism in Post-Communist Europe*.

Reinhard Heinisch is professor of Austrian politics in comparative European perspective and chair of the Department of Political Science at the University of Salzburg, Austria. He is also an affiliate faculty member of the University Center of International Studies at the University of Pittsburgh, where he had been on the faculty from 1994 to 2009. Reinhard Heinisch is the author of *Populism Proporz Pariah – Austria Turns Right* (2002) as well as of numerous publications. His main area of work includes comparative populism, Euroscepticism as well as research on corporatism under conditions of integration and internationalisation.

Gilles Ivaldi is a CNRS researcher at the University of Nice in the Center for Migration and Society. His research focuses on right-wing extremism, immigration and voting. He is a leading expert on the French National Front. He has published in leading international peer reviewed journals such as *Political Research Quarterly*, *International Journal of Forecasting*, *French Politics*, *West European Politics* and *Southern European Society and Politics*. He has a single authored book entitled *Droites populistes et extrêmes en Europe occidentale*, La Documentation française, collection 'Les Etudes', 2004, on the French National Front. He has also authored numerous chapters for edited collections.

Anders Ravik Jupskås is a senior researcher and deputy director at the Center for Research on Extremism (C-REX), University of Oslo. His PhD from 2015 was entitled 'Persistence of Populism: The Norwegian Progress Party, 1973–2009'. His main interests are political parties, right-wing extremism and ideologies. His research focuses on the ideological and organisational aspects of radical right parties in Europe in general and the Scandinavian region in particular. He has published in *Scandinavian Political Studies* and *Norsk statsvitenskapelig tidsskrift* as well as chapters in several recently published edited volumes on radical right-wing populism.

Sarah L. de Lange is professor of political science at the University of Amsterdam. She has the Dr. J.M. Den Uyl chair. Her main research interests include parties, party families and party systems, and her publications have appeared in *Acta Politica, Communist and Post-Communist Studies, Comparative European Politics, European Political Studies, Government and Opposition, Journal of Ethnic and Migration Studies, Party Politics, Political Studies* and *West European Politics*.

Oscar Mazzoleni is professor in political science and the director of the Research Observatory for Regional Politics at the University of Lausanne. His articles have been published in *Government and Opposition, Party Politics, Swiss Political Science Review, Federal and Regional Studies* and *Perspectives on European Politics and Society,* among others. On the Swiss People's Party, he has published a monography, *Nationalisme et populisme en Suisse. La radicalisation de l'Union démocratique du centre*, 2008 (first edition 2003), and chapters in edited books. He recently edited, with R. Heinisch, *Understanding Populist Party Organisation – The Radical Right in Western Europe* and, with S. Müller, *Regionalist Parties in Western Europe*.

Matthijs Rooduijn is assistant professor in the Department of Political Science at the University of Amsterdam. His research focuses on topics such as populism, voting behaviour, public opinion and polarisation. His work is published in journals such as the *European Journal of Political Research, Comparative Political Studies, European Union Politics, Party Politics* and *West European Politics*.

Dániel Róna (PhD) is assistant professor at Corvinus University of Budapest, Institute of Political Science. His PhD dissertation was entitled 'Reasons behind the Rise of Hungarian Radical Right'. He is a co-author of the article 'The Secret of Jobbik (Hungarian Extreme Right Party)' published in *Journal of East-European and Asian Studies* and of the chapter 'Rational Radicalism: Jobbik's Road to the Hungarian Parliament' in Grigorij Mesežnikov, Oľga Gyárfášová, Zora Bútorová (eds), *Alternative Politics? The Rise of New Parties in Central Europe*.

Bertjan Verbeek is professor of international relations at the Department of Political Science of the Institute for Management Research at Radboud University, Nijmegen, the Netherlands. His research interests include the impact of domestic politics on international relations and the changing role of intergovernmental organisations. His work is published in journals such as *European Journal of International Relations*, *Democratization*, *European Political Science Review*, *Acta Politica* and *Comparative European Studies*.

Steven Wolinetz is professor emeritus at Memorial University of Newfoundland in Canada. Wolinetz writes about parties and party systems and smaller democracies (especially the Netherlands and Belgium, and the European Union). His publications include *Parties and Party Systems in Liberal Democracies* (1988); 'Beyond the Catch-all Party: Approaches to the Study of Parties and Party Organization in Contemporary Democracies', in Linz, Montero, and Gunther, *The Future of Political Parties*; 'The Transformation of Western European Party Systems Revisited' and other articles on parties and party systems. He is currently working on a book, *Parties and Party Systems in the New Millennium*.

Andrej Zaslove is assistant professor of comparative politics at Radboud University (Nijmegen, the Netherlands), at the Department of Political Science, in the Institute for Management Research. His research focuses on comparative European politics, political parties, with a special emphasis on populism and the radical right. He has a published book on the Italian Northern League with McGill-Queens Press and articles in journals, such as *Comparative Political Studies*, *West European Politics*, *European Political Science Review* and *Democratization*.

www.ingramcontent.com/pod-product-compliance
Lightning Source LLC
Chambersburg PA
CBHW021808270326
41932CB00007B/102